Ideology and Modern Culture

Critical Social Theory in the Era of Mass Communication

John B. Thompson

Polity Press

Copyright © John B. Thompson 1990

First published 1990 by Polity Press
in association with Blackwell Publishers
Reprinted 1992

Editorial office:
Polity Press, 65 Bridge Street,
Cambridge CB2 1UR, UK

Marketing and production:
Blackwell Publishers
108 Cowley Road, Oxford OX4 1JF, UK

ISBN 0 7456 0081 6
ISBN 0 7456 0082 4 (pbk)

British Library Cataloguing in Publication Data

A CIP catalogue record for this book is available from the British Library

Typeset in 11½ on 12½ pt Bembo
by Joshua Associates Ltd, Oxford
Printed in Great Britain by
T. J. Press (Padstow) Ltd, Padstow, Cornwall

Contents

Preface

This book is a development of the ideas which were initially sketched in an earlier volume, *Studies in the Theory of Ideology*. The earlier volume was concerned primarily with the critical assessment of a number of outstanding contributions to contemporary social theory. In the course of that assessment I put forward some constructive ideas about the nature and role of ideology, its relation to language, power and social context, and the ways in which ideology can be analysed and interpreted in specific cases. My aim in this book is to take up these ideas, to develop them and incorporate them into a systematic theoretical account. This is an account which is certainly informed by the work of others – other theorists as well as others engaged in empirical and historical research. But I have tried to go beyond the material upon which I draw and to which I am indebted, in an attempt to stretch the existing frameworks of analysis and to provide some stimulus to further reflection and research.

While in many ways this book is a continuation of the project announced in *Studies*, there is one respect in which it differs significantly from the earlier volume: in this book I have sought to give much more attention to the social forms and processes within which, and by means of which, symbolic forms circulate in the social world. I have therefore devoted considerable space to the nature and development of mass communication, which I regard as a definitive feature of modern culture and a central dimension of modern societies. My analysis of the nature of mass communication and of the development of media institutions raises more issues than I can adequately address within the scope of this book, but they are issues which I plan to pursue further in a subsequent volume on social theory and mass communication.

In thinking about the ideas discussed in this book, I have benefited from the comments and criticisms of others. Anthony Giddens and David Held deserve particular mention: they have been partners in an ongoing dialogue which has been, and no doubt will continue to be, invaluable. Peter Burke, Lizbeth Goodman, Henrietta Moore and William Outhwaite read an earlier version of this text and gave me a great deal of helpful and encouraging feedback. I am also grateful to Avril Symonds for her skilful word-processing, to Gillian Bromley for her meticulous copy-editing, and to the many people at Blackwell–Polity and Stanford University Press who have contributed to the production and diffusion of this text. Finally, I should like to thank the friends who, in the course of the last couple of years, have helped to create the space for this book to be written: their generosity has meant much more to me than a few words of acknowledgement might suggest.

J.B.T., Cambridge, December 1989

Introduction

Today we live in a world in which the extended circulation of symbolic forms plays a fundamental and ever-increasing role. In all societies the production and exchange of symbolic forms – of linguistic expressions, gestures, actions, works of art and so on – is, and has always been, a pervasive feature of social life. But with the advent of modern societies, propelled by the development of capitalism in early modern Europe, the nature and extent of the circulation of symbolic forms took on a new and qualitatively different appearance. Technical means were developed which, in conjunction with institutions orientated towards capital accumulation, enabled symbolic forms to be produced, reproduced and circulated on a hitherto unprecedented scale. Newspapers, pamphlets and books were produced in increasing quantities throughout the seventeenth, eighteenth and nineteenth centuries; and, from the nineteenth century on, the expanding means of production and circulation were accompanied by significant increases in levels of literacy in Europe and elsewhere, so that printed materials could be read by a growing proportion of the population. These developments in what is commonly called mass communication received a further impetus from advances in the electrical codification and transmission of symbolic forms, advances which have given us the varieties of electronic tele-communication characteristic of the late twentieth century. In many Western industrial societies today, adults spend on average between 25 and 30 hours per week watching television – and this is in addition to whatever time they spend listening to the radio or stereo, reading newspapers, books and magazines, and consuming other products of what have become large-scale, trans-national media industries. Moreover, there are few societies in the world today which are not touched by the institutions and mechanisms of mass communication, and hence which are not open to the circulation of mass-mediated symbolic forms.

Despite the growing significance of mass communication in the modern world, its nature and implications have received relatively little attention in the literature of social and political theory. To some extent this neglect is due to a disciplinary division of labour: social and political theorists have been content, mistakenly in my view, to leave the study of mass communication to specialists in media and communications research. To some extent this neglect is also a consequence of the fact that the problems which preoccupy many theorists today are a legacy of nineteenth- and early twentieth-century thought. It is the writings of Marx and Weber, of Durkheim, Simmel, Mannheim and others which have, in many respects, set the agenda for contemporary theoretical debates. Of course, the legacy of these and other thinkers is not necessarily a millstone. As commentators on the social transformations and political upheavals which accompanied the develop- ment of industrial capitalism, these thinkers called attention to a range of social phenomena, and elaborated a series of concepts and theories, which remain relevant in many ways to the circumstances of the late twentieth century. But where there is insight and illumination, there is also blindness, over-simplification, wishful optimism. Part of the task that confronts social and political theorists today is to sift through this legacy and to seek to determine what aspects can be and should be retained, and how these aspects can be reconstructed to take account of the changing character of modern societies. In confronting social and political phenomena we do not begin with a *tabula rasa*: we approach these phenomena in the light of the concepts and theories which have been handed down from the past, and we seek in turn to revise or replace, criticize or reconstruct, these concepts and theories in the light of the developments which are taking place in our midst.

In the following chapters I shall take as my starting point the concept and theory of ideology. A notion which first appeared in late eighteenth-century France, the concept of ideology has undergone many transformations in the two centuries since then. It has been twisted, reformulated and recast; it has been taken up by social and political analysts and incorporated into the emerging discourses of the social sciences; and it has filtered back into the everyday language of social and political life. If I take the concept and theory of ideology as my starting point, it is because I believe that there is something worthwhile, and worth sustaining, in the tradition of reflection which has been concerned with ideology. Although there is much that is misleading and much that is erroneous in this tradition, we can nevertheless distil from it a residue of problems which retain their relevance and urgency today. The concept and theory of ideology define a terrain of analysis which remains central to the contemporary social sciences and which forms the site of continuous and lively theoretical debate.

I shall be concerned to argue, however, that the tradition of reflection on ideology also suffers from certain limitations. Most importantly, the writers who have concerned themselves with problems of ideology have failed to deal adequately with the nature and impact of mass communication in the modern world. Some of these writers have certainly acknowledged the importance of mass communication – indeed, they were among the first social and political theorists to call attention to the growing role of the mass media. But even these writers tended to take a rather dim view of the nature and impact of mass communication. They were inclined to regard the development of mass communication as the emergence of a new mechanism of social control in modern societies, a mechanism through which the ideas of dominant groups could be propagated and diffused, and through which the consciousness of subordinate groups could be manipulated and controlled. Ideology was understood as a kind of 'social cement', and mass communication was viewed as a particularly efficacious mechanism for spreading the glue. This general approach to the relation between ideology and mass communication is one which I shall criticize in detail. It is an approach which has, explicitly or implicitly, moulded many of the recent contributions to the ongoing debate about ideology and its role in modern societies, as well as some of the attempts to reflect theoretically on the nature and impact of mass communication. And yet it is, in my view, an approach which is fundamentally flawed.

One of my central aims in this book is to elaborate a different account of the relation between ideology and mass communication – or, to put it more precisely, to rethink the theory of ideology in the light of the development of mass communication. In pursuing this aim I shall adopt a three-stage argumentative strategy. I shall begin by reconsidering the history of the concept of ideology, retracing its main contours and its occasional detours. Against the backcloth of this brief analytical history, I shall formulate a particular conception of ideology which preserves something of the legacy of this concept while dispensing with assumptions which seem to me untenable. I shall then examine some of the general theoretical accounts which have been put forward in recent years concerning the nature and role of ideology in modern societies. I shall argue that these accounts are inadequate in numerous respects, particularly with regard to their treatment of mass communication and its significance for the theory of ideology.

In order to overcome this deficiency, we must shift the focus of analysis: this is the second stage of my argumentative strategy. I shall argue that we must elaborate a theoretical framework which enables us to understand the distinctive characteristics of mass communication and the distinctive course of its development. The key to this framework is what I shall call the *mediazation of modern culture*. By this I mean the general process by which the transmission of symbolic forms becomes increasingly mediated by the technical and institutional apparatuses of the media industries. We live in societies today in which the production and reception of symbolic forms is increasingly mediated by a complex, trans-national network of institutional concerns. The exploration of this process involves several considerations. Conceptually, we must examine the nature of symbolic forms and their relation to the social contexts within which they are produced, transmitted and received, an examination which falls within the domain traditionally demarcated by the concept of culture. Historically, we must reconstruct the development of some of the technical means of transmission and of the institutional forms within which these technical means have been, and currently are being, deployed. Theoretically, we must reflect on the nature of this general process of mediazation, its impact on social and political life in the modern world, its implications for social and political theory in general, and for the theory of ideology in particular.

The final stage of my argumentative strategy is at the level of methodo-logy. Here my concern is to draw out the methodological implications of the conceptual and theoretical arguments developed in earlier chapters, and to show that these arguments, however abstract they may seem, make a difference in practice – both in the practice of social research, and in the ways that we understand the relation between the practice of social research, on the one hand, and the everyday practices of the individuals who make up the social world, on the other. In pursuing these methodological issues, I try to show what is involved in the analysis of symbolic forms in general, and in the analysis of mass-mediated symbolic forms in particular. Drawing on my reformulated conception of ideology, I also attempt to show how this methodological framework can be employed for the analysis of ideology. These methodological reflections are not intended to replace or displace empirical research – nothing could be further from my intention. Rather, they are offered as a stimulus to empirical research and as a contribution to our understanding of what is involved in studying an object domain which consists of, among other things, subjects who produce, receive and understand symbolic forms as a routine part of their everyday lives.

In following through with this argumentative strategy, I shall develop a series of constructive proposals concerning ideology, culture, mass communication, interpretation and critique. My hope is that these proposals constitute a coherent and plausible approach to a range of issues, both theoretical and methodological, which are central to current debates in social and political theory, and in the social sciences generally. In the remainder of this Introduction, I shall concentrate on these constructive proposals. I shall aim to render explicit some of the ideas and assumptions which define the approach that I advocate and which underlie my criticisms of, and indicate my indebtedness to, the work of others.

The Concept and Theory of Ideology

When we employ the term 'ideology', whether in social and political analysis or in the discourse of everyday life, we draw upon a concept which has a long and complicated history. Part of the reason why this concept is so ambiguous today, has so many different uses and shades of meaning, is because the concept has travelled a long and circuitous route since it was introduced into European languages two centuries ago: the multiplicity of meanings which it displays today is a product of this historical itinerary. But there is a further factor which exacerbates the ambiguity of the concept of ideology. When we use the term 'ideology' today, or when we hear it used by others, we may not be entirely sure whether it is being used descriptively or prescriptively, whether it is being used simply to describe a state of affairs (e.g. a system of political ideas) or whether it is being used also, or perhaps even primarily, to evaluate a state of affairs. This ambiguity is evident in our everyday use of the term. Few people today would proudly proclaim themselves to be 'ideologists', whereas many would not hesitate to declare that they were conservatives or socialists, liberals or democrats, feminists or ecologists. Ideology is the thought of the *other*, the thought of someone other than oneself. To characterize a view as 'ideological' is, it seems, already implicitly to criticize it, for the concept of ideology seems to convey a negative, critical sense.

In the literature of social and political theory of the last two decades or so, there have been two common responses to the ambiguous heritage of the concept of ideology. One response has been to try to tame the concept. This has generally involved the attempt, explicit or implicit, to strip the concept of its negative sense and to incorporate it into a corpus of descriptive concepts employed by the social sciences. This has given rise to what may be called a *neutral conception* of ideology. According to this conception, ideologies can be regarded as 'systems of thought', 'systems of belief' or 'symbolic systems' which pertain to social action or political practice. No attempt is made, on the basis of this conception, to distinguish between the kinds of action or projects which ideology animates; ideology is present in every political programme and is a feature of every organized political movement. Armed with this conception, the analyst can seek to delineate and describe the major systems of thought or belief which animate social and political action. This line of inquiry is thus exemplified by the tendency to think of ideologies in terms of 'isms' – conservatism, communism,

Reaganism, Thatcherism, Stalinism, Marxism. These and other systems of thought or belief, these 'ideologies', can be categorized and analysed, broken down into their constituent elements and traced back to their original sources; and all this can be done, the analyst would claim, without making or implying any pejorative judgement concerning the systems of thought or belief.

A second response to the ambiguous heritage of the concept of ideology has been to dispense with the concept. The concept is simply too ambiguous, too controversial and contested, too deeply marred by a history in which it has been hurled back and forth as a term of abuse, to be salvaged today for the purposes of social and political analysis. In recent years this response has gained ground among some of the most original and perceptive social thinkers, partly as a result of the intellectual demise of Marxism, with which the concept of ideology has been closely linked. But this response, it seems to me, is shortsighted. Rather than sifting through the ambiguous heritage and seeking to determine whether there is a residue worthy of being sustained, this response prefers to abandon, or more commonly refuses to begin, the search. Rather than asking whether the tradition of reflection associated with the concept of ideology has highlighted a range of problems which continue to deserve our attention, even if it has also obscured these problems with misleading and untenable assumptions, this response chooses to drop the question or, more frequently, presumes an answer while avoiding the intellectual labour involved in trying to determine it.

The position I develop here differs from these two common responses to the ambiguous heritage of the concept of ideology. Unlike the second response, I maintain that the concept of ideology remains a useful and important notion in the intellectual vocabulary of social and political analysis. But unlike the first response, I argue that the concept cannot be so readily stripped of its negative, critical sense – or, more precisely, I argue that, in attempting to strip it of its negative sense, one overlooks a cluster of problems to which the concept, in some of its guises, sought to call our attention. It is this cluster of problems that I try to bring out in my reformulation of the concept of ideology. Since I do not try to eliminate the negative sense of the concept but rather take this sense as an index of the problems to which the concept refers, as an aspect which can be retained and creatively developed, this reformulation may be regarded as a *critical conception* of ideology. It preserves the negative connotation which has been conveyed by the concept throughout most of its history and binds the analysis of ideology to the question of critique.

In reformulating the concept of ideology, I seek to refocus this concept on a cluster of problems concerning the interrelations of meaning and power. I shall argue that the concept of ideology can be used to refer to the ways in which meaning serves, in particular circumstances, to establish and sustain relations of power which are systematically asymmetrical – what I shall call 'relations of domination'. Ideology, broadly speaking, is *meaning in the service of power*. Hence the study of ideology requires us to investigate the ways in which meaning is constructed and conveyed by symbolic forms of various kinds, from everyday linguistic utterances to complex images and texts; it requires us to investigate the social contexts within which symbolic forms are employed and deployed; and it calls upon us to ask whether, and if so how, the meaning mobilized by symbolic forms serves, in specific contexts, to establish and sustain relations of domination. The distinctiveness of the study of ideology lies in the latter question: it calls upon us to ask whether the meaning constructed and conveyed by symbolic forms serves, or does not serve, to maintain systematically asymmetrical relations of power. It calls upon us to study symbolic forms *in a certain light*: in the light of the structured social relations which their employment or deployment may serve, in specific circumstances, to create, nourish, support and reproduce.

If we reformulate the concept of ideology in this way, we bring the analysis of ideology into a domain of conceptual and methodological issues which is of more general scope and significance. The analysis of ideology can be regarded as an integral part of a broader concern with the characteristics of action and interaction, the forms of power and domination, the nature of social structure, social reproduction and social change, the features of symbolic forms and their roles in social life. This broader concern animates the arguments and proposals which I develop throughout this book. Some of the wider issues are pursued in chapter 3, where I examine some of the features of symbolic forms and explore their relation to social contexts which are structured in various ways. Other issues of a general methodological character are discussed in chapter 6, where I consider what is involved in studying an object domain which is at the same time a subject domain in which individuals produce, receive and understand symbolic forms that are meaningful for them as well as for the analyst who seeks to interpret them. By reformulating the concept of ideology in terms of the interrelations of meaning and power, we are invited and required to pursue these broader issues. In this book I cannot claim to have addressed these broader issues in all the detail and with all the rigour that they demand. At most I have indicated a path that can, I believe, be coherently and plausibly pursued.

The proposed reformulation of the concept of ideology enables us to avoid a number of tendencies which vitiate much of the recent theoretical literature. In the first place, it enables us to avoid the tendency, alluded to earlier, to view ideology as a kind of 'social cement' which succeeds in stabilizing societies by binding their members together and providing them with collectively shared values and norms. This assumption is pervasive in the contemporary literature, and yet it is based on assumptions which are dubious and probably untenable. There is little evidence to suggest that certain values or beliefs are shared by all (or even most) members of modern industrial societies. Moreover, there is little reason to suppose that the stability of complex industrial societies requires and depends upon a consensus concerning particular values and norms. In so far as our societies are 'stable' social orders, this stability could just as easily be the outcome of a diversity of values and beliefs, a proliferation of divisions between individuals and groups, a lack of consensus at the very point where oppositional attitudes might be translated into political action. In stressing this point I do not wish to suggest that there is no room for the social analysis of values and norms. But I wish to prise the concept of ideology apart from the search for collectively shared values, redirecting it towards the study of the complex ways in which meaning is mobilized for the maintenance of relations of domination.

The proposed reformulation also enables us to avoid the tendency, prevalent in the literature, to think of ideology as a characteristic or attribute of certain symbolic forms or symbolic systems *as such* (conservatism, communism, etc.). From the approach I develop here, it follows that symbolic forms or symbolic systems are not ideological in themselves: whether they are ideological, and the extent to which they are, depend on the ways in which they are used and understood in specific social contexts. In studying ideology we are not concerned simply with categorizing and analysing a system of thought or belief, nor with analysing a symbolic form or system taken in and for itself. Rather, we are concerned with some of what could be called *the social uses of symbolic forms*. We are concerned with whether, to what extent and how (if at all) symbolic forms serve to establish and sustain relations of domination in the social contexts within which they are produced, transmitted and received. This approach may lead us to regard a symbolic form or system as ideological in one context and as radical, subversive, contestatory in another; it may lead us to regard a discourse on human rights, for instance, as supportive of the status quo in one context and as subversive in another. The analysis of symbolic forms as ideological requires us to analyse these forms in relation to the specific social–historical contexts within which they are employed and take hold.

Further, the proposed reformulation of the concept enables us to avoid the tendency to think of ideology solely or even primarily in relation to the forms of power that are institutionalized in the modern state. The institutions of the modern state, and the numerous other organizations (political parties, pressure groups, etc.) which occupy the space commonly referred to as politics in modern societies, are extremely important sites of power and domination; but they are not the only sites, nor even necessarily the most important sites for most people most of the time. For most people, the relations of power and domination which affect them most directly are those characteristic of the social contexts within which they live out their everyday lives: the home, the workplace, the classroom, the peer group. These are the contexts within which individuals spend the bulk of their time, acting and interacting, speaking and listening, pursuing their aims and following the aims of others. These contexts are organized in complex ways. They involve inequalities and asymmetries of power and resources, some of which may be linked to broader inequalities and asymmetries which recur from one context to another, and which concern the relations between men and women, between blacks and whites, between those with wealth and property and those without. In studying ideology we are concerned as much with the contexts of everyday life as we are with that specific set of institutions which comprises the sphere of politics in the narrow sense. Of course, this does not mean that the sphere of politics in the narrow sense is irrelevant, nor does it mean that we should focus exclusively on the minute details of everyday life, ignoring broader structural features and constraints. It means only that we should not neglect the ways in which symbolic forms are employed and deployed, and the ways in which they intersect with relations of power, in the structured social contexts within which most of us spend most of our time.

If we reformulate the concept of ideology in terms of the interplay of meaning and power, we can also avoid the tendency, common in the theoretical literature as well as in everyday usage, to think of ideology as pure *illusion*, as an inverted or distorted image of what is 'real'. This view draws inspiration from a famous and oft-quoted passage in which Marx and Engels compare the operation of ideology to the workings of a *camera obscura*, which represents the world by means of an image turned upside down. But this view – appealing in its simplicity, alarming in its theoretical self-confidence – is likely to lead us astray. It inclines us to think of ideology as a realm of images or ideas which reflects inadequately a social reality that exists prior to and independently of these images or ideas. Yet the social world is rarely as simple as this view would suggest. As individuals we are immersed in sets of social relations and we are constantly involved in commenting upon them, in representing them to ourselves and others, in enacting, recreating and transforming them through actions, symbols and words. The symbolic forms through which we express ourselves and understand others do not constitute some ethereal other world which stands opposed to what is real: rather, they are partially constitutive of what, in our societies, 'is real'. By refocusing the study of ideology on the terrain of situated symbolic forms, on the ways in which symbolic forms are used to establish and sustain relations of power, we are studying an aspect of social life which is as real as any other. For social life is, to some extent, a field of contestation in which struggle takes place through words and symbols as well as through the use of physical force. Ideology, in the sense which I propose and develop here, is an integral part of this struggle; it is a creative and constitutive feature of a social life which is sustained and reproduced, contested and transformed, through actions and interactions which include the ongoing exchange of symbolic forms.

So far I have been discussing the concept of ideology, and the advantages and disadvantages of differing ways of responding to the ambiguous heritage of this concept. However, many of the authors who employ this concept today are interested primarily in substantive problems of social reproduction and social change. In their writings the concept of ideology plays a certain role within a broader theoretical framework or argument. These authors may employ the concept in a rather loose and imprecise way, and they can be legitimately criticized for this imprecision; but if we want to understand and appreciate their use of the concept, we must reconstruct and assess the broader theoretical framework within which it plays its role. This is the task which I confront in chapter 2. Here my concern is not so much with the historical trajectory of a concept and the prospects for its reformulation today, but rather with a range of theoretical frameworks or arguments, put forward by a variety of contemporary authors, and within which the concept of ideology performs a central role. I shall consider, for instance, the work of Aron, Bell and Gouldner, of Althusser and Poulantzas, of Horkheimer, Adorno and Habermas. By shifting the discussion on to this more general theoretical level, we can get a clearer sense of the ways in which contemporary social and political theorists have used the concept of ideology – what they have tried to highlight by means of this concept and what they have tried to use this concept to explain. We can also get a sense of what these theorists have neglected or failed to take adequately into account.

The key argument that I shall develop in this regard is that contemporary theorists who employ the concept of ideology have failed to deal adequately with the nature and development of mass communication, and with its role as a medium of ideology in modern societies. In some cases this is because the concept of ideology is part of a grand theoretical narrative concerning the cultural transformations associated with the rise of modern industrial societies. According to this grand narrative, the development of modern industrial societies was accompanied, in the sphere of culture, by the progressive secularization of beliefs and practices and the progressive rationalization of social life. As religion and magic lost their hold on individuals caught up in the restless activity of capitalist industrialization, the ground was prepared for the emergence of a new kind of belief system: for the emergence of secular belief systems which could mobilize individuals without reference to other-worldly values or beings. It is these secular belief systems which some contemporary theorists describe as 'ideologies'. In their view, the development of industrial capitalism gave rise to an 'age of ideologies' which was inaugurated by the French Revolution and which culminated with the radical revolutionary movements of the early twentieth century. The grand narrative of cultural transformation thus allocates a specific role to the concept of ideology (understood as a neutral conception, in the sense explained above). The concept of ideology is used to describe the systems of belief which – this theoretical narrative alleges – filled the cultural vacuum created by the decline of religion and magic, and which provided people with new forms of consciousness, new frames of meaning, in a world undergoing rapid and unprecedented social change.

The grand narrative of cultural transformation is deeply embedded in the discourse of social and political theory. It has served as a general, often implicit, theoretical construct within which many authors have viewed and analysed the development of modern societies. I think that this narrative contains some insights which are important for understanding the conditions under which modern societies emerged out of medieval and early modern Europe. But the narrative is also misleading in certain fundamental respects. One such respect is this: the theorists of the grand narrative, I shall argue, have mis-identified the major cultural transformation associated with the development of modern societies. Preoccupied with the alleged process of secularization and rationalization, these theorists have tended to neglect a process of far greater significance which was taking place before their eyes: namely, the rapid proliferation of institutions of mass communication and the growth of networks of transmission through which commodified symbolic forms were made available to an ever-expanding domain of recipients. This is the process that I describe as the mediazation of modern culture. This process constitutes, in my view, one of the key transformations associated with the rise of modern societies. Understanding this process is essential for understanding the world today, a world which is increasingly traversed by institutionalized networks of communication, and in which the experience of individuals is increasingly mediated by technical systems of symbolic production and transmission. Understanding this process will also provide an alternative theoretical framework within which a reformulated concept of ideology can play some role.

The Mediazation of Modern Culture

In seeking to understand the process which I describe as the mediazation of modern culture, I begin with the concept of culture. What are we referring to when we speak of 'culture', of that sphere of social life which has been, and continues to be, transformed by the development of mass communication? And how can we understand the development of mass communication as a development in the sphere of culture, as a cultural transformation? The concept of culture has a long and complicated history of its own, a history which has probably produced as many variants and as much ambiguity as the history of the concept of ideology. Nevertheless, I believe that the concept of culture remains an important and valuable notion and that, suitably reformulated, it defines a fundamental domain of social analysis. In chapter 3 I undertake the task of clarifying and reformulating the concept of culture. Following the work of anthropologists such as Geertz, I argue that the concept of culture can appropriately be used to refer, in a general way, to the symbolic character of social life, to the patterns of meaning embodied in the symbolic forms exchanged in social interaction. But this emphasis on the symbolic character of social life must be complemented by an emphasis on the fact – not always evident in the writings of Geertz – that symbolic forms are embedded in structured social contexts involving relations of power, forms of conflict, inequalities in terms of the distribution of resources, and so on. This dual emphasis defines what I call the 'structural conception' of culture. Cultural phenomena, on this account, may be seen as *symbolic forms in structured contexts*; and cultural analysis may be regarded as the study of the meaningful constitution and social contextualization of symbolic forms.

To view symbolic forms as contextualized phenomena is to regard them as generally produced and received by individuals situated in specific social–historical contexts and endowed with resources and capacities of various kinds. Symbolic forms may bear the traces of their social conditions of production – in the way, for instance, that an utterance may be marked by the accent, idiom and tone of a particular social class or regional background. The social contextualization of symbolic forms also implies that these forms may become the objects of complex processes of valuation, evaluation and conflict. Here I focus on what I call *processes of valorization* – that is, processes by which and through which symbolic forms are ascribed a certain 'value'. There are two types of value which are particularly important in this regard. One type is what may be called 'symbolic value': the value that symbolic forms have by virtue of the ways in which they are esteemed by the individuals who produce and receive them, by virtue of the ways in which they are praised or denounced, cherished or despised by these individuals. A second type of value is 'economic value', which we can construe as the value that symbolic forms acquire by virtue of being offered for exchange in a market. Not all symbolic forms have economic value in this sense, but the economic valorization of symbolic forms is an important process which has developed historically and assumed an increasingly important role in modern societies. When symbolic forms are subjected to economic valorization, they become commodities or, as I generally say, 'symbolic goods' which can be bought, sold or otherwise exchanged in a market. The development of a market for works of art, culminating in the establishment of galleries and auction houses in which works can change hands for extraordinary sums, offers a vivid example of the process of economic valorization.

In characterizing symbolic forms as meaningful phenomena which are both produced and received by individuals situated in specific contexts, we also imply that symbolic forms are generally transmitted, in one way or another, from producer to receiver. I shall describe this as *the cultural transmission of symbolic forms*, and I shall distinguish three aspects of this process. In the first place, cultural transmission involves the use of a technical medium, or material substratum, by means of which a symbolic form is produced and transmitted. The technical medium allows for a certain degree of fixation of meaningful content, as well as for a certain degree of reproduction of symbolic forms. The degree of fixation and reproduction depends on the nature of the medium – a message engraved in stone will generally have a much higher degree of fixation, but a much lower degree of reproduction, than a message inscribed or printed on paper. A second aspect of cultural transmission concerns the institutional apparatus within which a technical medium is deployed. The deployment of technical media is often part of a broader institutional context which includes systems of production of symbolic forms and channels of selective diffusion. A third aspect concerns what may be called, following authors such as Harold Innis and Anthony Giddens, the 'space–time distanciation' involved in cultural transmission. The transmission of a symbolic form necessarily involves the detachment, to some extent, of this form from the original context of its production: it is distanced from this context, both spatially and temporally, and inserted into new contexts which are located at different times and places. In this way symbolic forms acquire what I shall call an 'extended availability' in time and space. They are made available to an extended range of potential recipients who may be situated in contexts that are remote, both in time and in space, from the original contexts of production.

This theoretical reflection on the concept of culture and related issues provides a framework within which we can begin to think about the emergence and development of mass communication. We can broadly conceive of the emergence of mass communication in terms of the gradual establishment of a range of institutions based on certain technical means of cultural transmission, and orientated towards the large-scale production and generalized diffusion of commodified symbolic forms. The earliest forms of mass communication were based on techniques of printing and on the use of printed paper as a means of transmission. The key developments in this regard were those commonly associated with the goldsmith from Mainz, Johann Gutenberg, who invented a method for the replica-casting of metal letters and who adapted the traditional screw press to the purposes of manufacturing printed texts. By the end of the fifteenth century, printing presses had been set up in the major trading centres throughout Europe and the era of mass communication had begun.

In chapter 4 I trace the emergence and development of mass communication, from the fifteenth century to the present day, outlining the major institutional forms, describing the basic technical means and highlighting the most recent developmental trends. I try to show how, from the outset, the development of mass communication was closely interwoven with the expansion of commercial organizations and with the development of the modern state. Although I offer a broad historical account, I devote particular attention to the relatively recent emergence of broadcasting media – that is, media involving the transmission of messages via electromagnetic waves to an indeterminate and extended audience. Today the most important of the broadcasting media are those concerned with television transmission, and hence I consider these media in some detail. I also examine recent developments within the media industries as a whole, developments which are based on economic, political and technological factors. These developments include the growing concentration and diversification within the media industries, the increasing globalization of the activities of media concerns, and the deployment of new communication technologies, such as those associated with cable and satellite transmission. These processes have led to the formation of large-scale *communication conglomerates* which have major stakes in a variety of industries associated with the production and diffusion of information and communication. Multi-media and multi-national in character, these conglomerates sprawl across the globe, buying and selling particular media concerns at a feverish rate, transferring information and communication from one hemisphere to another instantaneously (or virtually so), and beaming messages into the living-rooms of countless individuals worldwide.

The developments and trends documented in chapter 4 are the institutional core, as it were, of the mediazation of modern culture. They have shaped, in a profound and irreversible way, the modes in which symbolic forms are produced, transmitted and received in modern societies, as well as the modes in which individuals experience the actions and events that take place in contexts from which they are spatially and temporally remote. These developments are partially constitutive of modern societies, and are partially constitutive of what is 'modern' about the societies in which we live today. That is, part of what constitutes modern societies as 'modern' is the fact that the exchange of symbolic forms is no longer restricted primarily to the contexts of face-to-face interaction, but is extensively and increasingly mediated by the institutions and mechanisms of mass communication. Of course, this process of the mediazation of modern culture is only one aspect of the formation of modern societies. It is a process which has gone hand-in-hand with the development of industrial capitalism (and alternative forms of industrial development) and with the rise of the modern state (and associated forms of political participation). These processes have overlapped with one another in complex ways; they have taken different paths in different historical and geographical contexts. But together they have defined the basic contours of the societies in which we live today, contours which are becoming increasingly global in character.

What are the characteristics of the new regime of cultural transmission created by the advent of mass communication? How should we understand the nature of mass communication, the ways in which it affects social interaction, the role which it plays, and ought to play, in social and political life? These are the questions which I address in chapter 5, where I sketch the beginnings of a social theory of mass communication. I emphasize the fact that, while mass communication involves the exchange of symbolic forms, the kinds of communication established thereby are quite different from those involved in ordinary, day-to-day conversation. For mass communication generally involves a one-way flow of messages from the producer to the receiver. Unlike the dialogical situation of a conversation, in which a listener is also a potential respondent, *mass communication institutes a fundamental break between the producer and the receiver*, in such a way that recipients have relatively little capacity to intervene in the communicative process and contribute to its course and content. Of course, recipients do have some capacity to intervene; they can, for instance, write letters to the editor, phone television companies and express their views, or vote with their feet. But while particular institutions and technical media admit of various kinds of recipient response, the fundamental asymmetry of the communicative process remains intact.

This asymmetry has implications for what I call *the interactional impact of technical media*. I use this expression to refer to the ways in which the technical media of mass communication have transformed, and are capable of transforming, the nature of social interaction in modern societies. The deployment of technical media should not be seen as a mere supplement to pre-existing social relations: rather, we should see this deployment as serving to *create* new social relations, new ways of acting and interacting, new ways of presenting oneself and of responding to the self-presentation of others. The creative character of technical media was highlighted by the so-called media theorists, most notably Marshall McLuhan; but the ways in which McLuhan elaborated this point were rather idiosyncratic and, in some respects, implausible. I therefore develop the theme in a different way. Focusing on electronically mediated mass communication, and primarily on television, I distinguish several dimensions of interactional impact and analyse each in some detail. At the most fundamental level, *the deployment of technical media separates social interaction from physical locale*, so that individuals can interact with one another even though they do not share a common spatial–temporal setting. This implication is characteristic of all technical media which involve some degree of space–time distanciation (a telephone conversation, for example); but in the case of mass communication, the interaction established thereby assumes a particular form. Since mass communication institutes a fundamental break between the production and reception of symbolic forms, it makes possible a specific kind of interaction across time and space which we may call 'mediated quasi-interaction'. It is 'interaction' because it involves individuals communicating to others who respond to them in certain ways and who may form bonds – sometimes intense – of friendship, affection or loyalty with them. But it is 'quasi-interaction' because the flow of communication is predominantly one-way and the modes of response available to recipients are strictly circumscribed.

By separating social interaction from physical locale, the deployment of technical media enables individuals to *act for distant others*. Technical media enable individuals to communicate with others who are spatially and temporally remote, and individuals adapt their communicative behaviour in order to concur with the opportunities offered by the deployment of new media. The existence of the medium of television has given rise to a new category of action which is carried out with the aim of being televisable, that is, capable of being transmitted via television to a spatially distant and potentially vast audience. By being televised, action (and the individuals who perform it) acquires a new kind of *visibility* that was simply not possible prior to the advent of mass communication in general, and of television in particular. This aspect of mass communication has long been recognized by individuals involved in the pursuit and exercise of power within the institutions of the state: *in the era of mass communication, politics is inseparable from the art of managing visibility*. But it is important to stress that the increased visibility afforded by mass communication is a source both of enormous political opportunities and of unprecedented political risks. Through the medium of television, political figures can communicate to a vast and widely dispersed audience, can present themselves and their views in a carefully controlled fashion. But this medium also allows for the possibility that political figures may appear incompetent, ill-informed, out of control, in ways and on a scale which never existed before. In the electronically mediated political arena, an impromptu remark or an emotional outburst can bring about the fall of an aspiring leader. We do not have to look far to find examples of the distinctive kind of political fragility created by mass-mediated visibility, a fragility which is intrinsic to societies in which the process of mediazation has penetrated and, to some extent, reconstituted the political arena.

If the deployment of technical media has transformed the ways in which individuals produce and transmit messages, it has also transformed the life conditions of the individuals who receive these messages as a routine part of their daily lives. This is true in the relatively straightforward sense in which the deployment of a technical medium like television can transform, and to a significant extent has transformed, the spatial and temporal organization of everyday life for most individuals in modern societies. The television set often occupies a central location within the home and becomes the point around which other spaces and activities are organized. The scheduling of particular programmes may determine the way in which individuals organize the temporal flow of their activities in the course of an evening, a day or a week. But the deployment of technical media can transform the life conditions of recipients in a more complicated, less evident sense. For it enables individuals to experience events which take place in locales that are spatially and temporally remote, and this experience may in turn inform or stimulate forms of action or response on the part of recipients, including forms of collective or concerted action. The reception of mediated events greatly expands the range of possible experience to which individuals are, in principle, exposed. It enables individuals in one part of the world to witness events which take place in another, and to respond, individually or collectively, to these events. When individuals in London or New York, in Moscow or Prague, turn on their televisions and watch Chinese troops assaulting students in Tiananmen Square, or East German border guards dismantling the Berlin Wall, they are witnessing events of major historical significance, even though these events may be taking place in distant regions of the world; and the events themselves are subjected thereby to a new kind of *global scrutiny* which never existed before. Individuals are able to participate in a realm of cultural experience which is no longer restricted by the sharing of a common locale, while the activities of states and other organizations are open to view in a way which is becoming increasingly global in scope.

While the realm of mediated experience brought into being by the development of mass communication is no longer restricted by the sharing of a common locale, nevertheless the nature and potential impact of this new realm of experience is shaped by the institutional arrangements and forms of power that characterize the contexts within which media messages are produced, transmitted and received. The traditional liberal arguments in favour of the 'freedom of the press' were based on the assumption that the forms of power likely to be most restrictive, and likely to hinder most the capacity of the emerging media to express a diversity of opinions and points of view, were the forms of power institutionalized in the modern state. For the early liberal thinkers like Jeremy Bentham, James Mill and John Stuart Mill, the establishment of an independent press which was free from state censorship and control was vital for the development of a democratic polity in which a diversity of opinions could be expressed, and in which the activities of those who rule could be scrutinized, criticized and, if necessary, restrained. There is much that can be said in favour of the arguments put forward by these early liberal thinkers, arguments which retain their relevance and urgency today, in a world where attempts by state officials to restrict the flow of information and the circulation of ideas have by no means disappeared, either in the West or in the East. But the traditional liberal theory of the free press is, I shall argue, of limited value today in thinking about the nature and role of media institutions in modern societies. By placing so much emphasis on the dangers of state power, the early liberal theorists did not take sufficient account of a threat stemming from a different source: from the unhindered growth of media industries *qua* commercial concerns. Moreover, the traditional liberal theory was developed primarily with regard to the newspaper and publishing industries, and it cannot be easily and directly transposed to those sectors of the media industries that have assumed such importance in the twentieth century, sectors which are based on different technical media and which have developed within fundamentally different institutional frameworks.

In an attempt to move beyond the traditional liberal theory of the free press and to think about the most appropriate institutional frameworks for the development of media industries in the late twentieth century, I argue in favour of what may be called *the principle of regulated pluralism*. By 'regulated pluralism' I mean a broad institutional framework which would both accommodate and secure the existence of a plurality of independent media institutions in the different spheres of mass communication. This principle calls for two concrete measures: the de-concentration of resources in the media industries, and the insulation of media institutions from the exercise of state power. The principle defines a broad institutional space – a space between the unhindered operation of market forces, on the one hand, and the direct control of media institutions by the state, on the other – within which media organizations can operate and develop. It is a space that can accommodate a variety of specific organizational forms, whether these are located within the public domain, the private domain or the domain of what may be described as intermediate organizations. But it is also a space which must be seen as existing on a trans-national scale. Media institutions have long since ceased to operate within the confines of a single nation-state; the trans-national character of the forms of transmission associated with satellite technology represents only the most recent, if perhaps the most dramatic, stage of a process of globalization which the development of mass communication has both promoted and reflected. If we are to make the most of the new opportunities afforded by the deployment of new technologies in the sphere of mass communication, and if we are to avoid the dangers which the development of mass communication hitherto has displayed, then the implementation of the principle of regulated pluralism will require a level of political will and international co-operation which is all too often absent from the contemporary political scene.

The development of a social theory of mass communication provides a backcloth against which we can reconsider the problems associated with the analysis of ideology in modern societies. If we conceive of ideology in terms of the ways in which the meaning mobilized by symbolic forms serves to establish and sustain relations of domination, then we can see that the development of mass communication has enormous consequences for the nature and scope of ideological phenomena. With the development of mass communication, the circulation of symbolic forms is increasingly severed from the sharing of a common physical locale, and hence the mobilization of meaning is increasingly capable of transcending the social context within which symbolic forms are produced. It is only with the development of mass communication that ideological phenomena could become *mass* phenomena, that is, phenomena capable of affecting large numbers of individuals in diverse and segregated settings. If mass communication has become a major medium for the operation of ideology in modern societies, it is because it has become a major medium for the production and transmission of symbolic forms, and because the symbolic forms thereby produced are capable of circulating on an unprecedented scale, reaching millions of individuals who may share little in common other than their capacity to receive mass-mediated messages. But while the significance of mass communication should not be underestimated, we must add two qualifications. Mass communication has become a major medium of ideology in modern societies, but it is by no means the only medium. It is important to stress that ideology - understood broadly as meaning in the service of power - operates in a variety of contexts in everyday life, from ordinary conversations between friends to ministerial addresses on prime time television. Those concerned with the theory and analysis of ideology would be mistaken to focus exclusively on mass communication, just as they would be misguided if they ignored it. The second qualification is this: while the development of mass communication has created a new set of parameters for the operation of ideology in modern societies, the question of whether particular mass-mediated messages are ideological is a question which cannot be answered abstractly, but which must be pursued within the framework of a systematic interpretative methodology. Only in this way can we avoid the tendency - all too common in the literature - to assume that certain media messages are ideological as such and efficacious throughout the social world. The elaboration of a systematic methodology will enable us to develop an approach to the ideological character of media messages which is both more rigorous and more restrained.

The Methodology of Interpretation

Most of this book is concerned with problems of a general theoretical nature - the concept and role of ideology, the concept of culture and the characteristics of cultural transmission, the development of mass communication and its implications for social and political life. But an essential part of my argument is that these general theoretical problems can be, and should be, conjoined with issues of a more concrete, methodological character. In chapter 6 I explore some of the connections between theory and methodology, between theoretical reflection and methodical, detailed inquiry. My aim is not so much to prescribe or proscribe particular methods of research, but rather to outline a broad methodological framework within which particular methods can be situated and related to one another, and within which their value (as well as their limits) can be appraised.

   In developing this framework, I draw on a particular tradition of thought, a tradition that is commonly known as hermeneutics. Why hermeneutics? What does this ancient tradition of thought, stemming from Classical Greece, have to offer the student of modern culture? We can answer this question on two levels. On a general level, this tradition calls our attention to what I shall describe as *the hermeneutical conditions of social-historical inquiry*. These conditions stem from the constitution of the object domain of social–historical inquiry, an object domain which differs in certain fundamental respects from the object domains of the natural sciences. For the object domain of social–historical inquiry is not only a concatenation of objects and events which are there to be observed and explained: it is also a subject domain which is made up, in part, of subjects who, in the routine course of their everyday lives, are constantly involved in understanding themselves and others, in producing meaningful actions and expressions and in interpreting the meaningful actions and expressions produced by others. In other words, the object domain of social–historical inquiry is a *pre-interpreted domain* in which processes of understanding and interpretation take place as a routine part of the everyday lives of the individuals who, in part, make up this domain. The pre-interpreted character of the social–historical world is a constitutive feature which has no parallel in the natural sciences. In pursuing social–historical inquiry we are seeking to understand and explain a range of phenomena which are, in some way and to some extent, already understood by the individuals who are part of the social–historical world; we are seeking, in short, to re-interpret a pre-interpreted domain.

While the tradition of hermeneutics can call our attention to these and other hermeneutical conditions of social–historical inquiry, it can also provide us, on a more concrete level, with some methodological guidelines for research. I develop these guidelines by means of what I call *the methodological framework of depth hermeneutics*. The idea of depth hermeneutics is drawn from the work of Paul Ricoeur, among others. The value of this idea is that it enables us to develop a methodological framework which is orientated towards the interpretation (or re-interpretation) of meaningful phenomena, but in which different types of analysis can play legitimate and mutually supportive roles. It enables us to see that the process of interpretation is not necessarily opposed to types of analysis which are concerned with the structural features of symbolic forms or with the social–historical conditions of action and interaction, but that, on the contrary, these types of analysis can be linked together and construed as necessary steps along the path of interpretation. It also enables us to see that particular methods of analysis may shed light on some aspects of a phenomenon at the expense of others, that their analytical strength may be based on strict limits, and that these particular methods may best be regarded as partial stages within a more comprehensive methodological approach.

I develop depth hermeneutics as a general methodological framework for the analysis of cultural phenomena, that is, for the analysis of symbolic forms in structured contexts. Depth hermeneutics, on this account, is a

methodological framework comprising three principal phases or procedures. The first phase, which may be described as 'social–historical analysis', is concerned with the social and historical conditions of the production,
circulation and reception of symbolic forms. This phase is essential because
symbolic forms do not subsist in a vacuum: they are contextualized social
phenomena, they are produced, circulated and received within specific
social–historical conditions which can be reconstructed with the aid of
empirical, observational and documentary methods. The second phase of the
depth-hermeneutical framework may be described as 'formal or discursive
analysis'. To undertake formal or discursive analysis is to study symbolic
forms as complex symbolic constructions which display an articulated
structure. This phase is essential because symbolic forms are contextualized
social phenomena *and* something more: they are symbolic constructions
which, by virtue of their structural features, are able to, and claim to,
represent something, signify something, say something about something. It
is this additional and irreducible aspect of symbolic forms which calls for a
different type of analysis, for an analytical phase which is concerned
primarily with the internal organization of symbolic forms, with their
structural features, patterns and relations. But this phase of analysis, while
perfectly legitimate, can become misleading when it is removed from the
framework of depth hermeneutics and pursued as an end in itself. Taken on
its own, formal or discursive analysis can become – and in many instances has
become – an abstract exercise, disconnected from social–historical conditions and oblivious to what is being expressed by the symbolic forms whose
structure it seeks to unveil.

The third and final phase of the depth-hermeneutical framework is what
may properly be called 'interpretation' (or 're-interpretation'). This phase is
concerned with the creative explication of what is said or represented by a
symbolic form; it is concerned with the creative construction of possible
meaning. The phase of interpretation builds upon the results of social–
historical analysis and formal or discursive analysis, but it moves beyond
them in a process of synthetic construction. It uses social–historical analysis
and formal or discursive analysis to shed light on the social conditions and
structural features of a symbolic form, and it seeks to interpret a symbolic
form in this light, to explicate and elaborate what it says, what it represents,
what it is about. This process of interpretation is at the same time a process
of re-interpretation, in the sense that it is a re-interpretation – mediated by
the phases of the depth-hermeneutical framework – of an object domain
which is already interpreted and understood by the subjects who make up
the social–historical world. In offering an interpretation of symbolic forms,
we are re-interpreting a pre-interpreted domain, and thus engaging in a

process which can, by its very nature, give rise to a conflict of inter-pretations.

The depth-hermeneutical approach, which I develop as a general framework for cultural analysis, can be adapted to the analysis of ideology. I regard the analysis of ideology as a specific form or version of depth hermeneutics. The specificity of this form consists in the fact that the various phases of the depth-hermeneutical approach are employed with the aim of highlighting the ideological character of symbolic forms, that is, with the aim of highlighting the ways in which meaning serves to establish and sustain relations of domination. Elaborated in terms of the methodological framework of depth hermeneutics, the phrase 'the interpretation of ideology' acquires a precise sense: to interpret ideology is to explicate the connection between the meaning mobilized by symbolic forms and the relations of domination which that meaning serves to maintain. The interpretation of ideology draws on the phases of social-historical analysis and formal or discursive analysis, but it gives them a critical emphasis: it employs them with the aim of disclosing meaning in the service of power. The interpretation of ideology is depth hermeneutics with a critical intent. The potential conflict inherent in the process of interpretation thus assumes a new and distinctive form when we are concerned with interpreting the ideological character of symbolic forms.

If we turn our attention to analysing symbolic forms in the context of mass communication, we must confront a new range of methodological problems. These problems stem primarily from the fact, noted earlier, that mass communication institutes a fundamental break between the pro-duction and reception of symbolic forms. In view of this characteristic, we must adopt a somewhat different approach to the analysis of mass-mediated symbolic forms. We must distinguish between three aspects or object domains of mass communication, and then apply the depth-hermeneutical procedures in differing ways to each. The three aspects are: first, the production and transmission or diffusion of mass-mediated symbolic forms; second, the construction of media messages; and third, the reception and appropriation of media messages. I describe this as the 'tripartite approach' to mass communication. All three aspects are involved in the production and circulation of mass-mediated symbolic forms. But since mass communica-tion institutes a break between production and reception, the conditions of production and transmission are generally distinct from the conditions of reception and appropriation, and must be analysed separately. While each aspect of mass communication can be analysed separately (and generally is in the empirical literature on mass communication), the tripartite approach highlights the fact that each aspect is defined by abstracting from the other aspects of a complex, integrated process. The tripartite approach reminds us that a comprehensive account of mass communication requires the capacity to analyse all three aspects and to show how these aspects relate to one another in the production, transmission and reception of mass-mediated symbolic forms.

The account I offer of the interpretation of ideology, combined with the tripartite approach to mass communication, enables us to pose in a new way the methodological problems involved in seeking to analyse ideology in the context of an increasingly mass-mediated culture. In much of the earlier literature on the ideological character of mass communication, analysts have tended to focus largely or exclusively on the structure and content of media messages, and have tried to 'read off' the consequences of these messages by reflecting on the messages themselves. This kind of analysis falls foul of what I call the 'fallacy of internalism', a fallacy which, in developing my methodological proposals, I am particularly concerned to avoid. In seeking to analyse the ideological character of mass-mediated symbolic forms, we must take account of all three aspects of mass communication – the production/ transmission, construction, and reception/appropriation of media messages – and we must give particular attention to what may be called *the everyday appropriation of mass-mediated products*. If we are interested in the way in which meaning serves to establish and sustain relations of domination, then we must examine how the meaning mobilized by mass-mediated symbolic forms is understood and appraised by the individuals who, in the course of their everyday routines, receive media messages and incorporate them into their lives. We must examine their everyday understanding, their routine practices of reception and appropriation, and the social–historical conditions within which these practices of reception and processes of understanding take place. We cannot take these practices and processes for granted; we cannot assume that a message constructed in a certain way will be understood in a certain way by all recipients in all contexts; we cannot claim or pretend to read off the consequences of media messages by attending to the structure and content of the messages alone. By examining the everyday appropriation of media messages in relation to the other aspects of mass communication, we can develop an interpretation of the ideological character of mass-mediated symbolic forms which avoids the fallacy of internalism, and which highlights the ways in which the meaning mobilized by media messages serves to sustain or disrupt, to establish or undermine, the structured social contexts within which individuals receive these messages and incorporate them into their everyday lives.

By reformulating the methodological issues in this way, we can avoid not only the fallacy of internalism, but also the myth that commonly accompanies it – the myth of the passive recipient. The idea that the recipients of media messages are passive onlookers who simply absorb what flashes before them on the screen, or what obtrudes from the page, is a myth that bears no resemblance to the actual character of appropriation as an ongoing process of understanding and interpretation, of discussion, appraisal and incorporation. The process of appropriation is an active and potentially critical process in which individuals are involved in a continuous *effort to understand*, an effort to make sense of the messages they receive, to relate to them and to share them with others. By engaging in this effort to understand, individuals are also engaging, however implicitly and unselfconsciously, in a process of self-formation and self-understanding, in a process of re-forming and re-understanding themselves through the messages they receive and seek to understand. In the course of receiving media messages and seeking to understand them, of relating to them and sharing them with others, individuals re-mould the boundaries of their experience and revise their understanding of the world and of themselves. They are not passively absorbing what is presented to them, but are actively, sometimes critically, engaged in a continuing process of self-formation and self-understanding, a process of which the reception and appropriation of media messages is today an integral part.

The critical potential inherent in the interpretation of ideology may be regarded, in part, as a contribution to this process of self-formation and self-understanding. In developing an interpretation of ideology, we are putting forward an interpretation which may diverge from the everyday under-standing of the individuals who make up the social world. The interpretation of ideology may enable individuals to see symbolic forms differently, in a new light, and thereby to see themselves differently. It may enable them to re-interpret a symbolic form in relation to the conditions of its production and reception, in relation to its structural features and organization; it may enable them to question or revise their prior understanding of a symbolic form, and thereby to alter the horizons of their understanding of themselves and others. I describe this process, the possibility of which is implicit in the interpretation of ideology, as *the interpretative transformation of doxa* – that is, the interpretative transformation of the everyday understandings, attitudes and beliefs of the individuals who make up the social world.

There is a second respect in which the interpretation of ideology implies a critical potential: it opens a path for a critical reflection, not only on the everyday understanding of lay actors, but also on the relations of power and domination within which these actors are enmeshed. The interpretation of ideology necessarily involves the social–historical analysis of structured relations of power, with reference to which the role of symbolic forms is considered. Hence the interpretation of ideology may serve to stimulate a critical reflection on relations of power and domination, their bases, their grounds and the modes by which they are sustained. It is in this sense that the interpretation of ideology bears an internal connection to what may be called *the critique of domination*: it is methodologically predisposed to stimulate a critical reflection on relations of power and domination. This is one of the reasons why the interpretation of ideology may elicit strong reactions from some of the individuals who make up the social world. It touches the nerves of power, it highlights the positions of those who benefit most and those who benefit least from existing social relations, and it examines some of the symbolic mechanisms by virtue of which these asymmetrical social relations are established and sustained in the day-to-day flow of social life.

The process of interpretation in general, and of the interpretation of ideology in particular, raises certain problems concerning the kinds of justification which are possible and appropriate in the realm of social-historical inquiry. My approach to these problems is piecemeal. I do not search for some general criterion which would magically resolve all disputes, but I ask, instead, what kinds of disputes we can expect to have in this realm of inquiry and how we might reasonably proceed to resolve them. This approach requires us to analyse the issues, break down the problems and try to define some of the conditions – however tentatively – under which conflicting interpretations and conflicting views could be compared and debated, under which different kinds of evidence and arguments could be adduced, and under which disagreements could, perhaps, be resolved. This piecemeal approach to problems of justification may disappoint those who long for certainty, who long for some 'foundation' (to use that fateful metaphor) upon which our knowledge of the social-historical world could be painstakingly and unshakeably built. But this quest for certainty is misguided; it is an epistemological impulse which wreaks havoc in an object domain that is too complex for intellectual criteria of this kind. On the other hand, the piecemeal approach I advocate may seem strangely old-fashioned to those who have long since abandoned the quest for certainty, seeing the modern (or 'post-modern') age as one in which we have, or should have, finally recognized that there are no valid criteria of justification and that all we have are multiple interpretations, competing with one another, playing off against one another, and surviving or slipping away by virtue of the power they possess. But these critics have, in my view, gone too far. We can reject the quest for certainty without abandoning the attempt to elucidate the conditions under which we can make reasonable judgements about the plausibility or implausibility of an interpretation, or the justness or otherwise of an institution. These conditions cannot determine our judgements, and these judgements may not be infallible. But in the sphere of social–historical inquiry, where we are seeking to understand an object domain already understood by the subjects who make up this domain, the exercise of reasonable judgement may be a particularly valuable gain.

1

The Concept of Ideology

For two centuries the concept of ideology has occupied a central, if at times inglorious, place in the development of social and political thought. Originally introduced by Destutt de Tracy as a label for a proposed science of ideas, the term 'ideology' quickly became a weapon in a political battle fought out on the terrain of language. Originally imbued with all of the confidence and positive spirit of the European Enlightenment, for which the science it described was supposed to represent a culminating stage, 'ideology' quickly became a term of abuse which alleged the emptiness, the idleness, the sophistry of certain ideas. The concept of ideology had a difficult birth and, as if this were not enough, the subsequent life history was hardly blissful. Taken up in differing ways by the emerging social sciences of the nineteenth and early twentieth centuries, the concept of ideology was pulled in one direction and pushed in another, and all the while it remained a term which played a role in the political battles of everyday life. When we use the concept of ideology today, we employ a concept which bears the traces, however faintly, of the multiple uses which characterize its history.

In this chapter I want to retrace the historical contours of the concept of ideology, with a view not only to highlighting the twists and turns of a complex intellectual itinerary, but also to preparing the way for a more constructive approach. I want to inquire, not only into the origins and development of this concept, but also into the prospects for reformulating the concept today, for re-conceptualizing ideology in a way which draws upon the accumulated sense of the concept while avoiding the many pitfalls which can be discerned in its past. My account of the history of the concept will, necessarily, be selective and will neglect many figures and diversions which would merit discussion in a more thorough survey.[1] But I shall aim to identify the main contours, the main lines of development in a history which has by no means drawn to a close. I shall begin by discussing the origins of the concept of ideology in late eighteenth-century France. Then I shall examine some of the ways in which the concept is employed in the work of Marx. While Marx is undoubtedly the most important figure in the history of the concept of ideology, his writings do not offer a single, coherent view. He uses this term occasionally and erratically; and one can discern several different themes which are associated with its use. In the third part of the chapter I shall consider the work of Karl Mannheim. Mannheim's *Ideology and Utopia* is a key text in this complex history; it focused the concept of ideology on the general problem of the social determination of thought, and thus treated the analysis of ideology as co-extensive with the sociology of knowledge. In the final sections of this chapter I shall resist the tendency, exemplified by Mannheim's work, to generalize the concept of ideology. I shall offer a formulation of the concept which preserves its negative character, which treats it as a critical concept but which rejects any suggestion that the analysis of ideology is a matter of pure polemics. I shall formulate a conception of ideology which draws on some of the themes implicit in the history of this concept, but which seeks to provide a basis for a constructive approach to the interpretation of ideology in modern societies.

Ideology and the Ideologues

The term 'ideology' was first used by the French philosopher Destutt de Tracy in 1796 to describe his project of a new science which would be concerned with the systematic analysis of ideas and sensations, of their generation, combination and consequences. Destutt de Tracy was a wealthy and educated nobleman who had studied the works of Enlightenment thinkers such as Voltaire, Holbach and Condillac. While de Tracy supported many of the reforms associated with the French Revolution, he, like other intellectuals of noble descent, was imprisoned during the Jacobin Terror.[2] To de Tracy and some of his fellow prisoners, it seemed as though Robespierre was seeking to destroy the Enlightenment. For these intellectuals, the barbaric anarchy of the Terror could be countered by a combination of philosophy and education based on the systematic analysis of ideas: this was how the legacy of the Enlightenment could be pursued in a revolutionary age. While many ex-nobles and intellectuals died or were put to death during the Terror, de Tracy was released from prison soon after the fall of Robespierre in 1794. In late 1795 de Tracy and his associates rose to a position of power in the new republic with the creation of the *Institut National*. The *Institut* was a replacement for the royal academies which had been abolished by Robespierre. In addition to an Academy of Sciences and a Class of Literature and Fine Arts, the *Institut* included a Class of Moral and Political Sciences. The latter class was headed by a section concerned with the analysis of sensations and ideas, a section to which de Tracy was elected in 1796.

Destutt de Tracy outlined the aims of the new discipline for which he had assumed responsibility in a series of memoirs delivered to the Class of Moral and Political Sciences in the course of 1796. Following Condillac, de Tracy argued that we cannot know things in themselves, but only the ideas formed by our sensations of them. If we could analyse these ideas and sensations in a systematic way, we could provide a firm basis for all scientific knowledge and draw inferences of a more practical kind. The name de Tracy proposed for this incipient and ambitious enterprise was 'ideology' – literally, the 'science of ideas'. Ideology was to be 'positive, useful, and susceptible of rigorous exactitude'.[3] Genealogically it was the 'first science', since all scientific knowledge involved the combination of ideas. It was also the basis of grammar, logic, education, morality and, ultimately, 'the greatest of the arts . . ., that of regulating society in such a way that man finds there the most help and the least possible annoyance from his own kind'.[4] Through a careful analysis of ideas and sensations, ideology would enable human nature to be understood, and hence would enable the social and political order to be re-arranged in accordance with the needs and aspirations of human beings. Ideology would place the moral and political sciences on a firm foundation and cure them of error and 'prejudice' – an Enlightenment faith that de Tracy inherited from Condillac and Bacon.

While de Tracy envisaged the possibility of extending the science of ideas to the social and political realm, most of his contributions were concerned with the analysis of intellectual faculties, forms of experience and aspects of logic and grammar. His four-volume *Élémens d'Idéologie*, published between 1803 and 1815, examined the faculties of thinking, feeling, memory and judgement, and the characteristics of habit, movement and the will, among other things. De Tracy became increasingly concerned with the develop-ment of a consistent and rigorous naturalism in which human beings are regarded as part of material reality, as one rather complex animal species among others. Hence, in de Tracy's view, 'Ideology is part of Zoology', and the analysis of human faculties is essential because 'our understanding of an animal is incomplete if we do not know its intellectual faculties'.[5] De Tracy's later writings continued the original project of ideology *qua* science of ideas, embedding this project within a thoroughgoing naturalism. But by the time these writings appeared, the term 'ideology' had acquired a new and quite different sense, a sense which would soon eclipse the grandiloquent aims of its inventor.

Destutt de Tracy and his associates in the *Institut National* were closely linked to the politics of republicanism. They generally shared Condorcet's vision of the perfectibility of human beings through education, and Condillac's method of analysing sensations and ideas. They attributed the excesses of the Revolution to the fanatical fervour of the Jacobins rather than to the revolutionary institutions as such, which they saw as pillars of progress and enlightenment. Given this close connection with republicanism, the fate of the doctrines of de Tracy and his associates was dependent to some extent on the fate of the Revolution itself. On his return from Egypt in 1799, Napoleon Bonaparte staged a successful *coup d'état* and became First Consul, a position which he held, with complete authority, for ten years. Napoleon drew on some of the ideas of de Tracy and his associates in devising a new constitution and rewarded some members of the *Institut* with lucrative political positions. But at the same time he distrusted them, for their affiliation with republicanism presented a potential threat to his autocratic ambitions. Hence Napoleon ridiculed the pretensions of 'ideology': it was, in his view, an abstract speculative doctrine which was divorced from the realities of political power. In January 1800 an article in the *Messager des relations extérieures* denounced the group which is 'called by the name metaphysical faction or "idéologues"' and which, having mishandled the Revolution, was now plotting against the new regime.[6] As public opinion began to turn against the Revolution, Napoleon – who later claimed to have coined the term '*idéologues*' – exploited this shift in order to disarm the representatives of republicanism.

Napoleon's opposition to the *idéologues* intensified during the following decade and reached a climax as the empire which he sought to establish began to collapse. The *idéologues* became the scapegoat for the failures of the Napoleonic regime. Returning to Paris in December 1812 after the disastrous Russian campaign, Napoleon accused the *idéologues* of undermining the state and the rule of law. Addressing the Council of State in a speech subsequently published in the *Moniteur*, he condemned ideology and characterized it as the very obverse of astute statecraft:

> We must lay the blame for the ills that our fair France has suffered on ideology, that shadowy metaphysics which subtly searches for first causes on which to base the legislation of peoples, rather than making use of laws known to the human heart and of the lessons of history. These errors must inevitably and did in fact lead to the rule of bloodthirsty men . . . When someone is summoned to revitalize a state, he must follow exactly the opposite principles.[7]

As Napoleon's position weakened both at home and abroad, his attacks on ideology became more sweeping and vehement. Nearly all kinds of religious and philosophical thought were condemned as ideology. The term itself had become a weapon in the hands of an emperor struggling desperately to silence his opponents and to sustain a crumbling regime.

With the abdication of Napoleon in April 1814 and the restoration of the Bourbon dynasty, Destutt de Tracy was returned to a position of political influence, but by then his original programme of ideology had been dissipated and tarnished by the conflicts of the Napoleonic period. Originally conceived of as the pre-eminent science, the science of ideas which, by providing a systematic account of the genesis, combination and communication of ideas, would provide a basis for scientific knowledge in general and would facilitate the natural regulation of society in particular, ideology had become one orientation among others and its philosophical claims had been compromised by its association with republicanism. Moreover, as the term 'ideology' slipped into the political arena and was hurled back at the philosophers by an emperor under siege, the sense and reference of the term began to change. It ceased to refer only to the *science of ideas* and began to refer also to the *ideas themselves*, that is, to *a body of ideas which are alleged to be erroneous and divorced from the practical realities of political life*. The sense of the term also changed, for it could no longer lay claim unequivocally to the positive spirit of the Enlightenment. Ideology *qua* positive and pre-eminent science, worthy of the highest respect, gradually gave way to ideology *qua* abstract and illusory ideas, worthy only of derision and disdain. One of the basic oppositions that have characterized the history of the concept of ideology – that between a positive or neutral sense, on the one hand, and a negative or critical sense, on the other – had already appeared in the first decade of its life, although the form and content of this opposition was to change considerably in the decades that followed.

The demise of Destutt de Tracy's original project of ideology seems hardly surprising today. The ambitious generality of this project, like that of others which preceded and succeeded it, was bound to give way to the development of specialized disciplines which could pursue particular fields of inquiry in depth, unhindered by the pretensions of a would-be foundational science. What is interesting about de Tracy's original project is not so much the nature and content of the project itself (indeed, his writings, already largely forgotten, would be totally neglected today had they not been linked to the concept of ideology) but the fact that this project highlights the conditions under which the concept of ideology emerged and began its circuitous history. The concept emerged as part of the attempt to develop the ideals of the Enlightenment in the context of the social and political upheavals that marked the birth of modern societies. However far the concept of ideology has travelled since the days of the *Institut National*, however varied its uses have become, nevertheless it remains tied to the ideals of the Enlightenment, in particular to the ideals of the rational understanding of the world (including the social–historical world) and of the rational self-determination of human beings. The ways in which this link is expressed vary considerably from one figure to another. If for de Tracy the link was direct and explicit (ideology was the pre-eminent science that would facilitate progress in human affairs), for Napoleon it was implicit and oppositional (ideology was the pretentious philosophy that incited rebellion by trying to determine political and pedagogical principles on the basis of abstract reasoning alone). The unique contribution of Marx consists in the fact that he took over the negative, oppositional sense conveyed by Napoleon's use of the term, but transformed the concept by incorporating it into a theoretical framework and political programme which were deeply indebted to the spirit of the Enlightenment.

Marx's Conceptions of Ideology

Marx's writings occupy a central position in the history of the concept of ideology. With Marx the concept acquired a new status as a critical tool and as an integral component of a new theoretical system. But in spite of the importance of Marx's work in this regard, the precise ways in which Marx employed the concept of ideology, and the ways in which he dealt with the many issues and assumptions surrounding its use, are by no means clear. Indeed, it is the very ambiguity of the concept of ideology in Marx's work which is partly responsible for continuing debates concerning the legacy of his writings. In this section I shall not attempt to examine all of the different shades of meaning which may be conveyed by Marx's varied uses of the term 'ideology', nor shall I trace the ways in which this term is employed by Marx's associates and followers, such as Engels, Lenin, Lukács and Gramsci.[8] I shall seek instead to identify several distinctive theoretical contexts in which the concept of ideology operates in the work of Marx. In doing so I shall attempt to elicit several distinct *conceptions* of ideology in Marx, conceptions which overlap with one another, of course, but which nevertheless relate to different issues and to different movements of thought. For Marx's work offers us not so much a single coherent vision of the social–historical world and its constitution, dynamics and development, but rather a multiplicity of views which cohere in some respects and conflict in others, which converge on some points and diverge on others, views which are sometimes explicitly articulated by Marx but which are sometimes left implicit in his arguments and analyses. I shall try to show that these different views create distinct theoretical spaces, as it were, in which several conceptions of ideology co-exist without being clearly formulated or cogently reconciled by Marx himself.

Ideology and the Young Hegelians: the polemical conception

Marx was familiar with the work of the French *idéologues* and with Napoleon's attack on it. During his exile in Paris in 1844–5 he had read and excerpted some of Destutt de Tracy's work. It was immediately after this period that Marx and Engels composed *The German Ideology*, a lengthy text in which they criticize the views of the 'Young Hegelians' such as Feuerbach, Bauer and Stirner. In characterizing the views of these thinkers as 'the German ideology', Marx and Engels were following Napoleon's use of the term 'ideology' and were drawing a comparison between the work of the *idéologues* and that of the Young Hegelians: the work of the Young Hegelians was the equivalent, in the relatively backward social and political conditions of early nineteenth-century Germany, of the doctrines of de Tracy and his associates. And just as Napoleon had poured scorn on these doctrines, thus giving the term 'ideology' a negative inflection, so too Marx and Engels derided the views of their compatriots. Like the *idéologues*, the Young Hegelians laboured under the illusion that the real battle to be fought was a battle of ideas, that, by taking up a critical attitude towards received ideas, reality itself could be changed. Marx's and Engels's critique of the Young Hegelians' 'critical thinking' was an attempt to disarm the approach of their erstwhile associates. Their aim was 'to debunk and discredit the philosophical struggle with the shadows of reality, which appeals to the dreamy and muddled German nation'.[9] The Young Hegelians thought they were radical but were in fact quite conservative, mere sheep who took themselves for wolves. In branding their views as 'the German ideology', Marx and Engels sought to discredit them by association with doctrines which had been fervently denounced in France several decades earlier.

In *The German Ideology* Marx and Engels thus employ the term 'ideology' in a polemical way. Their target is specific – the views of the Young Hegelians – and 'ideology' is used as a term of abuse. The views of the Young Hegelians are 'ideological' in the sense that they overestimate the value and role of ideas in history and in social life; they 'consider conceptions, thoughts, ideas, in fact all products of consciousness, to which they attribute an independent existence, as the real chains of men (just as the Old Hegelians declared them the true bonds of human society)'.[10] Hence the Young Hegelians oppose ideas with ideas, they fight phrases with phrases, and as a result they leave the real world unchanged. They fail to see the connection between their ideas and the social–historical conditions of Germany and they fail to give their criticism any practical, effective force. We may characterize this use of the term 'ideology' as the 'polemical conception': *ideology, on this account, is a theoretical doctrine and activity which erroneously regards ideas as autonomous and efficacious and which fails to grasp the real conditions and characteristics of social-historical life.* This polemical conception is indebted to Napoleon's attack on the pretensions of the *idéologues*, in so far as it shares Napoleon's contempt for the preoccupation with ideas divorced from practical politics, and in so far as it reflects the conviction that such ideas and preoccupations are illusory or misleading. But the way in which Marx and Engels develop their conception, and the uses to which they put it, go well beyond the aims and deliberations of Napoleon.

The originality of the polemical conception of ideology lies not so much in the conception itself as in the fact that it is linked to a series of assumptions concerning the social determination of consciousness, the division of labour and the scientific study of the social-historical world. These assumptions form what may be described as the conditions of possibility of the polemical conception of ideology. Let us examine each of these assumptions in turn. *Assumption 1a*: the forms of consciousness of human beings are determined by the material conditions of their life. Thinking, conceiving and, more generally, the production of ideas should be regarded, not as autonomous processes and even less as processes which prescribe the course of history, but rather as processes which are interwoven with, and essentially determined by, the mundane activity of human beings collectively producing their means of subsistence. In formulating this assumption Marx and Engels are primarily concerned to juxtapose their approach to what they regard as the idealistic philosophical practice of Hegel, his followers and critics: 'In direct contrast to German philosophy which descends from heaven to earth, here we ascend from earth to heaven.'[11] But they also want to claim that this idealistic philosophical practice – the fact that it is idealistic, that it takes ideas for causes rather than effects, that it therefore misunderstands its own character as well as the character of the social-historical world which it seeks to grasp, in a word, the fact that it is ideological – they want to claim that this is itself the product of particular material conditions. If we assume the social determination of consciousness, we can see that the ideology of the Young Hegelians is an expression of the relatively backward social, political and economic conditions of Germany. The point, moreover, can be generalized. This is what Marx and Engels propose in an oft-quoted passage: 'If in all ideology men and their circumstances appear upside-down as in a *camera obscura*, this phenomenon arises just as much from their historical life-process as the inversion of objects on the retina does from their physical life-process.'[12] While this passage is most memorable for the cryptic analogy with a *camera obscura*, an analogy which has ensnared more than one commentator,[13] the main point is the claim that the practice of regarding consciousness and ideas as autonomous and efficacious, and hence of regarding real individuals in their actual circumstances as the products of ideas rather than the producers of them, is itself the outcome of particular social–historical conditions and processes, just as 'the inversion of objects on the retina [arises] from their physical life-process.'

The polemical conception of ideology is also linked with an assumption concerning the division of labour. *Assumption 1b*: the development of theoretical doctrines and activities which regard ideas as autonomous and efficacious is made possible by the historically emergent division between material and mental labour. Marx and Engels posit a primeval state of human society in which individuals were conscious of little else than their own needs, their immediate environment and their limited interactions with other human beings. Consciousness, at this stage, was mere 'herd-consciousness', inextricably interwoven with the material conditions of life. But gradually a division of labour developed, initially as a division of labour in the sexual act and then as a division which developed spontaneously or 'naturally' by virtue of different needs and capacities, such as physical strength. Eventually a division emerged between material and mental labour, a division that enabled those individuals engaged in mental labour to produce ideas which seemed to have an independent existence, to be unconditioned by material life-processes and to have a history and a power of their own. The division between material and mental labour also prevented these individuals from seeing that they were labouring under the illusion of autonomy.

> From this moment onwards consciousness *can* really flatter itself that it is something other than consciousness of existing practice, that it *really* represents something without representing something real; from now on consciousness is in a position to emancipate itself from the world and to proceed to the formation of 'pure' theory, theology, philosophy, ethics, etc.[14]

The formation of 'pure' theory, theology, philosophy, ethics and 'all such muck', as Marx and Engels provocatively put it, marks the emergence of ideology in the sense of theoretical doctrines and activities which suppose themselves to be autonomous when, in fact, they are not.

The third assumption linked with the polemical conception concerns the project of a scientific study of the social–historical world. *Assumption 1c*: the theoretical doctrines and activities which constitute ideology can be explained by means of, and should be replaced by, the scientific study of society and history. They can be explained by means of such a science in the sense that they can be shown to be the product of particular social and historical circumstances, as the views of the Young Hegelians, for example, can be shown to be but a mirror of the real and wretched conditions of Germany. They should be replaced by such a science in the sense that, having been shown to be dependent on circumstances of which they are unaware and having thereby undermined their claim to autonomy, these theoretical doctrines and activities lose their credibility and give way to a successor discipline: the positive science of the social–historical world. 'Where speculation ends – in real life – there real, positive science begins: the representation of the practical activity, of the practical process of the development of men. Empty talk about consciousness ceases, and real knowledge has to take its place.'[15] This assumption indicates the proximity of Marx and Engels to the original project of Destutt de Tracy, in spite of the many differences that separate them from him. For although Marx and Engels regard de Tracy's project as the epitome of ideology in the sense of an abstract and illusory theoretical doctrine, they nevertheless share de Tracy's belief in the merits of positive science and, more generally, his faith in the ideals of the Enlightenment. It is one of the ironies of this complex conceptual history that what began life as the allegedly pre-eminent science, the 'science of ideas', became part of a theoretical approach which claimed the title to the throne of science while denouncing its progenitor as a traitor.

Ideology and class consciousness: the epiphenomenal conception

While the concept of ideology was initially employed by Marx and Engels in the context of their attack on the Young Hegelians, it subsequently acquired a more general role in their characterization of social structure and historical change. This more general role is already evident in *The German Ideology*, as Marx and Engels begin to link the production and diffusion of ideas to the relation between classes. 'The ideas of the ruling class', they remark at one point, 'are in every epoch the ruling ideas, i.e. the class which is the ruling *material* force of society, is at the same time its ruling *intellectual* force.'[16] This passage foreshadows the development of a new conception of ideology, a conception which emerges more clearly in Marx's 1859 Preface to *A Contribution to the Critique of Political Economy* and elsewhere. We may describe this new conception as the 'epiphenomenal conception', since it regards ideology as dependent on, and derived from, the economic conditions and class relations of production. *Ideology, according to the epiphenomenal conception, is a system of ideas which expresses the interests of the dominant class but which represents class relations in an illusory form*. Ideology expresses the interests of the dominant class in the sense that the ideas which compose ideology are ideas which, in any particular historical period, articulate the ambitions, concerns and wishful deliberations of the dominant social groups as they struggle to secure and maintain their position of domination. But ideology represents class relations in an illusory form in so far as these ideas do not accurately portray the nature and relative positions of the classes concerned; rather, they misrepresent these relations in a way which concurs with the interests of the dominant class.

With the formulation of the epiphenomenal conception, the notion of ideology acquires a systematic role in Marx's theoretical framework. This framework is sketched most succinctly, if somewhat simplistically, in the 1859 Preface. There is no need here to examine the Preface in detail, since its contentions are well known. But we shall gain a clearer view of the epiphenomenal conception of ideology by considering a short passage from this text. Having noted that a period of social revolution breaks out when the ever-expanding forces of production come into conflict with the existing relations of production, Marx elaborates as follows:

> In considering such transformations a distinction should always be made between the material transformation of the economic conditions of production, which can be determined with the precision of natural science, and the legal, political, religious, aesthetic or philosophic – in short, ideological forms in which men become conscious of this conflict and fight it out ... [we cannot] judge of such a period of transformation by its own consciousness; on the contrary, this consciousness must be explained rather from the contradictions of material life.[17]

From this and other passages in the Preface and elsewhere, we can elicit some of the assumptions which underlie the epiphenomenal conception. Once again, I shall focus on three key assumptions. *Assumption 2a*: in a given society we can distinguish between (i) the economic conditions of production, (ii) the legal and political superstructure and (iii) the ideological forms of consciousness. The precise content of each of these categories is not spelled out unambiguously by Marx (whether (iii) can always be clearly distinguished from (ii), for example, is a moot point); and the nature of the relations between these various aspects or levels of a society has been a matter of extensive debate. What can be said uncontroversially is that Marx assumes that the economic conditions of production have a primary role in determining the process of social–historical change and that they should therefore be regarded as a principal means of explaining particular social–historical transformations.

The first assumption leads directly to a second. *Assumption 2b*: ideological forms of consciousness are not to be taken at their face value but are to be explained by reference to the economic conditions of production. 'Just as our opinion of an individual is not based on what he thinks of himself,' comments Marx, 'so [we cannot] judge of such a period of transformation by its own consciousness'.[18] To understand social-historical change we must *begin* by examining the development of the economic conditions of production, 'which can be determined with the precision of natural science', and our knowledge of this development will then enable us to explain the ideological forms of consciousness characteristic of the period concerned. Moreover, by explaining ideological forms of consciousness in this way – by showing, for example, that declarations of the sanctity and universality of private property are expressions of the particular interests of a class whose dominance and livelihood depend on the possession of such property – we can also *unmask* these forms of consciousness. To unmask a form of consciousness is to show that it is illusory, mistaken or without rational justification; it implies not only that it can be explained by reference to socio-economic conditions, but also that it misrepresents these conditions or that it has no justification other than the empirically demonstrable fact that it expresses the particular interests of groups whose positions are determined by these conditions. The very characterization of a form of consciousness as 'ideological', according to this conception, implies that it can be explained and thereby unmasked as an expression of dominant class interests. Hence an inquiry that presents itself as a *science*, concerned with investigating the economic conditions of social life and explaining forms of consciousness on the basis thereof, can be harnessed in the service of a *critique* which unmasks forms of consciousness – and, more specifically, the theories and concepts of philosophers and others – as ideological.

The epiphenomenal conception of ideology is linked to a third assumption concerning the progressive character of the modern era. In previous forms of society the relations between classes were always interwoven with religious and sentimental ties, so that processes of exploitation were veiled by feelings of duty, honour and worth. But with the advent of capitalism, these traditional values are destroyed and social relations become visible, for the first time in human history, to the individuals involved in production. This radical transformation associated with the modern era is vividly described by Marx and Engels in the *Manifesto of the Communist Party*:

> Constant revolutionising of production, uninterrupted disturbance of all social conditions, everlasting uncertainty and agitation distinguish the bourgeois epoch from all earlier ones. All fixed, fast-frozen relations, with their train of ancient and venerable prejudices and opinions, are swept away, all

new-formed ones become antiquated before they can ossify. All that is solid melts into air, all that is holy is profaned, and man is at last compelled to face with sober senses, his real conditions of life, and his relations with his kind.[19]

Hence it is the very movement of the modern capitalist mode of production, the profound upheaval associated with its ceaseless expansion, which renders social relations transparent to individuals and compels them to face, 'with sober senses', their real conditions of life. *Assumption 2c*: the development of modern capitalism creates the conditions for a clear understanding of social relations and for the elimination of the class antagonisms upon which ideology depends. For the first time in history the subordinate class can understand its position as a class and its position within the historical process more generally. It can constitute itself as the revolutionary class, the class which, equipped with knowledge and experience, is able not merely to become a new dominant class, but to eliminate classes as such; the proletariat is a class which holds the universal interest of humanity in its grasp. The progressive, dynamic character of the modern era will ensure the ultimate victory of the proletariat; it may suffer temporary setbacks, but in the long run nothing, including the ideological notions of bourgeois apologists, can stand in its way. Indeed, as the hour of victory nears, a handful of 'bourgeois ideologists' will abandon their class and join forces with the proletariat, which they will come to recognize as the champion of humanity as a whole. The demise of bourgeois ideology is guaranteed by the movement of history itself, a movement in which the proletariat will inevitably emerge as the harbinger of a new era.

Ideology and the spirits of the past: a latent conception

There are parts of Marx's work, however, in which the movement of history appears to be somewhat less straightforward. The vision of a growing simplification of social antagonisms, the gradual reduction of all social conflicts to the opposition between bourgeoisie and proletariat and the progressive enlightenment of the proletariat itself: this vision is countered by a view which depicts the present as a scene of complexity rather than simplicity, of multiple schisms rather than one grand opposition, of individuals captivated by images and expressions from the past, acting out their historical roles on the basis of pre-given scripts rather than knowledge derived through experience and scientific investigation.[20] It is a view which tells a story of defeat and disappointment. It is also a view which suggests that, at a time when social relations are supposed to be increasingly visible to the individuals involved in production, these individuals may continue to look elsewhere, may long for something past or may cherish images and ideas which do not articulate their interests as a class. There are the elements here of a different conception of ideology, a conception which may be formulated as follows: *ideology is a system of representations which serves to sustain existing relations of class domination by orientating individuals towards the past rather than the future, or towards images and ideals which conceal class relations and detract from the collective pursuit of social change*. I shall describe this as a 'latent conception of ideology', for two reasons. First, Marx does not use the term 'ideology' in the contexts where this latent conception emerges. He speaks, instead, of 'illusions' and 'fixed ideas', of 'spirits' and 'ghosts' that lurk among the people and solicit their superstition and their prejudice. So we can speak of this as a conception of *ideology* in Marx only on condition of recognizing that we are extending the term 'ideology' to refer to a range of social phenomena which Marx described without naming, phenomena which he perceptively and disconcertingly portrayed in his concrete analyses but which, at the level of theory, he did not subsume under a discrete conceptual label.

The second reason why I shall describe this conception of ideology as 'latent' is that it refers to a range of phenomena which do not fit neatly into the theoretical framework sketched by Marx in the 1859 Preface and into the account of the modern era presented in the *Manifesto*. For the phenomena referred to by the latent conception of ideology are not mere epiphenomena of economic conditions and class relations; rather, they are symbolic constructions which have some degree of autonomy and efficacy. They constitute symbols and slogans, customs and traditions which move people or hold them back, propel them or constrain them, in such a way that we cannot think of these symbolic constructions as solely determined by, and fully explicable in terms of, the economic conditions of production. Moreover, the phenomena referred to by the latent conception of ideology attest to the persistence of traditional symbols and values, of that 'train of ancient and venerable prejudices and opinions' at the very heart of modern bourgeois society. These traditional symbols and values are not swept away once and for all by the constant revolutionizing of production; they live on, they modify and transform themselves, indeed they reappear as a potent reactionary force on the very eve of revolution itself. The latent conception of ideology calls attention to the fact that social relations may be sustained, and social change arrested, by the prevalence or diffusion of symbolic constructions. It calls attention to what we could describe as a *process of social conservation* within a society undergoing unprecedented social change, a process which Marx acutely discerned but the implications of which he was, perhaps, reluctant to draw out fully.

Let us consider for a moment Marx's account of the events leading up to the *coup d'état* of Louis Napoleon Bonaparte in December 1851, as presented in *The Eighteenth Brumaire of Louis Bonaparte*. Marx certainly portrays these events as conditioned by the development of forces and relations of production during the bourgeois monarchy of Louis Philippe. It was this development which had laid the foundations for the emergence of large-scale industry and an industrial proletariat, which had deepened the division between the Legitimists and the Orleanists and which had produced the economic crisis of 1847 that precipitated the political upheavals of 1848. But Marx's account is by no means couched exclusively in these terms. On the contrary, what is most striking about Marx's account is that it portrays the events of 1848–51, not as the inevitable outcome of processes working themselves out at the level of the economy, but rather as events caught up in images from the past, ensnared by traditions which persist *in spite of* the continuing transformation of the material conditions of life. Thus *The Eighteenth Brumaire* opens with this celebrated passage:

> The tradition of all the dead generations weighs like a nightmare on the brain of the living. And just when they seem engaged in revolutionising themselves and things, in creating something that has never yet existed, precisely in such periods of revolutionary crisis they anxiously conjure up the spirits of the past to their service and borrow from them names, battle cries and costumes in order to present the new scene of world history in this time-honoured disguise and this borrowed language.[21]

At the very moment when human beings are involved in creating their own history, in undertaking unprecedented tasks, they draw back before the risks and uncertainties of such an enterprise and invoke representations which assure them of their continuity with the past. At the very moment when continuity is threatened, they *invent* a past which restores the calm. From 1848 to 1851 it was the ghost of an old revolution which appeared in France, the bungling and lack-lustre Louis Bonaparte hiding behind the death mask of Napoleon. 'An entire people, which had imagined that by means of a revolution it had imparted to itself an accelerated power of motion, suddenly finds itself set back into a defunct epoch.'[22] While French society was convulsed by an economic crisis and seemingly on the threshold of a new revolution, it was drawn backwards by the weight of a tradition which, in the final moment, it could not shed.

It is significant that Marx, writing in 1850 of the events of 1848–9, had still envisaged the possibility of an imminent resurgence of revolutionary activity in France under the leadership of the proletariat.[23] Government measures, such as the re-introduction of the wine tax, were revolutionizing the peasantry and were, Marx suggested, driving them into a common front with their natural class ally, the proletariat. Two years later, however, writing in the aftermath of the *coup d'état* and with the benefit of hindsight, Marx's optimism was tempered. Revolution was still on the agenda, but the *coup d'état* had shown that, instead of being imminent, it was 'still journeying through purgatory'.[24] Why, instead of giving rise to a thoroughgoing revolution, had the events of 1848–51 given rise to a reactionary regime which parodied the past? What was the basis of this regime which had stolen the flame from the revolutionary hearth? Marx argues that Louis Bonaparte was able to stage his successful *coup* because, among other things, he represented the most numerous class in French society, the small-holding peasantry. While their class interests coincided with those of the proletariat, the small-holding peasants were not yet ready to take up arms with the proletariat in a common struggle. They were not yet capable of pursuing their own interests in their own name but required instead a *representative* who would compensate for the fragmentation of their life conditions by appearing above them as their *master*. And why should Louis Bonaparte, that bungling bureaucrat, be elevated to the position of being both the representative and the master of the peasantry?

> Historical tradition gave rise to the belief of the French peasants in the miracle that a man named Napoleon would bring all the glory back to them. And an individual turned up who gives himself out as the man because he bears the name of Napoleon . . . After a vagabondage of twenty years and after a series of grotesque adventures, the legend finds fulfilment and the man becomes Emperor of the French. The fixed idea of the Nephew was realised, because it coincided with the fixed idea of the most numerous class of the French people.[25]

The key to understanding why the events of 1848–51 culminated in a *coup d'état* rather than a revolutionary upheaval lies in the fact that the peasants, who comprised the largest class in France, lent their support to Louis Bonaparte; and they lent their support to him because they were captivated by the legend of Napoleon, they were entranced by a figure who presented himself as a saviour by donning the costumes of their one-time hero. The *coup d'état* can be explained, not by showing that the key classes acted in accordance with their alleged interests (which would have led to a quite different result), but rather by claiming that they acted in accordance with a tradition which was re-activated by the words and images of an impostor.

Marx's analysis of the events of 1848–51 thus ascribes a central role to the symbolic forms which comprise a tradition and which, at a time of crisis, may draw people back into the past, preventing them from perceiving their collective interests and from acting to transform a social order which oppresses them. A tradition can hold and take hold of a people, can lead them to believe that the past is their future and that a master is their servant, and can thereby sustain a social order in which the vast majority of people are subjected to conditions of domination and exploitation. 'Let the dead bury their dead,' implores Marx; 'the social revolution of the nineteenth century cannot draw its poetry from the past, but only from the future.'[26] But the dead are not buried so easily. For the symbolic forms transmitted from the past are constitutive of everyday customs, practices and beliefs; they cannot be disposed of like so many inert cadavers, since they play an active and fundamental role in people's lives. If Marx underestimated the significance of the symbolic dimension of social life, he nevertheless glimpsed its consequences in the context of mid-nineteenth-century France. In highlighting the ways in which words and images can re-activate a tradition that serves to sustain an oppressive social order and to bar the path of social change, he staked out the theoretical space for a new conception of ideology. It is a conception which shifts our attention away from the abstract ideas of philosophical and theoretical doctrines, focusing it instead on the ways in which symbols are used and transformed in specific social contexts. It is a conception which urges us to examine the ways in which social relations are created and sustained by the symbolic forms which circulate in social life, taking hold of people and orientating them in certain directions. Later in the chapter I shall return to this latent conception of ideology and try to develop it in a systematic way. But first we must consider some of the subsequent developments in the history of the concept.

From Ideology to the Sociology of Knowledge

After Marx the concept of ideology assumed a major role both within Marxism and within the emerging disciplines of the social sciences. In this context I cannot attempt to survey the multiple and varied uses of the term which can be discerned in this wide-ranging literature. I shall try instead to highlight a central tendency which is evident throughout this literature, a tendency which I shall describe as *the neutralization of the concept of ideology*. In the writings of Marx the concept of ideology preserved the negative, oppositional sense which it had acquired in the hands of Napoleon. This negative sense was inflected in differing ways by the various conceptions of ideology implicit in Marx's work, but the sense of negativity was common to all. The doctrines and ideas constitutive of ideology belonged to the realm of abstraction, misrepresentation and illusion; they expressed the interests of the dominant classes and they tended to sustain the status quo; they were phenomena which could be explained, unmasked and – according to at least one conception implicit in Marx's work – ultimately replaced by the scientific analysis of the material conditions of production and social change. There is no suggestion in Marx's work that ideology is a positive, progressive or unavoidable element of social life as such. Ideology, for Marx, is the symptom of an illness, not the normal trait of a healthy society and even less the medicine of a social cure. In subsequent literature, however, the concept of ideology tends to lose this negative sense. Both within Marxism and within the emerging disciplines of the social sciences, the concept of ideology is neutralized in various ways – even though, in the sphere of everyday social discourse, the term 'ideology' continues to convey a negative, even pejorative sense.

We can trace this process of neutralization by considering briefly, to begin with, the fate of the concept of ideology in some of the contributions to the development of Marxist thought after Marx. The neutralization of the concept of ideology within Marxism was not so much the result of an explicit attempt to transform the concept as the outcome of an implicit generalization of what I have called the epiphenomenal conception of ideology, a generalization which was part of the concern to elaborate strategies of class struggle in particular social–historical circumstances. Thus Lenin, analysing the polarized political situation in Russia at the turn of the century, called for the elaboration of a 'socialist ideology' which would combat the influence of bourgeois ideology and avoid the pitfalls of what he called 'spontaneous trade-union consciousness'.[27] Lenin was concerned to stress that the proletariat, left to itself, would not develop a genuine socialist ideology; rather, it would remain ensnared by bourgeois ideology and preoccupied with piece-meal reforms. Socialist ideology could only be elaborated by theoreticians and intellectuals who, detached from the demands of day-to-day struggle, are able to gain a broader view of developmental trends and overall goals. While not produced spontaneously by the proletariat, socialism is the ideology of the proletariat in the sense that it expresses and promotes the interests of the proletariat in the context of class struggle. A similar use of the term 'ideology' is evident in the work of Lukács. Reflecting in the early 1920s on the tasks and the problems facing the working-class movement, Lukács emphasized the importance of 'proletarian ideology' in determining the fate of the revolution. There can be no doubt, in Lukács's view, that the proletariat will eventually accomplish its world-historical mission; 'the only question at issue is how much it has to suffer before it achieves ideological maturity, before it acquires a true understanding of its class situation and a true class consciousness.'[28] Since the proletariat is immersed in the social-historical process and subject to the sway both of reification and of bourgeois ideology, the development of ideological maturity may require the mediation of a party which is organizationally separate from the class and which is able to articulate the interests of the class as a whole.

In this context I do not wish to examine the ramifications and refinements, the ambiguities, hesitations and inconsistencies, of the formulations of Lenin and Lukács. Such an examination would lead us away from the central theme which concerns us here; and, in any case, detailed commentaries on their views are readily available in the literature.[29] The central theme on which I wish to dwell is the way in which the use of the term 'ideology' in the writings of Lenin and Lukács involves an implicit neutralization of the concept of ideology. Drawing on Marx's epiphenomenal conception and adapting it to the exigencies of class struggle, both Lenin and Lukács effectively generalize this conception, in such a way that 'ideology' refers to ideas which express and promote the respective interests of the major classes engaged in conflict. While both Lenin and Lukács emphasize that the ideology of the proletariat is not necessarily produced by the proletariat in the ongoing course of events, they nevertheless stress the importance of elaborating and diffusing such an ideology in order to overcome the obstacles to revolution. Historical materialism, remarks Lukács, is 'the ideology of the embattled proletariat', and indeed is 'the most formidable weapon in this struggle'.[30] But to use the term 'ideology' in this way is to eliminate what we may call the 'asymmetrical aspect' of Marx's epiphenomenal conception. Marx's conception involves a certain asymmetry with regard to the basic classes involved in production. The ideas constitutive of ideology are ideas which express the interests of the *dominant* class; they are not ideas which express class interests as such. Marx never spoke of 'socialist ideology' or 'proletarian ideology' and he never characterized historical materialism as 'the ideology of the proletariat'. He did not suggest that such an ideology would endow the proletariat with a correct understanding of its class situation, interests and aims. Marx was too familiar with Napoleon's attack on the pretensions of the *idéologues* to employ the term 'ideology' with such an unequivocally positive sense. Far from staking out the privileged path along which the proletariat would march to victory, ideology, for Marx, was the realm of abstract doctrines and illusory ideas which could, perhaps, lead the proletariat astray. Far from being a *weapon* which the proletariat could deploy in its struggle, ideology was an *obstacle* which the struggle for socialism would, perhaps, have to overcome. In generalizing the use of 'ideology', Lenin and Lukács effectively eliminated the asymmetrical aspect of the epiphenomenal conception and neutralized the negative sense conveyed by the term in the writings of Marx.

In developing this argument my primary concern is to document an implicit transformation of the concept of ideology, not to level an attack at Lenin and Lukács or to call for an unqualified return to Marx. There are elements in the writings of Lukács - in particular his notion of reification - which are still important for the analysis of ideology and to which I shall return at a later stage. Moreover, Marx's comments on ideology are so elusive, ambiguous and fragmentary, so replete with speculative and questionable assumptions, that it would be credulous to call for an unqualified return to his views. If Marx helped to highlight some of the issues that must be addressed by the analysis of ideology today, such an analysis must be based on assumptions which are quite different from those made by Marx. If we may continue to draw from Marx the idea that the analysis of ideology is a *critical* activity, inseparable from a reflection on the relations of domination in which individuals are enmeshed, then we must also acknowledge that the way in which Marx proposed to conduct and justify the activity of critique can no longer be sustained today. I shall return to these issues in due course. But first I want to examine the treatment of the concept of ideology in the work of Karl Mannheim, whose *Ideology and Utopia* represents the first systematic attempt to elaborate, outside the tradition of Marxism, a neutral conception of ideology.

Mannheim was familiar with Lukács's work, having studied with Lukács at the University of Budapest and having been appointed by Lukács to a position at the University while the latter was deputy Commissar for Culture in the short-lived Hungarian Soviet Republic.[31] Like Lukács, Mannheim emphasized that all thought is situated within history and is part of the social–historical process which it seeks, in turn, to comprehend. But Mannheim was not directly and predominantly concerned with the theoretical and political problems of Marxism: he was primarily concerned to develop a way of studying the social conditions of knowledge and thought. Later in his career, following his forced emigration to England in 1933, he became increasingly preoccupied with pedagogical issues and with analysing the cultural aspects of social reconstruction and change. When Mannheim addressed the problem of ideology in the late 1920s, he did so within the context of an attempt to elaborate an interpretative method for studying socially situated thought. Mannheim harboured the hope that, by bringing to light what he called 'the social and activist roots of thinking', his methodological approach would make possible a new type of objectivity in social science and would 'answer the question as to the possibility of the scientific guidance of political life'.[32]

If, in expressing this hope, Mannheim appeared to reflect the aims of Destutt de Tracy's original programme of a science of ideas, it was a reflection that passed through the prism of Marx's work and acquired a new status in the context of early twentieth-century thought. It passed through the prism of Marx's work in the sense that Marx's discussion of ideology is seen by Mannheim as a decisive phase in the transition from a *particular* to a *total* conception of ideology. By a 'particular' conception of ideology Mannheim understands a conception which remains at the level of more or less conscious disguises, deceptions and lies. We imply the particular conception of ideology when we express scepticism towards the ideas and views advanced by our opponents and regard them as misrepresentations of the real nature of the situation. A 'total' conception of ideology emerges when we shift our attention to the characteristics of the total structure of mind of an epoch or of a social-historical group such as a class. We imply the total conception when we seek to grasp the concepts and modes of thought and experience, the *Weltanschauung* or 'world-view', of an epoch or group and to construe it as an outgrowth of a collective life-situation. The particular conception remains at the level of individuals engaged in deception and accusation, whereas the total conception has to do with collective thought systems which are related to social contexts.

In Mannheim's view, Marx was the first thinker to make the transition from the particular to the total conception of ideology, but he did so in a way which retained elements of the particular conception. He moved beyond the particular conception in so far as he sought to trace philosophical and theoretical doctrines and ideas back to the class position of their exponents, rooting these doctrines and ideas in the social-historical conditions of classes whose interests they express. But Marx's approach retained elements of the particular conception in so far as he sought to discredit bourgeois thought, to criticize the thought of his class adversary, while taking for granted the position from which this critical activity was carried out. Marx's approach was one-sided: he sought to interpret and criticize his opponent's thought in relation to its social context, but he did not apply the same approach to his own thought. Hence Mannheim draws a further distinction between what he calls the *special formulation* and the *general formulation* of the total conception of ideology. Marx practised the special formulation; what is now necessary is to make the final transition to the general formulation, such that the analyst 'has the courage to subject not just the adversary's point of view but all points of view, including his own, to the ideological analysis'.[33] *'Ideology', according to this general formulation, may be regarded as the interwoven systems of thought and modes of experience which are conditioned by social circumstances and shared by groups of individuals, including the individuals engaged in ideological analysis*. With the final transition to the general formulation, ideological analysis ceases to be the intellectual weapon of a party and becomes instead a method of research in social and intellectual history, a method which Mannheim describes as 'the sociology of knowledge'. The aim of this method is not to expose and discredit the thought of one's adversaries, but rather to analyse all of the social factors which influence thought, including one's own, and thereby 'to provide modern men with a revised view of the whole historical process'.[34]

While the transition to the sociology of knowledge involves a renunciation of the evaluative character of earlier conceptions of ideology, it nevertheless raises epistemological problems of its own. It is to Mannheim's credit that he confronts these problems in a direct and explicit way, even if the answers that he offers are ultimately unsatisfactory. The epistemological problems raised by Mannheim's approach are what may be described as *the epistemological problems of radical historicism*. If all knowledge, including the knowledge produced by the sociology of knowledge, is socially and historically situated and is intelligible only in relation to this situation, then how can we avoid the conclusion that all knowledge is merely relative to the social–historical situation of the knower? We can avoid this conclusion, Mannheim argues, by distinguishing between *relativism* and *relationism*. 'Relativism' is the result of combining the quite legitimate recognition of the social–historical conditioning of thought with an old and outdated theory of knowledge, a theory which takes propositions that are true analytically (e.g. mathematical formulae like '$2 \times 2 = 4$') as the paradigm of all knowledge. Compared with such a paradigm, forms of knowledge which are dependent on social–historical conditions are bound to appear as 'merely relative'. But if we reject this outdated theory of knowledge, then we can see that all historical knowledge is 'relational knowledge' and can only be formulated and understood with reference to the social–historical circumstances of the knower and the observer. The dependence of historical knowledge on social–historical circumstances is not a fault which vitiates this knowledge, but rather the condition of possibility of knowledge in the social–historical sphere.

Mannheim recognizes that relationism does not as such resolve the question of how one can discriminate between truth and falsity in the domain of historical knowledge. At most, relationism disposes of a misleading response to this question, a response based on an old theory of knowledge, and prepares the way for an alternative approach. But the alternative sketched by Mannheim in *Ideology and Utopia* is hardly more plausible than the response that he sought to put aside. The knowledge that we can acquire in our investigations, Mannheim suggests, is *partial* knowledge which is related to the larger body of knowledge and truth, and ultimately to the structure of historical reality itself, like so many parts of a whole. Although we cannot hope to grasp this whole in an immediate way, we can try to grasp as many partial perspectives as possible and to integrate them into a dynamic, comprehensive synthesis. The social group which stands the best chance of producing such a synthesis is the group that Alfred Weber referred to as the 'socially unattached intelligentsia'. Relatively classless and not too firmly rooted in the social order, the intelligentsia was exposed to differing viewpoints and increasingly sensitive to the dynamic, holistic character of society and history; by virtue of their very social position, they were able and inclined to produce a synthesis which would be free from any particular position.

This sociological Hegelianism provides Mannheim with a basis for a further, more normative undertaking: that of diagnosing the culture of an epoch. It is in this context that Mannheim introduces a somewhat different conception of ideology and contrasts it with the notion of utopia. Ideologies and utopias are conceptualized here as ideas which are 'discordant' or 'incongruous' with reality. Both ideologies and utopias transcend existing reality in the sense that they project modes of conduct which cannot be realized within the limits of the existing social order. But whereas ideologies never succeed *de facto* in realizing their projected modes of conduct, utopias realize their content to some extent and thereby tend to transform existing social reality in accordance with the modes of conduct which they project. Ideologies are pure projections which have no transforming effect on the social–historical world, whereas utopias are ideas which are eventually realized, to some extent, in this world. I shall refer to this notion of ideology as 'Mannheim's restricted conception', a conception which can be summarized as follows: *ideologies are ideas which are discordant with reality and unrealizable in practice*. Mannheim acknowledges that, in actual circumstances, it may be difficult to distinguish between ideologies in this sense and utopias, since the distinction presupposes a clear conception of social–historical reality and a hypothesis about whether certain ideas would eventually be realized or not. Since this hypothesis could only be confirmed retrospectively, the criterion of realization is at best a 'supplementary and retroactive standard for making distinctions between facts which as long as they are contemporary are buried under the partisan conflict of opinion'.[35]

There is no need to examine Mannheim's views in further detail here. His writings abound with difficulties and ambiguities which would require considerable space to analyse fully. What I wish to highlight is the way in which the central thrust of Mannheim's discussion results in a neutralization of the concept of ideology. Mannheim's primary concern is to move beyond the partisan character of earlier accounts and to transform the analysis of ideology into a sociology of knowledge which would be based on the general formulation of the total conception of ideology. 'Ideology', in this new programme, refers essentially to systems of thought or ideas which are socially situated and collectively shared; and ideological analysis is the study of the way in which these systems of thought or ideas are influenced by the social and historical circumstances in which they are situated. Mannheim's new programme thus seeks explicitly to put aside the critical, negative connotation associated with the concept of ideology since Napoleon, and to reconstruct the original project of a 'science of ideas' which would have practical, political consequences. But Mannheim knows that the project cannot be pursued in anything like the manner originally proposed by Destutt de Tracy. For as Marx has shown, ideas do not exist in an ethereal medium of their own but are always conditioned by social and historical factors, so that the study of ideas must be, in Mannheim's terms, a sociology of knowledge. Moreover, the study of ideas is itself socially and historically situated. Hence we cannot simply treat it as a 'science' and suppose that its criteria of validity are self-evident and beyond doubt. At the epistemological level, the sociology of knowledge must be explicated as a self-reflective historicism, rather than construed as a positive science in the mould of the Enlightenment.

We may justly ask, however, whether it is useful and helpful to regard the new programme for a sociology of knowledge as the legitimate heir to, or as co-extensive with, the analysis of ideology. Mannheim himself appears to be somewhat ambivalent in this regard. While in some contexts he emphasizes the limitations of earlier conceptions of ideology and advocates the general-ization of the ideological approach, in other passages he suggests that the study of ideology is necessarily limited and can therefore be distinguished from the sociology of knowledge. Indeed, at one point, he even suggests that it might be best to avoid using the term 'ideology' in the sociology of know-ledge, replacing it with the more neutral notion of 'perspective'.[36] But if this is so, then one may well doubt the success of Mannheim's attempt to generalize and neutralize the concept of ideology. Even in the wake of this attempt, Mannheim acknowledges that the general formulation of the total conception of ideology is not, perhaps, a conception of *ideology* after all, since it lacks the 'moral connotation' which is an essential aspect of that concept. Even in the wake of his attempt to extract the elements of the sociology of knowledge from the residue of problems traditionally associated with the concept of ideology, Mannheim concedes that these problems may, after all, deserve to be addressed separately, by an approach which is distinct from and complementary to the sociology of knowledge.

Can this residue of problems be adequately grasped by the more restricted conception of ideology introduced by Mannheim and juxtaposed to the notion of utopia? There is an interesting and important comparison to be made between the concept of ideology and that of utopia, but the specific way in which Mannheim makes this comparison is questionable. Apart from the evident problems associated with any attempt to apply the so-called 'criterion of realization', one may doubt whether Mannheim's more restricted conception of ideology is itself a plausible formulation. Ideologies, on this account, are ideas which are discordant with reality and unrealizable in practice; they are similar to utopias but are just more extreme – utterly inefficacious ideas, as it were. One may wonder whether, if one applied these criteria strictly, there would be anything that could be called 'ideology'. It is perhaps significant that the example which Mannheim adduces of an ideology in this sense is the idea of Christian brotherly love in feudal society, whereas a wide range of doctrines and ideas, from millenarianism to liberalism, conservatism to communism, are treated as utopias. But the point I wish to emphasize here is that Mannheim's restricted conception of ideology preserves the negative connotation associated with the term by focusing on two characteristics, those of discordance and unrealizability; *what is neglected by this account is the phenomenon of domination*. In the writings of Marx the concept of ideology was linked to the notion of domination, in the sense that the ideas or representations constitutive of ideology are in some way interwoven with – express, misrepresent, sustain – relations of class domination. This link with the phenomenon of domination is lost in Mannheim's restricted conception, which in this regard has more in common with the Napoleonic conception than with the conceptions of ideology that emerge in the writings of Marx. In the remaining sections of this chapter I shall attempt to recover the link between the concept of ideology and the phenomenon of domination and to develop this in a way which will provide a defensible conceptual basis for the analysis of ideology in modern societies.

Rethinking Ideology: A Critical Conception

In the previous sections I have analysed some of the principal phases in the history of the concept of ideology. I have highlighted some of the specific conceptions of ideology which emerge in the course of this history, from Destutt de Tracy's science of ideas to the various conceptions discernible in the writings of Marx and Mannheim. I now wish to move beyond this historical inquiry and develop an alternative formulation of the concept of ideology which draws on some of the contributions examined above. In so doing I shall not attempt to rehabilitate any particular conception of ideology, nor shall I propose some grand and sweeping synthesis. My aims are both more constructive and more modest. They are more constructive in the sense that I shall seek to develop a new formulation of the concept of ideology rather than rehabilitating some previous conception. This new formulation will capture the spirit of some earlier conceptions but will not adhere to the letter of any particular account. My aims are more modest in the sense that I shall make no attempt to synthesize the various conceptions highlighted above, as if the complex history of the concept of ideology could now be brought to a natural culmination; the formulation which I shall offer is a contribution to this history, not a bid to bring it to an end. My aims are also modest in the sense that I shall leave aside many of the assumptions and claims – sometimes very ambitious claims – that have been associated with the concept of ideology. There is no need to try to defend and justify the assumptions and claims of conceptions of ideology which are best treated as earlier episodes in a long and tangled history. Of course, the alternative formulation which I shall offer will imply assumptions of its own, and I shall undertake, in this chapter and elsewhere, to explicate and substantiate these assumptions.

Let me begin by distinguishing between two general *types* of conception of ideology. This distinction will enable us to classify the various conceptions of ideology into two basic categories and it will serve as a springboard for the development of an alternative view. One general type is what I shall call 'neutral conceptions of ideology'. Neutral conceptions are those which purport to characterize phenomena as ideology or ideological without implying that these phenomena are necessarily misleading, illusory or aligned with the interests of any particular group. Ideology, according to the neutral conceptions, is one aspect of social life (or form of social inquiry) among others, and is no more nor any less attractive or problematic than any other. Ideology may be present, for example, in every political programme, irrespective of whether it is orientated towards revolution, restoration or reform, irrespective of whether it aspires to the transformation or the preservation of the social order. Ideology may be as necessary to subordinate groups in their struggle against the social order as it is to dominant groups in their defence of the status quo. Like military hardware or tactical know-how, ideology may be a weapon which is orientated towards victory but towards no particular victor, since it is in principle available to any combatant who has the resources and skills to acquire and employ it.

We can distinguish neutral conceptions of ideology from a second general type, which I shall describe as 'critical conceptions of ideology'. Critical conceptions are those which convey a negative, critical or pejorative sense. Unlike neutral conceptions, critical conceptions imply that the phenomena characterized as ideology or ideological are misleading, illusory or one-sided; and the very characterization of phenomena as ideology carries with it an implicit criticism or condemnation of them. Critical conceptions of ideology differ in terms of the bases upon which they imply a negative sense. We may describe these differing bases as the *criteria of negativity* associated with particular conceptions of ideology. The distinction between neutral and critical conceptions of ideology, and the differentiation of criteria of negativity, enables us to classify the various conceptions of ideology examined earlier in terms of the schema presented in table 1.1. This schema indicates that the conceptions of ideology developed by Destutt de Tracy, Lenin, Lukács and Mannheim (in his general formulation of the total conception) share in common an important characteristic, in spite of the many differences that separate these thinkers. All of these conceptions of ideology are neutral conceptions, in the sense that they do not necessarily convey a negative, pejorative sense and do not necessarily imply that ideo-

Table 1.1

Classification of selected conceptions of ideology

	Critical conceptions	
Neutral conceptions	Conception of ideology	Criteria of negativity
Destutt de Tracy	Napoleon	AB
	Marx 1	AB
	Marx 2	BC
	Marx 3	BD
Lenin		
Lukács		
Mannheim 1	Mannheim 2	AB

Key:

Marx 1 — polemical conception
Marx 2 — epiphenomenal conception
Marx 3 — latent conception
Mannheim 1 — general formulation of total conception
Mannheim 2 — Mannheim's restricted conception

A — abstract or impractical
B — erroneous or illusory
C — expresses dominant interests
D — sustains relations of domination

logy is a phenomenon to be combated and, if possible, eliminated. By contrast, the conceptions of ideology offered by Napoleon, Marx and Mannheim (in what I have described as Mannheim's restricted conception) are all critical conceptions. They all convey a negative sense and imply that the phenomena characterized as ideology are susceptible of criticism.

The criteria of negativity, by virtue of which the different critical conceptions convey a negative sense, vary from one conception to another. In Napoleon's use of the term, 'ideology' conveyed a negative sense by suggesting that the ideas concerned were both erroneous and impractical, both misleading and divorced from the practical realities of political life. Marx's polemical conception of ideology retained these two criteria of negativity, while shifting the target of attack from de Tracy's science of ideas to the philosophical speculation of the Young Hegelians. With the transition to Marx's epiphenomenal conception, the criteria of negativity change: the ideas which constitute ideology are still illusory, but they are also regarded as ideas which express the interests of the dominant class. The latter criterion is replaced by another in what I described as the latent conception of ideology in Marx. Ideology, according to the latent conception, is a system of representations which conceal and mislead and which, in so doing, serve to sustain relations of domination. With the subsequent formulation of Mannheim's restricted conception, the criteria of negativity revert to those which were characteristic of Napoleon's use of the term and Marx's polemical conception.

This schema could be extended to encompass more recent contributions to the theory and analysis of ideology. I shall not, however, undertake to extend this schema here. I shall consider some recent contributions in the following chapter, but I shall do so with a slightly different aim in mind: I shall be less concerned with the specific conceptions of ideology employed by contemporary authors, and more concerned with their general accounts of the nature and role of ideology in modern societies. Nevertheless, as I have indicated in another context,[37] most contemporary authors who write on ideology – from Martin Seliger to Clifford Geertz, from Alvin Gouldner to Louis Althusser – employ some version of what I have described as a neutral conception of ideology. Ideology is conceived of, in a general way, as systems of beliefs or symbolic forms and practices; and in some cases these authors – like Mannheim several decades ago – seek explicitly to distance themselves from what they regard as a 'restrictive' or 'evaluative' conception of ideology. In developing an alternative approach to the analysis of ideology, my aim will be quite different. I shall seek to counter what I have described as the neutralization of the concept of ideology. I shall attempt to formulate a critical conception of ideology, drawing on some of the themes implicit in earlier conceptions while abandoning others; and I shall attempt to show that this conception can provide a basis for a fruitful and defensible approach to the analysis of ideology, an approach which is orientated towards the concrete analysis of social–historical phenomena but which, at the same time, preserves the critical character bequeathed to us by the history of the concept.

The analysis of ideology, according to the conception which I shall propose, is primarily concerned with the ways in which symbolic forms intersect with relations of power. It is concerned with the ways in which meaning is mobilized in the social world and serves thereby to bolster up individuals and groups who occupy positions of power. Let me define this focus more sharply: *to study ideology is to study the ways in which meaning serves to establish and sustain relations of domination.* Ideological phenomena are meaningful symbolic phenomena *in so far as* they serve, in particular social-historical circumstances, to establish and sustain relations of domination. *In so far as*: it is crucial to stress that symbolic phenomena, or certain symbolic phenomena, are not ideological as such, but are ideological only in so far as they serve, in particular circumstances, to maintain relations of domination. We cannot read the ideological character of symbolic phenomena off the symbolic phenomena themselves. We can grasp symbolic phenomena as ideological, hence we can analyse ideology, only by situating symbolic phenomena in the social–historical contexts within which these phenomena may, or may not, serve to establish and sustain relations of domination. Whether symbolic phenomena do or do not serve to establish and sustain relations of domination is a question which can be answered only by examining the interplay of meaning and power in particular circumstances, only by examining the ways in which symbolic forms are employed, cir-culated and understood by individuals situated in structured social contexts.

In formulating this conception of ideology I am drawing on what I have described as Marx's latent conception. However, I am retaining, in a modi-fied form, only one criterion of negativity as a defining feature of ideology: namely, the criterion of sustaining relations of domination. It is not essential for symbolic forms to be erroneous or illusory in order for them to be ideological. They *may* be erroneous or illusory, indeed in some cases ideo-logy *may* operate by concealing or masking social relations, by obscuring or misrepresenting situations; but these are contingent possibilities, not neces-sary characteristics of ideology as such. By treating error and illusion as a contingent possibility rather than a necessary characteristic of ideology, we can relieve the analysis of ideology of some of the epistemological burden with which it has been encumbered since Napoleon. Engaging in the analysis of ideology does not necessarily presuppose that the phenomena character-ized as ideological have been shown, or can be shown, to be erroneous or illusory. Characterizing symbolic phenomena as ideological does not necessarily impose on the analyst the burden of demonstrating that the phenomena so characterized are in some sense 'false'. What we are interested in here is not primarily and not initially the truth or falsity of symbolic forms, but rather the ways in which these forms serve, in particular circumstances, to establish and sustain relations of domination; and it is by no means the case that symbolic forms serve to establish and sustain relations of domination only by virtue of being erroneous, illusory or false. The analysis of ideology does, of course, raise important and complex questions of justification, and I shall consider these questions in a later chapter. But in order to address these questions in a fruitful way, it is vital to see that the characterization of symbolic phenomena as ideological does not directly and necessarily imply that these phenomena are epistemologically flawed.

There are two further respects in which the conception of ideology which I am proposing differs significantly from Marx's account. In Marx's work, the criterion of sustaining relations of domination is generally understood, explicitly or implicitly, in terms of *class* relations. For Marx, it is relations of class domination and subordination which constitute the principal axes of inequality and exploitation in human societies in general, and in modern capitalist societies in particular. For Marx, it is relations of class domination and subordination – primarily between the various factions of capital, on the one hand, and the downtrodden proletariat and fragmented peasantry, on the other – which are sustained by the persistence of the image and legend of Napoleon in mid-nineteenth-century France. But it is important to emphasize that class relations are only *one* form of domination and subordination, they constitute only *one* axis of inequality and exploitation; class relations are by no means the *only* form of domination and subordination. With the benefit of hindsight, it seems clear that Marx's preoccupation with class relations was misleading in certain respects. While Marx was right to stress the significance of class relations as a basis of inequality and exploitation, he tended to neglect or downplay the significance of relations between the sexes, between ethnic groups, between individuals and the state, between nation-states and blocs of nation-states; he tended to assume that class relations form the structural core of modern societies and that their transformation was the key to a future free from domination. These emphases and assumptions cannot be accepted as self-evident today. We live in a world today in which class domination and subordination continue to play an important role, but in which other forms of conflict are prevalent and, in some contexts, of equal or even greater significance. If we must qualify Marx's preoccupation with class relations, we must also sever the link between the concept of ideology and class domination. This link must be regarded as contingent rather than necessary. In studying ideology we *may* be concerned with the ways in which meaning sustains relations of class domination, but we may also be concerned with other kinds of domination, such as the structured social relations between men and women, between one ethnic group and another, or between hegemonic nation-states and those nation-states located on the margins of a global system.

A further respect in which my proposed conception of ideology differs from Marx's account is less clear-cut but important none the less. Since the latent conception of ideology was never explicitly formulated by Marx, it is difficult to attribute a clear and unambiguous sense to it. However, if my formulation of the latent conception is an accurate characterization of Marx's account, then there is another emphasis which is, in my view, misleading. When Marx turns his attention to the role of the Napoleonic tradition, of the legend of Napoleon which finds its fulfilment in the 'fixed ideas' of the peasantry, what interests him primarily is the ways in which this tradition serves to sustain a set of social relations which are established prior to, and independently of, the mobilization of meaning in symbolic forms. Classes exist 'in themselves', determined by objective relations of production and by circumstances which are primarily economic in character – although classes may not exist 'for themselves' without an appropriate form of symbolic representation in which, and through which, they can represent their interests and their aims to themselves. The difficulty with this account is that it tends to downplay the extent to which symbolic forms, and the meaning mobilized therein, are *constitutive of social reality* and are actively involved in creating as well as sustaining the relations between individuals and groups. Symbolic forms are not merely representations which serve to articulate or obscure social relations or interests which are constituted fundamentally and essentially at a pre-symbolic level: rather, symbolic forms are continuously and creatively implicated in the constitution of social relations as such. Hence I propose to conceptualize ideology in terms of the ways in which the meaning mobilized by symbolic forms serves *to establish and sustain* relations of domination: to establish, in the sense that meaning may actively create and institute relations of domination; to sustain, in the sense that meaning may serve to maintain and reproduce relations of domination through the ongoing process of producing and receiving symbolic forms.

In order to develop my proposed reformulation of the concept of ideology, there are three aspects which require elaboration: the notion of meaning, the concept of domination, and the ways in which meaning may serve to establish and sustain relations of domination. I shall discuss the notion of meaning and the concept of domination in some detail in chapter

3, so here I shall simply indicate the lines of analysis that will be developed later. In studying the ways in which meaning serves to establish and sustain relations of domination, the meaning with which we are concerned is the meaning of symbolic forms which are embedded in social contexts and circulating in the social world. By 'symbolic forms' I understand a broad range of actions and utterances, images and texts, which are produced by subjects and recognized by them and others as meaningful constructs. Linguistic utterances and expressions, whether spoken or inscribed, are crucial in this regard, but symbolic forms can also be non-linguistic or quasi-linguistic in nature (e.g. a visual image, or a construct which combines images and words). We can analyse the meaningful character of symbolic forms in terms of four typical aspects – what I shall call the 'intentional', 'conventional', 'structural' and 'referential' aspects of symbolic forms. There is a fifth aspect of symbolic forms, what I shall call the 'contextual' aspect, which indicates that symbolic forms are always embedded in socially structured contexts and processes. To describe these contexts and processes as 'socially structured' is to say that there are systematic differentials in terms of the distribution of, and access to, resources of various kinds. Individuals situated within socially structured contexts have, by virtue of their location, different quantities of, and different degrees of access to, available resources. The social location of individuals, and the entitlements associated with their positions in a social field or institution, endow them with varying degrees of 'power', understood at this level as a socially or institutionally endowed capacity which enables or empowers some individuals to make decisions, pursue ends or realize interests. We can speak of 'domination' when established relations of power are 'systematically asymmetrical', that is, when particular agents or groups of agents are endowed with power in a durable way which excludes, and to some significant degree remains inaccessible to, other agents or groups of agents, irrespective of the basis upon which such exclusion is carried out.

These initial characterizations of meaning and domination provide the backcloth against which we may pursue the third issue raised by the proposed reformulation of the concept of ideology: in what ways can meaning serve to establish and sustain relations of domination? There are innumerable ways in which meaning may serve, in particular social–historical conditions, to maintain relations of domination, and we can answer this question properly only by attending carefully to the interplay of meaning and power in the actual circumstances of social life. In a later chapter, I shall address the question in this way, providing a detailed analysis of some specific examples of empirical research. But here it may be helpful to identify certain general *modes of operation* of ideology and to indicate some of the ways in which they may be linked, in particular circumstances, with *strategies of symbolic construction*. In distinguishing these modes and developing these connections, my aim is not to provide a comprehensive account of the ways in which meaning may serve to establish and sustain relations of domination. Rather, my aim is simply to stake out, in a preliminary manner, a rich field of analysis which I shall pursue in greater detail in subsequent chapters.

I shall distinguish five general modes through which ideology can operate: 'legitimation', 'dissimulation', 'unification', 'fragmentation' and 'reification'. Table 1.2 indicates some of the ways in which these modes can be linked with various strategies of symbolic construction. Before unfolding the elements of this table, let me emphasize three qualifications. First, I do not want to claim that these five modes are the *only* ways in which ideology operates, or that they always operate independently of one another; on the contrary, these modes may overlap and reinforce one another, and ideology may, in particular circumstances, operate in other ways. Second, in associating certain modes of operation with certain strategies of symbolic construction, I do not wish to maintain that these strategies are *uniquely* associated with these modes, or that the strategies I mention are the *only* relevant ones. The most one could say is that certain strategies are *typically* associated

Table 1.2
Modes of operation of ideology

General modes	Some typical strategies of symbolic construction
Legitimation	Rationalization Universalization Narrativization
Dissimulation	Displacement Euphemization Trope (e.g. synecdoche, metonymy, metaphor)
Unification	Standardization Symbolization of unity
Fragmentation	Differentiation Expurgation of the other
Reification	Naturalization Eternalization Nominalization/passivization

with certain modes, while acknowledging that, in particular circumstances, any given strategy may serve other purposes and any given mode may be actualized in other ways; in mentioning various strategies, my aim is to exemplify, not to provide an exhaustive and exclusive categorization. The third qualification is that, in highlighting some typical strategies of symbolic construction, I do not want to maintain that these strategies are ideological *as such*. No such strategy is intrinsically ideological. Whether a given strategy of symbolic construction is ideological depends on how the symbolic form constructed by means of this strategy is used and understood in particular circumstances; it depends on whether the symbolic form so constructed is serving, in these circumstances, to sustain or subvert, to establish or undermine, relations of domination. Examining typical strategies of symbolic construction can alert us to some of the ways in which meaning may be mobilized in the social world, can circumscribe a range of possibilities for the operation of ideology, but it cannot take the place of a careful analysis of the ways in which symbolic forms intersect with relations of domination in particular, concrete circumstances.

Let me begin by considering *legitimation*. Relations of domination may be established and sustained, as Max Weber observed, by being represented as legitimate, that is, as just and worthy of support.[38] The representation of relations of domination as legitimate may be regarded as a *claim to legitimacy* which is based on certain grounds, expressed in certain symbolic forms and which may, in given circumstances, be more or less effective. Weber distinguished three types of grounds on which claims to legitimacy may be based: rational grounds (appealing to the legality of enacted rules), traditional grounds (appealing to the sanctity of immemorial traditions) and charismatic grounds (appealing to the exceptional character of an individual person who exercises authority). Claims based on such grounds may be expressed in symbolic forms by means of certain typical strategies of symbolic construction. One typical strategy is what we could call *rationalization*, whereby the producer of a symbolic form constructs a chain of reasoning which seeks to defend or justify a set of social relations or institutions, and thereby to persuade an audience that it is worthy of support. Another typical strategy is *universalization*. By means of this strategy, institutional arrangements which serve the interests of some individuals are represented as serving the interests of all, and these arrangements are regarded as being open in principle to anyone who has the ability and the inclination to succeed within them. Claims to legitimacy may also be expressed by means of the strategy of *narrativization*: claims are embedded in stories which recount the past and treat the present as part of a timeless and cherished tradition. Indeed traditions are sometimes *invented* in order to create a sense of belonging to a community and to a history which transcends the experience of conflict, difference and division.[39] Stories are told, both by official chroniclers and by individuals in the course of their everyday lives, which serve to justify the exercise of power by those who possess it and which serve to reconcile others to the fact that they do not. Speeches and documentaries, histories, novels and films are constructed as narratives which portray social relations and unfold the consequences of actions, in ways that may establish and sustain relations of power. In the mundane stories and jokes which fill so much of our everyday lives we are continuously engaged in recounting the way that the world appears and in reinforcing, through laughter which profits at another's expense, the apparent order of things. By telling stories and receiving (listening to, reading, watching) the stories told by others, we may be drawn into a symbolic process which may serve, in some circumstances, to create and sustain relations of domination.

A second *modus operandi* of ideology is *dissimulation*. Relations of domination may be established and sustained by being concealed, denied or obscured, or by being represented in a way which deflects attention from or glosses over existing relations or processes. Ideology *qua* dissimulation may be expressed in symbolic forms by means of a variety of different strategies. One such strategy is *displacement*: a term customarily used to refer to one object or individual is used to refer to another, and thereby the positive or negative connotations of the term are transferred to the other object or individual. This was the strategy of symbolic construction employed by Louis Bonaparte, who, as Marx so acutely observed, managed to re-activate a tradition of reverent respect for the imperial hero by presenting himself as the legitimate heir of the great Napoleon. It was 'this time-honoured disguise and this borrowed language' which veiled the new scene of world history, turned the peasantry towards the past rather than the future and prevented them, on Marx's account, from grasping their real conditions of life. Another strategy which facilitates the dissimulation of social relations is *euphemization*: actions, institutions or social relations are described or redescribed in terms which elicit a positive valuation. There are many well-known examples of this process: the violent suppression of protest is described as the 'restoration of order'; a prison or concentration camp is described as a 're-habilitation centre'; institutionalized inequalities based on ethnic divisions are described as 'separate development'; foreign labourers deprived of citizenship rights are described as 'guest workers'. But the process of euphemization is often more subtle than these well-known examples would suggest. Thus in 1982 we were told by Menachem Begin that the movement of thousands of troops and hundreds of tanks into Lebanon was not an 'invasion' because, according to Begin's definition of the term, 'you invade a land when you want to conquer it, or annex it, or at least conquer part of it. We don't covet even one inch.'[40] There is an openness, an indeterminate vagueness, in many of the words we use, so that euphemization may take place through a slight and even imperceptible shifting of sense.

Ideology *qua* dissimulation may be expressed through another strategy, or cluster of strategies, which we may subsume under the general label of *trope*.[41] By trope I mean the figurative use of language or, more generally, of symbolic forms. The study of trope is generally confined to the domain of literature, but the figurative use of language is much more widespread than this disciplinary specialization would suggest. Among the most common forms of trope are synecdoche, metonymy and metaphor, all of which may be used to dissimulate relations of domination. Synecdoche involves the semantic conflation of part and whole: one uses a term standing for part of something in order to refer to the whole, or uses a term standing for the whole in order to refer to part. This technique may dissimulate social relations by confusing or inverting the relations between collectivities and their parts, between particular groups and broader social and political forms – in the way, for example, that generic terms like 'the British', 'the Americans' and 'the Russians' are used to refer to particular governments or groups within a nation-state. Metonymy involves the use of a term standing for an attribute, adjunct or related characteristic of something to refer to the thing itself, although there is no necessary connection between the term and that to which one may be referring. Through the use of metonymy, the referent may be implied without being explicitly stated, or may be positively or negatively valued by association with something else; this is common practice, for instance, in advertising, where meaning is often mobilized in subtle and surreptitious ways, without making explicit the connections between the objects referred to or implied in the ad. Metaphor involves the application of a term or phrase to an object or action to which it is not literally applicable. Metaphorical expressions set up a tension within a sentence by combining terms drawn from different semantic fields, a tension which, if successful, generates a new and enduring sense. Metaphor may dissimulate social relations by representing them, or the individuals and groups embedded in them, as endowed with characteristics which they do not literally possess, thereby accentuating certain features at the expense of others and charging them with a positive or negative sense. Thus the former British Prime Minister Margaret Thatcher was often described as 'the Iron Lady', a metaphor which endowed her with a super-human determination and firmness of will. Or consider this comment by Margaret Thatcher herself, made in an interview with the Press Association in 1988 and reported in the British daily the *Guardian*: reflecting on her first eight years in office and on her perception of the changing status of Britain among the Western industrial nations, she observes that 'They used, when I first came in, to talk about us in terms of the British disease. Now they talk about us and say "Look, Britain has got the cure." '[42] The metaphor of disease and cure, combined with the language of 'us' and 'them', gives this comment a vivid and evocative character; it shrouds the process of social and economic development in the imagery of illness and health, while neglecting or glossing over the actual circumstances underlying and affecting this process. In calling attention to these various kinds of trope I do not want to suggest, of course, that the figurative use of language is always or even predominantly ideological. I wish only to claim that the figurative use of language is a fairly common feature of everyday discourse, that it is an effective way of mobilizing meaning in the social–historical world, and that, in certain contexts, the meaning mobilized thereby may be embroiled with power and may serve to create, sustain and reproduce relations of domination.

A third *modus operandi* of ideology is *unification*. Relations of domination may be established and sustained by constructing, at the symbolic level, a form of unity which embraces individuals in a collective identity, irrespective of the differences and divisions that may separate them. A typical strategy by means of which this mode is expressed in symbolic forms is the strategy of *standardization*. Symbolic forms are adapted to a standard framework which is promoted as the shared and acceptable basis of symbolic exchange. This is the strategy pursued, for example, by state authorities seeking to develop a national language in the context of diverse and linguistically differentiated groups. The establishment of a national language may serve to create a collective identity among groups and a legitimate hierarchy among languages and dialects within the boundaries of a nation-state. Another strategy of symbolic construction by means of which unification can be achieved is what we may describe as the *symbolization of unity*. This strategy involves the construction of symbols of unity, of collective identity and identification, which are diffused throughout a group or plurality of groups. Here again, the construction of symbols of national unity, such as flags, national anthems, emblems and inscriptions of various kinds, are evident examples. In practice the symbolization of unity may be interwoven with the process of narrativization, as symbols of unity may be an integral part of a narrative of origins which recounts a shared history and projects a collective fate. This is common not only in the case of large-scale social organizations such as the modern nation-state, but also in the case of smaller organizations and social groups which are held together, in part, by an ongoing process of symbolic unification through which a collective identity is created and continuously reaffirmed. By binding together individuals in a way which overrides differences and divisions, the symbolization of unity may serve, in particular circumstances, to establish and sustain relations of domination.

A fourth mode through which ideology may operate is *fragmentation*. Relations of domination may be maintained, not by unifying individuals in a collectivity, but by fragmenting those individuals and groups that might be capable of mounting an effective challenge to dominant groups, or by orientating forces of potential opposition towards a target which is projected as evil, harmful or threatening. Here a typical strategy of symbolic construction is *differentiation* – that is, emphasizing the distinctions, differences and divisions between individuals and groups, the characteristics which *dis*unite them and prevent them from constituting an effective challenge to existing relations or an effective participant in the exercise of power. Another pertinent strategy may be described as the *expurgation of the other*. This involves the construction of an enemy, either within or without, which is portrayed as evil, harmful or threatening and which individuals are called upon collectively to resist or expurgate. This strategy often overlaps with strategies orientated towards unification, since the enemy is treated as a challenge or threat, in the face of which individuals must unite. The portrayal of Jews and communists in the Nazi literature of the 1920s and 1930s, or the characterization of political dissidents in the Stalinist era as 'enemies of the people', are exemplary instances of the expurgation of the other, but this strategy is more commonplace than such examples might suggest. Consider an editorial remark in the mass-circulation newspaper the *Sun*: commenting on a possible strike by the train drivers' union ASLEF in summer 1982, the *Sun* reminds its readers that ASLEF may smash their own industry but will 'never break us', since, 'as the battle for the Falklands demonstrated so clearly, NOBODY can break this nation'.[43] This comment employs a complex strategy in which ASLEF is constructed as an other who is challenging the nation as a whole, and this opposition is superimposed on the conflicting forces in the Falklands War, so that ASLEF is identified with an alien power which is threatening a people who must unite in the face of adversity and whose will to resist evil is emphatically indomitable.

A fifth *modus operandi* of ideology is *reification*: relations of domination may be established and sustained by representing a transitory, historical state of affairs as if it were permanent, natural, outside of time. Processes are portrayed as things or as events of a quasi-natural kind, in such a way that their social and historical character is eclipsed. Ideology *qua* reification thus involves the elimination or obfuscation of the social and historical character of social–historical phenomena – or, to borrow a suggestive phrase from Claude Lefort, it involves the re-establishment of 'the dimension of society "without history" at the very heart of historical society'.[44] This mode may be expressed in symbolic forms by means of the strategy of *naturalization*. A state of affairs which is a social and historical creation may be treated as a natural event or as the inevitable outcome of natural characteristics, in the way, for example, that the socially instituted division of labour between men and women may be portrayed as the product of the physiological characteristics of and differences between the sexes. A similar strategy is what may be described as *eternalization*: social–historical phenomena are deprived of their historical character by being portrayed as permanent, unchanging and ever-recurring. Customs, traditions and institutions which seem to stretch indefinitely into the past, so that any trace of their origin is lost and any question of their end is unimaginable, acquire a rigidity which cannot be easily disrupted. They become embedded in social life and their apparently ahistorical character is re-affirmed by symbolic forms which, in their construction as well as their sheer repetition, eternalize the contingent.

Ideology *qua* reification may also be expressed by means of various grammatical and syntactic devices, such as *nominalization* and *passivization*.[45] Nominalization occurs when sentences or parts of sentences, descriptions of action and the participants involved in them, are turned into nouns, as when we say 'the banning of imports' instead of 'the Prime Minister has decided to ban imports'. Passivization occurs when verbs are rendered in the passive form, as when we say 'the suspect is being investigated' instead of 'police officers are investigating the suspect'. Nominalization and passivization focus the attention of the hearer or reader on certain themes at the expense of others. They delete actors and agency and they tend to represent processes as things or events which take place in the absence of a subject who produces them. They also tend to elide references to specific spatial and temporal contexts by eliminating verbal constructions or converting them into the continuous tense. These and other grammatical or syntactic devices may, in particular circumstances, serve to establish and sustain relations of domination by reifying social–historical phenomena. Representing processes as things, deleting actors and agency, constituting time as an eternal extension of the present tense: these are so many ways of re-establishing the dimension of society 'without history' at the heart of historical society.

By identifying these various modes of operation of ideology and some of the typical strategies of symbolic construction with which they may be associated and through which they may be expressed, I have called attention to some of the ways in which we can begin to think about the interplay of meaning and power in social life. I have called attention to some of the strategies and devices by virtue of which meaning can be constructed and conveyed in the social world, and some of the ways in which the meaning thus conveyed can serve to establish and sustain relations of power. As I have stressed, however, considerations of this kind are at best preliminary indications of a terrain to be explored; they should be regarded as rough guidelines which may facilitate inquiry of a more empirical or historical kind. For particular strategies of symbolic construction, or particular kinds of symbolic forms, are not ideological as such: whether the meaning generated by symbolic strategies, or conveyed by symbolic forms, serves to establish and sustain relations of domination is a question that can be answered only by examining the specific contexts within which symbolic forms are produced and received, only by examining the specific mechanisms by which they are transmitted from producers to receivers, and only by examining the sense which these symbolic forms have for the subjects who produce and receive them. Strategies of symbolic construction are the tools with which symbolic forms capable of creating and sustaining relations of domination can be produced; they are symbolic devices, as it were, which facilitate the mobilization of meaning. But whether the symbolic forms thereby produced serve to sustain relations of domination or to subvert them, to bolster up powerful individuals and groups or to undermine them, is a matter that can be resolved only by studying how these symbolic forms operate in particular social–historical circumstances, how they are used and understood by the subjects who produce and receive them in the socially structured contexts of everyday life. At a later stage I shall elaborate a methodological framework within which this kind of study can be carried out.

Reply to Some Possible Objections

In the previous section I proposed a conception of ideology which focuses on the ways in which meaning, as constructed and conveyed by symbolic forms of various kinds, serves to establish and sustain relations of domination. This is a conception which owes something to what I called Marx's latent notion of ideology, but which diverges from Marx's account in several fundamental respects. It is a conception which preserves the critical, negative sense associated with the concept of ideology since Napoleon, but which divorces this sense from the supposition of error and illusion. It is a conception which directs our attention towards the ways in which certain strategies of symbolic construction may facilitate the reproduction of relations of power, but which demands a systematic and detailed inquiry into the actual uses of symbolic forms in specific contexts and the ways in which they are understood by the individuals who produce and receive them. I shall pursue this inquiry further in due course. For the time being, I shall conclude this preliminary discussion of the concept of ideology by considering some possible objections which might be levelled against the reformulation proposed here.

Objection 1: 'You have focused the study of ideology on the ways in which meaning serves to establish and sustain relations of domination, but surely', the critic may object, 'the study of ideology should also be concerned with those symbolic forms, those doctrines and ideas, which challenge, contest and disrupt the status quo.' The study of ideology should indeed be concerned with contestatory symbolic forms, since these may help to highlight – as rebellion highlights an oppressive regime – those symbolic forms which serve to establish and sustain relations of domination. But contestatory symbolic forms are not ideological, according to the conception which I have proposed here. This conception retains the asymmetrical aspect which was characteristic of Marx's work. Ideology is not indifferent, as it were, to the nature of the power relations which symbolic forms express and support. Symbolic forms are ideological only in so far as they serve to establish and sustain systematically asymmetrical relations of power; and it is this activity in the service of dominant individuals and groups which both delimits the phenomenon of ideology, giving it specificity and setting it off from the circulation of symbolic forms in general, and endows the proposed conception of ideology with a negative sense. Ideology, according to this conception, is by nature hegemonic, in the sense that it necessarily serves to establish and sustain relations of domination and thereby to reproduce a social order which favours dominant individuals and groups. Ideological forms can of course be challenged, contested and disrupted, and they frequently are so challenged, both explicitly, in articulate and concerted attacks, and implicitly, in the mundane symbolic exchanges of everyday life. These challenging, disrupting interventions may be described as *contestatory symbolic forms* or, more specifically, as *incipient forms of the critique of ideology*. The very existence of ideology may call forth its obverse: rather than passively accepting ideological forms and the relations of domination which they serve to sustain, individuals may attack or denounce these forms and relations, may parody or satirize them, may seek to defuse whatever force ideological expressions may have in particular circumstances. In so doing these individuals are engaging, not in the promulgation of a new ideology (although, in other respects, they may be doing this as well), but rather in an incipient version of a form of critique which may be carried out in a more systematic way within the framework of a comprehensive interpretative methodology.

Objection 2: 'You have characterized the study of ideology as the study of the ways in which meaning serves to establish and sustain relations of domination, but relations of domination may be sustained in other ways, for example by apathy and indifference, or by the sheer repetitiveness of habit and routine. Surely the study of ideology should be concerned with the latter phenomena as well as with the mobilization of meaning in symbolic forms.' It is no doubt true that relations of domination are sustained in many different ways and by virtue of many different factors. In some circumstances, the apathy and indifference of subordinate individuals and groups, or even their willingness or their will to submit to servitude, may be vital. In other circumstances, relations of domination may be sustained by the fact that practices have been followed for so long and with such regularity that they have acquired the character of habits or routines which are neither discussed nor questioned; relations of domination may be reproduced, not because meaning is mobilized in support of them, but simply because this is how things have always been done. I do not wish to deny the importance of these considerations. I do not wish to claim, and it would be quite misleading to suggest, that social relations are sustained, that the social order is reproduced, by virtue of the mobilization of meaning in symbolic forms alone. What I do want to argue is that the mobilization of meaning in support of relations of domination is a social phenomenon worthy of systematic investigation, that it comprises some of the ways in which these relations are sustained, and that the investigation of these ways is the specific province of the study of ideology. The fact that relations of domination may be sustained in other ways does not imply that these other ways should also be regarded as forms of ideology. Indeed, in some circumstances, relations of domination may be sustained by the exercise of brute force, by beating, killing and forcefully repressing insurrection or protest, and it would hardly be sensible or illuminating to suggest that this way of sustaining relations of domination is yet another form of ideology. If the concept of ideology is to be useful, its sphere of application must be limited. I have proposed a limitation which focuses our attention on the ways in which the meaning mobilized in symbolic forms serves to establish and sustain relations of domination. It focuses our attention on an intersubjective space in which meaning intersects with power in certain ways. This proposed limitation makes no pretension to encompass all of the ways in which meaning intersects with power, nor all of the ways in which relations of domination may be sustained. But it defines a field of inquiry which bears some resemblance to the domain staked out by earlier conceptions of ideology and which is, without further extension, quite large enough.

Objection 3: 'In speaking of the ways in which meaning "serves to sustain" relations of domination, are you not implicitly adopting a functionalist standpoint and tying the study of ideology to a model of explanation which has long since been discredited?' In studying ideology we are indeed concerned, in a general sense, with the 'roles' that symbolic forms play in social life, with the ways in which they are used and understood by individuals and with the consequences of this usage and understanding for the reproduction of the social order. But we are not adopting a functionalist standpoint and we are not trying to explain ideology in functionalist terms. To explain ideology in functionalist terms we would have to proceed as follows: we would have to assume that the social order is a system which has certain 'needs', such as a set of needs which have to be met in order to maintain a stable equilibrium; we would have to assume that the end state of the system – e.g. maintaining a stable equilibrium – is a given; and we would have to argue that ideological symbolic forms can be explained by showing that they fulfil some of these needs. In other words, we would seek to explain ideological symbolic forms by showing that they satisfy certain indispensable needs. From a functionalist standpoint, ideology would be the *explanandum* (what is to be explained) and the pre-given needs of the system would be the *explanans* (that in terms of which it can be explained). This is not the standpoint which I am adopting. I am not trying to explain ideology in terms of some pre-given and un-questioned needs of a system (whatever that may be), but rather I am trying to focus attention on the nature and consequences of the ways in which symbolic forms are used and understood in particular circumstances. What we are concerned with, in a sense, are the social 'effects' of the usage and understanding of symbolic forms; and what we are concerned to explain, in part, is how the usage and understanding of symbolic forms contributes over time to the reproduction of relations of power and domination. But the language of cause and effect, of *explanandum* and *explanans*, is inadequate for the methodological tasks that confront us. For we are dealing with meaning and understanding as much as with cause and effect, we are seeking to inter-pret as much as to explain. To pursue the study of ideology, in the sense proposed here, we require a methodological framework which has left the standpoint of functionalism behind, and which is tailored to the specific characteristics of a meaningful object domain.

Objection 4: 'It's all very well in principle to define ideology in terms of the ways in which meaning serves to establish and sustain relations of domina-tion, but how can you ever tell in practice whether particular symbolic forms are serving to sustain or disrupt, to establish or undermine, relations of domination? How do you know what these symbolic forms mean to specific individuals, whether these individuals are in positions of domination or sub-ordination, and what (if any) relation there is between the meaning of these symbolic forms and the social positions of these individuals?' It is difficult to provide a general response to questions such as these. There are no simple rules of thumb which will determine, when applied to particular cases, the meaning that symbolic forms have for specific individuals or the nature of the social relations in which these individuals are enmeshed. But from this it does not follow that symbolic forms do not have determinate meanings for specific individuals or that these individuals are not enmeshed in determinate social relations. The fact that it is difficult to determine these phenomena does not imply that these phenomena are indeterminate. We can seek to illuminate relations of domination by employing various methods of social–historical analysis, for example by analysing the distribution of and access to scarce resources or institutional positions in relation to considerations such as class background, gender or ethnic origin. We can seek to elucidate the meaning that symbolic forms may have for individuals by examining the characteristics of these forms and, where possible, relating these characteristics to the accounts offered by the individuals who produce and receive them in the course of their everyday lives. We can try to show how the meaning conveyed by symbolic forms serves, in particular circumstances, to establish and sustain relations of domination by developing an interpretation which explicates the role that these symbolic forms play in, and the consequences that they have for, the lives of the individuals among whom they circulate. 'But an interpretation is not a proof.' Indeed it is not: if the critic is looking for proof, for incontestable demonstration, then he or she will be disappointed. But the disappointment stems more from the critic's expectations than from the analyst's results. In analysing ideology, in seeking to grasp the complex interplay of meaning and power, we are not dealing with a subject matter that admits of incontestable demonstration (whatever that may be). We are in the realm of shifting sense and relative inequalities, of ambiguity and word-play, of different degrees of opportunity and accessibility, of deception and self-deception, of the concealment of social relations and of the concealment of the very process of concealment. To approach this realm in the expectation that one could provide incontestable analyses is like using a microscope to interpret a poem.

Objection 5: 'But if the study of ideology is a matter of interpretation, then the characterization of particular symbolic forms as ideological seems little more than arbitrary. Perhaps Mannheim was right, after all, to contend that the only way to avoid arbitrariness and one-sidedness in the analysis of ideology is to generalize the approach and to subject the analyst's own position to ideological analysis.' Although interpretations are contestable, it does not follow that they are arbitrary. There may be good reasons for offering a particular interpretation and adhering to it, reasons which may be quite convincing in the circumstances even if they are not altogether conclusive. An interpretation may be plausible, and considerably more plausible than other interpretations, without purporting to exclude all doubt; there is a great deal of room on the spectrum between incontestable demonstration and arbitrary choice, and the interpretation of ideology, like all forms of interpretation, lies in the region in between. The interpretation of ideology does raise special problems, in so far as it is concerned with the interpretation of phenomena which are already understood in some sense by the individuals who produce and receive them and which are linked in complex ways to the interests and opportunities of these individuals. We can deal adequately with these problems only by attending carefully to the characteristics of this field of analysis and by examining the ways in which particular interpretations may be defended and criticized, challenged and sustained. Mannheim's proposal, however well-intentioned, is of no help in this task, since it conflates the analysis of ideology with the study of the social conditions of thought and since it culminates in the paradoxical position of seeking to overcome the epistemological problems of radical historicism by privileging a social group whose conditioned thought is relatively unconditioned. It is best to distance ourselves once and for all from Mannheim's approach to the analysis of ideology and its paradoxical consequences. We can seek to defend and criticize interpretations, to render some interpretations plausible and convincing and to try to show that others are not, without succumbing to the unhelpful and confused demand that every analysis of ideology must itself be analysed ideologically. This is not to say that the interpretation of ideology stands above all suspicion, that the interpreter usurps a privilege which is denied to all others. On the contrary, it is to say that any interpretation is open to suspicion, and it is precisely because of this that, in offering an interpretation, we must also offer reasons and grounds, evidence and arguments, which, in our view, render the interpretation plausible; and whether the interpretation is plausible, whether the reasons and grounds are convincing, is not a matter for the interpreter alone to judge.

In this chapter I have retraced the history of the concept of ideology with a twofold aim: with the aim of identifying some of the principal conceptions of ideology which have emerged in the course of this history and have contributed to the richness and the ambiguity of the term, and with the aim of preparing the groundwork for the formulation of an alternative conception. I have characterized this alternative conception as a critical conception, for it does not attempt to eliminate the negative sense which the term 'ideology' has acquired in the course of its history but rather retains this sense and construes it in a particular way. Hence ideology remains a critical concept, a critical tool which calls our attention to a range of social phenomena that can be – and that often are in the course of everyday life – subjected to criticism and embroiled in conflict. The concept of ideology, according to the formulation proposed here, calls our attention to the ways in which meaning is mobilized in the service of dominant individuals and groups, that is, the ways in which the meaning constructed and conveyed by symbolic forms serves, in particular circumstances, to establish and sustain structured social relations from which some individuals and groups benefit more than others, and which some individuals and groups have an interest in preserving while others may seek to contest. The study of ideology, understood in this sense, thus plunges the analyst into a realm of meaning and power, of interpretation and counter-interpretation, where the object of analysis is a weapon employed in a battle carried out on the terrain of symbols and signs.

In subsequent chapters I shall pick up and develop some aspects of this alternative approach to the study of ideology. I shall show how this approach can be integrated into a broader methodological framework for the analysis of contextualized symbolic forms. Before proceeding to these broader and more constructive concerns, however, I want to consider some of the most recent contributions to the theory and analysis of ideology. For Mannheim's work was by no means the last word on these matters. In recent years there has been an upsurge of interest in problems associated with the analysis of ideology and a veritable explosion of writings on this theme. I want to examine a selection of these writings in the following chapter. In doing so I shall shift my focus somewhat: I shall be less concerned with the differing ways in which contemporary authors employ the concept of ideology, the different shades of meaning which they give to this term, and I shall seek instead to highlight the role which this concept plays within their differing theoretical accounts of the nature and development of modern societies.

2

Ideology in Modern Societies

A Critical Analysis of Some Theoretical Accounts

In recent decades, problems associated with the analysis of ideology in modern societies have been central to social and political theory and debate. Many authors, of widely differing theoretical persuasions, have sought to analyse the concept of ideology, the characteristics of ideological forms and their role in social and political life. They have, in differing ways, sought to incorporate the concept of ideology into broader sets of assumptions concerning the nature and development of modern industrial societies. In this chapter I want to examine some of these contemporary writings on the theory and analysis of ideology. My aim will be not so much to trace the continuing vicissitudes of a concept, but rather to highlight some of the broader sets of assumptions on the basis of which the analysis of ideology is pursued today. Hence I shall be concerned with broad theoretical frameworks, with general and often implicit visions concerning the nature and development of modern societies. I shall try to show that, to some extent, these theoretical frameworks or visions are a legacy of nineteenth- and early twentieth-century social thought. Here, as in many contexts of social inquiry, the terms of reference of current debates were set a century ago. To a significant extent, writers such as Marx and Weber defined the problems that are still being debated; they put forward the concepts and theories that continue to guide research and discussion. While this in itself is not necessarily harmful – indeed, the transmission of a corpus of concepts and problems is part of what defines an intellectual tradition or discipline – nevertheless we must ask whether, in specific cases, the sets of assumptions handed down from the past are adequate for analysing the social forms and phenomena which confront us today. I shall argue that the principal assumptions which have guided many recent analyses of ideology in modern societies are inadequate in this regard.

In order to develop this argument, I shall begin by reconstructing two different sets of assumptions and examining the limitations of each. The first set of assumptions comprises a range of ideas which stem from the work of Marx and Weber, among others. Together these ideas constitute a general theoretical account of the cultural transformations associated with the rise of modern industrial societies. I shall call this account *the grand narrative of cultural transformation*. This narrative provides the framework within which much recent reflection on the nature and role of ideology in modern societies has taken place. The rise and fall of ideologies are phases of an historical drama which has been played out on the symbolic stage of modern societies, from their emergence in eighteenth-century Europe to the present day. Within the context of the grand narrative, ideology is understood as a particular kind of belief system characteristic of the modern age. I shall distinguish the grand narrative of cultural transformation from a second set of assumptions which has underpinned some recent work on the nature and role of ideology – especially work of a more explicitly Marxist persuasion. This second set of assumptions similarly constitutes a general theoretical account which has been both pervasive and deeply influential in social and political thought. I shall describe this account as *the general theory of state-organized and ideologically secured social reproduction*. Within the framework of this general theory, ideology is conceptualized as a cluster of values and beliefs which are produced and diffused by agencies of the state, and which serve to reproduce the social order by securing the adherence of individuals to it.

As I shall try to show, there are serious difficulties with both of the theoretical accounts which have guided much recent work on the analysis of ideology in modern societies. Both accounts rest on assumptions which are questionable or misleading in fundamental ways. While many of the criticisms that I shall make of these accounts are concerned with the assumptions specific to each, I shall argue that there is one major shortcoming which they share in common: both accounts fail to deal adequately with the nature and centrality of mass communication in modern societies. I shall argue that the *mediazation of modern culture* – that is, the ways in which symbolic forms in modern societies have become increasingly mediated by the mechanisms and institutions of mass communication – is a central feature of modern social life; and I shall maintain that a satisfactory analysis of ideology in modern societies must therefore be based, at least in part, on an understanding of the nature and development of mass communication.

It is one of the merits of the writings of the critical theorists associated with the Frankfurt Institute for Social Research – from Horkheimer and Adorno to Habermas – that they have sought to take account of the centrality of mass communication in modern societies. In their critical analysis of what they call 'the culture industry', Horkheimer and Adorno provide one of the first systematic accounts of the mediazation of modern culture, and they attempt to draw out the implications of this process for the analysis of ideology in modern societies. Similarly Habermas, especially in his early work on the public sphere, examines the ways in which political processes in modern societies have been profoundly transformed by the development of the media industries. In the final two sections of this chapter I shall examine the contributions of Horkheimer, Adorno and Habermas. I shall try to show that their work, while path-breaking and provocative in many respects, does not provide a satisfactory basis for rethinking the concept and analysis of ideology in the era of mass communication.

Ideology and the Modern Era

Let me begin by reconstructing a set of assumptions concerning the cultural transformations associated with the rise of modern industrial societies. These assumptions constitute a general theoretical framework, an overarching theoretical narrative, which has shaped many of the problems and debates in social and political analysis, including some of the debates concerned with the nature and role of ideology in modern societies. The original elements of this *grand narrative of cultural transformation* can be discerned in the writings of Marx and Weber, although it was not until the 1950s and 1960s that the story acquired a certain *dénouement*. In examining this theoretical narrative I shall not restrict myself to the work of any particular thinker. For this narrative is not so much a clearly formulated theoretical argument which can be discerned in the writings of one or several authors as a story which has to be gleaned from a variety of texts and which, when reconstructed in this way, offers a vision of the major cultural transformations associated with the development of modern societies. Within this narrative, ideologies have a role to play, as secular belief systems which emerged in the wake of the demise of religion and magic and which served to mobilize political action in a world stripped of tradition. I want to reconstruct this narrative and to examine the twists and turns of its dramatic plot, not only because it offers a vision which has been deeply influential in social and political theory, but also because it presents an account of the cultural transformations associated with the development of modern societies, and in particular of the nature and role of ideology in these societies, which is, in my view, misguided in certain fundamental respects.

We can summarize the key elements of the grand narrative in terms of three main points.

1 The rise of industrial capitalism in Europe and elsewhere was accompanied by the decline of religious and magical beliefs and practices, which were prevalent in pre-industrial societies. The development of industrial capitalism at the level of economic activity was accompanied, in the sphere of culture, by the secularization of beliefs and practices and by the progressive rationalization of social life.

2 The decline of religion and magic[1] prepared the ground for the emergence of secular belief systems or 'ideologies', which serve to mobilize political action without reference to other-worldly values or beings. The religious and mythical consciousness of pre-industrial society was replaced by a practical consciousness rooted in social collectivities and animated by secular systems of belief.

3 These developments gave rise to the 'age of ideologies' which culminated in the radical revolutionary movements of the late nineteenth and early twentieth centuries. These movements – according to some theorists writing in the 1950s and 1960s – were the last manifestations of the age of ideologies. Today politics is increasingly a matter of piecemeal reform and the pragmatic accommodation of conflicting interests. Social and political action is less and less animated by secular belief systems which call for radical social change. Hence we are witnessing, according to some proponents of this view, not only the end of the age of ideologies, but the end of ideology as such.

Let me elaborate briefly on each of these points.

1 The idea that the rise of industrial capitalism was accompanied by the decline of religious and magical beliefs and practices is an idea that was shared by many nineteenth- and early twentieth-century thinkers, including Marx and Weber. For Marx, the type of society brought about by the emergence of industrial capitalism is radically different from earlier precapitalist societies. Whereas precapitalist societies were basically conservative in their mode of production, modern capitalist society is constantly expanding, changing, transforming itself; modern capitalist society also dissolves the traditions and cultural forms – including the religious traditions – which were characteristic of precapitalist societies. In the previous chapter I highlighted this emphasis – which is particularly striking in the *Manifesto of the Communist Party* – on the progressive, demystifying character of the modern era. The restless, ceaseless activity of the capitalist mode of production strips social relations of that 'train of ancient and venerable prejudices and opinions' which shrouded them in the past; 'all that is solid melts into air, all that is holy is profaned'.[1] The demystification of social relations

is, on Marx's account, an inherent aspect of the development of capitalism. It is this process of demystification which enables human beings, for the first time in history, to see their social relations for what they are – namely, relations of exploitation. It is this process which places humanity at the threshold of a new era, one that can be and will be ushered in by an *enlightened* transformation of society, that is, a transformation based on a shared knowledge of demystified social relations. The process of demystification inherent in the development of capitalism is thus an essential precondition for the ultimate elimination of exploitative class relations – even if, as I indicated in the previous chapter, Marx sometimes acknowledged that symbolic forms transmitted from the past may persist at the heart of the present and deflect the trajectory of revolutionary social change.

Weber was also concerned to highlight the links between the development of industrial capitalism and the transformation of culture and tradition. Like Marx, he saw an association between the rise of industrial capitalism and the dissolution of traditional values and beliefs. But Weber's account differs from that of Marx in several important respects. In the first place, Weber argued that changes in the sphere of culture and tradition were not merely by-products of the autonomous development of capitalism: on the contrary, certain transformations in religious ideas and practices were the cultural preconditions for the emergence of capitalism in the West. Moreover, Weber goes on to argue that, once industrial capitalism had established itself as the predominant form of economic activity in the course of the seventeenth and eighteenth centuries, it acquired a momentum of its own and dispensed with the religious ideas and practices that had been necessary for its emergence. The development of capitalism, together with the associated rise of the bureaucratic state, progressively rationalized action and adapted human behaviour to criteria of technical efficiency. The purely personal, spontaneous and emotional elements of traditional action were squeezed out by the demands of purposive-rational calculation and technical efficiency. Whereas the early Puritans had pursued rational economic activity as a calling, for subsequent generations this activity became a necessity, an impersonal power which circumscribed the lives of individuals and constrained them with the inexorability of an iron cage.

> Since asceticism undertook to remodel the world and to work out its ideals in the world, material goods have gained an increasing and finally an inexorable power over the lives of men as at no previous period in history. To-day the spirit of religious asceticism – whether finally, who knows? – has escaped from the cage. But victorious capitalism, since it rests on mechanical foundations, needs its support no longer. The rosy blush of its laughing heir, the Enlighten-

ment, seems also to be irretrievably fading, and the idea of duty in one's calling prowls about in our lives like the ghost of dead religious beliefs.[2]

While both Marx and Weber discerned a connection between the development of industrial capitalism and the dissolution of traditional religious beliefs, the tone of their accounts is altogether different. Whereas Marx spoke of the *demystification* of social relations and regarded this as the precondition for the ultimate emancipation from exploitative class relations, Weber spoke instead of the *disenchantment* of the modern world, in which some of the traditional and distinctive values of Western civilization were submerged beneath the increasing rationalization and bureaucratization of social life, and he regarded this, with some regret, as the 'fate of modern times'.

2 The views of Marx and Weber, among others, provide the backcloth against which some thinkers have argued that the formation and diffusion of ideologies is a distinctive characteristic of the modern era. This argument, evident already in the work of Mannheim, has been developed in recent years by a variety of authors.[3] Here I shall try to reconstruct the argument in a general way, without adhering too closely to the work of any particular theorist. During the late eighteenth and early nineteenth centuries – so the argument goes – the process of secularization was beginning to take hold in the industrial heartlands of Europe. As more and more people were swept off the land and into the cities to form a labour force for the expanding factories of industrial capitalism, the old traditions, religions and myths began to lose their grip on the collective imagination. The old ties of bondage between lord and serf, ties shrouded in the veil of loyalty and mutual obligation, were increasingly called into question, as individuals were thrust into a new set of social relations based on the private ownership of the means of production and the exchange of commodities and labour power in the market. At the same time as this new set of social relations was being formed, political power was increasingly concentrated in the institutions of a secularized state – that is, a state based on a notion of sovereignty and the formal rule of law and justified by an appeal to universal values, rules and rights, rather than by an appeal to some religious or mystical value or being which would endow political power with the authority of a divine will. The modern state is distinguished from the political institutions of the *ancien régime* by, among other things, the fact that it is located entirely *within* the social–historical world, and hence the struggle for and exercise of power becomes a mundane matter which is embedded in the language of reason and science, interests and rights.

The secularization of social life and of political power created the conditions for the emergence and diffusion of 'ideologies'. In this context 'ideologies' are understood primarily as secular belief systems which have a mobilizing and legitimating function. The late eighteenth and early nineteenth centuries marked the beginning of the 'age of ideologies' in this sense, as expressed in the great political revolutions in France and America and in the proliferation of political doctrines or 'isms', from socialism and communism to liberalism, conservatism and nationalism. The diffusion of political doctrines was facilitated, and their efficacy enhanced, by two further developments characteristic of the eighteenth and nineteenth centuries: the expansion of the newspaper industry and the growth of literacy. These developments increasingly enabled individuals to read about the social and political world and to share the experience of others with whom they did not interact in their everyday lives. The horizons of individuals were thereby expanded; they became potential participants of a 'public sphere' in which issues were debated and positions were challenged or supported by means of reasons and arguments. It was in the cleared space of the public sphere that the discourse of ideologies appeared, constituting organized systems of beliefs which offered coherent interpretations of social and political phenomena, and which served to mobilize social movements and to justify the exercise of power. Ideologies thus provided frames of meaning, as it were, which enabled individuals to orientate themselves in a world characterized by a certain sense of *groundlessness*, a sense produced by the destruction of traditional ways of life and by the demise of religious and mythical world-views.

3 If the cultural transformations associated with the rise of modern industrial societies created a new space within which ideologies could flourish, this was a space which could, in the view of some theorists, be closed down by the subsequent development of modern societies. The idea that the age of ideologies has come to an end is not a new idea, nor is it an idea which is shared by all theorists who have argued that ideologies are a distinctive feature of the modern era; it is an idea which could be seen as constituting a particular, but by no means generally shared, twist to the grand narrative of cultural transformation. The so-called 'end of ideology' thesis was originally put forward by a range of liberal and conservative thinkers, including Raymond Aron, Daniel Bell, Seymour Lipset and Edward Shils, although an echo of this thesis can be heard today in ongoing theoretical debates.[4] In its original formulation, the end of ideology thesis was an argument about the alleged decline of radical or revolutionary political doctrines in the developed industrial societies of both Eastern Europe and the West. In the wake of the Second World War, the defeat of Fascism and Nazism, the

Moscow trials, the denunciation of Stalinism and other political developments and atrocities of recent years, the old ideologies stemming from the
late eighteenth and nineteenth centuries had lost, it was argued, much of
their persuasive power. These ideologies had taken hold primarily among
groups of intellectuals who had become disaffected with existing social and
political institutions, and who had expressed their disaffection by calling for
radical change. But the political events of the early twentieth century had
exposed the naïvety and the danger of such calls. It was becoming
increasingly clear to intellectuals and others that the problems confronting
developed industrial societies could not be resolved by the kind of radical
social change espoused by Marxism and communism, since this kind of
change gave rise to similar problems and to new forms of violence and
repression. Hence the end of ideology theorists discerned the emergence of a
new consensus: the old 'ideological politics' were giving way to a new sense
of pragmatism in the developed industrial societies. Revolutionary passion
was waning and was being replaced by a pragmatic, piecemeal approach to
social change within the framework – in the West at least – of a mixed
economy and a redistributive welfare state. The end of ideology theorists
generally recognized that ideologies would continue to flourish in less
developed societies, and they did not altogether rule out the possibility that
revolutionary passions might occasionally reappear as isolated and incon-
sequential outbursts in the developed industrial societies. But they
maintained that, as a general situation in which the political arena is
animated by radical and revolutionary doctrines which arouse passion and
heated conflict, the age of ideologies is over and ideology has ceased to be a
significant feature of modern industrial societies.

Of course, the end of ideology theorists were using the term 'ideology' in a
very special sense. Ideologies, in their view, were not secular belief systems of
any kind: rather, they were comprehensive, totalizing doctrines which offer a
coherent vision of the social–historical world and which demand a high
degree of emotional attachment. For most of these theorists, Marxism was
the epitome of ideology in this sense. Marxism offered a systematic,
totalizing vision of the social–historical world. It predicted a future which
would be radically different from the present, and which could only be
realized through the dedicated action of individuals who believed un-
flinchingly in their cause. These were the characteristics of ideology:
totalizing, utopian, impassioned, dogmatic. The end of ideology in this sense
was not necessarily the end of political debate and conflict, of contrasting
political programmes which expressed genuine differences of interest and
opinion. But these debates, conflicts and programmes would no longer be
animated by totalizing, utopian visions which incited individuals to

revolutionary action and blinded them to any considerations which were contrary to their view. With the passing of the age of ideologies, political processes could be increasingly institutionalized within a pluralistic framework in which political parties or groups competed for power and implemented pragmatic policies of social reform. Ideologies were not so much an endemic feature of the modern era as a passing symptom of modernization, a symptom which would gradually disappear as industrial societies reached a stage of economic and political maturity.

I have reconstructed this grand narrative of cultural transformation in order to raise a series of issues about the nature and role of ideology in modern societies. It is a narrative with different elements and several sub-plots and – as I indicated earlier – I do not want to suggest that the whole story can be found in the work of any single author. I have abstracted from detailed variations and elaborations in order to sketch a general line of argument which is deeply embedded in the literature of social and political theory, and which continues to structure debates about the nature and role of culture and ideology in modern societies. I now want to turn from reconstruction to critical assessment. In so doing I do not want to suggest that there is nothing of enduring value in the grand narrative: my aim is not to dismiss this narrative in its entirety, but rather to highlight certain respects in which it is, in my view, misleading. I shall restrict my attention to two main issues. There are many other issues that could be addressed in this context: a line of argument so broad in scope is bound to raise many questions and problems. But my concern is less with detailed difficulties than with general short-comings; I want to try to show that, for reasons of a fundamental kind, the grand narrative of cultural transformation is not a suitable framework within which to analyse the nature and role of ideology in modern societies.

The first major shortcoming of the grand narrative is that, by characteriz-ing the cultural transformations associated with the rise of modern industrial societies primarily in terms of the processes of secularization and rationaliza-tion, this account downplays the significance of what I have called the mediazation of modern culture. The problem here is not simply that the processes of secularization and rationalization may have been less sweeping and less uniform than earlier social theorists sometimes suggested – though it is probably the case that these processes were over-emphasized, and that religious beliefs and practices are more persistent features of modern societies than the early social theorists imagined.[5] More importantly, the problem is that the preoccupation with processes of secularization and rationalization has tended to occlude a development which was of much greater significance for the nature of cultural forms in modern societies –

namely, the development of a range of institutions concerned with the mass production and mass distribution of symbolic goods. I shall document this development and draw out some of its implications in subsequent chapters. Here it will suffice to say that, in so far as the traditional narrative neglects this development, it offers a seriously misleading account of the cultural transformations associated with the rise of modern societies. The institutions and processes of mass communication have assumed such fundamental significance in modern societies that no account of ideology and modern culture can afford to neglect them.

It is of course true that some of the theorists who could be associated with the grand narrative of cultural transformation have commented on the development of mass communication. For instance, Alvin Gouldner, drawing on Habermas's early work, discusses the ways in which the development of printing and the newspaper industry facilitated the formation of a public sphere in which political issues were debated and ideologies flourished. But Gouldner's account is limited and partial at best; and he hardly considers the implications of more recent forms of mass communication, particularly those involving electronic storage and transmission. Indeed, Gouldner tends to conceive of ideologies as discrete symbolic systems which are realized above all in *writing*, and which serve, as written, rational discourse, to animate public projects of social reconstruction. Hence Gouldner is led to the conclusion that the growth of electronic media, such as radio and television, marks the *decline* of the role of ideology in modern societies. Ideology is increasingly displaced from society as a whole, where consciousness is shaped more and more by the products of the electronic media; ideology is increasingly confined to the restricted sphere of the universities, where intellectuals continue to cultivate the written word.[6] This is not exactly a version of the end of ideology thesis, since Gouldner acknowledges a continuing, albeit restricted, role for ideology in contemporary societies. But to argue that ideology bears a privileged relation to writing and hence cannot be implicated in the development of electronic communication is at best a shortsighted view, for it severs the analysis of ideology from the very forms of mass communication which are of greatest significance today. So while the development of mass communication has not been altogether neglected by some authors who could be associated with the grand narrative of cultural transformation, we may doubt whether they have provided a satisfactory account of this development and of its implications for the analysis of ideology.

The second major shortcoming of the grand narrative concerns the ways in which the concept of ideology is employed within it. This concept is used in differing ways by different thinkers and it would be erroneous to suggest that it has a clear, univocal sense within the grand narrative. But if we abstract from the differences of usage, we can see that this concept is generally used to refer to discrete belief systems or symbolic systems which emerged in the wake of secularization and which have served to mobilize political movements and/or legitimate political power in modern societies; the general usage, in other words, is consistent with what I have called a neutral conception of ideology. This general usage is given a specific inflection by particular theorists or groups of theorists. We have seen, for example, that Gouldner tends to use 'ideology' to refer to symbolic systems which are realized primarily in writing, and which animate public projects of social reconstruction by means of rational discourse. The end of ideology theorists, by contrast, tend to use the term to refer to that specific sub-set of discrete political belief systems or doctrines which are comprehensive and totalizing, such as Marxism and communism. It is this restriction of the term that enables them to predict – with a confidence that no doubt contains a good deal of wishful thinking – that the age of ideologies is now over.

The main problem with this general usage of the term 'ideology' and its specific inflections is that it tends to downplay or dissolve the link between ideology and domination. In the previous chapter I examined this link and situated it in relation to the principal conceptions of ideology which have emerged in the course of the last two centuries. If we draw upon this analysis here and accept the critical conception of ideology proposed in the previous chapter, we can see that the general usage of 'ideology' in the grand narrative is questionable in two key respects. In the first place, it obliges us to regard ideology as an essentially *modern* phenomenon, that is, as a phenomenon unique to those societies which emerged in the course of capitalist industrialization during the seventeenth, eighteenth and nineteenth centuries. But this, it seems to me, is an overly restrictive view. It is not necessary to define the concept of ideology in terms of a particular body of political doctrines, belief systems or symbolic systems which are characteristic of certain societies only at a certain stage of their historical development. The concept admits, as we have seen, of many other definitions, and it is by no means clear that restricting the concept to modern societies is the most plausible or illuminating way to proceed. Must we accept that it *makes no sense* to speak of ideology in societies which preceded capitalist industrialization in Europe, that it makes no sense to speak of ideology in pre-industrial Europe, or in non-industrial societies elsewhere in the world? I think not. It seems to me to be perfectly possible to elaborate a justifiable conception of ideology which is not restricted to a particular body of doctrines that have emerged in the modern era.

The general usage of 'ideology' in the grand narrative is also misleading in so far as it directs our attention towards discrete political doctrines, belief systems or symbolic systems, and it therefore turns our attention away from the multiple ways in which symbolic forms are used, in the varied contexts of everyday life, to establish and sustain relations of domination. There is no clear and convincing justification that can be drawn, either from the history of the concept of ideology or from a reflection on the ways in which power is maintained, for restricting the analysis of ideology to the study of discrete political doctrines, belief systems or symbolic systems. To do so would be to take an overly narrow view of the nature and role of ideology in modern societies, and to neglect a wide range of symbolic phenomena which support forms of power in the social contexts of everyday life. Once again, it could not be said that all of the authors associated with the grand narrative espouse a consistent conception of ideologies as discrete political doctrines, belief systems or symbolic systems. More often than not, each of these authors uses the term 'ideology' in differing ways in different works, or even within the covers of a single work. But it is unquestionably the case that the conception of ideologies as discrete political doctrines features prominently among these uses, and it is primarily as such that the alleged rise and fall of ideologies in the modern era is traced. It we put aside this conception, we can also put aside the view that ideologies first appeared with the dawn of the modern era and have since disappeared from the social and political domain, and we can re-orientate the study of ideology towards the multiple and varied ways in which symbolic forms have been used, and continue to be used, in the service of power, whether in modern Western societies or in social contexts that are situated elsewhere in time and space.

Ideology and Social Reproduction

So far I have been examining a general theoretical narrative about the cultural transformations associated with the rise of modern industrial societies, a narrative which offers a distinctive account of the nature and role of ideology in modern societies. I have criticized this narrative both for its portrayal of cultural transformation and for its account of ideology. I now want to turn to a second set of assumptions which have underpinned much recent work on the analysis of ideology. This work is different in many ways from the writings which have been strongly influenced by the grand narrative of cultural transformation: it is generally less historical in orientation, and it is more concerned with analysing the conditions under which societies in general, and contemporary capitalist societies in particular, are sustained and reproduced. Much of this work is Marxist in orientation and is generally regarded as a contribution to a Marxist theory of ideology and the state. The writings of Althusser and Poulantzas have been particularly influential in this regard;[7] and partially as a result of their efforts, the writings of Gramsci have also featured prominently in recent debates.[8] The ideas of these theorists have been taken up and elaborated by many different authors in Europe and elsewhere.[9] Here I shall not attempt to examine the ideas of these theorists, or the work of their followers and critical commentators, in any detail. Detailed examinations of this kind are already available in the literature.[10] However, I do want to consider some of the assumptions which underlie the work of Althusser, Poulantzas and others, for these assumptions form part of a general theoretical account which is widespread in contemporary social and political theory. I shall describe this account as *the general theory of state-organized and ideologically secured social reproduction*. This is not a theory which is explicitly articulated by any particular author, but the assumptions which comprise this theory can be discerned in the writings of particular authors. Moreover, these assumptions are sufficiently widespread in the contemporary literature, and have sufficient influence on the ways in which problems of politics and ideology are conceived, that it is worthwhile to formulate the assumptions explicitly, to reconstruct the general theoretical argument which, taken together, they constitute, and to assess their strengths and weaknesses.

The general theory of state-organized and ideologically secured social reproduction may be seen as a partial answer to the following question: why do societies in general, and contemporary capitalist societies in particular, persist in spite of the divisions and inequalities which characterize them? The theory offers a partial answer to this question by attempting to identify some of the *mechanisms* which secure the reproduction of existing social relations. We can reconstruct the theory in terms of three main steps.

1 The reproduction of existing social relations requires not only the reproduction of the material conditions of social life (food, housing, machinery, etc.), but also the reproduction of collectively shared values and beliefs.
2 Some of the collectively shared values and beliefs constitute the elements of a dominant ideology which, by being diffused throughout society, secures the adherence of individuals to the social order.
3 The production and diffusion of the dominant ideology is one of the tasks of the state, or of particular agencies and officials of the state. In carrying out this task, the state acts in the long-term interests of the class or classes which benefit most from existing social relations - that is, it acts in the long-term interests of the dominant class or classes.

This general theoretical account has a certain prima facie plausibility. It emphasizes the importance of collectively shared values and beliefs, as diffused by agencies and officials of the state, in helping to sustain social order in societies based on divisions of class. Despite this prima facie plausibility, however, I think it can be shown that this general theoretical account is seriously deficient. Let me consider each step in turn.

1 The account begins with the claim that social reproduction requires both the reproduction of the material conditions of social life and the reproduction of collectively shared values and beliefs. It requires the reproduction of the material conditions of social life in the sense that the means of production (tools, machinery, factories, etc.) and the means of subsistence for producers (housing, clothing, food, etc.) must be continuously provided and renewed as an ongoing aspect of social life. There is more than a hint of functionalism in this contention, but it can also be construed in a counterfactual way: if the means of production and subsistence were not continuously provided and renewed, then existing social relations would break down and crisis and conflict would ensue. Here I do not wish to examine in further detail the logic of this argument, and the plausibility of this counterfactual construal, as my main concern is with a different issue. Social reproduction requires not only the reproduction of the material conditions of social life, but also the reproduction of collectively shared values and beliefs – that is, it requires the continuous provision and renewal of symbolic forms which are, to some extent, collectively shared and which serve, to some extent, to mould the actions and attitudes of individuals. It is this continuous provision and renewal of symbolic forms which ensures – so the argument goes – the ongoing submission of individuals to the normative rules and conventions of the social order. They are moulded to fit the parts which are scripted for them in the great play of social reproduction.

This account is a particular version of what we may describe as *the consensual theory of social reproduction*. According to this theory, the ongoing reproduction of social relations depends in part on the existence of values and beliefs which are collectively shared and accepted by individuals, and which thereby bind individuals to the social order. This theory admits of many variations, but we can distinguish between two main variants: *the core consensual theory*, which maintains that there are certain core values and beliefs (freedom, democracy, equality of opportunity, the sovereignty of parliament, etc.) which are widely shared and firmly accepted; and *the differentiated consensual theory*, which places less emphasis on the existence of core values and beliefs and stresses instead the importance of values and beliefs which are specific to the roles and positions of individuals who are differentially located in the division of labour. These two variants are often combined in the writings of particular authors, but they do not necessarily entail one another. Both variants of the consensual theory nevertheless suffer from serious limitations. Let us consider some of these.

The main difficulty with the core consensual theory is that it exaggerates the extent to which particular values and beliefs are shared and accepted by individuals in modern industrial societies. Although the relevant evidence is far from conclusive, it tends to indicate a much higher degree of dissensus and disaffection, of scepticism and cynicism, than the core consensual theory would suggest. One study of a range of empirical material from Britain and the United States found that the material showed no significant degree of consensus concerning values and beliefs. The study also found that the degree of dissensus varied from one class to another, with working-class respondents displaying less consensus and less internal consistency in their values and beliefs than middle-class respondents.[11] Other studies, carried out in Britain in the 1960s and 1970s, suggest that many working-class people reject values and rights associated with capital accumulation and property ownership; many think that big business has too much power in society and that there is one law for the rich and another for the poor; and many believe that they have no significant influence on government and that the political system is not responsive to what ordinary people think and want.[12] These findings, while limited, tentative and now somewhat dated in nature, cast considerable doubt on the core consensual theory of social reproduction. It cannot be plausibly assumed that there is a core set of values and beliefs which are widely shared and firmly accepted by individuals in modern industrial societies, and which thereby bind individuals to a common normative framework, for it seems likely that most core values and beliefs are contested and that there is a fairly high degree of disagreement and disaffection. If social reproduction were dependent on a generalized acceptance of core values and beliefs, then the ongoing reproduction of the social order would seem very improbable indeed.

The differentiated consensual theory does not suffer from the same difficulty. This theory does not assume the existence of a core set of values and beliefs which are widely shared; rather, it assumes only that there exist different sets of values and beliefs which are specific to particular roles and positions, such that an individual situated in or destined for a particular role or position will acquire the appropriate values and beliefs. The 'consensus' which exists is not so much a consensus among a plurality of individuals about a core set of values and beliefs, but rather a consensus between a role-specific set of values and beliefs, on the one hand, and the values and beliefs of the individual incumbents of the role or position, on the other. It is the consensus of an orchestrated performance in which individuals have learned their respective parts so well that they can play without a score and without the explicit orchestration of a conductor. By virtue of the fact that individuals have acquired role-specific sets of values and beliefs and play their parts so effectively in the routine course of their day-to-day lives, the social order of which their routine activity is part is reproduced. There is no need for all or most individuals to share a core set of values and beliefs, so long as all or most individuals have acquired the role-specific sets of values and beliefs which enable them (and impel them) to perform successfully their respective parts.

No doubt there is some plausibility to the account of social reproduction offered by the differentiated consensual theory (or some version thereof). It is no doubt the case that processes of socialization, as well as the routine and continuous inculcation of values and beliefs, play a vital role in endowing individuals with the social skills and attitudes which govern their subsequent behaviour. However, there are two respects in which this account tends to overemphasize the extent to which individuals are moulded by social processes. Individuals are treated essentially as the products of, or as 'constituted by', the processes of socialization and inculcation to which they are subjected. But individuals are never simply the sum total of processes of socialization and inculcation; they are never simply actors who obediently perform the roles which are scripted for them. It is part of their very nature *qua* human agents that they are capable, to some extent, of distancing themselves from the social processes to which they are subjected, of reflecting on these processes, criticizing them, contesting them, ridiculing them and, in some circumstances, rejecting them. It is important to see, however, that this critical and contestatory relation to processes of socialization and inculcation does not necessarily disrupt social reproduction – and this brings us to the second respect in which the differentiated consensual theory can be misleading. In the course of their everyday lives individuals typically move through a multiplicity of social contexts and are subjected to conflicting social pressures and processes. Rejecting one set of values and norms may coincide with accepting another, or may facilitate their participation in social activities which serve, *ipso facto*, to reproduce the status quo. Willis provides an excellent illustration of how the reproduction of the social order can be an unintentional outcome of the *rejection* of the values and norms propagated by the official agencies of secondary socialization, i.e. the schools.[13] In his study of a group of working-class boys he shows that their cynical and contestatory view of school authorities, and their rejection of the individualistic ethos and non-manual career orientation espoused by the educational system, makes them more (rather than less) suitable for post-school employment in working-class jobs. The reproduction of manual labour is not the outcome of a seamless fit between the values and beliefs of individuals and a role-specific set of values and beliefs which is provided, as it were, by the educational system; on the contrary, it is precisely because these teenagers do *not* incorporate the values and beliefs propagated by the educational system that they accept so readily the burdens of manual labour.

Both variants of the consensual theory of social reproduction therefore suffer from certain limitations. While the differentiated consensual theory is more sophisticated and more plausible than the core consensual theory, both accounts place too much emphasis on consensus and convergence in terms of values and beliefs, and both downplay the prevalence and significance of dissensus and disagreement, of scepticism and cynicism, of contestation and conflict. Both variants of the consensual theory assume that social reproduction is the outcome in part of a consensus concerning values and beliefs (whether core or role-specific), but the ongoing reproduction of the social order is probably more dependent on the fact that individuals are embedded in a variety of different social contexts, that they carry out their lives in routine and regularized ways which are not necessarily animated by overarching values and beliefs, and that there is a *lack of consensus* at the very point where oppositional attitudes might be translated into coherent political action. The prevalence of sceptical and cynical attitudes, and the rejection of values and beliefs propagated by the principal agencies of socialization, do not necessarily represent a challenge to the social order. Scepticism and hostility are often interfused with traditional and conservative values and are often tempered by a sense of resignation. Divisions are ramified along the lines of gender, ethnicity, skill and so on, forming barriers which obstruct the development of movements which could threaten the status quo. The reproduction of the social order does not require some deep underlying consensus concerning values and beliefs, so long as there is sufficient dissensus to prevent the formation of an effective oppositional movement.

2 The consensual theory of social reproduction is readily linked to a particular conception of ideology. Some of the values and beliefs about which a consensus is presumed to exist are regarded as constituting the elements of a dominant ideology which secures the adherence of individuals to the social order. The dominant ideology provides the symbolic glue, as it were, which unifies the social order and binds individuals to it. By virtue of the pervasive presence of the dominant ideology, individuals from all social strata are incorporated into a social order which is structured in unequal ways. It is the pervasiveness of the dominant ideology which explains – so the

argument goes – both the ease with which dominant groups dominate and the resignation with which dominated groups accept their domination. The dominant ideology is a symbolic system which, by incorporating individuals from all strata into the social order, helps to reproduce a social order which serves the interests of dominant groups.

In previous discussions I have already raised some of the points which weigh most heavily against this so-called 'dominant ideology thesis', and there is no need to dwell on them extensively now.[14] Let me briefly elaborate the essential points. First, the dominant ideology thesis presumes what we could describe as *the social cement theory of ideology*. That is, it presumes that ideology works like a kind of social cement, binding individuals to a social order which oppresses them. But, as we have seen, there is not much evidence to support the claim that individuals from different strata are bound to the social order in this way. It may be that dominant values and beliefs are shared by some members of dominant groups, endowing these groups with a certain cohesiveness, but there is little evidence to support the view that such values and beliefs are widely shared by members of subordinate groups. Hence the dominant ideology thesis, in so far as it presumes that dominant values and beliefs comprise an ideology which works like cement, fails to explain what it seeks to explain, namely, why it is that members of subordinate groups act in ways which do not undermine the social order.

To criticize the dominant ideology thesis in this way is not to deny that certain symbolic forms have a great deal of symbolic value in our societies, nor is it to deny that these symbolic forms may, in certain circumstances, serve to establish, sustain and reproduce relations of domination; even less is it to suggest that the concept of ideology has no useful role to play in the analysis of social and political life. The problem with the dominant ideology thesis is simply that it offers a much too simple account of how ideology works in modern societies. It assumes that a particular set of values and beliefs constitutes the elements of a dominant ideology which, by being diffused throughout society, binds individuals of all strata to the social order; but the ways in which symbolic forms serve to maintain relations of domination are far more complicated than this account would suggest. The notion of social cement is a conceptual convenience which obscures the very issues that must be examined by a more satisfactory approach to the phenomenon of ideology. Rather than assuming that a particular set of values and beliefs serves *ipso facto* to bind individuals of all strata to the social order, a more satisfactory approach must examine the ways in which individuals differentially situated in the social order respond to and make sense of particular symbolic forms, and how these symbolic forms, when analysed in relation to the contexts in which they are produced, received and understood, serve (or do not serve) to establish and sustain relations of domination. To short-circuit this analysis with a general assumption about the cementing properties of symbolic forms (or of symbolically transmitted values and beliefs) is to bolster up an implausible theory of social reproduction with what is, at best, a very partial account of ideology and its mode of operation in modern societies.

3 The production and diffusion of the dominant ideology is generally regarded as one of the tasks and accomplishments of the state, or of particular agencies and officials of the state. Which agencies are regarded as particularly important in this regard varies from one author to another. Let us consider briefly the work of Althusser. In an influential article Althusser distinguishes between the 'repressive state apparatus', which comprises the government, the civil service, the police, the courts, the prisons, the armed forces, etc., and the 'ideological state apparatuses', which include the churches, the schools, the family, the legal system, the political system, the trade unions, the system of mass communication, and cultural activities like sports and the arts. One might reasonably doubt whether it is helpful or sensible to regard such a broad range of institutions as part and parcel of the state. But Althusser argues that the apparently diverse body of institutions and activities which make up the ideological state apparatuses are unified by the fact that the ideology which is realized in them and through them is primarily the ideology of the dominant class – that is, they are all essentially mechanisms for the propagation of the dominant ideology.[15] Other ideological elements may be present within these apparatuses, but the ideological field is structured in favour of the ideology of the dominant class, which exercises control over the ideological state apparatuses. Hence, on this account, various institutions of the state are regarded as the means through which the dominant ideology is produced and diffused, and through which the reproduction of the relations of production – and of individuals *qua* subjects who duly submit to the existing order of things – is secured.

For our purposes here, there is no need to examine further the details of Althusser's account, or to examine the permutations that may be found in the work of authors influenced by him. Nor is there any need to demonstrate, through detailed textual analysis, the extent to which the criticisms made in previous paragraphs can be levelled at Althusser's account. At this stage I want simply to use Althusser's account as a basis on which to raise three final objections to the general theory of state-organized and ideologically secured social reproduction. The first objection is that this theory tends to adopt a *class-reductionist approach to the modern state*. That is, the state is seen, primarily and ultimately, as an institutional mechanism through which class power is sustained. It is commonly acknowledged – following some occasional remarks of Engels and some of Marx's more substantive analyses[16] – that the various institutions of the state may have a degree of autonomy from the immediate interests and activities of the dominant class or class factions; but this autonomy is always limited by the fact that, 'in the last instance', as the saying goes, the state operates within a set of boundary conditions which are defined by the class character of the production process. The role or function of the state coincides with the long-term interests of the dominant class, although the state may best fulfil this role by maintaining a certain distance, a 'relative autonomy', from the immediate aims of the dominant class and its factions.

The main problem with this approach to the state is not that it leaves unresolved the questions of how much autonomy is 'relative autonomy', and what it means to speak of the state and its apparatuses as determined 'in the last instance' by the economic mode of production. These questions are unresolved and probably unresolvable, but they are also largely of scholastic interest. The main problem is that this approach does not do justice to the historical development and distinctive character of the modern state. This approach conceives of the modern state and its institutions primarily in terms of their role or function of sustaining a system of social relations based on class exploitation, a role which is carried out in part by the propagation of a dominant ideology through the ideological state apparatuses. But this is an overly narrow and one-sided conception of the modern state. It is no doubt the case that some aspects and activities of the state can be understood in terms of the long-term interests of the dominant class, but it could hardly be maintained that state institutions are unresponsive to the demands of other classes and major interest groups, nor could it be plausibly argued that *all* aspects and activities of the modern state, including some of the most important aspects and activities, can be analysed in terms of class interests and class relations. As Max Weber and others have observed, the modern state is concerned not only with the regulation of social and economic activity and the exercise of political rule, but also with the maintenance of order within a given territory and the maintenance of territorial boundaries *vis-à-vis* other nation-states.[17] The modern state has an effective monopoly on the legitimate use of force or violence within a given territory, and violence is used by the state both for the purposes of internal control or pacification, and for the purposes of external defence or offence *vis-à-vis* other nation-states. States have developed a variety of institutions and agencies which are concerned, directly or indirectly, with the maintenance of internal order and external boundaries, agencies which rely extensively on the accumulation and control of information. These activities of the state can, and often do, come into conflict with the activities of other state organizations, as well as with the activities of individuals and organizations in other domains of social life. Any attempt to understand the diverse activities of modern states, and the conflicts which they engender, exclusively or even primarily in terms of *class* analysis would be a gross over-simplification of the issues involved.

If the general theory of state-organized and ideologically secured social reproduction tends to adopt a class-reductionist approach to the modern state, it also tends to assume a *class-reductionist approach to ideology*. That is, ideology is conceptualized primarily and essentially in relation to the classes or class factions which make up the social order, and it is the 'ruling ideology', or the ideology of the dominant class, which organizes the ideological field and expresses itself in the ideological state apparatuses. The ruling or dominant ideology may incorporate elements drawn from subordinate groups or classes, and there may be ideologies or 'ideological sub-systems' which correspond to subordinate groups or classes and which have a 'relative autonomy' with regard to the dominant ideology. But these ideological sub-systems are constrained by the dominant ideology; they are part of an ideological field which is ultimately structured by the ideology of the dominant class. It is in this way – to employ Gramsci's term – that the dominant class secures 'hegemony': through the structuring of the ideological field, the dominant class or class faction is able to exercise political leadership based on the 'active consent' of subordinate classes and to integrate the various factions of the dominant class into a relatively stable power bloc.

Some of the objections raised earlier against consensual theories of social reproduction could be raised again here, as this account of ideology and hegemony clearly involves certain assumptions about the integration of individuals into the social order and their consent to, or 'constitution by', particular values or beliefs. But here I want to focus on a different short-coming: namely, the extent to which this account relativizes ideology, and the analysis of ideology, to class relations. Ultimately it is the ideology of the dominant class or class faction which structures the ideological field, and the analysis of ideologies or ideological sub-systems is carried out primarily with reference to the various classes and class factions which make up the social order. It is certainly the case that relations of domination and subordination between classes and class factions are of major importance for the analysis of ideology, but it would be quite misleading, in my view, to maintain that class relations are the *only*, or in all circumstances the *primary*, structural feature of social contexts with reference to which the analysis of ideology should be carried out. On the contrary, it seems to me essential to recognize that there are systematically asymmetrical relations of power which are based on considerations other than class – which are based, for instance, on considerations of sex, age, or ethnic origin; and it seems to me essential to broaden the framework for the analysis of ideology to take account of these considerations. The general theory of state-organized and ideologically secured social reproduction, in so far as it gives primary emphasis to class relations and regards the ideological field as ultimately structured by the ideology of the dominant class or class faction, tends to over-value the importance of class in the analysis of ideology and to marginalize other types of domination as well as the symbolic forms which serve to sustain them.

The final objection, or series of objections, that I wish to raise concerns the ways in which the nature and role of mass communication are generally characterized by this account. The institutions of mass communication are generally regarded by proponents of this account as part of the system of ideological state apparatuses, that is, as one of the mechanisms, or as a cluster of mechanisms, through which the ideology of the dominant class is realized and the reproduction of the relations of production is secured. It may be acknowledged that these institutions possess some degree of autonomy *vis-à-vis* one another and *vis-à-vis* other aspects of the state; it may be acknowledged that the ideology diffused by the mass media may contain conflicting and contradictory elements, may incorporate elements drawn from subordinate groups, classes or class factions; but, ultimately, the institutions of mass communication are defined by their function of securing social cohesion and reproduction by means of the transmission and inculcation of the dominant ideology.[18] While this account rightly calls attention to the importance of mass communication, the characterization which it offers is, I think, misleading. The institutions of mass communication are treated in a relatively peripheral way, as some among a broad range of ideological state apparatuses; but this perspective fails to do justice to the mediazation of modern culture and, in general, to the centrality of mass communication in modern social and political life. Today the activities of states and governments, of their organizations and officials, take place within an arena that is to some extent *constituted by* the institutions and mechanisms of mass communication. The media of mass communication are not simply one among several mechanisms for the inculcation of a dominant ideology; rather, these media are partially constitutive of the very— forum within which political activities take place in modern societies, the forum within which, and to some extent with regard to which, individuals act and react in exercising power and in responding to the exercise of power by others. These are issues to which I shall return in a subsequent chapter.

The theory of state-organized and ideologically secured social reproduction not only fails to do justice to the centrality and constitutive
character of mass communication: it also begs some of the key questions
concerning the nature and role of media institutions in modern societies. By
assigning a principal role or function to the institutions of mass communication within a social order conceptualized essentially in terms of class
relations and divisions, it prejudges a whole range of issues concerning the
ways in which these institutions have developed historically, the ways in
which they are organized and operate routinely in the production and
diffusion of symbolic goods, and the ways in which the symbolic goods thus
produced are received and understood by individuals in the course of their
everyday lives. By defining the institutions of mass communication as part of
the state (broadly conceived), this account obscures and misconstrues the
nature of the conflicts and tensions which characterize the relations between
the various institutions of mass communication, on the one hand, and the
agencies and organizations of the state, on the other. These conflicts and
tensions can be adequately understood only by attending more carefully to
the specific activities and aims of the institutions of mass communication, by
analysing how and why these activities and aims may clash with the conduct
of the agencies and organizations of the state, and by acknowledging that the
latter agencies and organizations have a variety of concerns which cannot be
reduced to the function of securing the reproduction or cohesion of a social
order based on class exploitation.

In the previous paragraphs I have examined some of the key claims which
make up what I have described as the general theory of state-organized and
ideologically secured social reproduction. I have tried to show that, in certain
respects, these claims are dubious: they present an implausible account of
social reproduction (the consensual theory of social reproduction), a partial
account of the nature and role of ideology (the social cement theory of ideology), and a misleading account of the ways in which the development of mass
communication has affected social and political life. I have also argued that, in
the writings of some of the authors who have been most influential in recent
debates (such as Althusser and Poulantzas), these shortcomings are combined
with a class-reductionist approach to ideology and the state. Although these
authors avoid a strictly instrumentalist interpretation of ideology and the state
as tools or weapons of the dominant class, emphasizing instead the structured
complexity of the ideological field and the relative autonomy of the state,
nevertheless their analyses are guided by the assumption that, ultimately,
ideology and the state are mechanisms which secure the cohesion and reproduction of a social order based on class exploitation.

   In the remainder of this chapter I want to move away from the two sets of assumptions which have guided much recent work on the analysis of ideology in modern societies. I want to turn my attention to two theoretical approaches which have been less central and less influential in recent debates, but which are of considerable interest in themselves and which seek, in an explicit and innovative way, to take account of the nature and role of mass communication in modern societies. These two approaches are the critique of the culture industry as developed by Horkheimer and Adorno, and Habermas's early work on the structural transformation of the public sphere. These approaches are, of course, closely linked, and both are generally regarded as variants of the critical theory of the Frankfurt School. However, there are significant differences between the views of the earlier generation of critical theorists, which included Horkheimer and Adorno, and the views of later critical theorists such as Habermas. I shall not attempt here to explore in detail the similarities and differences between the views of these thinkers. Rather, I shall look in turn at those aspects of their work which bear directly on the issues which concern us in this chapter.

The Critique of the Culture Industry

The writings of the early Frankfurt School theorists offer a distinctive and original account of the nature and role of ideology in modern societies. This account is part of a far-reaching analysis of the developmental characteristics of modern societies and of the fate of the individual in modern times. In examining this account I shall focus on the work of Horkheimer and Adorno, although the work of other individuals associated with the early Frankfurt School, such as Benjamin, Marcuse, Lowenthal and Kracauer, is also of interest in this regard.[19] Horkheimer and Adorno gave particular attention to the rise of what they called 'the culture industry', a process which has resulted in the increasing commodification of cultural forms. Hence, unlike most of the authors associated with the grand narrative of cultural transformation, the early Frankfurt School theorists stressed the importance of the development of mass communication and attempted to rethink the nature and role of ideology in relation to this development. As I shall try to show, however, this account of mass communication was strongly influenced by a theme which is also central to the grand narrative, namely, the theme of rationalization; and this among other things resulted in an exaggerated view of the cohesive character of modern societies and an overly pessimistic prognosis concerning the fate of the individual in the modern era.

The views of the early critical theorists were shaped by historical events and developments in Europe and the United States in the 1920s, 1930s and 1940s. The suppression of revolutionary upheavals in Europe at the end of the First World War, the development of Stalinism in the Soviet Union and the rise of Fascism in Germany were interpreted by the critical theorists as so many signs that the revolutionary potential which Marx had discerned in modern societies was capable of being contained, thwarted or deflected towards reactionary ends. The social–historical and social–psychological dynamics underlying this process were analysed by Horkheimer and Adorno in terms of a general logic of enlightenment and domination whose roots could be traced back through the history of the human species.[20] With the growth of knowledge, human beings increased their mastery of nature – both external nature and the inner nature of human subjectivity – and they increasingly subordinated the natural world to the exercise of technical control. Mythical and animistic beliefs were progressively eliminated in favour of a scientific, instrumental reason which objectifies the world from the viewpoint of technical control. Human beings themselves become part of this objectified world, and their subordination to the logic of domination is enhanced by the commodification of labour power under capitalism. But human nature resists complete subordination; it rebels against the processes of objectification, rationalization and bureaucratization characteristic of the modern world. It is this quasi-instinctual rebellion which is taken up and exploited by Fascism. Fascist leaders employ a variety of carefully constructed techniques to tap the repressed anger and anxiety of the masses. They mobilize these irrational feelings, stirring them by frenzied attacks on ostracized groups and transforming them into a new mechanism for the domination of the very individuals whose quasi-instinctual rebellion was the source of the Fascists' success.

This general account of the logic of enlightenment and domination provides the backcloth against which Horkheimer and Adorno analyse the nature and consequences of the culture industry. Horkheimer and Adorno use the term 'culture industry' to refer to the commodification of cultural forms brought about by the rise of the entertainment industries in Europe and the United States in the late nineteenth and early twentieth centuries. Among the examples they discuss are film, radio, television, popular music, magazines and newspapers.[21] Horkheimer and Adorno argue that the rise of the entertainment industries as capitalistic enterprises has resulted in the standardization and rationalization of cultural forms, and this process has in turn atrophied the capacity of the individual to think and act in a critical and autonomous way. The cultural goods produced by these industries are designed and manufactured in accordance with the aims of capitalist accumulation and profit realization; they do not arise spontaneously from the masses themselves, but rather are tailored for consumption by the masses. 'The culture industry intentionally integrates its consumers from above . . .the masses are not primary, but secondary, they are an object of calculation; an appendage of the machinery.'[22] The goods produced by the culture industry are not determined by their intrinsic characteristics as an artistic form, but by the corporate logic of commodity production and exchange. Hence the goods are standardized and stereotyped, mere permutations of basic genres or types – the Western, the mystery, the soap. They affect an air of individuality, for example by featuring great personalities and stars, but this gesture does nothing to mitigate the fact that the goods themselves are standardized objects produced for profit and devoid of artistic content.

The products of the culture industry are very different from the traditional work of art. In the eighteenth century and before, the work of art could maintain a certain autonomy from the marketplace, thanks to a system of patronage which shielded the artist from the immediate demands of survival. This autonomy enabled the work of art to maintain some distance from existing reality, to express suffering and contradiction and thereby retain some grasp on the idea of the good life. But with the progressive commodification of cultural goods, this autonomy is destroyed. Art is increasingly subsumed to the logic of commodity production and exchange, and it therefore loses the critical potential inherent in the very purposelessness of traditional artistic forms. 'The work of art, by completely assimilating itself to need, deceitfully deprives men of precisely that liberation from the principle of utility which it should inaugurate.'[23] The contemplation and enjoyment of a work of art are replaced by the exchange of a commodity which is valued primarily for its exchangeability, rather than for its intrinsic aesthetic character. The *coup de grâce* of the culture industry is thoroughly to have commodified art while, at the same time, presenting it to the consumer as unsaleable. Thus when a concert by Beethoven is heard on the radio or an opera by Verdi is seen on television, no cash changes hands. But the apparent absence of exchange is an illusion made possible by a whole series of commercial transactions which take place outside the act of consumption itself. The consumer is left with the impression of an unmediated encounter with the work of art, while the culture industry reaps the profits from a series of transactions which have taken place behind the consumer's back.

Most of the products of the culture industry no longer make any pretension to be works of art, however. For the most part they are symbolic constructs which are moulded according to certain pre-established formulae and impregnated with stereotypical settings, characters and themes. They do not challenge or diverge from existing social norms; rather, they reaffirm these norms and censure any actions or attitudes that deviate from them. The products of the culture industry present themselves as a direct reflection or reproduction of empirical reality, and by virtue of this 'pseudo-realism' they normalize the status quo and curtail critical reflection on the social and political order. What people read, see and hear is familiar and banal, and into this symbolic sphere of repetitive familiarity is inserted a string of homespun slogans – 'all foreigners are suspect', 'a pretty girl can do no wrong', 'success is the ultimate aim of life' – which appear as self-evident and eternal truths. The collective authors of *Aspects of Sociology* sum up the ideological character of the culture industry as follows:

> If one were to compress within one sentence what the ideology of mass culture actually adds up to, one would have to represent this as a parody of the injunction: 'Become that which thou art': as the exaggerated duplication and justification of already existing conditions, and the deprivation of all transcendence and all critique. In this limiting of the socially effective spirit to once again presenting to the human beings only what in any case already constitutes the conditions of their existence, but at the same time proclaiming this present existence as its own norm, the people are confirmed in their faithless faith in pure existence.[24]

Unlike earlier forms of ideology, whose ideological character consisted in their alleged but illusory independence from social reality, the new ideology of the culture industry lies in the very absence of this independence. The products of the culture industry are moulded to fit and reflect a social reality which is reproduced without the need of an explicit and quasi-independent justification or defence, since the very process of consuming the products of the culture industry induces individuals to identify with the prevailing social norms and to continue to be as they already are.

In the vision of Horkheimer and Adorno, the development of the culture industry is an intrinsic part of the process of increasing rationalization and reification in modern societies, a process which is rendering individuals less and less capable of independent thinking and more and more dependent on social processes over which they have little or no control. Here the impact of Max Weber is evident: Weber's 'iron cage' of rationalized, bureaucratized action is replaced by the 'iron system' of the culture industry, in which individuals are surrounded by a universe of objects that are essentially identical and thoroughly commodified. Rather than providing a symbolic space within which individuals could cultivate their imagination and critical reflection, could develop their individuality and autonomy, this commodified universe channels the energy of individuals into the collective consumption of standardized goods. Individuals are adapted and adjusted to the existing social order by their very desire for the objects produced by it, and by the pleasure they experience in consuming these objects. 'Before the theological caprices of commodities, the consumers become temple slaves. Those who sacrifice themselves nowhere else can do so here, and here they are fully betrayed.'[25] The development of the culture industry, and of consumer culture more generally, has thus brought about the incorporation of individuals into a rationalized and reified social totality; it has stunted their imagination, stifled their revolutionary potential and rendered them vulnerable to manipulation by dictators and demagogues. Those who were swept along by the rhetoric of Nazism and Fascism are those who had already been crumpled beneath the footsteps of the culture industry. They were not so much individuals as social atoms who had become increasingly dependent on the collectivity, and whose repressed anger and resistance could be exploited by leaders who shrewdly employed the very techniques which had produced their dependence. Fascist propaganda needed only to activate and reproduce the existing mentality of the masses; it simply took people for what they were – the children of the culture industry – and employed the techniques of this industry to mobilize them behind the aggressive and reactionary aims of Fascism.[26] Thus the process of enlightenment, which had sought to control the world through the technical domination of nature, culminated in a rationalized and reified social totality in which human beings are not the masters but the servants and victims, whose consciousness has been fettered by the products of the culture industry. Whether human beings are still capable of cultivating a critical and responsible attitude, are still capable of becoming autonomous, independent individuals who can exercise reasoned judgement, is a question about which Horkheimer and Adorno are at times pessimistic, but which ultimately they leave as an open issue. They do not rule out the possibility that the processes of rationalization and reification which have brought about the destruction of the individual will be arrested or curtailed in the future, and that individuality will eventually re-emerge as an element of a more humane and democratic form of life. But they do not predict this outcome either.

Horkheimer's and Adorno's analysis of the culture industry represents one of the most sustained attempts by social and political theorists to come to terms with the nature and consequences of mass communication in modern societies. They are right, in my view, to emphasize the importance of mass communication and to seek to examine its impact on social and political life. They are also right, I think, to suggest that this process has transformed the nature and role of ideology in modern societies. The mass media have become major channels for the circulation of information and communication of various kinds, and any attempt to rethink the nature and role of ideology in modern societies must take full account of this development. But I want to argue that the analysis offered by Horkheimer and Adorno is ultimately and irredeemably flawed. It provides a helpful point of departure, but it cannot be regarded as a satisfactory basis for examining the relations between mass communication and ideology in modern societies. I shall focus my critical remarks on three themes in the writings of Horkheimer and Adorno: (1) their characterization of the culture industry; (2) their account of the nature and role of ideology in modern societies; and (3) their totalizing and often pessimistic conception of modern societies, and the fate of the individual within them.

1 Horkheimer and Adorno use the term 'culture industry' to refer in a general way to the industries concerned with the mass production of cultural goods. They seek to highlight the fact that, in certain key respects, these industries are no different from the other spheres of mass production which churn out increasing quantities of consumer goods. In all cases the goods are produced and distributed in accordance with rationalized procedures and for the purpose of profit realization; in all cases the goods themselves are standardized and stereotyped, even if they are given a tinge of individuality – the uniqueness of a brand name, the personality of a star – in order to increase their appeal; in all cases the recipients are regarded as little more than potential consumers whose needs and desires can, with suitable means, be manipulated, stimulated and controlled. Horkheimer and Adorno recognize that cultural forms also have special features, in so far as they offer images and representations which may or may not be a source of reflection, an object of identification or a schema of interpretation. I shall come back later to some of the issues raised by these special features. But first I want to consider whether this general approach to the culture industry is a satisfactory framework within which to analyse the institutions and characteristics of mass communication.

If we bear in mind the diversity and complexity of the forms of mass communication which have emerged since the sixteenth century, the broad traits of which I shall outline in a later chapter, I think we can see that the general approach adopted by Horkheimer and Adorno is too limited. Their approach is determined largely by their attempt to tie together the theme of rationalization, adapted from Weber, with the themes of commodification and reification, taken over from Marx and Lukács, and to situate these themes within an overall vision of history which emphasizes the increasing entanglement of human beings in the webs of domination which they and their predecessors have unwittingly spun. The forms and institutions of mass communication are but another strand of this ever-expanding web, albeit a central and particularly efficacious one. But this is at best a partial view of the nature of mass communication and its impact. It focuses our attention on certain aspects of mass communication – those which pertain to the commodification of symbolic forms by the media industries; and even within this restricted focus it analyses the developmental processes in a rather abstract way, stressing general features like standardization, repetition and pseudo-personalization but not examining in detail the social organization and everyday practices of media institutions, or the differences between one branch of the media and another. Moreover, in focusing our attention on these aspects of mass communication, the approach of Horkheimer and Adorno tends to neglect other equally important characteristics. In chapter 5 I shall argue that mass communication involves several distinct characteristics: it involves the institutionalized production and diffusion of symbolic goods; it involves an instituted break between production and reception; it involves the extension of availability of symbolic forms in time and in space; and it involves the circulation of these forms in a public domain. The work of Horkheimer and Adorno sheds light on the first of these characteristics but not on the latter three. Their approach is so strongly shaped by the traditional themes of rationalization, commodification and reification that they fail to do justice to what is *new and distinctive* about the development of mass communication, and therewith the mediazation of modern culture. Horkheimer and Adorno seek to *apply* to mass communication a logic of development which has already invaded other spheres of modern society, but in so doing they neglect those characteristics of mass communication which are distinctive and unprecedented, and which endow the institutions of mass communication with a unique and Janus-faced role in modern societies.

2 The second theme I want to examine concerns Horkheimer's and Adorno's account of the nature and role of ideology in modern societies. Although Horkheimer and Adorno do not offer a sustained discussion of the concept of ideology (the most extensive analysis is to be found in the collaborative volume prepared by the Institute, *Aspects of Sociology*) they use the term frequently in their writings and they clearly employ it in a critical way. Here I do not want to examine their varied uses of the term, but want to focus instead on the transformation of the nature and role of ideology which is associated, in their view, with the development of the culture industry. Previous ideologies often existed in the form of distinct doctrines which claimed some independence from the social reality that they sought to justify. This alleged independence was both the source of their 'untruth' (because the alleged independence was more apparent than real) and the

basis for some exercise of the critical spirit (because ideologies did not merely reflect what exists but went beyond it, projecting possibilities or ideals which did not exist in fact). With the development of the culture industry, however, the pretension to independence is destroyed. The culture industry gives rise to a new form of ideology which no longer claims to be independent of social reality: rather, it presents itself as *part of social reality*. It is immanent in the products of the culture industry, in so far as these products are moulded for the entertainment and gratification of individuals who, in consuming these products, reproduce the social reality which the products so faithfully reflect. Ideology today is not so much a clearly articulated doctrine which stands above the social world and overshadows it, throwing its institutions into stark relief; rather, it is that characteristic of mass-produced cultural objects which turns them into a kind of 'social cement'. By becoming purely objects of exchange and sources of pleasure, devoid of any critical, transcending quality, the products of the culture industry acquire an ideological role which is both more pervasive than previous ideologies and more obscure. At every level of society and in the very act of pleasurable consumption, the products of the culture industry bind individuals to the social order which oppresses them, providing the social cement which renders modern societies increasingly rigid, uniform and unshakeable.

Horkheimer and Adorno are right, in my opinion, to argue that the development of mass communication has had a fundamental impact on the nature of culture and ideology in modern societies. They are also right to maintain that the analysis of ideology can no longer be limited to the study of political doctrines but must be broadened to take account of the diverse symbolic forms which circulate in the social world. But it must also be said that there are serious shortcomings to their account of the new form of ideology engendered by the culture industry. Here I shall restrict myself to two main criticisms. The first criticism is that it is by no means clear that the reception and consumption of the products of the culture industry have the consequences that Horkheimer and Adorno suggest. That is, it is by no means clear that, by receiving and consuming these products, individuals are impelled to adhere to the social order, to identify with the images projected and to accept uncritically the proverbial wisdom that is meted out. This criticism is similar to that which I have levelled at more recent versions of the social cement theory of ideology. Here, as in more recent versions, the social cement theory takes too much for granted. It is one thing to show that the products of the culture industry are characterized by standardized formats, pseudo-realism and so on; it is quite another to show that, in receiving and consuming these products, individuals are impelled to act in an imitative and conforming way, or to act in a way which serves in general to bind them to the social order and to reproduce the status quo. The social cement theory of ideology assumes that what looks like cement will work like cement, and yet it is well known – if we can press the metaphor a little further – that some materials do not respond to cement.

This raises a general methodological problem to which I shall return in a later chapter. The problem is that Horkheimer and Adorno try to read off the consequences of cultural products from the products themselves. I shall describe this endeavour as *the fallacy of internalism*. It is a fallacy because it cannot be assumed that the characteristics which the analyst discerns in a particular cultural product will have a given effect when that product is received and appropriated by individuals in the course of their everyday lives. The reception and appropriation of cultural products is a complex social process which involves an ongoing activity of interpretation and the assimilation of meaningful content to the socially structured background characteristics of particular individuals and groups. To attempt to read off the consequences of cultural products from the products themselves is to neglect these ongoing activities of interpretation and assimilation; it is to speculate about the impact of these products on the attitudes and behaviour of individuals without examining this impact in a systematic way. Of course, Horkheimer and Adorno are aware that their analyses are often of a speculative, tentative kind. In his content analysis of the astrology column of the *Los Angeles Times*, Adorno remarks that 'our results must by necessity be regarded as tentative. They provide us with formulations, the validity of which can and should only be established by reader research.'[27] This qualification is indisputable. The problem, however, is that the necessary reader research never took place, and that this and other analyses of cultural products have, in practice, stood on their own as accounts of how a new form of ideology, engendered by the culture industry, has induced obedient and conformative behaviour, strengthened the sense of fatality and dependence, dulled the imagination and atrophied the critical spirit of the masses, and thereby served to reproduce the status quo.

My second criticism of Horkheimer's and Adorno's account of the new form of ideology is that this account presents an overly restrictive view of the ways in which ideology operates in modern societies. I have described this view as the social cement theory of ideology, since ideology is regarded primarily as a kind of symbolic substance which circulates in the social world and binds individuals to the social order, so that the latter is rendered increasingly rigid and resistant to social change. It may be the case that some symbolic forms in modern societies do play this role, but it would be unnecessarily restrictive to regard this role as the only or even the primary way in which ideology operates in modern societies. If we conceptualize ideology in terms of the ways in which meaning serves to establish and sustain relations of domination and we attempt to distinguish different modes of operation, as I did in the previous chapter, then we can see that the social cement theory highlights only some of the ways in which ideology may operate. It highlights some of the ways in which symbolic forms may secure the unification and reification of social relations, but it neglects the modes of legitimation, dissimulation and fragmentation. Ideology is not the only factor involved in the reproduction of relations of domination, and unification and reification are not the only modes involved in the operation of ideology. In portraying the new form of ideology as a kind of social cement, Horkheimer and Adorno offer an overly restricted view of the ways in which ideology operates, a view which is linked to their totalizing and often pessimistic conception of modern societies and the fate of individuals within them.

3 The third theme I want to address concerns this conception of modern societies and the associated notion of the atrophy of the individual. Horkheimer and Adorno project an image of modern societies as increasingly integrated and unified, as propelled along a path of development which, if it were to continue uninterrupted, would lead to a wholly rationalized, reified and administered world. The processes of rationalization, commodification and reification have fused together to produce an almost inexorable trend. While the mechanisms of capitalist production and exchange are an intrinsic aspect of this development and have accelerated the process of commodification and reification, the trend discerned by Horkheimer and Adorno has a generality which goes beyond the specific dynamics of capitalism. It is part of a general process of rationalization that was set in motion well before the capitalist mode of production had fully taken hold in the West. This general process of rationalization involves the increasing subordination of nature – both external and inner nature – to the exercise of technical control; it is a deep-rooted human project, a quasi-anthropological human adventure, in which human beings, in pursuing the lofty ideals of knowledge and truth, find themselves ensnared in an ever-expanding web of domination. Indeed, the very ideals they had set themselves were already tainted by the logic of domination. The great Enlightenment thinkers who called for the pursuit of positive science as a way of freeing human beings from the burden of tradition and myth were, in spite of their lofty ideals, propelling humanity into a new and more extensive form of domination. For 'what men want to learn from nature is how to use it in order wholly to dominate it and other men. That is the only aim.

Ruthlessly, in despite of itself, the Enlightenment has extinguished any trace of its own consciousness.'[28] As the pursuit of scientific knowledge became coupled with the expansion of bourgeois commodity production, human beings were increasingly turned into the appendages of a machine which grinds on relentlessly. Like the oarsmen in the myth of Odysseus, their ears have been plugged so that they can no longer hear the beauty of the Sirens' song: deaf and dumb, they concentrate on the task which confronts them in the division of labour, ignoring whatever lies to one side. Enlightenment has become the wholesale deception of the masses, whose critical sensibilities have become so atrophied that their capacity to resist, to overthrow the yoke of domination and achieve some reconciliation with an alienated nature, must remain in doubt.

There are some characteristics of modern societies which might appear to lend plausibility to the sweeping historical perspective sketched by Horkheimer and Adorno. The growing bureaucratization of many domains of social life, the persistence of relations of domination and inequality in modern capitalist societies as well as in those societies which claim (or have claimed) to be socialist in some sense, the increasing significance of ecological issues and the heightened awareness of the dangers of the uncontrolled exploitation of nature: these and other characteristics of modern societies might be regarded as developments which are consistent with the general trend discerned by Horkheimer and Adorno. But this interpretation would be a generous one and would overlook the serious limitations of their approach. Here I shall highlight two such limitations. In the first place, Horkheimer and Adorno overemphasize the integrated and unified character of modern societies. The image they project is that of a society in which every element is increasingly tailored to fit into the whole, in which every aspect has its place, and in which any form of deviance or incipient criticism is either normalized or excluded. It is a Kafkaesque image of instrumental reason gone wild; the individual is increasingly locked within a world of total administration. But this image is surely exaggerated. While it is certainly true that modern societies are interconnected in many ways and at many levels both nationally and internationally, it is also the case that a great deal of diversity, disorganization, dissensus and resistance exists, and is likely to continue to exist, within modern societies. How could we explain the groundswell of popular rebellion in Eastern Europe in 1989, and the speed with which the political regimes collapsed, if modern societies were really as integrated and unified as Horkheimer and Adorno suggest? Faced as they were with the persistence of a social order which satisfies some people but fulfils very few, Horkheimer and Adorno were inclined to conclude, erroneously and prematurely I think, that the sources of social instability have been brought under control and that all voices of serious dissent have been smothered.

The second limitation concerns Horkheimer's and Adorno's account of the decline of the individual. In previous societies the idea of individuality – an idea emphasizing the spontaneity, autonomy and uniqueness of the human being – had been nurtured by philosophical and religious thought, but had only been very partially realized in practice. The idea of individuality was sustained as an unfulfilled promise of philosophical thought. In the modern era, however, with the rise of large-scale industrial organizations and the spread of mass culture, individuals have become increasingly absorbed in a social totality which makes no concessions to the traditional idea of individuality. Individuals become more and more dependent on economic and social forces which lie beyond their control. They sacrifice themselves to the huge organizations upon which they depend for their very survival. They lose the capacity for critical thinking and the will to struggle for an alternative social order. They become so thoroughly integrated into the existing order that their spontaneity, autonomy and uniqueness are repressed or virtually eliminated. The products of the culture industry contribute to this integration by reaffirming the existing order and by furnishing popular icons which enable the masses to experience vicariously the residues of an individuality which in practice they are denied. Modern society has become a vast and well-oiled machine in which individuals are little more than functional parts. The only question which remains open for Horkheimer and Adorno is whether the repressed desires and longings of human beings, the residue of their humanity which smoulders beneath the surface of society, can be released in a constructive and progressive way, or whether the frustrations engendered by an aborted individuality will be exploited by reactionary forces and demagogues.

The main difficulty with this account is that it greatly over-estimates the extent to which individuals have been successfully integrated into the existing social order. Just as Horkheimer and Adorno project an overly consensual image of modern societies, so too they project an overly integrated conception of the modern individual. It is by no means clear that all or even most individuals in modern industrial societies are neatly integrated into the social order, their intellectual faculties so severely stunted that they are no longer capable of critical, independent thought. Moreover, the assumption that the reception and consumption of cultural products serves merely to reinforce conformity to the status quo, to liquidate what is already an atrophied individuality, is too simple. This assumption rests on the fallacy of internalism and it over-simplifies the processes involved in receiving cultural products, in appropriating them and integrating them into the social contexts and interpretative frameworks of the recipients. These processes are more varied and complex than Horkheimer and Adorno allow. It is likely that stereotypical images and repetitive patterns in cultural products contribute to some extent to the socialization of individuals and the formation of their identity. But it is also likely that individuals are never completely moulded by these and other processes of socialization, and that they are able to maintain at least some distance, intellectually and emotionally, from the symbolic forms that are constructed of them, for them and around them. Even children, it seems, have a shrewd sense of fact and fantasy, of what is real, unreal and utterly silly in the television cartoons which occupy so much of their time, and in watching these cartoons they are engaged in a complex process of interpretation.[29] To assume, as Horkheimer and Adorno do, that the reception and consumption of cultural products are but nails in the coffin of the individual, who is more or less doomed to an unceremonious burial by the developmental tendencies of modern societies, is to overestimate the extent to which individuality has been crushed by the culture industry (among other things) and to over-simplify the processes involved in the reception and appropriation of the products of these industries.

The Transformation of the Public Sphere

I now wish to consider, in this final section of the chapter, some of the writings of the most influential contemporary exponent of critical social theory, Jürgen Habermas. While Habermas has been strongly influenced by the views of the earlier critical theorists, he never takes up uncritically the ideas of his intellectual progenitors: even when the influence of Horkheimer, Adorno or Marcuse is clear, Habermas typically recasts their views in a new framework and gives them a new sense. Habermas's early work on the structural transformation of the public sphere takes up some of the themes of the critique of the culture industry, but reworks these themes in a new and insightful way. Paying greater attention to the development of media institutions from the seventeenth century to the present day, Habermas retraces the emergence and subsequent disintegration of what he calls 'the public sphere'.[30] As a realm of communication and debate that was stimulated by the emergence of mass communication in the form of a relatively small-scale and independent press, the bourgeois public sphere created a forum in which the authority of the state could be criticized and called upon to justify itself before an informed and reasoning public. But this was a restricted and fragile forum and it was effectively undercut by the development of the state and of non-state social institutions in the nineteenth and twentieth centuries. The growth of the state and of large-scale commercial organizations in the domain of mass communication have transformed the emerging public sphere in a fundamental way, so that the critical potential inherent in this sphere has been curtailed or pushed underground and retains its value today more as a promise, as an imminent principle of criticism, than as an institutionalized reality.

In this section I want to examine Habermas's argument in some detail. In doing so I shall be concentrating primarily on Habermas's early work, and especially on the arguments developed in *The Structural Transformation of the Public Sphere*.[31] These arguments, while crucial for understanding Habermas's more recent writings, have not yet received the attention they deserve in the English-speaking world.[32] But more importantly, my reason for concentrating on Habermas's early work is that it represents one of the few systematic attempts to develop an historically informed social theory of mass communication, and to rethink the nature and role of ideology within this framework. In this respect, Habermas's early work offers something that is missing from his more recent writings. For the latter become increasingly preoccupied with problems of social rationalization; the development of mass communication is lost from view, while a particular version of the grand narrative of cultural transformation assumes an increasingly prominent role. I shall comment later on this shift in Habermas's work.

In *The Structural Transformation of the Public Sphere* Habermas observes that, although the public–private distinction dates from Classical Greece, it assumed a new and distinctive form in seventeenth- and eighteenth-century Europe, in the context of a rapidly developing capitalist economy and the establishment of a bourgeois constitutional state. 'Public authority' in the narrow sense came to refer increasingly to state-related activity, that is, to the activities of a state system which had legally defined spheres of jurisdiction and which had a monopoly on the legitimate use of violence. 'Civil society' emerged as a domain of privatized economic relations which were established under the aegis of public authority. The 'private' realm thus comprised both the expanding domain of economic relations, and the intimate sphere of personal relations which became increasingly disengaged from economic activity and anchored in the institution of the conjugal family. Between the realm of public authority, on the one hand, and the private realm of civil society and the intimate sphere, on the other, there emerged a new sphere of 'the public': a bourgeois public sphere which consisted of private individuals who had come together to debate among themselves and with state authorities concerning the regulation of civil society and the conduct of the state. The medium of this confrontation was significant and unprecedented: it was the public use of reason, as articulated by private individuals engaged in argument that is *in principle* open and unconstrained. This unique constellation of public–private relations, as it emerged in early modern Europe, is summarized in Table 2.1.

Table 2.1
The social context of the bourgeois
public sphere

Private realm	Bourgeois public sphere	Realm of public authority
Civil society (domain of commodity production and exchange	Public sphere in political realm	State
Intimate sphere (conjugal family)	Public sphere in literary realm	Court

Source: Adapted from Habermas, *The Structural Transformation of the Public Sphere*, p. 30.

The bourgeois public sphere developed initially in the realm of literature, and was subsequently transformed into a public sphere bearing directly on political issues. In the late seventeenth and early eighteenth centuries, the salons and coffee houses of Paris and London became centres of discussion and debate; they were the principal locales in which private individuals could meet to discuss literary matters and, increasingly, issues of general concern. These discussions were facilitated by the development of the newspaper industry. Whereas the early news sheets and newspapers were concerned primarily with the transmission of information of various kinds, in the course of the eighteenth century they became increasingly orientated towards the expression of political views. The press became a key forum of critical political debate, offering an ongoing commentary on, and criticism of, the actions of officials of the state. This development was particularly prominent in Britain, where the press enjoyed greater liberties than in some other parts of Europe. In France and Germany, the press was periodically subjected to stringent censorship and control by state officials, and it was only with the development of the constitutional state that some degree of freedom of the press, as well as other features and functions of the public sphere (freedom of opinion and speech, freedom of assembly and association, etc.) were formally embodied in law.

Although the bourgeois public sphere was *in principle* open to all private individuals, it was *in practice* restricted to a limited section of the population. The effective criteria of admission were property and education: the public sphere comprised, in practice, the bourgeois reading public of the eighteenth century. The two effective criteria of admission tended to circumscribe the same group of individuals, for education was largely determined by one's entitlement to property. The class bias inherent in the actual constitution of the bourgeois public sphere was perceived and criticized by Marx – for instance, in his scathing attack on 'the so-called *rights of man*' in *On the Jewish Question*.[33] But if some aspects of the bourgeois public sphere were a veiled and disingenuous expression of class interests, nevertheless it embodied, argues Habermas, ideas and principles that went beyond the restricted historical forms in which it was realized. It embodied the idea that a community of citizens, coming together as equals in a forum which is distinct both from the public authority of the state and the private realms of civil society and family life, was capable of forming a *public opinion* through critical discussion, reasoned argument and debate. It embodied what Habermas describes as a principle of 'publicness' or 'publicity' (*Prinzip der Öffentlichkeit*): namely, that the personal opinions of private individuals could evolve into a public opinion through the rational–critical debate of a public of citizens which was open to all and free from domination.

If the ideas and principles embodied in the bourgeois public sphere were never fully realized in the propitious historical conditions of eighteenth-century Europe, then they were all but eclipsed by the subsequent development of the state and of other social organizations. The emergent public sphere was progressively squeezed by, on the one hand, the expansion of an interventionist state which increasingly assumed a wide range of welfare functions and, on the other, the massive growth of industrial organizations which increasingly assumed a semi-public character. These parallel developments gave rise to a re-politicized social sphere in which organized interest groups struggle for a larger share of available resources, in a way that largely eliminates the role for ongoing public debate among private individuals. At the same time, the institutions which once provided a forum for the bourgeois public sphere either died out or underwent radical transformation. The salons and coffee houses gradually declined in significance, and the institutions of mass communication developed increasingly into large-scale commercial organizations. The commercialization of mass communication altered its character in a fundamental way: what was once a privileged forum of rational–critical debate became just another domain of cultural consumption, and the emergent public sphere collapsed into a sham world of pseudo–privacy that is fashioned and control-led by the culture industry. As Habermas remarks,

> When the laws of the market governing the sphere of commodity exchange and of social labor also pervaded the sphere reserved for private people as a public, rational–critical debate had a tendency to be replaced by consumption, and the web of public communication unraveled into acts of individuated reception, however uniform in mode.[34]

The commercialization of mass communication progressively destroyed its character as a medium of the public sphere, for the content of newspapers and other products was depoliticized, personalized and sensationalized as a means of increasing sales, and recipients were treated more and more as the consumers both of media products and of those products from which the media organizations derived their advertising revenue.

In addition to the commercialization of mass communication, new techniques of 'opinion management' were developed and increasingly employed in those areas of mass communication which still bore directly on political issues. These techniques address individuals as private citizens rather than consumers and they exploit the idea of a public of private individuals using their reason, but they turn this idea to their own ends. Beneath the veil of an alleged public interest, the opinion-moulding services promoted the particular aims of organized interest groups. The residues of the bourgeois public sphere have thus taken on a quasi-feudal character: new techniques are employed to endow public authority with the kind of aura and personal prestige which was once bestowed by the staged publicity of the feudal courts. This *refeudalization of the public sphere* turns the latter into a theatre and turns politics into a managed show in which leaders and parties routinely seek the acclamatory assent of a depoliticized population. Once a critical principle employed by private individuals against the established power of public authority, 'publicity has been transformed into a principle of managed integration (wielded by staging agencies – the administration, special-interest groups, and above all the parties).'[35] The mass of the population has become a managed resource which is effectively excluded from public discussion and decision-making processes, and from which leaders and parties occasionally seek to elicit, with the aid of media techniques, sufficient assent to legitimate their political programmes and compromises.

Although the developments of the nineteenth and twentieth centuries have undermined the bourgeois public sphere and transformed the principle of publicity into a tool of vested interests, Habermas does not rule out the possibility that the ideas and principles originally embodied in the public sphere could be reconstituted on a different basis in the future. In *The Structural Transformation of the Public Sphere* his remarks on this subject are fragmentary and allusive at best, but the general line of argument is fairly clear: under today's conditions, a public sphere could be reconstituted only by (1) affirming and implementing a critical principle of publicity *within* the organizations and interest groups (including political parties) which have come to assume a major role in the social domain; (2) restricting and controlling the bureaucratic decision-making processes of the state; and (3) relativizing structural conflicts of interest 'according to the standard of a universal interest everyone can acknowledge'.[36] The critical principle of publicity which emerged with the bourgeois public sphere has not been altogether eliminated from contemporary political consciousness; it continues to animate some opposition to the transformed and deformed version of publicity which is little more than a theatrical display for the purposes of acclamation. Like the idea of democracy with which it was in some ways linked, the critical principle of publicity retains its value as a yardstick by which the shortcomings of existing institutional arrangements can be critically assessed and the possibilities for a more rational social order can be imaginatively explored.

This thoughtful and wide-ranging argument concerning the formation and disintegration of the bourgeois public sphere raises many issues which remain relevant to contemporary social and political analysis. Although *The Structural Transformation of the Public Sphere* is one of Habermas's earliest works and has, in certain respects, been supplemented and displaced by the subsequent development of his views, it is clear that the idea of a public sphere, as a community of individuals who are united by their participation in rational–critical debate, remains a guiding thread in his work. Moreover, this early study brings to the fore, in a way that is largely absent from Habermas's subsequent writings and from most other contributions to contemporary social and political thought, the role of mass communication as a formative factor in the development of modern societies. It is primarily this aspect of the study that I want to focus on here. I want to argue that, while Habermas is right to emphasize the importance of mass communication, his account of the disintegrative consequences of the development of media institutions is one-sided and overly negative. I shall elaborate this argument by considering four main points: (1) the notion of the refeudalization of the public sphere; (2) the conception of recipients as consumers; (3) Habermas's account of the new ideology; and (4) the contemporary relevance of the idea of the public sphere.

1 The commercialization of media institutions and the use of quasi-commercial techniques in the presentation of political issues has, Habermas argues, undermined the bourgeois public sphere and replaced it with an arena which is quasi-feudal in character. As with the feudal courts of the *ancien régime*, modern politics has become a managed show in which leaders and parties seek to secure, at regular intervals, the acclamatory assent of a depoliticized population. There is no doubt some truth in the suggestion that politics today has increasingly become a matter of *staging*, of cultivating images and controlling their diffusion; but the mediazation of modern culture and its impact on institutionalized politics cannot, I think, be satisfactorily interpreted as a refeudalization of the public sphere. The development of mass communication has created new opportunities for the production and diffusion of images and messages, opportunities which exist on a scale and are executed in a manner that precludes any serious comparison with the theatrical practices of feudal courts. By virtue of the technical media of transmission, images and messages are made available to audiences which are greatly extended in time and space; unlike courtly behaviour, which was largely orientated towards individuals who shared the same immediate milieu, the images and utterances of mediated messages are – especially with the development of television – receivable and perceivable by large numbers of individuals who are spatially and temporally dispersed. This new situation endows the communicator with unprecedented opportunities for reaching and influencing a large number of individuals. But it should also be emphasized that this situation greatly increases the visibility of political leaders, and limits the extent to which they can control the conditions of reception of messages and the ways in which these messages are interpreted by recipients. Moreover, since the development of mass communication in the nineteenth and twentieth centuries has been accompanied by processes of democratization in many countries, the individuals who receive mediated messages have acquired new forms of power and a new awareness of rights. Hence the development of mass communication has not only created new stages for the carefully managed presentation of leaders and their views: it has also given these leaders a new visibility and vulnerability before audiences which are more extensive and endowed with more information and more power (however intermittently expressed) than ever before. To interpret this scenario as a refeudalization of the public sphere is to focus on a relatively superficial aspect of politics in the era of mass communication – namely, the cultivation of image and the preoccupation with showy presentation – and to neglect the fundamental changes in terms of information availability and political power which have both accompanied the development of mass communication and been facilitated by it.

2 A second and related shortcoming of Habermas's account is that it tends to treat the recipients of media messages as passive consumers who are enthralled by the spectacle, manipulated by clever techniques and numbed into acquiescent acceptance of the status quo. The active participation of citizens in rational–critical debate has been replaced by the passive consumption of images and messages, and individuals are subjected to, and swayed by, an array of techniques which are employed to fabricate opinion and consensus without participation and debate. Here again, this argument has some plausibility; it is certainly true that an array of techniques, some borrowed from advertising, are used to cultivate the images and promote the ideas of political leaders and parties. But this argument can be easily overstated. It is all too easily assumed that, because individuals have been treated as the passive consumers of images and ideas, they have *become* passive consumers – that is, they have become a depoliticized mass which is effectively moulded and manipulated by the media and other organizations. This assumption, which is evident in Habermas's account, is dubious. It commits the fallacy of internalism: it unjustifiably infers, on the basis of the production and characteristics of a particular cultural product, that this product will have a given effect when it is received by individuals in the course of their everyday lives. It exaggerates the passivity of individuals and the extent to which they are orientated towards, and swayed by, the consumption of media messages. There is little justification for this aspect of Habermas's account. Moreover, by taking for granted the political efficacy of media messages, Habermas's argument tends to overlook the new kind of *fragility* which political processes acquire in the era of mass communication. As I shall argue in more detail later, it is because political processes take place today in a social environment which is 'information-rich' – that is, in which individuals have greater access than ever before to information and communication transmitted via technical media – that political leaders and state officials seek increasingly to control, and are rendered increasingly vulnerable by their inability completely to control, the diffusion of the images and information upon which the exercise of their power in part depends.

3 In treating the recipients of media messages as passive consumers who are enthralled by the spectacle and manipulated by media techniques, Habermas shares the perspective adopted by Horkheimer and Adorno in their critical analysis of the culture industry. Habermas also shares their perception of the 'new ideology' to which the development of mass communication has allegedly given rise – and this, I shall argue, is a third shortcoming of Habermas's account. According to this view, ideology no longer takes the

form of a coherent system of discrete ideas or beliefs, like the old political ideologies of the nineteenth century, but rather is inherent in the products of the media industries in so far as these products replicate the status quo and integrate individuals into it, eliminating any element of transcendence and critique. The media industries engender a 'false consciousness' and a 'false consensus'. 'Intelligent criticism of publicly discussed affairs gives way before a mood of conformity with publicly presented persons or personifications; consent coincides with good will evoked by publicity.'[37] To the extent that a consensus prevails in modern societies, it is a false and fabricated consensus, for it is more the effect of the opinion-moulding techniques employed by the media industries than the outcome of processes of argumentation and deliberation among citizens employing their critical faculties.

This account of the new ideology engendered by the media industries suffers from weaknesses similar to those that vitiate the writings of Horkheimer and Adorno. Ideology is viewed essentially as a kind of social cement which circulates in the social world via the products of the media industries, and which integrates and incorporates individuals into the social order, thereby reproducing the status quo. This account, like that of Horkheimer and Adorno, presents an overly restrictive conception of ideology and of its mode of operation in modern societies. Like Horkheimer and Adorno, Habermas offers an account of the new ideology which overemphasizes the extent to which cultural products are capable of, and have succeeded in, integrating individuals into a social order which is supposedly reproduced thereby. But Habermas's account raises additional problems, in so far as he employs terms such as 'false consciousness' and 'false consensus' without fully clarifying and justifying their use. To some extent his subsequent work could be seen as an attempt to respond to these problems, disposing of some and pursuing others in ways which have led to a substantial revision of his views. Today, I doubt whether Habermas would wish to sustain in any detail the account of the new ideology presented in *The Structural Transformation of the Public Sphere*. The notions of ideology and false consciousness no longer feature significantly in his writings, and the phenomena of mass communication have become increasingly peripheral to his core concerns. The earlier analyses have given way to a wide-ranging preoccupation with the conditions, characteristics and consequences of the processes of rationalization which define the modern era, a preoccupation in which the influence of Max Weber looms large.[38] In his more recent work Habermas offers an account of the development of modern societies which converges in many respects with what I have called the grand narrative of cultural transformation. Indeed, in volume II of *The Theory of Communicative Action*, Habermas goes so far as to endorse a version of the end of ideology thesis, arguing that the rationalization of the lifeworld has stripped everyday communicative practice of the synthetic and totalizing tendencies inherent in traditional world-views, and has thereby eliminated the basis for the formation of ideologies. Individuals may still be prevented from grasping the structures of domination characteristic of modern societies, the processes of enlightenment may still be blocked; but if so, it is not because of the operation of ideology but rather because the basis for the operation of ideology has been destroyed. '*Everyday consciousness* is robbed of its power to synthesize; it becomes *fragmented* . . . In place of "false consciousness" we today have a "fragmented consciousness" that blocks enlightenment by the mechanism of reification.'[39]

There are some aspects of Habermas's revised position which are, I think, a definite improvement on his earlier views. Habermas is certainly right to leave the problematic of 'false consciousness' behind, and he is right to emphasize the importance of fragmentation and reification in analysing the nature and impact of symbolic forms in modern societies. But it seems to me misleading to suggest that, in shifting the emphasis in this way, one is no longer dealing with the analysis of ideology – and indeed to suggest, as Habermas now seems inclined to do, that ideology no longer plays any significant role in societies which have been propelled into cultural modernity. These suggestions are based on a rather narrow conception of ideology, understood as synthetic and totalizing world-views addressed to political activists, a conception which shares much in common with that of the end of ideology theorists and which I criticized earlier. Moreover, Habermas's suggestions are based on the claim that processes of social and cultural rationalization have rendered everyday communicative practice so transparent to individuals that it 'no longer affords any niches for the structural violence of ideologies'.[40] Today, argues Habermas, the imperatives of autonomous sub-systems are imposed on the action domains of the lifeworld from outside, 'like colonial masters coming into a tribal society', and they instigate a process of assimilation that can be understood as a 'colonization of the lifeworld'.[41] Whatever the merits of this particular thesis, I do not think it is helpful or plausible to maintain that the communicative practice of everyday life has become effectively transparent to individuals to the extent that it no longer offers any foothold for the operation of ideology. The texture of everyday communication is much more complex and multi-layered, and much more infused with relations of power, than Habermas's argument would suggest. If we develop a broader conception of ideology, as I tried to do in the previous chapter, then everyday communicative action can continue to be analysed as a site, indeed a central site, of ideology: Habermas's recent proclamations concerning the end of ideology are, like so many that have been uttered before, decidedly premature.

4 Finally, let me return to Habermas's account of the transformation of the public sphere and address a fourth issue that emerges from this study: to what extent can the idea of the public sphere be used as a model for thinking about the development of political and media institutions in modern societies? Habermas recognizes that industrial societies have changed so much that there could be no question of re-establishing the bourgeois public sphere as it existed in eighteenth-century Europe. But he contends that the *idea* of the public sphere still has value today as a critical yardstick, and he even suggests, however tentatively, that a public sphere could be reconstituted in the future, albeit on a different institutional basis. I shall argue that the idea of the public sphere does retain some value today as a critical yardstick; it calls our attention, for instance, to the importance of a sphere of social communication which is neither wholly controlled by the state nor concentrated in the hands of large-scale commercial organizations. I shall take up this point at a later stage. But here I want to ask whether, apart from general considerations of this kind, the idea of the public sphere has any value today as a model for institutional reorganization. Is it plausible to suggest, however tentatively, that a public sphere could be reconstituted in the conditions of modern industrial societies? I shall argue that this suggestion is implausible and that the idea of the public sphere is largely inapplicable to the circumstances of the late twentieth century. There are two aspects of this idea which severely limit its contemporary relevance.

The first limitation stems from the fact that the idea of the public sphere emerged, as Habermas shows, under the conditions of a relatively restricted circulation of printed materials and the discussion of them in public fora such as salons and coffee-houses. The original idea of the public sphere was thus bound to the medium of print and to the conduct of face-to-face discussion – stimulated and informed by printed materials – in fora that were 'public' (i.e. open in principle to all) but were distinct from institutionalized political power. Habermas suggests that, while the traditional fora that nurtured the public sphere have long since declined or disappeared, the idea of the public sphere could be reactivated on a different institutional basis. The problem with this suggestion is that the development of technical media has dramatically altered the nature of mass communication and the conditions under which it takes place, so much so that the original idea of the public sphere could not simply be reactivated on a new footing. The media of print have increasingly given way to electronically mediated forms of mass communication, and especially television; and these new media have transformed the very conditions of interaction, communication and information diffusion in modern societies. The original idea of the public sphere, bound to the medium of print and to the conduct of face-to-face interaction in a shared physical locale, cannot be directly applied to the conditions created by the development of new technical media. If we are to make sense of these conditions and of the opportunities afforded by them, we must pay closer attention than Habermas does to the nature of technical media and their impact on social and political life.

The second reason why the idea of the public sphere is of limited relevance today is that the idea is linked fundamentally to a notion of participatory opinion formation. The idea of the public sphere assumes that the personal opinions of individuals will become *public opinion* through, and only through, participation in a free and equal debate which is open in principle to all. But this assumption, whatever relevance it may have had to eighteenth-century political life (and this may have been considerably less than Habermas suggests), is far removed from the political realities and possibilities of the late twentieth century. There are, of course, many areas of social life in which individuals could assume a greater role in decision-making processes, and it may be the case that increased participation in these processes would facilitate the formation of what Habermas calls 'public opinion'. But at the level of national and international politics, and at the upper levels in which power is exercised in large-scale civil and commercial organizations, it is difficult to see how the idea of participatory opinion formation could be implemented in any significant way. What we may hope for at best is a greater diffusion of information concerning the activities of powerful individuals and organizations, a greater diversity in channels of diffusion and a greater emphasis on the establishment of mechanisms through which these activities can be rendered accountable and controlled. We live in a world today in which the sheer scale and complexity of decision-making processes limits the extent to which they can be organized in a participatory way. Hence the original idea of the public sphere, in so far as it is linked to the notion of participatory opinion formation, is of limited relevance today.

For these reasons, we must treat with some scepticism Habermas's suggestion that the public sphere could be reconstituted today on a different institutional basis. It seems to me that we should put this suggestion aside and look afresh at the two processes of the mediazation of modern culture and the democratization of modern politics, processes which have overlapped to a significant extent and created in part the social and political conditions of life in the modern age. While Habermas's early work on the structural transformation of the public sphere does not offer a satisfactory account of these processes, it represents a valuable, if somewhat neglected, contribution to such an account, the development of which remains as urgent as ever.

My principal aim in this chapter has been to examine some recent theoretical perspectives on the nature and role of ideology in modern societies. I began by reconstructing two general accounts which have been deeply influential in framing recent debates – what I called the grand narrative of cultural transformation, on the one hand, and the general theory of state-organized and ideologically secured social reproduction, on the other. I argued that, apart from a number of specific criticisms that can be made of each, both of these accounts fail to do justice to the centrality of mass communication in modern societies. It is to the credit of the early critical theorists, including Horkheimer and Adorno, and to the credit of Habermas (in his early work at least) that they emphasized the importance of mass communication and sought to re-conceptualize the nature of ideology in relation to it. But, as I have tried to show, their contributions are deficient in various ways and cannot be regarded as a suitable basis upon which to rethink the analysis of ideology in the era of mass communication.

Part of my concern in the remainder of this book is to elaborate an alternative approach to the issues which have been raised in this chapter but which have not, in my view, been addressed satisfactorily by existing theoretical accounts. I shall take, as my guiding theme, the process I have described as the mediazation of modern culture; by pursuing this theme, I shall aim to give mass communication a more central role in the development of modern societies than it has customarily been given in the literature of social and political thought. Before turning to the analysis of mass communication, however, we must give further attention to the nature of symbolic forms and their relation to the social contexts in which they are produced and received. For the emergence and development of mass communication may best be viewed as the emergence and development of a range of institutions concerned with the production and diffusion of symbolic forms – concerned, that is, with the commodification of culture and with the extended circulation of symbolic forms in time and space.

The Concept of Culture

In the literature of the social sciences, the study of symbolic forms has generally been conducted under the rubric of the concept of culture. While there may be little agreement concerning the meaning of the concept itself, many analysts would agree that the study of cultural phenomena is a concern of central importance for the social sciences as a whole. For social life is not merely a matter of objects and events which occur like happenings in the natural world: it is also a matter of meaningful actions and expressions, of utterances, symbols, texts and artefacts of various kinds, and of subjects who express themselves though these artefacts and who seek to understand themselves and others by interpreting the expressions they produce and receive. In the broadest sense, the study of cultural phenomena may be construed as the study of the social–historical world as a meaningful domain. It may be construed as the study of the ways in which meaningful expressions of various kinds are produced, constructed and received by individuals situated in the social–historical world. Construed in this way, the concept of culture refers to a range of phenomena and a set of concerns which are shared today by analysts working in a variety of disciplines, from sociology and anthropology to history and literary criticism.

The concept of culture has not always been used in this way, however. It is a concept with a lengthy history of its own, and the sense which it conveys today is to some extent a product of this history. By retracing some of the main episodes in the development of the concept of culture, we can gain a deeper understanding into what is involved, and what is to be avoided, in the contemporary study of cultural phenomena. I shall therefore begin this chapter by offering a brief overview of this development. My aim is not to provide a comprehensive survey of the many uses, past and present, of the concept of culture, but rather to highlight some of the main lines of usage.[1] I shall distinguish, for the sake of simplicity, between four basic senses. The first sense is that which was apparent in the early discussions of culture, especially those that took place among German philosophers and historians during the eighteenth and nineteenth centuries. In these discussions the term 'culture' was generally used to refer to a process of intellectual or spiritual development, a process that differed in certain respects from that of 'civilization'. We can describe this traditional usage of the term as the *classical conception* of culture. With the appearance of the discipline of anthropology in the late nineteenth century, the classical conception gave way to various anthropological conceptions of culture. Here I distinguish two such conceptions, what I call the *descriptive conception* and the *symbolic conception*. The descriptive conception of culture refers to the varied array of values, beliefs, customs, conventions, habits and practices characteristic of a particular society or historical period. The symbolic conception shifts the focus to a concern with symbolism: cultural phenomena, according to this conception, are symbolic phenomena, and the study of culture is essentially concerned with the interpretation of symbols and symbolic action.

The symbolic conception is a suitable starting point for the development of a constructive approach to the study of cultural phenomena. But the weakness of this conception – in the form that it appears, for instance, in the writings of Geertz – is that it gives insufficient attention to the structured social relations within which symbols and symbolic actions are always embedded. Hence I formulate what I call the *structural conception* of culture. Cultural phenomena, according to this conception, may be understood as symbolic forms in structured contexts; and cultural analysis may be construed as the study of the meaningful constitution and social con-textualization of symbolic forms. Most of this chapter is concerned with the elaboration of the two features implied by the structural conception of culture – namely, the meaningful constitution of symbolic forms and their social contextualization.

By viewing symbolic forms in relation to the structured social contexts within which they are produced and received, the structural conception of culture provides a basis upon which we can begin to think about what is involved in the emergence and development of mass communication. For mass communication is concerned, in certain ways and by virtue of certain means, with the production and transmission of symbolic forms. Mass communication is certainly a matter of technology, of powerful mechanisms of production and transmission; but it is also a matter of symbolic forms, of meaningful expressions of various kinds, which are produced, transmitted and received by means of the technologies deployed by the media industries. Hence the emergence and development of mass communication may be viewed as a fundamental and continuing transformation of the ways in which symbolic forms are produced and circulated in modern societies. It is in this sense that I speak of the mediazation of modern culture. What defines our culture as 'modern' is the fact that the production and circulation of symbolic forms have, since the late fifteenth century, become increasingly and irreversibly caught up in processes of commodification and transmission that are now global in character. These are developments that I shall examine in the next chapter.

Culture and Civilization

Let me begin by retracing the history of the concept of culture. Deriving from the Latin word *cultura*, the concept acquired a significant presence in many European languages during the early modern period. The early uses in European languages preserved something of the original sense of *cultura*, which meant primarily the cultivation or tending of something, such as crops or animals. From the early sixteenth century on, this original sense was gradually extended from the sphere of husbandry to the process of human development, from the cultivation of crops to the cultivation of the mind. However, the use of the independent noun 'culture', referring to a general process or to the product of such a process, was not common until the late eighteenth and early nineteenth centuries. The independent noun first appeared in French and English; and in the late eighteenth century the French word was incorporated into German, spelled first as *Cultur* and then later as *Kultur*.

By the early nineteenth century the word 'culture' was being used as a synonym for, or in some cases in contrast with, the word 'civilization'. Derived from the Latin word *civilis*, meaning of or belonging to citizens, the term 'civilization' was initially used in French and English in the late eighteenth century to describe a progressive process of human development, a movement towards refinement and order and away from barbarism and savagery. Behind this emergent sense lay the spirit of the European Enlightenment and its confident belief in the progressive character of the modern era. In French and in English the uses of the words 'culture' and 'civilization' overlapped: both were used increasingly to describe a general process of human development, of becoming 'cultivated' or 'civilized'. In German, however, these words were often contrasted, in such a way that *Zivilisation* acquired a negative connotation and *Kultur* a positive one. The word '*Zivilisation*' was associated with politeness and the refinement of manners, while '*Kultur*' was used more to refer to the intellectual, artistic and spiritual products in which the individuality and creativity of a people were expressed.

The Germanic contrast between *Kultur* and *Zivilisation* was linked to patterns of social stratification in early modern Europe. This link has been examined in some detail by Norbert Elias.[2] In eighteenth-century Germany, observes Elias, French was the language of the courtly nobility and of the upper layers of the bourgeoisie; to speak French was a status symbol of the upper classes. Distinct from these upper classes was a small, German-speaking stratum of intellectuals recruited mainly from the courtly officialdom and occasionally from the landed nobility. This intelligentsia conceived of its own activity in terms of its intellectual and artistic achievements; it derided the upper classes which achieved nothing in this sense but expended their energies in refining manners and imitating the French. The polemic against the upper classes was expressed in terms of the contrast between *Kultur* and *Zivilisation*. 'We become cultivated through art and science,' remarked Kant, 'we become civilized [by acquiring] a variety of social graces and refinements.'[3] The German intelligentsia used the term '*Kultur*' to express its peculiar position and to distinguish itself and its achievements from the upper classes, to which it had no access. In this respect, the situation of the German intelligentsia differed significantly from that of the French. In France there was also a rising group of intellectuals, including Voltaire and Diderot, but they were assimilated by the large court society of Paris, whereas their counterparts in Germany were excluded from courtly life. The German intelligentsia therefore sought its fulfilment and found its pride elsewhere, in the realms of scholarship, science, philosophy and art, in the realm, that is, of *Kultur*.

In the late eighteenth and early nineteenth centuries, the term 'culture' was also commonly used in works which sought to provide universal histories of the development of humankind. This usage was particularly strong in the German literature, for example in the works of Adelung, Herder, Meiners and Jenisch; it was in Adelung's work of 1782 that the expression '*Cultur-Geschichte*' – 'history of culture' – first appeared.[4] In these histories the term 'culture' is generally used in the sense of the cultivation, improvement and ennoblement of the physical and spiritual qualities of a person or a people. The histories of culture thus expressed the Enlightenment belief in the progressive character of the modern era, while at the same time conveying the positive connotation of 'culture' as the genuine development and ennoblement of the human faculties. The most well known of these early histories of culture was J. G. von Herder's four-volume work, *Ideen zur Philosophie der Geschichte der Menschheit*, originally published between 1784 and 1791.[5] In this wide-ranging work Herder preserved some of the emphases of his contemporaries, though he was critical of the ethnocentrism characteristic of many works that presented themselves as universal histories. In response to what he regarded as a misunderstanding of his ideas, Herder remarked:

> It had never entered into my mind, by employing the few figurative expressions, the *childhood, infancy, manhood* and *old age* of our species, the chain of which was applied, as it was applicable, only to a few nations, to point out a highway, on which the *history of culture*, to say nothing of the *philosophy of the history of humanity as a whole*, could be traced with certainty. Is there a people upon earth which is totally without culture? And how contracted must the scheme of Providence be, if every individual of the human species were to be formed to what *we* call culture, for which refined weakness would often be a more appropriate term? Nothing can be more vague, than the term itself; nothing more apt to lead us astray, than the application of it to whole nations and ages.[6]

Herder preferred to speak of 'cultures' in the plural, calling attention to the particular characteristics of different groups, nations and periods. This new sense of 'culture' was subsequently taken up and elaborated by Gustav Klemm, E. B. Tylor and others in the nineteenth century, whose ethnographic writings provided, as we shall see, a stimulus to the development of anthropology.

The concept of culture which emerged in the late eighteenth and early nineteenth centuries, and which was articulated primarily by German philosophers and historians, may be described as the 'classical conception'. This conception can be broadly defined as follows: *culture is the process of developing and ennobling the human faculties, a process facilitated by the assimilation of works of scholarship and art and linked to the progressive character of the modern era*. It is evident that certain aspects of the classical conception – its emphasis on the cultivation of 'higher' values and qualities, its appeal to works of scholarship and art, its link with the Enlightenment idea of progress – remain with us today and are implicit in some of the everyday uses of the word 'culture'. However, it is the very restrictiveness and narrowness of the classical conception which are also the sources of its limitations. The classical conception privileges certain works and values over others; it treats these works and values as the means by which individuals can be cultivated, that is, ennobled in mind and spirit. This privilege accorded to certain works and values was linked to the self-affirmation and self-image of the German intelligentsia and, more generally, to the confident belief in progress associated with the European Enlightenment. The concept of culture could not carry the weight of these assumptions for long. I have already noted the reservations expressed by Herder. But the decisive shift came in the late nineteenth century, with the incorporation of the concept of culture into the new emerging discipline of anthropology. In this process the concept of culture was stripped of some of its ethnocentric connotations and adapted to the tasks of ethnographic description. The study of culture was now less concerned with the ennoblement of the mind and spirit within the heart of Europe, and more concerned with unravelling the customs, practices and beliefs of those societies that were Europe's *other*.

Anthropological Conceptions of Culture

The concept of culture has been so closely associated with the development of the discipline of anthropology that they are sometimes regarded as virtually co-extensive: anthropology, or at least one major branch of anthropology, *is* the comparative study of culture. In view of the centrality of the concept of culture in the anthropological literature, it is perhaps not surprising that the concept has been used in a variety of ways and has been linked to many different assumptions and methods. I shall not undertake a detailed survey or analysis of these uses; for my purposes it will suffice to distinguish between two basic usages, which I shall refer to as the 'descriptive conception' and the 'symbolic conception'. This distinction inevitably involves some simplification, not only because it neglects nuances which may be discerned in different uses of the term, but also because it accentuates the differences between the two conceptions and therefore overlooks similarities. Nevertheless, the distinction is a useful analytical device which will enable us to examine some of the principal uses of the concept of culture in the anthropological literature.

The descriptive conception

The descriptive conception of culture can be traced back to the writings of nineteenth-century cultural historians who were concerned with the ethnographic description of non-European societies. Among the most important of these was Gustav Klemm, whose ten-volume work, *Allgemeine Cultur-Geschichte der Menschheit*, was published between 1843 and 1852. Klemm sought to provide a systematic and wide-ranging account of 'the gradual development of mankind' by examining the customs, skills, arts, tools, weapons, religious practices and so on of peoples and tribes throughout the world.[7] Klemm's work was familiar to E. B. Tylor, Professor of Anthropology at the University of Oxford, whose major work, *Primitive Culture*, was published in two volumes in 1871. In the English context, the contrast between 'culture' and 'civilization' was not as marked as it was in Germany. Tylor employed these terms interchangeably, offering, at the outset of *Primitive Culture*, this classic definition:

> Culture or Civilization, taken in its wide ethnographic sense, is that complex whole which includes knowledge, belief, art, morals, law, custom, and any other capabilities and habits acquired by man as a member of society. The condition of culture among the various societies of mankind, in so far as it is capable of being investigated on general principles, is a subject apt for the study of laws of human thought and action.[8]

Tylor's definition contains the key elements of the descriptive conception of culture. According to this conception, culture may be regarded as the interrelated array of beliefs, customs, laws, forms of knowledge and art, etc. which are acquired by individuals as members of a particular society and which can be studied scientifically. These beliefs, customs, etc. form a 'complex whole' which is characteristic of a certain society, distinguishing this society from others that exist at different times and places. One of the tasks of the study of culture, on Tylor's account, is to dissect these wholes into their component parts and to classify and compare them in a systematic way. It is a task similar to that undertaken by the botanist and the zoologist: 'Just as the catalogue of all the species of plants and animals of a district represents its Flora and Fauna, so the list of all the items of the general life of a people represents that whole which we call its culture.'[9]

As the latter remark makes clear, Tylor's approach involves a series of methodological assumptions about how culture is to be studied. These assumptions constitute culture as the object of a systematic, scientific inquiry; they produce what we may describe as the *scientization of the concept of culture*. Whereas the earlier, classical conception of culture was primarily a humanistic notion concerned with the cultivation of the human faculties through works of scholarship and art, the descriptive conception of culture, as it emerged in the writings of Tylor and others, was regarded as the mainstay of an emerging scientific discipline concerned with the analysis, classification and comparison of the constitutive elements of different cultures. However, the scientization of the concept of culture did not eliminate the earlier emphasis on the idea of progress; in many cases it simply embedded this idea in an evolutionary framework. This is evident in the work of Tylor, for whom the cultural conditions of differing societies were regarded as 'stages of development or evolution, each the outcome of previous history, and about to do its proper part in shaping the history of the future'.[10] In addition to analysing, classifying and comparing, the study of culture should seek, according to Tylor, to reconstruct the development of the human species, with a view to re-assembling the steps that led from savagery to civilized life. Hence Tylor's preoccupation with what he calls 'survival in culture': that is, with those residues of previous cultural forms which persist into the present, and which attest to the primeval and barbaric origins of contemporary culture.

The scientific and evolutionary character of Tylor's work was consistent with the general intellectual climate of the late nineteenth century, when the methods of the positive sciences were being adapted to new fields of inquiry and when the impact of Darwin's ideas was pervasive. In the writings of subsequent anthropologists these emphases were somewhat tempered, or sometimes partially displaced by other concerns. Thus Malinowski, writing in the 1930s and 1940s, espoused a 'scientific theory of culture' and endorsed a qualified evolutionary perspective; but his main concern was to develop a functionalist approach to culture, in which cultural phenomena could be analysed in terms of the satisfaction of human needs.[11] The conception of culture employed by Malinowski is a version of what I have called the descriptive conception. Human beings vary, he observes, in two respects. In the first place, they vary in terms of their bodily structure and physiological characteristics; the study of these variations is the task of physical anthropology. They also vary in terms of their 'social heritage' or culture, and these variations are the concern of 'cultural anthropology'. 'Culture comprises inherited artefacts, goods, technical processes, ideas, habits and values. . . Culture is a reality *sui generis* and must be studied as such.'[12] The study of culture must seek to break this social heritage down into its component elements and relate these elements to one another, to the environment and to the needs of the human organism. According to Malinowski, the examination of the functions of cultural phenomena, of the ways in which they satisfy human needs, must precede any attempt to formulate stages of social development and evolutionary schemata.

Despite the different emphases which are evident in the writings of Tylor, Malinowski and others, they share a common view of culture and of the tasks – or at least some of the tasks – of the study of cultural phenomena. I have characterized this view as the 'descriptive conception' of culture, a conception which may be summarized as follows: *the culture of a group or society is the array of beliefs, customs, ideas and values, as well as the material artefacts, objects and instruments, which are acquired by individuals as members of the group or society*; and the study of culture involves, at least in part, the scientific analysis, classification and comparison of these diverse phenomena. However there are, as we have seen, differing views about how the study of culture should proceed – whether, for instance, it should be pursued within an evolutionary framework, or whether it should give priority to functional analysis. The main difficulties with the descriptive conception of culture, as it has emerged within the anthropological literature, have more to do with these associated assumptions about the study of culture than with the conception of culture itself. There are many grounds on which these assumptions could be questioned, and indeed have been questioned, both by anthropologists and by others concerned with the logic and methodology of social inquiry; and if these assumptions are called into question, then the descriptive conception of culture loses much of its value and utility, since the main point of this conception was to define a range of phenomena that could be analysed in a systematic, scientific way. Without further specification of the method of analysis, the descriptive conception of culture may be left spinning in air. Moreover, we might well have some reservations about the very *breadth* of the concept of culture, as it is employed by Malinowski and others. Used to embrace everything that 'varies' in human life, apart from the sheer physical and physiological characteristics of the human being, the concept of culture becomes co-extensive with anthropology itself, or more precisely with 'cultural anthropology'. The concept becomes vague at best and redundant at worst; in any case, it runs the risk of losing the kind of precision that would befit a discipline seeking to establish its intellectual credentials. The concern to counter this risk has been one of the motives behind the formulation of a somewhat different concept of culture within anthropology.

The symbolic conception

It has long been argued that the use of symbols is a distinctive feature of human life. Whereas non-human animals can emit and respond to signals of various kinds, only human beings, it is argued, have fully developed languages by virtue of which meaningful expressions can be constructed and exchanged. Human beings not only produce and receive meaningful linguistic expressions, but also bestow meaning on non-linguistic con-structions – on actions, works of art, material objects of various kinds. The symbolic character of human life has been a constant theme of reflection among philosophers concerned with, and practitioners involved in, the development of the social sciences and humanities. Within the context of anthropology, this reflection has taken the form of elaborating what we may describe as a 'symbolic conception' of culture. One such conception was outlined in the 1940s by L. A. White in *The Science of Culture*. Beginning from the premise that the use of symbols, or 'symbolling' as he calls it, is the distinctive feature of the human being, White argues that '"culture" is the name of a distinct order, or class, of phenomena, namely, those things and events that are dependent upon the exercise of a mental ability, peculiar to the human species, that we have termed "symbolling"'.[13] White goes on to divide up the broad category of cultural phenomena into three systems – the technological, the sociological and the ideological – and to place these systems within a broad evolutionary framework that emphasizes the role of technology. But in developing his account in this way, White loses much of the interest and originality of his conception of culture. While his writings helped to prepare the way for a conception which emphasized the symbolic character of human life, it was left to other authors to develop this conception in a plausible and effective way.

In recent years the symbolic conception of culture has been placed at the centre of anthropological debates by Clifford Geertz, whose magisterial work, *The Interpretation of Cultures*, represents an attempt to draw out the implications of this conception for the nature of anthropological inquiry. Geertz describes his concept of culture as 'semiotic' rather than 'symbolic', but this difference in terminology is not significant here. For Geertz's overriding concern is with questions of meaning, symbolism and inter-pretation. 'Believing, with Max Weber, that man is an animal suspended in webs of significance he himself has spun, I take culture to be those webs, and the analysis of it to be therefore not an experimental science in search of law but an interpretive one in search of meaning.'[14] Culture is a 'stratified hierarchy of meaningful structures'; it consists of actions, symbols and signs, of 'twitches, winks, fake-winks, parodies' as well as utterances, conversations and soliloquies. In analysing culture we are engaged in unravelling layers of meaning, describing and re-describing actions and expressions which are *already meaningful for* the very individuals who are producing, perceiving and interpreting these actions and expressions in the course of their everyday lives. Analyses of culture – that is, the ethnographic writings of anthropo-logists – are interpretations of interpretations, second-order accounts, as it were, of a world which is already constantly described and interpreted by the individuals who make up this world. The ethnographer 'inscribes' social discourse, that is, he or she writes it down. In so doing, the ethnographer transforms it from a fleeting, transient event into a durable, perusable text. Borrowing a formula from Paul Ricoeur, Geertz describes this process as the fixation of the 'said' of social discourse: ethnography is an interpretative activity in which the interpreter is seeking to grasp what is 'said' in social discourse, its meaningful content, and to fix this 'said' in a written text. As such, the analysis of culture has little to do with the formulation of laws and predictions, let alone with the construction of grand evolutionary schemes;

it is more like interpreting a literary text than observing some empirical regularity. The analyst is seeking to make sense of actions and expressions, to specify the meaning they have for the actors whose actions they are, and, in so doing, to venture some suggestions, some contestable considerations, about the society of which these actions and expressions are part.

Geertz's interpretative approach to the study of culture is of great interest, representing a development within anthropology which converges in certain respects with developments elsewhere in the social sciences and humanities. Underlying this approach is a conception of culture which I have described as the 'symbolic conception', and which may be characterized broadly as follows: *culture is the pattern of meanings embodied in symbolic forms, including actions, utterances and meaningful objects of various kinds, by virtue of which individuals communicate with one another and share their experiences, conceptions and beliefs*. Cultural analysis is, first and foremost, the elucidation of these patterns of meaning, the interpretative explication of the meanings embodied in symbolic forms. Viewed in this way, the analysis of cultural phenomena becomes an activity quite different from that implied by the descriptive conception, with its associated assumptions concerning scientific analysis and classification, concerning evolutionary change and functional interdependence. The study of culture, on Geertz's account, is an activity more akin to interpreting a text than to classifying flora and fauna. What it requires is not so much the attitude of an analyst seeking to classify and quantify, but rather the sensitivity of an interpreter seeking to discern patterns of meaning, to discriminate between shades of sense, and to render intelligible a way of life which is already meaningful for those who live it.

Geertz's work offers, in my view, the most important formulation of the concept of culture to emerge from the anthropological literature. He has re-orientated the analysis of culture towards the study of meaning and symbolism and highlighted the centrality of interpretation as a methodological approach. It is precisely because I find Geertz's approach so attractive that I want to spend some time examining what seem to me to be difficulties and weaknesses in his work. I shall restrict myself to three main criticisms. First, although I have attempted to formulate a precise characterization of the symbolic conception of culture, in fact Geertz uses the term 'culture' in several different ways, not all of which appear to be entirely consistent. For example, at one point Geertz defines 'culture' as 'an historically transmitted pattern of meanings embodied in symbols', whereas in another passage culture is conceived of as 'a set of control mechanisms – plans, recipes, rules, instructions (what computer engineers call "programs") – for the governing of behavior'.[15] According to this latter conception, culture is more like a template or blueprint for the organization of social and psychological processes, a template which is necessary, argues Geertz, because human behaviour is 'extremely plastic'. Be that as it may, it is by no means clear how this conception of culture, as rules, plans or 'programs' which govern behaviour, relates to the symbolic conception of culture *qua* patterns of meaning embodied in symbolic forms. Nor is it evident that the *analysis* of culture, conceived of as the elucidation of rules, plans or 'programs', would be the same as the interpretative explication of meaning. Elucidating the rules, plans or 'programs' which govern human behaviour may require attention to patterns of meaning, but it may also require attention to other factors, such as regulations and routines, relations of power and inequality and broader social trends; analysing patterns of meaning may not, in and by itself, illuminate the rules, plans or 'programs' which govern human behaviour. Hence Geertz's use of the term 'culture', and his view of the nature and tasks of cultural analysis, are not as clear and consistent as they might at first seem.

A second difficulty in Geertz's work concerns the notion of the text, which plays a central role in his approach. As I mentioned earlier, Geertz borrows this notion from Paul Ricoeur, who has attempted to define the key characteristics of the text and to develop a theory of interpretation on this basis.[16] Geertz appears to employ this notion in two different ways, both of which give rise to problems. In some contexts, Geertz suggests that cultural analysis is concerned with texts in the sense that the practice of ethnography is the production of texts: the texts we are dealing with are *ethnographic texts*, which 'fix' the 'said' of social discourse. Now there can be no doubt that writing ethnography involves the production of texts. But where are the arguments to support the claim that what ethnographic texts are doing, or should seek to do, is to 'fix' what is 'said' in the social discourse of the subjects who form the object of ethnographic inquiry? The arguments cannot be found in the writings of Ricoeur, whose proposals concerning the fixation of meaning have nothing to do with the relation between the social scientific researcher and the subject/object of his or her research. Moreover, Geertz's own practice as an ethnographer is sometimes difficult to reconcile with this methodological injunction. For example, in his 'Deep Play: Notes on the Balinese Cockfight' – a brilliant and imaginative essay in interpretative ethnography – Geertz construes the cockfight as an 'art form' in which and through which the Balinese experience and dramatize their status concerns; it is, to use Goffman's arresting phrase, a 'status bloodbath' which provides the Balinese with a way of perceiving and enacting their status relations without running the risk of actually modifying or disrupting these relations.[17] Brilliant and imaginative though this interpretation is, Geertz does not provide any convincing defence of the claim that this is what the cockfight means to the Balinese who participate in it. He does not conduct interviews with a representative sample of participants (or if he does, he doesn't tell us), nor does he offer his interpretation to the Balinese to see whether they would regard it as an accurate rendition of their own understanding. There are methodological problems here that deserve discussion in their own right;[18] but the point I wish to stress is simply that the relation between the ethnographic text and the subject matter about which the ethnographer is writing may be considerably more complex than Geertz's methodological precept would suggest.

However, Geertz also employs the notion of the text in a rather different way. He sometimes maintains that cultural analysis is concerned with texts, not simply because writing ethnography involves the production of texts, but also because the patterns of meaning which the ethnographer is seeking to grasp are themselves *constructed like a text*. Culture can be seen as 'an assemblage of texts', as 'acted documents', as 'imaginative works built out of social materials'.[19] The purpose of this text analogy is to focus our attention on the ways in which meaning is inscribed in cultural forms and to enable us to regard the analysis of these forms as similar, in essential respects, to the interpretation of a literary text. 'To see social institutions, social customs, social changes as in some sense "readable" is to alter our whole sense of what such interpretation is and shift it toward modes of thought rather more familiar to the translator, the exegete, or the iconographer than to the test giver, the factor analyst, or the pollster.'[20] Understood in this general way, the text analogy is a salutary methodological device; problems arise, however, as soon as one probes the analogy in detail and examines the assumptions on which it is based. Geertz does not state these assumptions in a clear and explicit way, relying instead on occasional references to Ricoeur as sufficient grounds for his use of the analogy. But Ricoeur's conceptualization of the text, his arguments in favour of treating action as a text and his theory of interpretation can all be questioned in certain fundamental respects. As I have argued elsewhere, I think it can be shown that Ricoeur's approach involves an unjustifiable reification of action and a misleading abstraction from the social–historical circumstances in which actions, utterances and, indeed, texts are produced, transmitted and received.[21] Geertz's use of the text analogy, however salutary it may be at a general level, neglects these difficulties of detail; it simply skates over a cluster of problems which, if confronted more directly, would cast considerable doubt on any attempt to view culture *en masse* as 'an assemblage of texts'.

The third difficulty with Geertz's approach is that it gives insufficient attention to problems of power and social conflict. Cultural phenomena are viewed above all as meaningful constructs, as symbolic forms, and the analysis of culture is understood as the interpretation of the patterns of meaning embodied in these forms. But cultural phenomena are also embedded in relations of power and conflict. Everyday utterances and actions, as well as more elaborate phenomena such as rituals, festivals or works of art, are always produced or enacted in particular social–historical circumstances, by specific individuals drawing on certain resources and endowed with varying degrees of power and authority; and these meaningful phenomena, once produced or enacted, are circulated, received, perceived and interpreted by other individuals situated in particular social–historical circumstances, drawing on certain resources in order to make sense of the phenomena concerned. Viewed in this way, cultural phenomena may be seen as expressing relations of power, as serving in specific circumstances to sustain or disrupt relations of power, and as subject to multiple, perhaps divergent and conflicting interpretations by the individuals who receive and perceive these phenomena in the course of their everyday lives. None of these considerations figures prominently in Geertz's approach. His emphasis is on meaning rather than power, and on *the* meaning rather than the divergent and conflicting meanings that cultural phenomena may have for individuals situated in different circumstances and endowed with differing resources and opportunities. In this regard, Ricoeur's model of the text is likely to be somewhat misleading. For the key characteristic of the text, according to Ricoeur, is its 'distanciation' from the social, historical and psychological conditions of its production, in such a way that the interpretation of the text can be based on an analysis of its internal structure and content alone. But to proceed in this way is to ignore the ways in which the text, or the analogue of the text, is embedded in social contexts within which, and by virtue of which, it is produced and received; it is to disregard the sense that it has for the very individuals involved in creating and consuming this object, the very individuals for whom this object is, in differing and perhaps divergent ways, a meaningful symbolic form. The symbolic conception of culture, especially as elaborated in the writings of Geertz, fails to give sufficient attention to problems of power and conflict and, more generally, to the structured social contexts within which cultural phenomena are produced, transmitted and received.

Rethinking Culture: A Structural Conception

The foregoing analyses of different conceptions of culture provide the backcloth against which I want to outline an alternative approach to the study of cultural phenomena. In developing this approach I shall draw upon the symbolic conception as formulated by Geertz, while seeking to avoid the difficulties and limitations evident in his work. I shall put forward what may be called a 'structural conception' of culture, by which I mean a conception of culture that emphasizes *both* the symbolic character of cultural phenomena *and* the fact that such phenomena are always embedded in structured social contexts. We may offer a preliminary characterization of this conception by defining 'cultural analysis' as *the study of symbolic forms – that is, meaningful actions, objects and expressions of various kinds – in relation to the historically specific and socially structured contexts and processes within which, and by means of which, these symbolic forms are produced, transmitted and received*. Cultural phenomena, on this account, are to be seen as *symbolic forms in structured contexts*; and cultural analysis – to use an abbreviated formula which I shall explain more fully later – may be regarded as the study of the *meaningful constitution and social contextualization of symbolic forms*. As symbolic forms, cultural phenomena are meaningful for actors as well as for analysts. They are phenomena which are routinely interpreted by actors in the course of their everyday lives and which call for interpretation by analysts seeking to grasp the meaningful characteristics of social life. But these symbolic forms are also embedded in specific social–historical contexts and processes within which, and by means of which, they are produced, transmitted and received. Such contexts and processes are structured in various ways. They may be characterized, for instance, by asymmetrical relations of power, by differential access to resources and opportunities, and by institutionalized mechanisms for the production, transmission and reception of symbolic forms. The analysis of cultural phenomena involves the elucidation of these socially structured contexts and processes as well as the interpretation of symbolic forms; or, as I shall try to show in more detail in a later chapter, it involves the interpretation of symbolic forms *by means of* the analysis of socially structured contexts and processes.

In describing this conception of culture as a 'structural' conception, I wish to highlight the concern with the socially structured contexts and processes within which symbolic forms are embedded. But I do not want to suggest that this concern exhausts the tasks of cultural analysis: on the contrary, what is crucial is the way in which this concern is linked to the activity of interpretation. The structural conception of culture is not so much an alternative to the symbolic conception as a modification of it, that is, a way of modifying the symbolic conception by taking account of socially structured contexts and processes. The term 'structural', as I am using it here, should not be confused with 'structuralist'. The latter term is generally used to refer to a variety of methods, ideas and doctrines associated with French thinkers such as Lévi-Strauss, Barthes, Greimas, Althusser and – in some phases of his work at least – Foucault. Later I shall examine in some detail the strengths and weaknesses of structuralist methods. For the time being it will suffice to draw a distinction between the *internal structural features* of symbolic forms, on the one hand, and the *socially structured contexts and processes* within which symbolic forms are embedded, on the other. Structuralist methods are traditionally and primarily concerned with the former – that is, with the internal structural features of symbolic forms – whereas the structural conception of culture is concerned to take account of socially structured contexts and processes. I shall argue later that structuralist methods can be useful as a means of analysing internal structural features, such as the structure of the narrative deployed in a text. But I shall also argue that these methods are, for various reasons, strictly limited in terms of their usefulness and validity. The structur*al* conception of culture is concerned to avoid the limitations of structural*ist* approaches. While employing structuralist methods when it is useful to do so, the methodological framework that I shall outline later will seek to combine, in a systematic way, the twin concerns with meaning and context that are conveyed by the structural conception of culture.

We can begin to elaborate the structural conception of culture by discussing some of the characteristics of symbolic forms. I shall distinguish five characteristics of symbolic forms, which I shall describe as their 'intentional', 'conventional', 'structural', 'referential' and 'contextual' aspects. I want to suggest that these five aspects are typically involved in the constitution of symbolic forms, although the specific ways in which they are involved, and the relative importance of one aspect *vis-à-vis* another, may vary considerably from one type or instance of symbolic form to another. The intentional, conventional, structural and referential aspects all have to do with what is commonly conveyed by the terms 'meaning', 'sense', and 'significance'. It is not my aim here to offer a general survey of the literature dealing with these much-contested terms, let alone to offer anything so grand as a Theory of Meaning. My aim is much more modest: to distinguish some of the key characteristics by virtue of which symbolic forms may be regarded as 'meaningful phenomena', in such a way that, at a later point, we can examine what is involved in the interpretation of symbolic forms. The fifth aspect of symbolic forms, the 'contextual' aspect, is also relevant to questions of meaning and interpretation; but it calls our attention to socially structured characteristics of symbolic forms which are often neglected in discussions of meaning and interpretation, characteristics which are, none the less, crucial to the analysis of culture. I shall focus on the contextual aspect of symbolic forms in the following section. Here I want to begin by offering a preliminary clarification of the intentional, conventional, structural and referential aspects. In this preliminary discussion I shall not examine in detail the differences that may exist between 'linguistic' and 'non-linguistic' meaning, or the variations that may be found among different types of symbolic forms. I shall use the term 'symbolic forms' to refer to a broad range of meaningful phenomena, from actions, gestures and rituals to utterances, texts, television programmes and works of art. In the following chapter I shall draw some distinctions between different types of symbolic forms, in the course of analysing some of the modalities of cultural transmission.

Let me consider first the 'intentional' aspect of symbolic forms. What I mean by this is that *symbolic forms are expressions of a subject and for a subject (or subjects)*. That is, symbolic forms are produced, constructed or employed by a subject who, in producing or employing such forms, is pursuing certain aims or purposes and is seeking to express himself or herself, what he or she 'means' or 'intends', in and by the forms thus produced. The producer-subject is also seeking to express himself or herself *for* a subject or subjects who, in receiving and interpreting the symbolic form, perceive it *as* the expression of a subject, *as* a message to be understood. Even in the limiting case of a diary which is not intended for circulation, the producer-subject writes for a subject, namely for the very same subject who writes the diary and who alone possesses the key. In this respect, symbolic forms differ from natural patterns of stones on the seashore or of clouds in the sky. Such patterns are generally not symbolic forms precisely because they are not expressions of a subject and are not perceived as such. In certain animistic belief systems, natural patterns may acquire a symbolic character and may be regarded as 'meaningful' in some sense; however, natural patterns acquire this character in so far as they are seen as the expression of an intentional, purposeful subject, whether a human, quasi-human or supernatural being. The constitution of objects as symbolic forms presupposes that they are produced, constructed or employed by a subject for a subject or subjects, and/or that they are perceived as so produced by the subject or subjects who receive them.

In describing this aspect of symbolic forms as 'intentional', I do not wish to suggest that the 'meaning' of symbolic forms, or of the constituent elements of symbolic forms, can be analysed exclusively or exhaustively in terms of what the producer-subject 'intended' or 'meant'. Various attempts have been made to analyse meaning in terms of the producer-subject's intentions, from Grice to E. D. Hirsch.[22] There is no need here to examine the strengths and weaknesses of these various attempts, nor is there any need to try to determine, in a general and all-embracing way, the relation between the meaning of symbolic forms and the intentions of a producer-subject. It will suffice to make two general observations. First, the constitution of objects as symbolic forms – that is, their constitution as 'meaningful phenomena' – presupposes that they are produced, constructed or employed by a subject capable of acting intentionally, or at least that they are perceived as produced by such a subject. To say that an object was produced by, or perceived as produced by, a subject capable of acting intentionally is *not* to say, however, that this subject produced this object intentionally, or that this object is what this subject intended to produce; rather, it is to say simply that this object was produced by, or perceived as produced by, a subject about whom we could say, on some occasion, 'he or she did that intentionally'. The second observation we may make is this: the 'meaning' of a symbolic form, or of constituent elements of a symbolic form, is not necessarily identical with what the producer-subject 'intended' or 'meant' in producing the symbolic form. This potential divergence is present in everyday social interaction, as is evident in the indignant retort, 'That may be what you *meant*, but it's certainly not what you *said*.' But the divergence may be even more common in the case of symbolic forms which are not linked to a dialogic situation. Thus written texts, ritualized actions or works of art may have or acquire a meaning or sense which could not be fully explicated by determining what the producer-subject intended or meant in producing the symbolic form. The meaning or sense of a symbolic form may be far more complex and ramified than the meaning that could be derived from what the producer-subject originally intended. Moreover, what the producer-subject intended or meant in any particular case may be unclear, confused, inchoate or inaccessible; the subject may have had various intentions, conflicting intentions, 'unconscious' intentions or simply no clear intention. These variations and conflations in the producer-subject's intentions are not necessarily reflected at the level of the symbolic form as such. The meaning of a symbolic form, or of constituent elements of a symbolic form, is a complex phenomenon that depends on, and is determined by, a variety of factors. What the producer-subject intended or meant in producing the symbolic form is certainly one (or some) of these factors and may, in some circumstances, be of crucial importance. But it is not the only factor and it would be quite misleading to suggest that the producer-subject's intentions could or should be taken as the touchstone of interpretation.

The second characteristic of symbolic forms is the 'conventional' aspect. By this I mean that *the production, construction or employment of symbolic forms, as well as the interpretation of symbolic forms by the subjects who receive them, are processes that typically involve the application of rules, codes or conventions of various kinds*. These rules, codes or conventions range from rules of grammar to conventions of style and expression, from codes which link particular signals to particular letters, words or states of affairs (e.g. the Morse code) to conventions which govern the action and interaction of individuals seeking to express themselves or to interpret the expressions of others (e.g. the conventions of courtly love). To apply rules, codes or conventions in producing or interpreting symbolic forms is not necessarily to be aware of these rules or to be able to formulate them clearly and accurately if called upon to do so. These rules, codes or conventions are generally applied in a *practical state*, that is, as implicit and taken-for-granted schemes for generating and interpreting symbolic forms. They constitute part of the tacit knowledge which individuals employ in the course of their everyday lives, constantly creating meaningful expressions and making sense of the expressions created by others. While generally tacit, this knowledge is nevertheless social, in the sense that it is shared by more than one individual and is always open to correction and sanction by others. If we produce an utterance that is grammatically incorrect, or if we express our emotions in a way that is abnormal in terms of prevailing conditions, our utterance or expression may be corrected or sanctioned in certain ways. The possibility of correcting or sanctioning the production and interpretation of symbolic forms attests to the fact that these processes typically involve the application of social rules, codes or conventions.

It is important to distinguish more sharply than I have done so far between the rules, codes or conventions involved in the production, construction or employment of symbolic forms, on the one hand, and those involved in the interpretation of symbolic forms by the subjects who receive them, on the other. In the former case we may speak of the rules of *encoding*, whereas in the latter case we may speak of the rules of *decoding*. It is important to draw this distinction in order to emphasize the fact that these two sets of rules need not coincide nor even co-exist. They need not coincide in so far as a symbolic form encoded in accordance with certain rules or conventions may be decoded in accordance with other rules or conventions. For example, a text produced in accordance with the conventions of scientific discourse may be interpreted by subsequent readers in differing ways, as a work of philosophy or mythology or as a work which breaks with scientific conventions and inaugurates something new; or a spectacle enacted as an occasion of state may be interpreted by spectators as a warning or a threat, as a blunder or a farce. Moreover, the rules of encoding and decoding need not co-exist in the sense that a symbolic form may be encoded but never in practice decoded, as with a diary that is never read or an artefact that is never seen. Similarly, a symbolic form may be decoded in accordance with certain rules or conventions even though it was never in fact encoded. The animistic interpretation of natural patterns or events is one example of the decoding of unencoded forms; but this practice is also common in the everyday interpretation of human action and events. Thus an action may be interpreted as an act of resistance or a threat to the social order, as a sign of exhaustion or as a symptom of mental illness, even though the action was not encoded in accordance with any particular rule or convention. The failure to distinguish clearly between the rules of encoding and the rules of decoding is one of the problems that vitiates the writings of Winch and other philosophers who, under the influence of the later Wittgenstein, have argued that the key feature of social life is its 'rule governed' character.[23] In his concern to emphasize the connection between rules and meaningful action, Winch ends up by populating the world with rules to govern each and every action which is 'meaningful' in some sense, whereas in fact the relevant rules already existed in another form, namely as rules of decoding rather than as rules of encoding. By distinguishing clearly between these two sets of rules, we can avoid the kind of problems encountered by Winch and others and we can prepare the way for a more detailed investigation into the relations between the rules, codes or conventions involved in the production of symbolic forms and those involved in the interpretation of these forms by the subjects who receive them.

The third characteristic of symbolic forms is the 'structural' aspect, by which I mean that *symbolic forms are constructions which display an articulated structure*. They display an articulated structure in the sense that they typically consist of elements which stand in determinate relations with one another. These elements and their interrelations comprise a structure which can be analysed formally, in the way, for example, that one can analyse the juxtaposition of words and images in a picture or the narrative structure of a myth. We may distinguish here between the *structure* of a symbolic form, on the one hand, and the *system* which is instantiated in particular symbolic forms, on the other. To analyse the structure of a symbolic form is to analyse the specific elements and their interrelations which may be discerned in the symbolic form in question; to analyse the system instantiated in a symbolic form is, by contrast, to abstract from the form in question and to reconstruct a general constellation of elements and their interrelations, a constellation which is exemplified in particular cases. The structure of a symbolic form is a pattern of elements which can be discerned in actual instances of expression, in actual utterances, expressions or texts. A symbolic system, by contrast, is a constellation of elements – we may describe these as 'systemic elements' – which exist independently of any particular symbolic form but which are realized in particular symbolic forms. The Swiss linguist Ferdinand de Saussure was primarily concerned with symbolic systems in this sense. By distinguishing between language (*la langue*) and speech (*la parole*), Saussure sought to isolate language as a symbolic system, as a 'system of signs', so as to study its basic elements and principles of functioning.[24] While we may distinguish in this way between symbolic systems and the structure of particular symbolic forms, the analysis of the latter may be facilitated by, and may in turn facilitate, the study of the former. Thus the analysis of a particular text may be facilitated by an understanding of the constellation of pronouns characteristic of a linguistic system such as English or French; and, conversely, we can reconstruct the constellation of pronouns characteristic of such systems by attending to the ways in which pronouns are used in particular texts and other instances of language use.

The analysis of the structural features of symbolic forms, and the relation between these features and the characteristics of symbolic systems, is an important but limited part of the study of symbolic forms. It is important because the meaning conveyed by symbolic forms is commonly *constructed with* structural features and systemic elements, so that by analysing these features and elements we can deepen our understanding of the meaning conveyed by symbolic forms. Consider a familiar example from Barthes.[25] The cover of *Paris-Match* is illustrated with the picture of a young black soldier in French uniform; the soldier is saluting, eyes slightly uplifted, as if fixed on the tricolour at full mast. This rich juxtaposition of images forms a structure through which the meaning of the message is conveyed. Change one aspect of the picture – change the black soldier to a white soldier, or dress him in a guerrilla outfit instead of a French uniform, or put the picture on the cover of *Libération* rather than *Paris-Match* – and the meaning conveyed by this message would change. By analysing the structural features of the picture, we can elucidate a meaning which is constructed with these features and conveyed, often implicitly, to readers or viewers.

Although the analysis of structural features and systemic elements is important, the value of this kind of analysis is also limited. Here I shall note two key respects in which the limits of this kind of analysis can be discerned; in a later chapter I shall draw out the methodological implications of these points. In the first place, while the meaning conveyed by symbolic forms is commonly constructed with structural features and systemic elements, such meaning is never *exhausted by* these features and elements. Symbolic forms are not only concatenations of elements and their interrelations: they are also typically representations *of* something, they present or portray something, they say something *about* something. This characteristic of symbolic forms, which I shall describe below as their 'referential' aspect, cannot be grasped by the analysis of structural features and systemic elements alone. The *referent* of an expression or figure is by no means identical to the 'signified' (*signifié*) of a sign, for the latter, on Saussure's account, is merely the concept that is correlated with the sound-image or 'signifier' (*signifiant*); both signified and signifier are an integral part of the sign.[26] The referent, by contrast, is an extra-linguistic object, individual or state of affairs. Grasping the referential aspect of a symbolic form requires a creative interpretation which moves beyond the analysis of internal features and elements and which seeks to explicate what is represented or what is said. A second respect in which the analysis of structural features and systemic elements is limited is this: by focusing on the internal constitution of symbolic forms, this kind of analysis not only neglects the referential aspect of symbolic forms, but also abstracts from the social–historical context and processes within which these forms are embedded. The analysis of structural features and systemic elements thus disregards what I have called the 'contextual' aspect of symbolic forms; and, as I shall try to show, it thereby disregards some of the characteristics which are crucial for the cultural analysis of symbolic forms.

The fourth characteristic of symbolic forms is the 'referential' aspect, by which I mean, as indicated above, that *symbolic forms are constructions which typically represent something, refer to something, say something about something*. Here I am using the term 'referential' very broadly, to embrace the general sense in which a symbolic form or element of a symbolic form may, in a certain context, stand for or represent some object, individual or state of affairs as well as the more specific sense in which a linguistic expression may, on a given occasion of use, refer to a particular object. Consider some examples: a figure in a painting from the Renaissance may stand for or represent the devil, human evil or death; a cartoon figure in a modern daily newspaper, facial features slightly exaggerated, may refer to a particular individual or to a composite political actor such as a nation-state; the expression 'I' in the sentence 'I am committed to improving the conditions of our members' refers to the individual who uttered this sentence at a particular time and in a particular place. As these examples suggest, figures and expressions acquire their *referential specificity* in differing ways. By 'referential specificity' I mean the fact that, on a given occasion of use, a particular figure or expression refers to a specific object or objects, individual or individuals, state of affairs or states of affairs. Some figures or expressions acquire their referential specificity only by virtue of their use in certain circumstances. For example, pronouns such as 'I' or 'you' are free-floating referential terms; they refer to specific individuals only by being used in particular contexts, by being uttered or inscribed by an individual on a given occasion. By contrast, the referential specificity of proper names is fixed to some extent independently of their use on a given occasion. Thus the name 'Richard M. Nixon' refers by virtue of an accumulated set of conventions and practices which link this name to a particular individual (or relatively small set of individuals).

However, even proper names possess a certain ambiguity or *referential opacity*. There may be more than one possible referent of a name, and a name may be used on a given occasion to refer to an individual other than the referent fixed by the relevant conventions and practices (a slip of the tongue, an ironical allusion), in which cases the referential specificity can be fixed, and the opacity removed, only by attending to the particular circumstances in which the expression is used.

In highlighting the referential aspect of symbolic forms, I wish to call attention not only to the ways in which figures or expressions refer to or represent some object, individual or state of affairs, but also to the way in which, having referred to or represented some object, symbolic forms typically say something about it, that is, assert or state, project or portray. We can illustrate this point by returning to some of the examples previously used. In uttering the sentence 'I am committed to improving the conditions of our members', the speaker refers to a specific individual, namely to himself or herself as the referent of 'I', and, having so referred, he or she says something about this individual, namely that he or she is committed to doing something. He or she has said something, stated or asserted something, about which we could say 'That's true' (or 'That's not true', as the case may be); for 'true', in this context, is a predicate that we attribute to statements.[27] Or consider again the example from Barthes. 'I see very well', says Barthes, commenting on the cover of *Paris-Match*, 'what it signifies to me: that France is a great Empire, that all her sons, without any colour discrimination, faithfully serve under her flag, and that there is no better answer to the detractors of an alleged colonialism than the zeal shown by this Negro in serving his so-called oppressors.'[28] The picture projects a possible meaning which Barthes seeks to grasp and express through interpretation. Barthes offers an interpretation, a creative construction of possible meaning. The interpretation articulates: 'that France is a great Empire, that all her sons . . ., that there is no better answer . . .'. The interpretation attempts to re-assert what is projected by the picture, to explicate and articulate what the picture may represent and portray. In using this example to illustrate the referential aspect of symbolic forms, I do not want to suggest that we can derive from Barthes's work an adequate account of this aspect or of the nature and role of interpretation. Barthes's work suffers from some of the limitations of the analysis of structural features and systemic elements, limitations which I discussed briefly above; and if in this example he is led beyond a purely formal analysis of structural elements and their interrelations, is led to explore the links between symbolic forms and that which they portray or that about which they speak, is led to engage in a creative construction of possible meaning, then this example may be less a vindication of Barthes's general approach than an indication that his practical analyses burst the bounds of this approach.

The fifth characteristic of symbolic forms to which I want to call attention is the 'contextual' aspect. By this I mean, as I indicated earlier, that *symbolic forms are always embedded in specific social–historical contexts and processes within which, and by means of which, they are produced, transmitted and received*. Even a simple phrase, uttered by one person to another in the course of everyday interaction, is embedded in a structured social context and may bear the traces – in terms of accent, intonation, mode of address, choice of words, style of expression, etc. – of the social relations characteristic of this context. More complex symbolic forms, such as speeches, texts, television programmes and works of art, generally presuppose a range of specific institutions within which, and by means of which, these forms are produced, transmitted and received. What these symbolic forms are, the way that they are constructed, circulated and received in the social world as well as the sense and the value that they have for those who receive them, all depend to some extent on the contexts and institutions which generate, mediate and sustain them. Thus the way that a speech is interpreted by particular individuals, the perception of it as a 'speech' and the weight that is accorded to it, are conditioned by the fact that these words are uttered by this individual on this occasion in this setting and are transmitted by this medium (a microphone, a television camera, a satellite); change the elements of this setting – suppose, for instance, that the same words are uttered by a child to a group of admiring parents – and the same words will acquire a different sense and a different value for those who receive them. It is important to stress that, in highlighting the contextual aspect of symbolic forms, we are moving beyond the analysis of the internal structural features of symbolic forms. In the above example, the setting and the occasion of the speech, the relations between the speaker and the audience, the mode of transmission of the speech and the ways that it is received by the audience are not so many aspects of the speech itself, aspects which could be discerned by analysing the structural features and systemic elements of the speech alone. On the contrary, these aspects can be discerned only by attending to the social contexts, institutions and processes within which the speech is uttered, transmitted and received and by analysing the relations of power, forms of authority, kinds of resources and other characteristics of these contexts. These are issues which I shall examine further in the following section.

The Social Contextualization of Symbolic Forms

In examining the contextual aspect of symbolic forms, I shall seek to highlight those features of symbolic forms which derive from the fact that they are always embedded in structured social contexts. The embedding of symbolic forms in social contexts implies that, in addition to being the expressions of a subject, these forms are generally produced by agents situated within a specific social–historical context and endowed with resources and capacities of various kinds; symbolic forms may bear the traces, in differing ways, of the social conditions of their production. The embedding of symbolic forms in social contexts also implies that, in addition to being expressions for a subject (or subjects), these forms are generally received and interpreted by individuals who are also situated within specific social–historical contexts and endowed with various kinds of resources; how a particular symbolic form is understood by individuals may depend on the resources and capacities they are able to employ in the process of interpreting it. A further consequence of the contextual embedding of symbolic forms is that they are often the object of complex processes of valuation, evaluation and conflict. Symbolic forms are constantly valued and evaluated, acclaimed and contested, by the individuals who produce and receive them. They are the object of what I shall call *processes of valorization*, that is, processes by which and through which they are ascribed certain kinds of 'value'. Moreover, as social phenomena, symbolic forms are also exchanged between individuals located in specific contexts, and this process of exchange requires certain means of transmission. Even a simple exchange of utterances in a face-to-face situation presupposes an array of technical conditions and apparatuses (larynx, vocal cords, lips, air waves, ears, etc.), and many symbolic forms presuppose other conditions and apparatuses which are specially constructed and deployed. I shall describe different types of conditions and apparatuses as *modalities of cultural transmission*. In the remainder of this chapter I want to focus on the characteristics of social contexts within which symbolic forms are produced and received, and on the processes of valorization to which symbolic forms may be subjected. I shall defer until the next chapter the analysis of modalities of cultural transmission.

I have stressed that the production and reception of symbolic forms are processes that take place within structured social contexts. These contexts are spatially and temporally specific: they involve particular *spatio-temporal settings*, and these settings are partially constitutive of the action and interaction which take place within them. The spatial and temporal characteristics of the context of production of a symbolic form may coincide or overlap with the characteristics of the context of reception, as in the case of the exchange of utterances in a face-to-face interaction. In face-to-face situations, the speaker and the hearer share the same locale, and the features of the locale are routinely incorporated into symbolic forms and the interaction of which they are part (for instance, in providing referential specificity for deictic expressions and pronouns). But the spatial and temporal characteristics of the context of production may diverge significantly or entirely from the characteristics of the context of reception. This is the typical situation of symbolic forms which are transmitted via technical media of some kind – for example, a letter which is written in one context and read in another, or a television programme which is produced in one context and watched in a plurality of other contexts dispersed in time and space. I shall return to this circumstance of symbolic forms, which I regard as a fundamental feature of cultural transmission, in the following chapter.

The social contexts of symbolic forms are not only spatially and temporally specific: they are also *structured* in various ways. The concept of structure is essential for the analysis of social contexts, but it is a complex and highly contested concept which has been widely used, and sometimes overused, in the literature of the social sciences. Here I do not wish to review and appraise the differing usages of this concept.[29] I shall restrict myself to outlining a conceptual framework for the identification and analysis of some of the typical characteristics of social contexts.[30] Within this framework, the notion of social structure can be assigned a specific role, as a notion which highlights a certain range of phenomena and calls our attention to a certain level of analysis. In outlining this framework, I do not want to suggest that the analysis of social contexts is an activity altogether divorced from the study of the individuals who act and interact within these contexts, who produce symbolic forms in certain contexts and receive them in others. On the contrary, as I shall try to show, the analysis of these contexts is an activity indispensable to the study of action and interaction, production and reception, just as the analysis of contexts would be partial and incomplete without a consideration of the actions and interactions that take place within them.

We can begin to clarify the typical characteristics of social contexts by introducing the concept of *fields of interaction*. The concept of field has been developed by Pierre Bourdieu and employed in a range of illuminating studies.[31] I shall not examine Bourdieu's use of this concept in any detail; but here, and later in this chapter, I shall draw upon his work in so far as it is relevant to my concerns.[32] Following Bourdieu, a field of interaction may be conceptualized synchronically as a space of positions and diachronically as a set of trajectories. Particular individuals are situated at certain positions within this social space and they follow, in the course of their lives, certain trajectories. These positions and trajectories are determined to some extent by the volume and distribution of various kinds of *resources or 'capital'*. For our purposes here we can distinguish between three principal kinds of capital: 'economic capital', which includes property, wealth and financial assets of various kinds; 'cultural capital', which includes knowledge, skills and differing types of educational qualifications; and 'symbolic capital', which includes the accumulated praise, prestige and recognition associated with a person or position. Within any given field of interaction, individuals draw upon these differing kinds of resources in order to pursue their particular aims. They may also seek opportunities to convert resources of one type into resources of another – as, for example, when accumulated family wealth is used to obtain educational qualifications for children who may be able thereby to secure well-paid jobs.[33]

In pursuing their aims and interests within fields of interaction, individuals also typically draw upon *rules and conventions* of various kinds. These rules and conventions may be explicit and well-formulated precepts, as in the case of the written rules which guide the action of individuals in an office or on a factory floor. But explicit and well-formulated precepts of this kind are the exception; when they exist, and where they exist, they may be ignored as often as they are respected. To a large extent, the rules and conventions which guide much of the action and interaction in social life are implicit, unformulated, informal, imprecise. They may be conceptualized as *flexible schemata* which orientate individuals in the course of their everyday lives, without ever being raised to the level of explicit and well-formulated precepts. They exist in the form of practical knowledge, gradually inculcated and continuously reproduced in the practices of everyday life, in much the way, for example, that conventions of cleanliness or good manners are inculcated from birth. These flexible schemata are not so much 'drawn upon' by individuals as implicitly implemented by them. They are socially inculcated and socially differentiated conditions of action and interaction, conditions which are, to some extent, fulfilled and reproduced every time that an individual acts – e.g. utters an expression, makes a gesture, acquires and consumes food, dresses himself or herself and prepares his or her body for presentation to others. But in implementing schemata, and in drawing upon rules and conventions of various kinds, individuals also extend and adapt these schemata and rules. Every application involves responding to circumstances which are, in some respects, new. Hence the application of rules and schemata cannot be understood as a mechanical operation, as if actions were rigidly determined by them. Rather, the application of rules and schemata is a creative process which often involves some degree of selection and judgement, and in which the rules and schemata may be modified and transformed in the very process of application.

We can distinguish fields of interaction, and the various kinds of resources, rules and schemata characteristic of them, from what may be called *social institutions*. Social institutions may be understood as specific and relatively stable clusters of rules and resources, together with the social relations that are established by them and within them. A particular enterprise, such as the Ford Motor Company, or a particular organization, such as the BBC, is an institution in this sense. Enterprises and organizations like these are characterized by certain kinds and quantities of resources, and certain rules, conventions and flexible schemata which govern the use of resources and the conduct of individuals within the organization. They are also typically characterized by hierarchical relations between individuals, or between the positions that they occupy. Some of the characteristics of institutions may be formalized by being given an explicit status in law, or by being brought into line with laws that already exist (e.g. the legal statutes which govern the activities of the BBC). For analytical purposes we can distinguish between *specific* institutions, like the Ford Motor Company or the BBC, and what we could call *generic* or *sedimented* institutions. By the latter I mean the configurational form of specific institutions, a form which can be abstracted from specific institutions and which persists through the ebb and flow of particular organizations. So, for example, the Ford Motor Company is one instance of a large-scale productive enterprise, of which numerous other examples can be found, and the BBC is one instance of a broadcasting institution. In studying institutions we may be concerned as much with the generic features of sedimented institutions, features which highlight broad patterns or trends, as we are with the specific features of particular organizations. Social institutions can be seen as constellations of rules, resources and relations which are situated within, and at the same time create, fields of interaction. When a specific institution is set up, it gives shape to pre-existing fields of interaction, and at the same time it creates a new set of positions and possible trajectories. For most individuals in modern societies, the very idea of a 'career' is inseparable from the existence of institutions which seek, as part of their own goal-orientated activity, to recruit individuals and assign them to an institutionally based life trajectory. While social institutions are an integral part of fields of interaction, they are not co-extensive with the latter. There are many actions and interactions which take place within fields but outside of specific institutions – for example, a casual encounter between acquaintances in the street. But the fact that many actions and interactions take place outside of specific institutions does not imply, of course, that these actions and interactions are unaffected by power and resources, rules and schemata. For all action and interaction involves the implementation of social conditions which are characteristic of the fields within which they take place.

So far I have been concerned to distinguish fields of interaction from social institutions, and to clarify the constituents of each. I now want to draw a further distinction between fields of interaction and social institutions on the one hand, and what I shall call *social structure* on the other. Here I shall use the term 'social structure' to refer to the relatively stable asymmetries and differentials which characterize fields of interaction and social institutions. To say that a field of interaction or social institution is 'structured', in this sense, is to say that it is characterized by relatively stable asymmetries and differentials in terms of the distribution of, and access to, resources of various kinds, power, opportunities and life chances. To analyse the social structure of a field or institution is to determine the asymmetries and differentials that are relatively stable – that is, systematic and likely to endure – and to try to ascertain the criteria, categories and principles which underlie them. Hence the analysis of social structure involves in part the positing of categories and distinctions which may help to organize and illuminate the evidence of systematic asymmetries and differentials. In this way we can seek to determine some of the factors which structure fields of interaction and the institutions located within them. So, for instance, the field of higher education in Britain or the United States is characterized by a set of specific institutions (specific universities, colleges, polytechnics, etc., in determinate relations to one another) which give shape to this field; and, like the field as a whole, these institutions are structured by the systematic asymmetries and differentials (e.g. those between men and women, between white and black, between working-class and middle-class youths, etc.) which constitute in part the social structure of the field.

Figure 3.1 summarizes the key terms in the conceptual framework I have sketched so far. The concepts on the left – i.e. spatio-temporal settings, fields of interaction, social institutions, social structure – refer to different aspects of social contexts and define different levels of analysis. They enable us to grasp the social features of the contexts within which individuals act and interact. These features are not merely the elements of an environment within which action takes place, but are *constitutive of action and interaction*, in the sense that individuals routinely and necessarily draw upon, implement and employ the various aspects of social contexts in the course of acting and interacting with one another. Contextual features are not simply restrictive and limiting: they are also productive and enabling.[34] They do circumscribe the range of possible action, defining some courses as more appropriate or

Spatio-temporal settings

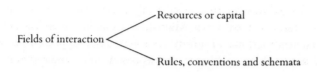

Social institutions: Relatively stable clusters of rules, resources and relations

Social structure: Relatively stable asymmetries and differentials

Figure 3.1 Typical Characteristics of Social Contexts

more feasible than others and ensuring that resources and opportunities are distributed unevenly. But they also *make possible* the actions and interactions which take place in everyday life, constituting the social conditions upon which these actions and interactions necessarily depend.

This analysis provides a backcloth against which we can consider what is involved in the exercise of *power*. In the most general sense, 'power' is the ability to act in pursuit of one's aims and interests: an individual has the *power to act*, the power to intervene in the sequence of events and to alter their course. In so acting, an individual draws upon and employs the resources available to him or her. Hence the ability to act in pursuit of one's aims and interests is dependent on one's position within a field or institution. 'Power', analysed at the level of a field or institution, is a capacity which *enables* or *empowers* some individuals to make decisions, pursue ends or realize interests; it empowers them in such a way that, without the capacity endowed by their position within a field or institution, they would not have been able to carry out the relevant course. Individuals endowed with varying capacities of this kind, and hence with varying degrees of power, may stand in determinate social relations with one another. When established relations of power are *systematically asymmetrical*, then the situation may be described as one of *domination*. Relations of power are 'systematically asymmetrical' when particular individuals or groups of individuals are endowed with power in a durable way which excludes, and to some significant degree remains inaccessible to, other individuals or groups of individuals, irrespective of the basis upon which such exclusion is carried out. In such cases we can speak of 'dominant' and 'subordinate' individuals or groups, as well as those individuals or groups which, by virtue of their partial access to resources, occupy intermediate positions in a field.

Among the instances of domination which are particularly important are those which are linked to structural features that recur from one context to another. The strength of traditional Marxist analysis lay in its concern to demonstrate that domination and subordination in past and present societies was structured in just this way: that is, it was based on a fundamental class division which recurs from one context to another, a division which, in modern capitalist societies, assumes the form of the capital/wage-labour relation. There can be no doubt that class relations and divisions remain an important basis of domination and subordination in modern societies: classes and class conflict have by no means disappeared from the social landscape of the late twentieth century. But it would be a serious mistake to assume that the relation between classes is the only important basis of domination and subordination in modern societies, or that it is the most important in all circumstances. The overemphasis on class relations – an overemphasis which is evident in Marx's work as well as that of some of his followers – may obscure or misrepresent those forms of domination and subordination which are not based on class division and cannot be reduced to it. A satisfactory analysis of domination and subordination in modern societies would – without minimizing the importance of class – have to give attention to other equally fundamental divisions, such as those between the sexes, between ethnic groups and between nation-states.

The various characteristics of social contexts are constitutive not only of action and interaction, but also of the production and reception of symbolic forms. Like action more generally, the production of symbolic forms involves the use of available resources, and the implementation of rules and schemata of various kinds, by an individual or individuals situated at a certain position or positions within a field or institution. An individual employs resources, draws on rules and implements schemata in order to produce a symbolic form for a particular recipient or range of potential recipients; and the anticipated reception of the form comprises part of the conditions of its production. The position occupied by an individual in a field or institution, and the anticipated reception of a symbolic form by the individuals to whom it is addressed, are social conditions of production which mould the symbolic form produced. So, for instance, a linguistic utterance may bear the traces – in terms of accent, style, words employed and mode of delivery – of the socially structured position of the speaker. An utterance may also bear the traces of its anticipated reception by the individuals to whom it is addressed, as when an adult modifies the tone of an utterance addressed to a child. It is not difficult to find other examples of the ways in which the anticipated reception of symbolic forms is routinely incorporated into their conditions of production. An artist may modify the style of his or her work with a view to reaching a certain clientele; an author may modify the content of a book in the hope of appealing to a certain readership (or in the hope of not offending another); and a television producer may alter a programme in the light of expectations about the nature and size of the audience.

If the characteristics of social contexts are constitutive of the production of symbolic forms, they are also constitutive of the ways in which symbolic forms are received and understood. Symbolic forms are received by individuals who are situated in specific social–historical contexts, and the social characteristics of these contexts mould the ways in which the forms are received, understood and valued by them. The process of reception is not a passive process of assimilation; rather, it is a creative process of interpretation and evaluation in which the meaning of a symbolic form is actively constituted and reconstituted. Individuals do not passively absorb symbolic forms but creatively and actively *make sense of them*, and thereby produce meaning in the very process of reception. Even a relatively simple utterance, exchanged between friends in a casual encounter, is typically understood in relation to a continuing history of which this encounter is part. In receiving and interpreting symbolic forms, individuals draw upon the resources, rules and schemata which are available to them. Hence the ways in which symbolic forms are understood, and the ways in which they are valued and appraised, may differ from one individual to another, depending on the positions which they occupy in socially structured fields or institutions. These variations are particularly evident in the case of symbolic forms – such as fine art and classical music – whose interpretation and appreciation require a specialized set of conventions which are traditionally restricted to certain privileged sectors of the population.

In receiving and interpreting symbolic forms, individuals are involved in an ongoing process of constituting and reconstituting meaning, and this process is typically part of what may be called *the symbolic reproduction of social contexts*. The meaning that is conveyed by symbolic forms and reconstituted in the course of reception may serve to sustain and reproduce the contexts of production and reception. That is, the meaning of symbolic forms, as received and understood by recipients, may serve in various ways to maintain the structured social relations characteristic of the contexts within which the symbolic forms were produced and/or received. Figure 3.2 illustrates this process. The symbolic reproduction of social contexts is a particular kind of social reproduction: it is social reproduction mediated through the everyday understanding of symbolic forms. It is not the only kind of social

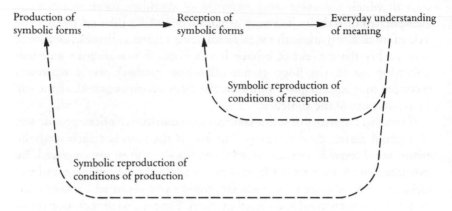

Figure 3.2 The Symbolic Reproduction of Social Contexts

reproduction, nor even necessarily the most important. Social relations are also typically reproduced through the use or threatened use of force, as well as through the sheer routinization of everyday life. But the symbolic reproduction of social contexts is an important phenomenon worthy of analysis in its own right. It is at this point that our discussion of symbolic forms rejoins the problem of ideology. For the study of ideology, as I defined this notion in chapter 1, is the study of the ways in which the meaning mobilized by symbolic forms serves, in specific circumstances, to establish, sustain and reproduce social relations which are systematically asymmetrical in terms of power. At a later stage I shall consider in more detail what is involved in the study of ideology.

The Valorization of Symbolic Forms

One consequence of the contextualization of symbolic forms is, as I mentioned earlier, that they are frequently subjected to complex processes of valuation, evaluation and conflict. They are the objects, in other words, of what I shall call *processes of valorization*. We can distinguish between two principal types of valorization which are of particular importance. The first type is what we can call 'symbolic valorization': it is the process through which symbolic forms are ascribed a certain 'symbolic value' by the individuals who produce and receive them. Symbolic value is the value that objects have by virtue of the ways in which, and the extent to which, they are *esteemed by* the individuals who produce and receive them – that is, praised or denounced, cherished or despised by these individuals. The ascription of symbolic value can be distinguished from what we may call 'economic valorization'. Economic valorization is the process through which symbolic forms are ascribed a certain 'economic value', that is, a value for which they could be exchanged in a market. Through the process of economic valorization, symbolic forms are constituted as *commodities*; they become objects which can be bought and sold on a market for a price. I shall refer to commodified symbolic forms as 'symbolic goods'. In the following chapter I shall trace the historical process through which symbolic forms became increasingly commodified in this sense, an historical process which is an essential part of the emergence and development of mass communication.

Both types of valorization are commonly accompanied by distinctive forms of conflict. Symbolic forms may be ascribed different degrees of symbolic value by the individuals who produce and receive them, in such a way that an object which is praised by some may be denounced or despised by others. We can describe this as a *conflict of symbolic valuation*. Such conflicts always take place within a structured social context which is characterized by asymmetries and differentials of various kinds. Hence the symbolic valuations offered by different individuals who are differentially situated are rarely of equal status. Some valuations carry more weight than others, by virtue of the individual who offers them and the position from which he or she speaks; and some individuals are in a better position than others to offer valuations and, if need be, to impose them. The words of the Director of the Tate Gallery, speaking on BBC television about the work of a new artist, are likely to carry more weight than the comments of a passer-by in the street. In acquiring symbolic value, a work may acquire a degree of legitimacy – that is, it may be recognized as legitimate not only by those who are well positioned to ascribe symbolic value, but also by those who recognize and respect the position of those who ascribe it. To the extent that a work is recognized as legitimate, the producer of the work is endowed with honour, prestige or respect. He or she is recognized as an artist, a writer, a film director, a man or woman of style or taste. But this process of valorization is rarely consensual or conflict-free. The continuing controversies surrounding the work of 'pop artists' like Andy Warhol, or the varying and often barbed reviews of books and films which can be found in newspapers, journals and literary supplements, are ample testimony to the conflictual character of symbolic valorization.

The process of economic valorization is also commonly accompanied by conflict. Symbolic goods may be economically valued in differing degrees by different individuals, in the sense that some individuals may regard them as being worth more or worth less than what others regard them as being worth. We can describe this kind of conflict as a *conflict of economic valuation*. Such conflicts always take place in structured social contexts in which some individuals may be able and willing to pay more than others in order to acquire or control symbolic goods. The bidding and counter-bidding which takes place in the auction of works of art offers a vivid, if somewhat exceptional, example of conflicts of economic valuation – vivid because the conflicting valuations are expressed openly and directly in competition with one another, exceptional because most conflicts of economic valuation do not take place within a clearly defined space and a strictly regulated temporal framework in which individuals or their proxies engage in open competition for the acquisition of symbolic goods. With the growing commodification of symbolic forms and their incorporation into institutions of mass communication, most conflicts of economic valuation take place within an institutional framework comprised of media organizations. These organizations are routinely concerned with the economic valorization of symbolic forms and with the resolution of conflicts of economic valuation. So, for instance, in producing a symbolic good such as a book, a publishing organization is transforming a symbolic form into a commodity and offering it for exchange in a market. Depending on the anticipated sales of the book, the publisher will generally ascribe a certain economic value to the symbolic form, an ascription which may, and frequently does, differ from the ascriptions of others, such as authors and agents. Such conflicts of economic valuation are routinely confronted and resolved as part of the everyday operation of media organizations.

Although we can distinguish analytically between symbolic and economic valorization, and between the forms of conflict typically associated with them, in actual circumstances these forms of valorization and conflict frequently overlap in complex ways. In some cases, the acquisition of symbolic value, whether ascribed by others or derived from the accumulated prestige of the producer, may increase the economic value of a symbolic good. This direct relation between symbolic value and economic value is evident, for instance, in the sale of paintings by well-known artists, or in the sale of rights for books or films by well-known authors or directors. In other cases, however, the acquisition of symbolic value may not significantly increase the economic value of a symbolic good, and may even depress its economic value. In certain fields of symbolic production and exchange, the symbolic value of a good may be inversely related to its economic value, in the sense that, the less 'commercial' it is, the more worthy it is seen to be. Thus some forms of opera and ballet, which depend heavily on grants and subsidies from public funds, may be viewed by some people as among the highest forms of art; and the lower their economic value, the more they may be ascribed symbolic value, since they can be seen as increasingly untainted by commercial interests. Similarly, academics who write books which are highly successful in commercial terms may be regarded with suspicion by their colleagues, who may construe the commercial success of a work as an indication of its lack of intellectual worth.

The individuals involved in the production and reception of symbolic forms are generally aware of the fact that symbolic forms can be subjected to processes of valorization, and they may pursue strategies orientated towards the augmentation or reduction of symbolic or economic value. The pursuit of such strategies may be an explicit aim of individuals – as, for example, when an individual expressly seeks to ridicule or put down another, or openly competes to win a prestigious prize. But the pursuit of such strategies may also be an implicit aim, a goal which is sought but not acknowledged, an outcome which is desired but not expressly or openly pursued. An individual who seeks to gain recognition among colleagues may, if this is his or her *avowed* aim, be regarded as opportunistic. The strategies pursued by individuals may be orientated towards the augmentation or reduction of symbolic value, towards the augmentation or reduction of economic value, or towards a combination of the two. The latter involves what can be described as *cross-valorization* – that is, the use of symbolic value as a means of increasing or decreasing economic value, and vice versa. Cross-valorization is an essential part of the strategy pursued by advertisers when they use well-known film stars, pop stars or public figures as a means of promoting particular products: the aim is to increase sales by association, to increase economic value by association with a figure of high symbolic value, even though there is no necessary connection between the two. Cross-valorization is also part of the strategy pursued by individuals when they seek to convert their recognition in a field into a more lucrative job, or when they publicly attack or malign someone in an attempt to deprive him or her of promotion or of a job. Strategies of cross-valorization thus overlap with what I referred to earlier as strategies of capital conversion, whereby individuals seek to convert one kind of capital into another, and to reconvert it at a later stage in the life cycle, in order to preserve or improve their overall social position.

The strategies pursued by individuals are linked to the positions they occupy within particular fields of interaction. The kinds of strategies typically pursued by individuals, and their capacity to succeed in them, depend on the resources available to them and their relation to other individuals in the field. I shall illustrate this point by focusing on some of the strategies that individuals typically pursue in ascribing symbolic value. I shall distinguish several typical *strategies of symbolic valuation* and show how they are linked to different positions in a field. In distinguishing these typical strategies, I do not want to suggest that these are the only courses open to individuals, nor that these are the courses always pursued by individuals located in the positions concerned. On the contrary, individuals are constantly involved in devising new strategies, in finding new ways to pursue their aims or to prevent others from pursuing theirs, and these strategies can be fully analysed only by considering specific cases. Nevertheless, we can identify certain typical strategies of symbolic valuation and show how they may be linked to different positions in a field. In doing so I shall draw upon studies of a more detailed kind by Bourdieu and others, and I shall highlight some relations which could, in turn, help to guide research of a more concrete character. Table 3.1 summarizes some of these typical strategies and their links to different positions in a field.

Table 3.1
Some typical strategies of symbolic valuation

Positions within a field of interaction	Strategies of symbolic valuation
Dominant	Distinction
	Derision
	Condescension
Intermediate	Moderation
	Pretension
	Devaluation
Subordinate	Practicality
	Respectful resignation
	Rejection

Individuals who occupy dominant positions within a field of interaction are those who are positively endowed with, or who have privileged access to, resources or capital of various kinds. In producing and appraising symbolic forms, individuals in dominant positions typically pursue a strategy of *distinction*, in the sense that they seek to distinguish themselves from individuals or groups who occupy positions subordinate to them.[35] Thus they may attribute high symbolic value to goods which are scarce or expensive (or both) and which are therefore largely inaccessible to individuals less well endowed with economic capital. High symbolic value may be accorded, for instance, to classical works of art, which can be fully appreciated only by individuals of educated taste and considerable wealth. Similarly, in the realm of *haute couture*, the most exclusive brand names and the most elegant styles are a mark of distinction for those who can afford to display them. Individuals in dominant positions may also seek to distinguish themselves by pursuing a strategy of *derision*: that is, by regarding the symbolic forms produced by those below them as brash, gauche, immature or unrefined. This attitude was evident among the courtly aristocracy of eighteenth-century Europe, who sought to protect their privileges by regarding the conduct of the rising bourgeois strata as vulgar and uncontrolled.[36] A more subtle variant of the latter strategy is *condescension*. By praising symbolic forms in a way which puts down their producers and reminds them of their subordinate position, condescension enables individuals in dominant positions to reaffirm their dominance without openly declaring it.

Intermediate positions within a field are those which offer access to one kind of capital but not another, or which offer access to different kinds of capital but in quantities which are more limited than those available to dominant individuals or groups. An intermediate position may be characterized by a large quantity of economic capital but a low quantity of cultural capital (the *nouveaux riches*), or by a low quantity of economic capital and a large quantity of cultural capital (the intelligentsia or the *avant-garde*), or by moderate quantities of both (the rising bourgeois strata of eighteenth- and nineteenth-century Europe). The strategies of symbolic valuation pursued by individuals in intermediate positions are often characterized by *moderation*: individuals positively value those goods which they know to be within their reach; and, as individuals whose futures may not be entirely secure, they may value most those symbolic forms which enable them to employ their cultural capital while preserving their limited economic resources. Thus, in the sphere of fashion, they may seek maximum style with minimum expense, searching for good buys and making the most of annual or bi-annual sales. But individuals in intermediate positions may also be orientated towards dominant positions, producing symbolic forms *as if* they were the products of dominant individuals or groups, or appraising them *as if* they were being appraised by the latter. Individuals in intermediate positions may thus pursue a strategy of *pretension*, pretending to be what they are not and seeking thereby to assimilate themselves to positions which are superior to their own. For example, individuals in intermediate positions may adopt the accent, vocabulary and speech mannerisms of dominant individuals and groups, producing symbolic forms which display dominant characteristics and which attest to their ambition, their insecurity or both.[37]

In some circumstances, however, individuals in intermediate positions may pursue a quite different strategy towards dominant individuals or groups, seeking to *devalue* or debunk the symbolic forms produced by them. Rather than reproducing the valuations of dominant individuals and groups in order to assimilate themselves to dominant positions, they may denounce the symbolic forms produced by dominant individuals and groups in an attempt to elevate themselves above these positions. Thus the rising bourgeoisie of eighteenth- and nineteenth-century Europe sometimes portrayed the old aristocracy as extravagant, degenerate and irresponsible, as incapable of organizing economic and political affairs and as superficial in its social life.[38] Once the bourgeoisie had succeeded in displacing the old aristocracy and creating new positions of dominance, the principal site of its symbolic warfare shifted to the boundaries that separated it from the groups below it, from the groups least endowed with economic and cultural capital and, subsequently, from the new emerging middle strata.

Subordinate positions within a field are those which offer access to the smallest quantities of capital of differing kinds. The individuals in these positions are those who are least endowed with resources and whose opportunities are most restricted. The strategies of symbolic valuation pursued by individuals in subordinate positions are typically characterized by *practicality*: as individuals who are more preoccupied than others with the necessities of survival, they may ascribe more value than others do to objects which are practical in design and functional in everyday life.[39] Thus they may value clothing which is practical, durable and inexpensive, 'good value for money'; and they may prefer interior designs which are functional and easy to maintain. The positive valuation of practical objects may go hand in hand with a *respectful resignation* concerning the symbolic forms produced by individuals who occupy superior positions in a field. This strategy is one of respect in the sense that the forms produced by individuals occupying superior positions are regarded *as superior*, that is, as worthy of respect; but it is a strategy of resignation in so far as the superiority of these forms, and hence the inferiority of one's own products, is accepted as inevitable. Thus individuals in subordinate positions may acknowledge classical works of art or literature as great works, while at the same time accepting that they are not the kind of works which they would wish to (or be able to) consume and enjoy. They may value symbolic forms which are practical, accessible and relatively cheap, while at the same time acknowledging that these forms are inferior to certain forms which, while more valuable, are not for them. In contrast with this strategy of respectful resignation, individuals in subordinate positions may pursue various strategies of *rejection*. They may reject or ridicule the symbolic forms produced by individuals in superior positions, in the way, for example, that working-class boys may parody the language of authorities and may reject educational activities and 'mental work' as 'effeminate'.[40] In so doing, individuals in subordinate positions may not necessarily be seeking to elevate themselves above the positions of their superiors (as those pursuing a strategy of devaluation are typically seeking to do); given their position within the field, to try to raise themselves in this way may not be a realistic aim. But by rejecting the symbolic forms produced by their superiors, individuals in subordinate positions may find a way of affirming the value of their own products and activities without fundamentally disrupting the unequal distribution of resources characteristic of the field.

So far I have been examining some typical strategies of symbolic valuation, with the aim of highlighting the relations between these strategies and the positions of individuals within a field of interaction. But I have not considered the ways in which such strategies may be affected by the development of institutions which are concerned in part with the ascription and renewal of symbolic value (e.g. schools, universities, museums, etc.) or by the development of institutions which are orientated essentially towards the economic valorization of symbolic forms (art galleries, institutions of mass communication, etc.). The development of such institutions is accompanied by the accumulation of resources, the fixation of positions of valuation and the differentiation of cultural spheres. Particular institutions emerge in which resources of various kinds are amassed – not only economic capital, but also accumulated forms of knowledge and prestige. By virtue of their location within these institutions, individuals assume a position of valuation which confers a certain authority on the valuations they offer. They speak *as* a professor of a university, *as* a director of a museum, *as* a correspondent for a television network, and as such the valuations they offer will carry an authority derived from the institution which they represent. The development of institutions is also accompanied by the differentiation of cultural spheres in the sense that, with the emergence of institutions concerned with producing, transmitting and accumulating symbolic forms, different types of symbolic form emerge in relation to one another, differentiated in terms of their modes of production, transmission and reception and in terms of the symbolic and economic value accorded to them. Thus, within the domain of written texts, the emergence and perpetuation of a canon of great literature is linked to the development of an educational system in which practices of literary criticism are institutionalized. These institutionalized practices operate as a selective filter for the extraction of certain works from the extensive domain of written texts, and for the constitution of these works as 'literature'.[41] The emergence of a sphere of 'popular literature' was the product both of these mechanisms of exclusion, through which popular literature was constituted as literature's 'other', and of the development of institutions of mass communication and mass education, which created the conditions for the large-scale production and widespread circulation of symbolic forms.

In this chapter I have been concerned primarily to develop a distinctive conception of culture which emphasizes the meaningful constitution and social contextualization of symbolic forms. I have followed Geertz's injunction to think of cultural analysis as the study of the symbolic character of social life; but I have argued that this orientation must be conjoined with a systematic account of the ways in which symbolic forms are embedded in structured social contexts. To grasp the meaningful constitution of symbolic forms we must examine the intentional, conventional, structural and referential aspects of symbolic forms. The social contextualization of symbolic forms requires us to pay attention to certain social aspects of contexts (spatio-temporal aspects, the distribution of resources within fields of interaction, etc.), as well as to certain processes of valorization and to what I shall call 'modalities of cultural transmission'.

The account presented in this chapter provides us with a framework for analysing the emergence and development of mass communication. For the emergence of mass communication may be understood as the appearance, in late fifteenth- and early sixteenth-century Europe, of a range of institutions concerned with the economic valorization of symbolic forms and with their extended circulation in time and space. With the rapid development of these institutions and the exploitation of new technical devices, the production and circulation of symbolic forms was increasingly mediated by the institutions and mechanisms of mass communication. This process of the mediazation of culture was pervasive and irreversible. It is a process that accompanied the rise of modern societies, that partially constituted these societies and that defined them, in part, as modern. And it is a process that continues to take place around us and to transform the world in which we live today.

4

Cultural Transmission and Mass Communication

The Development of the Media Industries

The production and circulation of symbolic forms in modern societies is inseparable from the activities of the media industries. The role of media institutions is so fundamental, and their products are such pervasive features of everyday life, that it is difficult today to imagine what it would be like to live in a world without books and newspapers, without radio and television, and without the countless other media through which symbolic forms are routinely and continuously presented to us. Day by day, week by week, newspapers, radio and television present us with a steady flow of words and images, information and ideas, concerning events which take place beyond our immediate social milieu. The figures who feature in films and television programmes become common points of reference for millions of individuals who may never interact with one another, but who share, by virtue of their participation in a mediated culture, a common experience and a collective memory. Even those forms of entertainment which have existed for many centuries, such as popular music and competitive sports, are today interwoven with the media of mass communication. Pop music, sports and other activities are largely sustained by the media industries, which are involved not merely in the transmission and financial support of pre-existing cultural forms, but also in the active transformation of these forms.

The media industries have not always played such a fundamental role. The emergence and development of these industries was a specific historical process that accompanied the rise of modern societies. The origins of mass communication can be traced back to the late fifteenth century, when the techniques associated with Gutenberg's printing press were taken up by a variety of institutions in the major trading centres of Europe and exploited for the purposes of producing multiple copies of manuscripts and texts. This was the beginning of a series of developments which, from the sixteenth century to the present day, was to transform radically the ways in which symbolic forms were produced, transmitted and received by individuals in the course of their everyday lives. It is this series of developments which underlie what I call the mediazation of modern culture. This is a process which has gone hand-in-hand with the expansion of industrial capitalism and with the formation of the modern nation-state system. Together these processes are constitutive of the modern industrial societies of the West. They are also processes which have profoundly affected the development of societies elsewhere in the world, societies which in the past have been interwoven to varying degrees with one another, and which are becoming increasingly interwoven today. The growing interconnection of societies in the contemporary world is an outcome of the very processes – including the mediazation of modern culture – which have shaped social development since the early modern period.

In this chapter I want to examine the emergence and development of the media industries. I shall begin from the conception of culture elaborated in the previous chapter. The circulation of symbolic forms in specific social-historical contexts involves a series of characteristics which I have not yet examined in any detail. I shall treat these characteristics as different aspects of *cultural transmission* – that is, the process by which symbolic forms are transmitted from producers to receivers. By focusing on the process of cultural transmission, we can highlight a series of characteristics which are crucial for understanding the nature and development of mass communication. On the basis of this preliminary conceptual analysis, I shall then trace the development of some of the principal kinds of technical media of cultural transmission, and some of the major institutional apparatuses within which these media have been deployed. I shall discuss the significance of writing and the introduction of technical media for the fixation of written messages, giving particular attention to the emergence of the printing industry in Europe and to the appearance of mass circulation newspapers in the nineteenth and twentieth centuries. Next I shall discuss the emergence of broadcasting and the development of broadcasting institutions in Britain and the USA. In the final two sections of the chapter I shall examine some recent trends in the media industries and consider the social impact of new communication technologies.

Aspects of Cultural Transmission

Symbolic forms are social phenomena: a symbolic form that is received only by the very same individual who produced it is the exception rather than the rule. The exchange of symbolic forms between producers and receivers generally involves a series of characteristics that we can analyse under the heading of cultural transmission. I shall distinguish three aspects of cultural transmission: (1) the *technical medium* of transmission, (2) the *institutional apparatus* of transmission, and (3) the *space-time distanciation* involved in transmission. The exchange of symbolic forms typically involves each of these aspects, in varying ways and degrees. With the emergence and development of mass communication, these aspects assume new forms and acquire a new significance. They become combined in specific ways for the production, commodification and extended circulation of symbolic forms. I shall refer to these specific combinations as 'modalities of cultural transmission'. What is commonly regarded as a particular medium – such as newspapers or television – can be conceptualized more rigorously as a specific modality of cultural transmission which combines, in a distinctive way, a technical medium, an institutional apparatus and a certain kind of space–time distanciation. Let me consider each of these aspects in turn.

1 The technical medium of transmission is the material substratum of a symbolic form, that is, the material components with which, and by virtue of which, a symbolic form is produced and transmitted. These components vary enormously, of course, from the material conditions of face-to-face conversation to the electronic systems of audio amplification and diffusion, from stone and chisel to paper and printing press. I shall discuss some of these components later in the chapter. Here I want to focus on some of the general attributes of technical media, with a view to highlighting those features that are of particular importance for the development of mass communication. One attribute of the technical medium is that it allows for a certain degree of *fixation* with regard to the symbolic form being transmitted. The degree of fixation varies from one substratum to another. In the case of conversation, including conversation transmitted by technical media such as loudspeakers or telephones, the degree of fixation may be very low or non-existent; any fixation that does occur may be dependent on the faculty of memory, or on the inculcation of routine or ritualized practices, rather than on any distinctive properties of the technical medium as such. In the cases of writing, engraving, painting, filming, recording, etc., there may be a relatively high degree of fixation, depending on the specific medium employed – a message written in stone, for example, will be more durable than one written on parchment or paper. By virtue of this fixation of symbolic forms, technical media may be regarded as differing kinds of *information storage mechanisms*. That is, they have differing capacities to store information or, more generally, 'meaningful content', and to allow this information or meaningful content to be preserved for subsequent use. The storage capacity of technical media enables them to be employed as a

resource for the exercise of power, since they may confer restricted access to information that can be used by individuals for the pursuit of particular interests or aims.

A second attribute of the technical medium is that it allows for a certain degree of *reproduction* of a symbolic form. In the case of writing, the development of the printing press was decisive in this regard, in that it allowed written messages to be reproduced on a scale that had not been possible previously. Similarly, the development of lithography, photography and the gramophone were significant not only because they allowed visual and acoustic phenomena to be fixed in a durable medium, but also because they fixed these phenomena in a form that could in principle be reproduced. The reproducibility of symbolic forms is one of the key characteristics that underlies the commercial exploitation of technical media by institutions of mass communication, and the commodification of symbolic forms which these institutions pursue and promote. In order to exploit technical media effectively, commercial organizations must develop ways to control the reproduction of symbolic forms – for example, by increasing their capacity to reproduce symbolic forms while restricting, through the protection of copyright or other means, the capacity of other organizations to do the same. With the emergence of technical media which allow symbolic forms to be reproduced and commodified on a large scale, the idea of an 'original' or 'genuine' work or symbolic form acquires a new significance. The original or genuine work is that which is not reproduced; it is, of course, reproducible, but the reproduction is not the same as the original and generally commands less value on the market of symbolic goods.[1] The eighteenth- and nineteenth-century disputes over the artistic value of engraving and photography are indicative of a more fundamental conflict to control the process of economic valorization at a time when the emergence of new technical media were making possible the mass reproduction of symbolic forms.[2]

A third attribute of the technical medium concerns the nature and extent of the *participation* that it allows for, and requires of, the individuals who employ the medium. Different media require individuals to utilize different skills, faculties and resources in order to encode and decode messages in the medium concerned. The skills, faculties and resources required in order to write and read a personal letter, for example, are different from those involved in writing and reading a literary text, and these in turn are different from those involved in scripting, producing, transmitting and watching a television programme. Consider for a moment some of the differences between reading a literary text and watching a television programme. An individual reading can move back and forth between chapters, re-reading passages or jumping forward to get a sense of where the story is going. But the effort of reading is considerable, requiring concentration over an extended period of time; and a difficult text may be particularly demanding for individuals who have not acquired the cultural capital typically employed in the appreciation of literary works. An individual watching a television programme, by contrast, has no control over the time and pace of watching (unless, of course, he or she is equipped with a video recorder, in which case the technical medium itself has been modified). The linguistic component of the programme is generally spoken in a conversational style, rather than inscribed in a literary form, and it is generally integrated with a visual component, so that the symbols available to the subject are complex audio-visual constructions. A programme is commonly watched in a social context, with friends or members of a family, and may be watched with differing degrees of attentiveness, from intense involvement to a dim awareness of the fact that the television is on in the background and a particular programme is showing. This brief comparison amply illustrates the fact that different technical media are linked to different skills, faculties and resources, in such a way that a technical medium cannot be fully dissociated from the social contexts in which it is employed by individuals involved in the encoding and decoding of symbolic forms.

2 In addition to the technical medium, the exchange of symbolic forms often involves an institutional apparatus of transmission. By 'institutional apparatus' I mean a determinate set of institutional arrangements within which the technical medium is deployed and the individuals involved in encoding and decoding symbolic forms are embedded. These arrangements are characterized by rules, resources and relations of various kinds; they typically involve hierarchical relations of power between individuals occupying institutionalized positions. By virtue of such arrangements, individuals are endowed with differing degrees of control over the process of cultural transmission. Consider, for example, some of the institutional arrangements involved in the transmission of a literary text. Among the specific institutions which may be relevant to this process are the publishing organization, the distribution network, media institutions and the educational system. The decision to publish a literary text, and hence to make it available as a symbolic good, lies ultimately with the publishing organization, which is able to employ accumulated resources in order to produce and promote the book. However, the extent to which a text is effectively transmitted also depends on the ways in which it is taken up and diffused by other institutions, such as those concerned with sales and distribution (bookshops, book clubs, etc.), those concerned with the

production of newspapers or journals in which the text may be featured or reviewed, and those concerned with teaching literature and literary skills. These various institutions constitute what I shall describe as the *channels of selective diffusion* of symbolic forms, that is, the set of institutional arrangements through which symbolic forms are circulated, in differing ways and to differing extents, in the social world. With the commodification of symbolic forms, the channels of selective diffusion acquire a key role in the process of economic valorization, as they become the mechanism through which symbolic goods are exchanged in the market.

The institutional apparatus of transmission constitutes not only the channels of selective diffusion: it also constitutes a framework within which symbolic forms can be used in, and are affected by, the exercise of power. By virtue of the storage capacity of technical media, symbolic forms can be employed as a resource in the pursuit of particular interests and aims – in the way, for instance, that recorded information about a population may be used by state officials to regulate and control the population. Moreover, the diffusion of symbolic forms is itself a process which can be regulated and controlled in various ways. In order to bring out these aspects of the interplay between symbolic forms and power, I shall say that the institutional apparatus of transmission constitutes a set of *mechanisms for the restricted implementation* of symbolic forms. When symbolic forms involve the storage of information which may be useful in commercial transactions, or which may be perceived as beneficial or harmful to particular individuals or organizations, then the mechanisms for restricted implementation assume a major role and may serve to limit or deflect the diffusion of symbolic forms. Similarly, the history of the regulation of mass communication can be understood as the history of attempts by state officials to construct and impose mechanisms for the restricted implementation of symbolic forms. By suppressing information, monitoring output, controlling access to technical media and punishing offenders, state officials have devised a variety of institutional mechanisms which circumscribe the flow of symbolic forms and, in some cases, link the restricted implementation of symbolic forms to the pursuit of overt political aims.

3 A third aspect of cultural transmission is what may be called the space–time distanciation involved in transmission. In discussing this aspect and relating it to other developments later in this chapter, I shall draw on the work of Harold Innis and Anthony Giddens, both of whom have emphasized the importance of space and time to social theory and to the analysis of systems of communication.[3] The transmission of a symbolic form necessarily involves the detachment of this form, to varying degrees, from the context of

its production: it is distanced from this context, both spatially and temporally, and inserted into new contexts which may be located at different times and places. We can use the term 'distanciation' to refer to this process of distancing.[4] The nature and extent of distanciation varies from one technical medium to another. In the case of ordinary conversation, unaided by electronic or other synthetic equipment, there is relatively little space-time distanciation. The conversation takes place in what can be called a *context of co-presence*; the availability of the symbolic form is limited to the participants of the conversation, or to individuals located in the immediate proximity, and the form will not endure beyond the transient moment of its utterance or the rapidly fading memory of its content. The supplementation of speech by certain technical media, such as loudspeakers, telephones or systems of radio broadcasting and reception, may facilitate spatial distanciation while preserving temporal co-presence: an utterance may be transmitted across vast distances in a way which is both virtually instantaneous and transient. Other technical media, such as the tape recorder, provide a way of fixing speech which makes temporal distanciation possible. The tape recorder generally operates in a context of spatial co-presence; but when coupled with other technical media, such as systems of radio broadcasting and reception, it may facilitate distanciation on both a temporal and a spatial plane.

When symbolic forms are transmitted beyond a context of co-presence, we may speak of the *extension of availability* of symbolic forms in time and space, where the nature and degree of availability-extension are dependent on both the technical medium of transmission and the institutional apparatus in which the medium and its users are embedded. Different media favour different kinds of availability-extension, although the degree to which they effectively extend availability depends also on the institutions involved in their deployment. Prior to the development of telecommunications, the extension of availability in space generally required the physical transportation of symbolic forms: with a few notable exceptions (e.g. semaphore), significant spatial distanciation could be achieved only by transporting symbolic forms from one place to another. Hence the media favouring the extension of availability in space tended to be relatively light and transportable, such as papyrus and paper. With the development of telecommunications, however, significant spatial distanciation could be secured without physically transporting symbolic forms, giving rise to new possibilities for cultural transmission and, therewith, for the exercise of power across spatial distances. The extension of availability in time generally requires the fixation of symbolic forms and it is therefore facilitated by media which allow a relatively high degree of fixation and which are relatively durable. Inscriptions in clay and stone are among the most durable, although written or printed texts and, more recently, symbolic forms stored on film, tape or disc also make possible the extension of availability in time and, therewith, the exercise of power across temporal distances. Some of the most important developments in new communication technologies, such as computer-based communication networks and direct broadcasting by satellite, may be understood in part as developments which extend availability in space and time while also giving the users of these technologies greater flexibility in, and control over, the conditions of their use.

I have distinguished three basic aspects of cultural transmission – the technical medium, the institutional apparatus, and space–time distanciation – and examined some of the attributes of each. These aspects and attributes are summarized in figure 4.1. In the historical development of technical media, these various aspects and attributes are combined in certain ways to form specific modalities of cultural transmission. The development of postal systems, of the publishing industry and the associated retail book trade, of the film industry and the associated cinema chains, of radio and television broadcasting networks and so on are examples of the emergence of modalities of cultural transmission. Each modality is based on certain technical media which endow the relevant symbolic forms with certain kinds of fixation and reproducibility. Each modality involves distinctive types of institutions – what I called, in the previous chapter, generic or

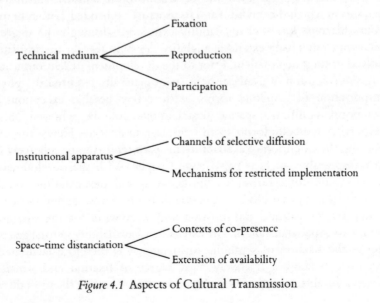

Figure 4.1 Aspects of Cultural Transmission

sedimented institutions – within which symbolic forms are produced and diffused. Each modality is associated with a certain degree of space–time distanciation which is made possible by the specific combination of technical medium and institutional apparatus. In the remainder of this chapter I shall examine, in a more concrete and historical way, the development of some modalities of cultural transmission. I shall begin by discussing some of the early technical media employed for the fixation of written messages, and then concentrate on the development of modalities associated with the rise of mass communication.

Writing, Printing and the Rise of the Trade in News

Among the key developments in the early history of cultural transmission were the invention of written scripts and the introduction of new technical media for the fixation of written messages. Prior to the invention of writing, most cultural transmission took place in contexts of co-presence, although some extension of availability was achieved through rudimentary forms of inscription such as pictography and through the production and trans-mission of material artefacts. It is generally accepted that the first complete system of writing was developed by the Sumerians in southern Mesopotamia around 3000 BC, and that a somewhat different system was developed, slightly later but probably independently, by the Ancient Egyptians of the Nile delta.[5] In both cases it seems likely that the development of written scripts was closely linked to the task of recording information relevant to the exchange of goods, the conduct of trade and the exercise of political and religious power. The evidence suggests that the earliest forms of Sumerian writing consisted of clay tags or labels which were fastened to objects and which served as markers for the identification of property. More extensive lists and inventories were inscribed on clay tablets and apparently employed for the purposes of administration. Ledgers were developed to keep records of agricultural surpluses, transported to and stored in the cities, and of manufactured goods sent to the countryside. The clay tablets were produced by marking moist clay and then baking them in fire to make them durable. During the second half of the third millenium, cuneiform writing began to appear. Cuneiform was produced with a triangular stylus which enabled the user to make a series of wedges in the tablet. By 2900 BC a script, involving around 600 signs, had been developed. A stratum of scribes emerged who kept records of commercial transactions and accounts of religious and civil life. Clay tablets were accumulated as local and durable records of the activities of relatively dispersed city-states.

The Sumerian system of writing was taken over and developed by the Semites, Akkadians and Assyrians and continued to be used into the first millenium BC. Recording information relevant to trade and administration remained a central concern, but writing was also used as a means of inscribing religious, scientific, legal and literary ideas. During the fifth century BC, cuneiform fell into disuse and eventually disappeared. It was replaced by the alphabetic script, which was probably invented during the second millenium BC and spread rapidly throughout the Near East and the Mediterranean. As cuneiform disappeared, clay tablets were gradually replaced by papyrus and parchment as technical media of transmission. Papyrus sheets were originally developed in Egypt around 2600 BC. They were made from a plant (*cyperus papyrus*) which grew in the Nile delta; the stems were transformed into writing material by being hammered together with a mallet and allowed to dry. As a material substratum for writing, it was much lighter than stone or clay; it could be transported more easily and it allowed a scribe to write much more rapidly. Papyrus became the principal medium of administration during the New Kingdom in Ancient Egypt, enabling officials to keep records of reserves as well as rents and tributes collected from peasants. Papyrus sheets were also exported throughout the eastern Mediterranean and, together with parchment, they eventually replaced entirely the use of clay tablets. Papyrus was used by both the Aramaeans and the Phoenicians who, from about the twelfth century BC, extended their influence throughout the Near East and the Aegean respectively. The Aramaeans and the Phoenicians were centrally involved in trade and both developed alphabetic scripts which were widely used during the second half of the first millenium BC and which had a major influence on subsequent scripts, including Arabic and Greek.

Papyrus was used as a major medium of transmission until the development of the technique of paper production. Paper was invented in China around AD 105.[6] Textiles were broken down into fibres, soaked in water and then matted into paper and dried. A writing brush made from hairs, and ink made from lampblack, were used to inscribe an elaborate system of ideographs employing several thousand characters. The use of paper gradually spread westward and, by the end of the fifth century, it was in general use throughout central Asia. In the eighth century the Arabs defeated the Chinese army in what is now known as Turkestan and took as prisoners several papermakers, who taught the Arabs the art of papermaking. Paper mills were established in Baghdad and, subsequently, in Damascus, which became the main source of supply for Europe. The technique of paper manufacture spread via Egypt to Morocco and Spain. In 1276 the first Italian paper mill was established at Montefano. Italian paper manufacture expanded rapidly; by 1283 there were at least 12 paper mills in Fabriano, and in the fourteenth century Italy became the major source of paper for Europe.

As with the invention of paper, techniques of printing were developed originally in China. Block printing emerged gradually from processes of rubbing and stamping and was probably first used during the eighth century. By the ninth century relatively advanced techniques had been developed and were used to print religious texts. Improved methods were introduced during the Sung dynasty (960–1280). The new methods included an early version of movable type, the invention of which is generally attributed to Pi Sheng in 1041. The use of movable type was developed further by printers in Korea, who replaced earthenware characters with metal type. Although there is no direct evidence of the transfer of printing techniques from China and Korea to Europe, these methods may have spread with the diffusion of paper money and playing cards printed in China.[7] Block prints began to appear in Europe in the latter part of the fourteenth century and block-printed books appeared in 1409. However, the developments commonly associated with Gutenberg differed from the original Chinese method in two key respects: the use of alphabetic type, rather than ideographic characters; and the invention of the printing press. Johann Gutenberg, who worked as a goldsmith in Mainz, began experimenting with printing work around 1440, and by 1450 he had developed his techniques far enough to exploit them commercially.[8] Gutenberg developed a method for the replica-casting of metal letters, so that large quantities of type could be produced for the composition of extended texts. He also adapted the screw press, known in Europe since the first century AD, to the purposes of manufacturing printed texts. This combination of techniques enabled a page of type to be composed, held together and handled as a single block, to which ink could be added and paper pressed. The basic principles of Gutenberg's press remained in use, without fundamental modification, for more than three centuries.

During the second half of the fifteenth century, the techniques of printing spread rapidly and presses were set up in the major trading centres throughout Europe. This was the dawn of the era of mass communication. It coincided with the development of early forms of capitalist production and trade, on the one hand, and with the beginnings of the modern nation-state, on the other. The early presses were generally small-scale commercial enterprises which were concerned primarily with the reproduction of manuscripts of a religious or literary character, and with the production of texts for use in law, medicine and trade. The process gradually took over, transformed and greatly expanded a range of activities which had previously been the preserve of scribes and copyists. Combining the activities of printing, publishing and bookselling, the early presses became part of a flourishing new book trade in Europe. By the end of the fifteenth century, presses had been established in most parts of Europe and at least 35,000 editions had been produced, resulting in perhaps 15 or 20 million copies in circulation.

One of the largest of these early presses was that of Anton Koberger, who founded his establishment in 1470 in Nuremberg. Between 1473 and 1513 he printed at least 236 books, mostly in the areas of theology and scholastic philosophy. Koberger was an entrepreneur who expanded his business in response to the growing demand for books. By 1509 he ran 24 presses and employed about 100 compositors, proof-readers, press-men, engravers, binders and other workers. As demand outstripped the capacity of his own workshop, he went into partnership with printer-publishers in Basle, Strasburg and Lyons. In order to market his books, he established an extensive commercial network, with agents based in the most important cities throughout Europe – Frankfurt, Leipzig, Vienna, Budapest, Warsaw, Florence and Paris, among others.

Printing was introduced into England by William Caxton. A merchant from London, he learned the craft of printing in Cologne in 1471–2 and set up a press in the abbey precincts at Westminster when he returned to England in 1476. He printed and published more than 90 books, many of them translations, and he also imported books from abroad and sold them in England. Caxton's business continued after his death and by 1535 it had published around 800 items, about two-fifths of which were intended for use in grammar schools. The number of printers in England increased throughout the sixteenth century – although many were initially foreigners, and much of the equipment was imported from abroad. The number of books produced in England rose steadily: 550 books were printed between 1520 and 1529; 739 between 1530 and 1539; and 928 between 1540 and 1549. By 1590 there were nearly 100 separate establishments, publishing as many as 150 titles annually. Although the printing industry expanded significantly in England during the sixteenth century, the rate of production remained relatively low compared to other European countries, partly because state officials in England, anxious about the possible proliferation of seditious pamphlets, exercised tighter control over the number and output of the presses.

In addition to printing and publishing books, the early presses printed pamphlets, periodicals and news sheets of various kinds. The earliest news sheets appeared in the early sixteenth century; they were *ad hoc* publications concerned with particular events, such as military encounters, and they were not followed by subsequent issues of a series. Periodical news sheets began to appear in the second half of the sixteenth century. But it was not until the beginning of the seventeenth century that regular, and relatively frequent, journals of news began to appear. In 1609 the *Avisa-Relation oder Zeitung* was printed in Wolfenbüttel, and the *Relation* appeared in Strasburg. There is some evidence to suggest that a weekly paper may have appeared somewhat earlier (1607) in Amsterdam; in any case, by 1620 Amsterdam had become the centre of a rapidly expanding *trade in news* through which information concerning military, political and commercial activities was regularly diffused to various European cities. While stimulated by the development of the Thirty Years' War and the growing demand for news about it, the early trade in news also played an increasingly important role in the expansion of the system of capitalist production and exchange and in the emergence of early forms of capitalist financing and credit.

The first English coranto – the term normally used to describe these single-sheet compilations of news – was probably produced by the Dutch printer Pieter van den Keere in 1620 and exported to London.[9] It seems likely that the first coranto printed in England was produced by the London stationer Thomas Archer in the summer of 1621. The newspaper industry in England developed rapidly during the second half of the seventeenth century, subject to government controls of various kinds. By the beginning of the eighteenth century there were around twenty papers appearing weekly, twice-weekly or thrice-weekly in London. The first daily paper in England, the *Courant*, appeared in 1702 and was soon followed by several others. The number of dailies in England rose from about six in the 1730s to about nine in the 1770s. During the early decades of the eighteenth century circulation was low, probably less than 1,000 copies per issue, and distribution was restricted to central London. By mid-century the circulation of the more successful dailies had increased substantially and probably hovered around 3,000 copies per issue.[10] The increase in circulation was closely linked to the improvement of roads and the growing efficiency of the General Post Office, which facilitated the distribution of London-based newspapers to provincial cities and towns.

The early development of printing and publishing was interwoven in complex ways with the exercise of political power by authorities within the administrative apparatuses of the emerging nation-states. The new state authorities actively made use of newspapers to communicate official proclamations of various kinds, but they also sought to restrict or suppress the publication of material deemed to be heretical or dangerous. The exercise of censorship was not a new phenomenon. Throughout the Middle Ages, ecclesiastical authorities had monitored the output of scribes and copyists, with a view to suppressing heretical material; but this regulatory activity was *ad hoc* and irregular, reflecting to some extent the irregular output of the scriptoria. With the advent of printing, the concern with regulation became more systematic and more secular. An early sign of this concern appeared in 1485, when the Archbishop of Mainz asked the town council of Frankfurt to examine the books to be exhibited at the Lenten Fair and to collaborate with the ecclesiastical authorities in suppressing publications thought to be dangerous. The first edict issued by the Frankfurt censor was aimed at the suppression of translations of the Bible into the vernacular. The subsequent history of censorship, and of the conflict-ridden relations between state authorities and the institutions of the press, varied from one country to another.[11] In sixteenth-century France the restrictions on publications were particularly severe, whereas in The Netherlands the regulations were more lenient; this enabled The Netherlands to consolidate its position as a centre of the early publishing industry, printing books in many different languages and exporting them throughout Europe. Faked imprints and fictitious places of publication were used in an attempt to evade the censors in the countries of origin and destination. In England a complicated framework of official control developed in the course of the sixteenth and seventeenth centuries and, with the Printing Act of 1662, the press was subjected to parliamentary control and to a system of licensing. The Act and the system of licensing fell into abeyance at the end of the seventeenth century and was replaced in 1712 by the first of a series of Stamp Acts. Subsequent Acts were introduced to broaden the basis for the application of the law and to control the activities of those who were flouting it. The Acts were widely and bitterly opposed as restricting both trade and the dissemination of knowledge – as 'taxes on knowledge' – and the taxes were progressively reduced from the 1830s onwards. The struggle against state control of the press, whether in the form of overt censorship or in the form of stamp duties, became a central theme of nineteenth-century liberal and democratic thought, a point to which we shall return in the following chapter.

The development of the newspaper industry in the nineteenth and twentieth centuries was characterized by two main trends: first, *the growth and consolidation of mass circulation newspapers*; and second, *the growing internationalization of news-gathering activities*. We can illustrate the first trend with reference to the British newspaper industry, although similar developments can be discerned in many of the major industrializing countries.[12] In the course of the nineteenth century, the newspaper industry became increasingly commercial in character, seeking to increase circulation as a means of increasing the revenue generated through sales and advertising. Of course, commercialization was not a new phenomenon; the early presses, as we have seen, were predominantly commercial concerns orientated towards the production of printed materials for sale in the marketplace. But in the course of the nineteenth century, the scale of commercialization, especially in the newspaper industry, increased significantly. The rapid expansion of the newspaper industry was made possible by the improvement in methods of production and distribution, the growth in literacy and the abolition of taxes. The development of Koenig's steam press, first used on *The Times* in 1814, increased the rate of production from about 250 copies per hour to around 1,000; and the introduction of the rotary printing press in 1848 increased the rate to as much as 12,000 impressions per hour. These technical innovations were crucial for the dramatic augmentation of reproductive capacity in the newspaper industry. They enabled the production of newspapers to be subjected to a set of processes – including the use of power machinery, the ramified division of labour within a factory system, etc. – which were revolutionizing other spheres of commodity production. Moreover, the development of the railways in the 1830s greatly facilitated the distribution of papers throughout the country, creating new and more effective channels of diffusion. During the nineteenth century there was also a substantial increase in population and a gradual extension of literacy, resulting in a steadily expanding market for newspapers and books.

As a result of these and other developments, the circulation of newspapers increased steadily and significantly. The expansion in the circulation of the Sunday papers, which generally led the field in this regard, was particularly striking. The first Sunday paper in Britain, the *Sunday Monitor*, appeared in 1779 and was soon followed by others, including the *Observer* in 1791. By 1810 the Sunday papers had circulations well above the dailies; by 1854 the leading Sunday papers had circulations of around 110,000, whereas the leading daily, *The Times*, had a circulation of 38,000 in 1851.[13] Moreover, the readership of newspapers, and especially the Sunday papers, was probably much larger than their actual sale, since they were widely read in coffee-houses, taverns, newsrooms and clubs. By the end of the nineteenth century the leading Sunday paper, *Lloyd's Weekly News*, had a circulation of about 1 million. The daily papers also increased their circulation substantially in the course of the nineteenth century, and by 1890 the *Daily Telegraph* had reached a circulation of 300,000.

The rapid expansion in circulation was accompanied by significant changes in the nature and content of newspapers.[14] Whereas the earlier newspapers of the seventeenth and eighteenth centuries had been aimed primarily at a restricted, relatively well-off and well-educated sector of the population, the newspaper industry of the nineteenth and twentieth centuries became increasingly orientated towards a broader public. Technological developments and the abolition of taxes enabled prices to be reduced; and newspapers adopted a lighter and livelier style of journalism, as well as a more vivid style of presentation, in order to attract a wider readership. Following the lead of the Sunday papers, the dailies gave greater attention to crime, sexual violence, sport and gambling – these were the staples of the 'new journalism'. At the same time, commercial advertising assumed an increasingly important role in the financial organization of the industry. Newspapers became a crucial mechanism in facilitating the sale of other goods and services, and their capacity to secure advertising revenue was directly linked to the size and profile of their readership. The exploitation of the link between advertising and mass circulation news-papers – what is sometimes referred to as the 'Northcliffe Revolution' – became increasingly important in the early decades of the twentieth century. Northcliffe began the halfpenny *Daily Mail* in 1896 and the *Daily Mirror* in 1903; both papers derived a significant proportion of their revenue from advertising the goods of department stores. By 1911 the *Daily Mirror* had reached a circulation of 1 million – the first daily paper to do so. Other papers, employing the same formula of low price, extensive advertising and mass circulation, were established in the wake of Northcliffe's success. At the same time, newspapers increasingly became large-scale commercial ventures which required relatively large quantities of capital to initiate and sustain in the face of increasingly intense competition. Hence the traditional proprietor–publisher, who owned one or two newspapers as a family concern, increasingly gave way to the development of large-scale, multi-newspaper and multi-media organizations.

The change in the economic basis of newspapers was the beginning of a period of consolidation and concentration. During the first half of the twentieth century, the newspaper industry in Britain witnessed a substantial growth in overall circulation accompanied by a decline in the number of newspapers published. The total circulation of the national dailies rose from just under 15 million in 1920 to nearly 20 million in 1937. The trends since then are illustrated table 4.1. The national dailies continued to increase their circulation throughout the 1940s, reaching a peak of nearly 30 million in the mid-1950s, after which the circulation declined to around 20 million in the early 1980s. The pattern for the Sunday papers is roughly similar: they rose to an aggregate circulation of around 32 million by 1957, but since then the circulation has fallen to below 20 million. These trends have been accompanied by a decline in the number of newspapers published, as shown in table 4.2. The number of national dailies fell from 12 in 1921 to 9 in 1937, while the number of Sunday papers fell from 21 in 1921 to 17 in 1937, and then to 12 in 1975. The major losses occurred among the provincial daily papers, which fell from 130 in 1921 to 80 in 1987. The decline in the number

Table 4.1
Newspaper circulation in UK, 1937–1982 (figures in millions)

	1937	*1947*	*1957*	*1961*	*1975*	*1982*
National and provincial Sundays	15.3	28.3	32.0	25.4	19.7	19.0
National dailies	14.6	25.3	29.0	25.5	22.5	22.0
Provincial dailies	6.0	9.5	10.2	8.6	8.3	7.0
Weeklies	8.6	11.9	–	12.7	12.3	–

The term 'daily' includes morning and evening papers. The term 'provincial' refers to England, Scotland and Wales and excludes Northern Ireland.

Source: Adapted from Graham Murdock and Peter Golding, 'The Structure, Ownership and Control of the Press, 1914–76', in George Boyce, James Curran and Pauline Wingate (eds), *Newspaper History from the Seventeenth Century to the Present Day* (London: Constable, 1978), p. 132 and Jeremy Tunstall, *The Media in Britain* (London: Constable, 1983), p. 70

Table 4.2
Number of newspapers published in UK 1921–1987

	1921	*1937*	*1947*	*1975*	*1987*
National and provincial Sundays	21	17	16	12	13
National dailies	12	9	9	9	11
Provincial dailies	130	107	100	95	80
Weeklies	–	1,348	1,307	1,097	359

Source: Adapted from Murdock and Golding, 'The Structure, Ownership and Control of the Press, 1914–76', p. 132 and Ralph Negrine, *Politics and the Mass Media in Britain* (London: Routledge, 1989), p. 48

of papers was indicative of increasing concentration in the newspaper industry, with fewer organizations commanding larger shares of the market. In 1948 the top three press groups were Beaverbrook Newspapers, Associated Newspapers and Kemsley Newspapers and, between them, they controlled 43 per cent of the circulation in the general newspaper market. By 1974 the top three groups – then Beaverbrook, Reed International and News International – controlled 65 per cent of the market. Concentration rose even more dramatically among the Sunday papers, so that by 1974 the top three groups controlled 80 per cent of the Sunday market. As we shall see later in this chapter, the increasing concentration in the newspaper industry is part of a broader series of changes taking place within the media industries, whereby large international conglomerates, associated with names such as Rupert Murdoch and Robert Maxwell, have acquired interests in a wide range of communications and commercial sectors.

The second main trend characteristic of the newspaper industry in the nineteenth and twentieth centuries was the growing internationalization of news-gathering activities. The early news sheets and newspapers had always been concerned with the transmission of information from one trading centre to another; to some extent, they conveyed information across the boundaries that were taking shape with the rise of the nation-state system in early modern Europe. But the international flow of information assumed a new institutional form in the course of the nineteenth century: *news agencies* were established in the major commercial centres of Europe, and these agencies became increasingly responsible for supplying foreign information to client newspapers. The first news agency was established in Paris by Charles Havas in 1835. A wealthy entrepreneur, Havas acquired what was primarily a translating office, the *Correspondance Garnier*, and turned it into an agency which collected extracts from various European papers and delivered them daily to the French press.[15] By 1840 the agency catered for clients in London and Brussels as well, supplying news by coach and by means of a regular pigeon service. Among Havas's employees were two individuals – Julius Reuters and Bernhard Wolff – who, in the late 1840s, left Havas's agency to set up rival news-gathering services in London and Berlin. With the development of telegraph technology, the agencies made increasing use of cable systems to transmit information across vast distances at great speed. The competition among the three agencies intensified in the 1850s, as each agency sought to secure new clients and to expand its domain of operation. In order to avoid unrestricted and damaging conflict, the three agencies eventually entered into a series of treaties which enabled them to divide up the world into mutually exclusive territories for the collection and distribution of news. By virtue of the Agency Alliance Treaty of 1869, Reuter obtained the territories of the British Empire and the Far East; Havas acquired the French Empire, Italy, Spain and Portugal; and Wolff was granted the exclusive right to exploit Austria, Scandinavia and Russia. While the agencies were independent commercial organizations, their domains of operation corresponded to the spheres of economic and political influence of the major European imperial powers. Each agency collaborated closely with government officials in the state which served as its home base, and the economic and political expansion of these states was facilitated by the communication services provided by the agencies.

The triple agency cartel dominated the international collection and dissemination of news until the outbreak of the First World War. Many other news agencies were established in the latter half of the nineteenth century, but they had, for the most part, aligned themselves with one of the three principals. In the wake of the First World War, however, the triple agency cartel was effectively broken by the international expansion of two American agencies, Associated Press (AP) and the United Press Association (UPA, subsequently transformed into United Press International or UPI). Associated Press was a co-operative established in 1848 by six New York daily papers. The United Press Association was founded by E. W. Scripps in 1907, partly in order to break the hold of AP in the domestic US news market. AP joined the European cartel in 1893, agreeing to supply the European agencies with news from America in return for the exclusive right to distribute news in the United States. UPA set up independent offices in South America and sold news to South American and Japanese newspapers. During the First World War and its aftermath, both AP and UPA expanded their activities worldwide, placing increasing pressure on the cartel arrangements. By the early 1930s the triple agency cartel was effectively at an end; in 1934 Reuters signed a new agreement with AP which gave the American agencies a free hand to collect and distribute news throughout the world. In the new era of free competition, the American agencies expanded rapidly. The capitulation of France in 1940 brought about the dissolution of Havas, although this was eventually replaced by a new agency, the Agence France-Presse (AFP), which took over many of the assets and connections of its predecessor. With the rise of Nazism in Germany, the Wolff agency was turned into an official government organ and subsequently lost its position of influence in the international domain.

In the post-Second World War period, the four major agencies – Reuters, AP, UPI and AFP – have expanded and consolidated their positions in the international system for the dissemination of news. They are concerned not only with the supply of information to newspapers, but also with the provision of financial news and, increasingly, with the supply of material to radio and television stations and networks. Although there are many other news agencies operating in various parts of the world today, the four majors retain a dominant role. Many newspapers and broadcasting organizations throughout the world depend heavily on the four majors for international news, as well as for news of their own geopolitical regions. In 1977 Reuters provided news services to 150 countries and AFP provided services to 129; AP and UPI services were supplied to 108 and 92 countries respectively. By contrast with the fairly wide dispersion of client countries, the locations of the overseas news-gathering bureaux tend to be concentrated in the more developed regions of the world. In 1971 more than 40 per cent of AP's 60 overseas bureaux were located in Europe, while less then 10 per cent were based in Africa; a third of UPI's 65 foreign bureaux were in Europe, while 10 per cent were in Africa and the Middle East.[16] This imbalance in the geographical distribution of news-gathering bureaux, coupled with the heavy dependence of Third World countries on information provided by the major agencies, has helped to fuel calls for a concerted reorganization of the international information order. However, we can appreciate the full significance of this issue only if we place it within the broader context of the development of other media industries, and especially of the industries associated with the development of broadcasting.

The Development of Broadcasting

The emergence of broadcasting ushered in a new era in the history of cultural transmission. The technical basis for broadcasting was first developed by Marconi at the end of the nineteenth century. The possibility of using electrical energy for communication purposes had been known since the 1840s, when the first successful telegraph line was established in the United States. But Marconi's invention, by employing electromagnetic waves and disposing of the need for transmission wires, greatly increased the potential of this medium and transformed the nature of electrically mediated communication. Marconi applied for a British patent in 1896 and set up the Marconi Wireless Telegraph and Signal Company in 1897. By 1899 he succeeded in sending messages across the English Channel, and by 1901 signals had been sent across the Atlantic. Wireless technology developed rapidly during the First World War, when it was used as a means of communication for military purposes. Following the war, British Marconi and its American counterpart began experimental work on *broadcasting* – that is, the transmission of signals via electromagnetic waves to an indeterminate and potentially vast audience, rather than to a specific recipient. The development of broadcasting during the next 40 years was rapid and pervasive. The specific patterns of development varied from one national context to another, depending on the extent to which, and the ways in which, they were animated by commercial concerns and restricted by government regulations. In order to illustrate the development of broadcasting institutions, I shall focus primarily on Britain, although I shall also consider briefly the emergence of broadcasting in the USA and elsewhere.[17]

The first steps in large-scale radio broadcasting were taken in the United States in the early 1920s. The first commercially licensed broadcasting station, KDKA, was launched by Westinghouse in November 1920. The other major communication concerns – General Electric, AT&T and RCA – were quick to enter the field and more than 570 stations had been licensed by early 1922. The early stations and their parent organizations derived revenue from a variety of sources: initially by selling transmitters and receivers, then by selling air-time to broadcasters and advertisers and by sub-licensing programmes through networks of stations. In 1926 the first nationwide broadcasting network, the National Broadcasting Company, was established jointly by RCA, General Electric and Westinghouse; and the following year the Columbia Phonographic Broadcasting System – the precursor of CBS – was established. By 1928 the basic elements of the American broadcasting system were in place: stations were integrated into competitive national networks which controlled the syndication of programmes, and revenue was raised primarily by selling air-time to advertisers. Some non-commercial stations, often sponsored by educational institutions, existed from the outset, but they tended to have low power and unfavourable time slots. The allocation of time slots was the prerogative of the Secretary of Commerce who, under the Radio Act of 1912, was mandated to grant licences to stations. With the rapid growth in the number of stations, however, the 1912 Act proved inadequate and was replaced by a new Radio Act in 1927. The 1927 Act established a Federal Radio Commission consisting of five members appointed by the President and approved by the Senate. Among other things, the Commission was concerned with standardizing channel designation and controlling the number of stations in operation. In 1934 the powers of the Commission were strengthened and it was given jurisdiction over radio transmission between states and with foreign countries.

The development of broadcasting in Britain followed a somewhat different pattern, to some extent in reaction against the distinctive American constellation of economic dependence on advertising, the syndication of programmes by national networks and relatively loose government control. In the early 1920s British observers commented on the chaos of the fledgling American radio industry and recommended a more cautious and regulated approach.[18] Experimental broadcasts from the Marconi Laboratories at Chelmsford were banned in 1920, but continuing pressure from radio enthusiasts and commercial organizations eventually led to the foundation of the British Broadcasting Company in 1922. The company was a consortium of manufacturers of domestic receivers and their purpose in organizing and financing broadcasts was to increase the sale of radio sets. From the outset the company was supervised closely by officials and technical experts from the Post Office and other government ministries. The company was limited to a profit of 7.5 per cent, which was to be earned from a licence fee on receivers which would be collected by the Post Office. For various reasons the original arrangements proved unsatisfactory and the constitutional basis of the organization was modified in 1926, when the British Broadcasting Corporation was established. The corporation was overseen by a Board of Governors, each appointed for five years in the first instance by the government of the day. John Reith, who had been General Manager of the British Broadcasting Company since 1922, was appointed Director General of the Corporation and remained at the head of the BBC until 1937. The idea of 'public service broadcasting', which had been espoused by Reith with an almost missionary zeal, became an operative principle embedded in both the charter and the practice of the BBC.

Systems of broadcasting were revolutionized in the 1940s and 1950s by the advent of television. Experiments with television transmission had begun in both Britain and the USA during the 1930s, but the full-scale exploitation of the television medium did not take place until after the Second World War. In Britain, responsibility for television broadcasting was vested in the BBC and broadcasting recommenced in June 1946. Judged in terms of the number of licences issued, the early television audiences were relatively small; but the rate of growth was rapid, rising from under 15,000 licences in 1947 to over 340,000 by 1950 – a growth of more than 20-fold in three years.[19] The single-channel BBC monopoly on television broadcasting continued until 1954, when the then Conservative government's Television Act provided for the establishment of a second channel organized on a commercial basis. The Act established an Independent Television Authority (later to become the Independent Broadcasting Authority or IBA) which issued contracts to independent television companies; these companies were granted a franchise to make and broadcast programmes within particular regions of the country. Under the terms of the Act, the IBA owns and operates transmission facilities which are rented by the companies, while the companies, in turn, raise revenue primarily by selling air-time to advertisers within their respective regions of operation. Independent television – or ITV, as it is generally called – began broadcasting in the London region in September 1955. As more ITV companies began broadcasting in the ensuing months, the audiences expanded and competition between ITV and the BBC became more intense. By 1954 the number of television licences issued was just over 3 million; by 1958 this figure had risen to 8 million, and by 1968 to 15 million. In 1950 only 10 per cent of homes in Britain had television sets, but by 1963 only 10 per cent of homes were without them.[20] In a short span of about fifteen years, television had become one of the most important media of cultural transmission in Britain and in other Western industrial societies.

The rapid rise of television undoubtedly had important consequences for the other media industries, although it is difficult to assess the precise nature and extent of the impact. Some industries suffered from loss of revenue due to lower sales of their products, which now faced new and serious competition from television. The cinema industry was probably the major victim in this regard. Although cinema admissions began falling significantly in the immediate post-Second World War period, before television had become a widely used medium, the decline during the period 1954–64 was particularly dramatic. In 1954 admissions to cinemas in Britain were still around 25 million per week, having fallen from a 1946 peak of around 32 million; by 1964 the weekly admissions had fallen to just over 6 million, or about 25 per cent of the figure of a decade earlier. The decline continued, albeit more gradually, throughout the 1960s and 1970s, so that by 1983 admissions were just over 1 million per week.[21] It is likely that the rise of television was a major contribution to the decline of the cinema, but no doubt it was not the only factor; and it should also be remembered that, while its impact on cinema admissions was detrimental, the television industry has provided new stimulants for the production of films and new channels for their distribution.

A second respect in which the rise of television has affected other media industries is in terms of competition for advertising revenue. Newspapers derive a substantial proportion of their revenue from advertising; and prior to the rise of television, a high percentage – in 1954, 88 per cent – of British advertising expenditure was absorbed by newspapers and related printed media. The decline in this proportion is illustrated in table 4.3. By 1962 television had captured 25 per cent of media advertising expenditure, while the press share had fallen to under 70 per cent; the regional newspapers and other printed material, such as magazines and periodicals, witnessed the largest decline in share. By 1982 the press share had fallen below 64 per cent, while the television share had risen to nearly 30 per cent. Of course, commercial television helped to generate higher levels of advertising expenditure, especially during the 1950s. But in recent years the media industries have engaged in an increasingly competitive struggle to maintain or increase their share of the available advertising revenue.[22]

Since 1960 the main institutional changes in British broadcasting involved the establishment of two additional television channels. The second BBC channel – BBC2 – was established in the wake of the Pilkington Committee's report and began broadcasting in April 1964. Both BBC channels are financed primarily by a licence fee collected by the Post Office.

Table 4.3
UK media advertising expenditure, 1954–1982

	1954	1962	1972	1982
National newspapers	17.2	19.8	18.4	16.5
Regional newspapers	31.2	23.0	26.5	23.6
Other press	39.6	25.9	25.4	23.5
Total press	88.0	68.7	70.3	63.5
Television	–	25.0	24.9	29.7
Poster and transport	8.9	4.6	3.7	4.0
Cinema	2.5	1.4	1.0	0.6
Radio	0.7	0.3	0.1	2.2
Total media	100.0	100.0	100.0	100.0

Source: Adapted from Tunstall, *The Media in Britain*, pp. 72–3

The expansion of BBC services and the growth in capital expenditure associated with BBC2 and other technical changes have increased the financial pressures on the BBC in recent years. Increasing costs have been met to a large extent by substantial increases in the licence fee, which must be approved by the Home Secretary. But the trends were sufficiently worrying to induce the Home Secretary to establish the Peacock Committee in 1985 to inquire into the financial basis of the BBC. The Peacock Committee advised against the introduction of advertising on BBC television under current arrangements, recommending that the licence fee should be maintained for the time being and linked to a cost-of-living index, while envisaging the possibility that, in the long term, the licence fee might be replaced by a subscription system.[23] In the late 1970s discussions were under way concerning the establishment of a fourth channel, which began broadcasting in autumn 1982. Channel 4, as it is called, is a wholly owned subsidiary of the IBA. The channel does not make its own programmes, but commissions them from independent sources, including the ITV regional companies. Channel 4 is financed out of subscriptions paid by the ITV companies; in return, the ITV companies gain revenue from the sale of advertising time on the channel. During the first few years of operation, the revenue earned from the channel through advertising was less than the subscriptions paid by the ITV companies, so that the ITV companies effectively subsidised Channel 4. By 1987 it appeared that the channel was beginning to break even, fuelling controversy about whether it should be floated off as a self-financing company.

In the late 1980s the system of television broadcasting in the UK is thus characterized by a basic division between the BBC and the independent television network, each of which controls two channels. Figure 4.2 summarizes the main institutional features of the television broadcasting system in Britain. The BBC is both a production and a transmission company. It produces and transmits programmes via its two channels, and derives the bulk of its income from the licence fee (supplemented by revenue from publications, the sale of subsidiary rights and government grants). The ITV companies operate under the umbrella of the IBA, which issues licences to the ITV companies and which, in turn, receives rental fees for the use of its transmission facilities; companies which make high profits are liable to pay an additional levy to the IBA. There are 15 ITV companies operating in different regions of the country. Five of these – Thames, London Weekend, Central, Granada and Yorkshire – operate in the most heavily populated regions and are the most important institutions of independent television production, supplying programmes to other regional companies as well as to Channel 4. Unlike the other ITV companies, Channel 4 does not make its own programmes but rather commissions them from independent pro-duction companies, as well as acquiring material from the ITV companies and from independent film producers. The principal form of income for Channel 4 is the subscription fee, paid by the ITV companies in return for the right to advertise on the channel.

In terms of audience shares, BBC1 and ITV have the highest proportions, while BBC2 and Channel 4 cater to some extent to minority interests. Table 4.4 indicates the audience shares obtained by the different channels in 1985. ITV secured the largest share, with an average viewing of 12 hours 23 minutes per head of population per week, which represented 46.6 per cent of total viewing time. BBC1 achieved an average viewing of 9 hours 16 minutes and captured 34.9 per cent of viewing time. BBC2 and Channel 4 fell well behind, representing 11.1 per cent and 7.4 per cent respectively of viewing time. Taken together, ITV and Channel 4 have a slightly larger share of the audience than the two BBC channels (with a ratio of 54:46), a lead that has remained fairly stable over recent years. The audiences for different channels display significant variations in terms of class composition. When the class profiles of the channels are compared with that of the population as a whole, it can be seen that the middle class is well represented in both BBC audiences but under-represented in that for ITV, whereas the unskilled manual workers are under-represented in the BBC audiences and over-represented among ITV viewers.[24]

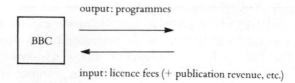

output: programmes

BBC

input: licence fees (+ publication revenue, etc.)

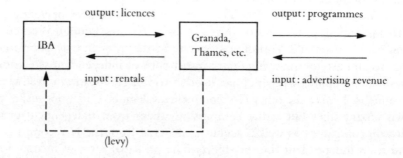

output: licences   output: programmes

IBA   Granada,
             Thames, etc.

input: rentals   input: advertising revenue

(levy)

– licenses 15 ITV companies operating in regions
– monitors output of ITV companies
– owns and monitors Channel 4

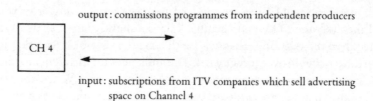

output: commissions programmes from independent producers

CH 4

input: subscriptions from ITV companies which sell advertising
        space on Channel 4

Figure 4.2 The Social Organization of British Television Broadcasting

Table 4.4
Average amount of viewing and channel shares in UK, 1985

	Average viewing per head of population per week (hrs:mins)	*Share of total viewing (%)*
BBC1	9:16	34.9
BBC2	2:57	11.1
Total BBC	12:13	46.0
ITV	12:23	46.6
Channel 4	1:57	7.4
Total ITV	14:20	54.0
Total TV	26:33	100.0

Source: Adapted from Julia Lamaison and Judy Moreton, 'Trends in Viewing and Listening 1985', *Annual Review of BBC Broadcasting Research Findings*, 12 (1986), p. 9

The British broadcasting system, while it remained relatively stable throughout the 1980s, is likely to change in certain respects during the coming decade. The Conservative government's 1988 White Paper on the future of broadcasting called for the abolition of the IBA and its replacement by an Independent Television Commission (ITC) which will regulate a more extensive independent sector.[25] The White Paper also proposed that the allocation of ITV franchises should be subjected to a process of competitive tendering. According to this procedure, independent companies would be invited to submit sealed bids for an ITV licence, and the ITC would then award the licence to the highest bidder, provided that it passed a certain quality threshold. Not surprisingly, this proposal met fierce resistance from the established ITV companies, who perceived it as a threat to their long-term interests and argued that it would undermine their capacity to produce high-quality programmes. When the first results of the new system of allocation were announced in October 1991, it became clear that the ITC would take account of considerations other than the size of the bid. But the system produced anomalous and unsatisfactory results, with some un-opposed companies retaining their licences for minimal fees while other companies in contested regions paid well over the odds.

The development of television broadcasting in the United States occurred within a similar time span but assumed a different institutional form. Rapid expansion of the television industry began in 1948 and within a decade there were nearly as many television sets in use as there were families in the United

States. The Federal Communications Commission was responsible for licensing stations and assigning them to channels within their operating regions. Many of the stations became affiliated to the three major networks – NBC, CBS and ABC – as shown in table 4.5. By 1974 more than 60 per cent of television stations were affiliated to the major national networks, compared with 34 per cent of radio stations. The networks thus constitute a key institutional aspect of the American television system. They provide programmes to their affiliates, arrange interconnection facilities for programme distribution, and sell advertising time in the national market on behalf of their affiliates. As payment for these services, an affiliate allocates around 20 hours of free broadcasting per week to the network, charges about 30 per cent of its regular rate for the remaining hours used by the network, and receives only a small proportion of the revenue derived by the network from the sale of national advertising time.[26] But the programmes provided by the network enable the affiliates to obtain good rates for local and non-network advertising, which are their major sources of revenue. Generally the networks provide sufficient programmes to fill about 60 per cent of affiliates' schedules, leaving them to acquire rights on non-network material from independent producers and programme suppliers to fill the remaining time. The unaffiliated television stations, by contrast, must fill their entire schedules and must compete both with other unaffiliated stations, and with

Table 4.5
US commercial network affiliates, 1974

	Number of affiliates	
Network	Radio	Television
ABC	1,479	168
CBS	249	192
NBC	216	211
MBS	620	–
Total affiliates	2,564	571
Unaffiliated	4,936	363
Percentage affiliated	34%	61%

Source: Adapted from Sidney W. Head, *Broadcasting in America: A Survey of Television and Radio* (Boston: Houghton Mifflin, 1976), p. 169

the networks and their affiliates, for advertising and for the rights to non-network material.

In addition to commercial stations and networks, a range of channels in the USA is reserved for educational or non-commercial broadcasting. In 1962 Congress established the Corporation for Public Broadcasting (CPB) to facilitate and oversee the development of non-commercial television. The CPB is a federal body which is governed by fifteen Presidential appointees. It makes grants to independent stations, production companies and a network – the Public Broadcasting Service or PBS – which links the non-commercial stations. Although local stations have the option to broadcast or ignore PBS material, more than 70 per cent of an average non-commercial station's programming is provided by the network. PBS obtains material from several large production-orientated stations within the network as well as from outside suppliers, including foreign suppliers such as the BBC. The stations pay PBS varying levels of fees for the programmes supplied, depending on the overall budget of the station concerned. The principal sources of support for the non-commercial stations are taxes, which accounted for nearly 60 per cent of stations' revenue in 1971–2; non-tax sources, including foundations, subscribers, business gifts and corporate underwriters, accounted for 32 per cent.[27] Corporate underwriting, mainly by oil companies, accounts for about one-quarter of PBS programme contributions and plays a particularly prominent role in prime-time programming. Compared to the major commercial networks, however, public television in the United States remains a small-scale operation. Public broadcasting stations operate on relatively small budgets and spend substantially less per hour on broadcasting. Their share of the television audience is minute – about 3 per cent in prime time – and their viewers tend to be relatively well educated and well off. So while public television plays an important role in the American broadcasting system, it is also a very limited role in terms of overall levels of finance and audience, and on most evenings the three commercial networks combined usually account for more than 90 per cent of all viewers.

In examining the development of broadcasting I have concentrated on the institutional features of the British and American systems; a more comprehensive account would have to consider the differing institutional forms which have emerged in other countries. It is important to stress, however, that the systems of broadcasting which developed in Britain and the USA have been highly influential in the establishment of broadcasting systems elsewhere in the world. The British model of a public service corporation, operating with an exclusive franchise or in tandem with a carefully regulated independent sector, was effectively exported to many of the territories of the British Empire, and this model formed the institutional basis for the development of broadcasting in many countries that were formerly British colonies.[28] Thus the Nigerian Broadcasting Corporation, which was the first broadcasting organization to be established in the British colonies, was closely modelled on the BBC. In some ex-colonial countries, however, the governments have exercised a much tighter control over broadcasting organizations than Reith, in originally formulating the idea of public service broadcasting, had envisaged. In other regions of the developing world, such as Latin America and parts of Asia, the American system of broadcasting has been particularly influential. Many countries of South and Central America were already within the economic and political sphere of influence of the USA when broadcasting technology became available for commercial exploitation, and the regulatory frameworks adopted in these countries were very similar to those developed in the United States. Much of the technological hardware and training was provided by American corporations such as RCA. Local entrepreneurs developed commercial broadcasting stations which, through mergers and acquisitions, were gradually integrated into oligopolistic family empires. By the early 1960s the US model of broadcasting was well-established in many Latin American countries, although political upheavals in the 1960s and 1970s have resulted in more direct political control of broadcasting institutions in some cases.

While broadcasting institutions developed fairly rapidly in the countries of Africa, Asia and Latin America, the diffusion of receiving equipment has proceeded more slowly. The extent of ownership of radio and television sets in these countries is much lower than in the industrial societies of Europe and North America. In 1975 there were 68 radios and 6 TV sets per 1,000 people in Asia; this compares with 1,813 radios and 530 TV sets per 1,000 people in the USA, and 700 radios and 530 TV sets per 1,000 in Britain in 1975.[29] However, these broad figures conceal significant differences in terms of rates of penetration between urban and rural areas. In Africa and Asia the ownership of receiving equipment, and especially TV sets, is heavily concentrated in the major urban centres, where reception is best and incomes are higher. Hence the ownership of receiving equipment in the rural areas of developing countries is likely to be significantly lower than broad comparative figures would suggest. To some extent the low level of penetration in rural areas may be offset by the development of more collective forms of reception activity, such as the community viewing centres set up by the Broadcasting Corporation of Northern Nigeria. Moreover, it is likely that levels of penetration will increase steadily and significantly in the coming decades, as developing countries become increasingly urbanized and electrified, and as the producers of receiving equipment seek to exploit an expanding market for their goods.

Recent Trends in the Media Industries

The media industries, including television broadcasting, are currently undergoing major changes which are having a significant impact on the nature of media products and the modes of their production and diffusion. These changes are the outcome of developments occurring at two levels: at the level of political economy, and at the level of technology. The media industries in Western societies are, in most cases, commercial or quasi-commercial organizations operating in a competitive marketplace and subject to financial pressures and incentives of various kinds; hence changes in the media industries are, to some extent, responses to the economic imperatives and political constraints affecting these industries *qua* commercial concerns. But the media industries are also heavily dependent on technology and technological innovation. Recent developments in telecommunications and computing have created new possibilities for the transmission, storage and recall of information, developments which are transforming the media industries and increasingly integrating them into a broader range of industries concerned with the diffusion and control of information and communication. I shall consider some of these techno-logical developments in the following section. But first I want to examine some of the changes that are currently taking place at the level of political economy. I shall focus on four main trends: (1) the increasing *concentration* of the media industries; (2) their growing *diversification*; (3) the increasing *globalization* of the media industries; and (4) the trend towards *deregulation*. In order to illustrate these trends, I shall draw examples primarily from Britain and the United States, although these developments are by no means specific to these countries and, indeed, are increasingly trans-national in character.

1 As with other industrial sectors in Western societies, productive resources in the media industries have become increasingly concentrated in the hands of a relatively small number of large corporations. The growing concentra-tion of the media industries has been fairly well documented in a range of studies carried out in different countries.[30] In the USA in 1981, 46 large corporations controlled most of the business in daily newspapers, magazines, books, television and film; by the end of the 1980s, the number of firms controlling half or more of the business in these media had shrunk by half, from 46 to 23. Although there were more than 1,600 daily newspapers in the United States in 1989, half of the total circulation was controlled by only 14 corporations, including Gannett (with *USA Today* and 87 other dailies), Knight-Ridder, Inc. (with the Miami *Herald* and 28 others) and Newhouse

Newspapers (with the Staten Island *Advance* and 25 other papers).[31] If we consider developments in Britain, we can see that concentration has increased significantly during the last 70 years, although the rate and extent of concentration varies from one domain of the media industries to another. In the newspaper and cinema industries, concentration occurred at a rapid pace in Britain in the 1920s, 1930s and 1940s, so that by 1929 half the daily newspaper circulation was controlled by four concerns, and by 1944 a third of all cinema seats were controlled by three chains. Concentration continued in these and other media industries in the 1950s and 1960s, at a time when markets for some media products were expanding significantly. The extent of concentration in different media industries in Britain in 1972 is indicated in table 4.6, which estimates the proportion of the market controlled by the five leading companies in each sphere. In 1972 86 per cent of national morning papers and 88 per cent of national Sunday papers were sold by the top five companies in each sphere. By 1981, the top five companies controlled 95 per cent of the total circulation of mornings and Sundays, and the top three controlled more than 80 per cent. In 1972 seven out of ten paperback books were sold by the top five companies concerned; the concentration of resources in the publishing industry has increased further since then, by virtue of a series of spectacular and well-publicized takeovers involving large corporations on both sides of the Atlantic. The high levels of concentration in spheres such as publishing and the music industry has not prevented the emergence of small independent companies catering for

Table 4.6

Proportion of total domestic UK market accounted for by the five leading companies in each medium, 1972 (%)

Medium	% Share
National morning newspaper circulations	86
National Sunday newspaper circulations	88
Commercial television (% of television homes served)	73
Paperback books (% of market)	70
Mid-price records (% of market)	69
Cinema (% of box office takings, top four circuits)	80

Source: Adapted from Graham Murdock and Peter Golding, 'For a Political Economy of Mass Communications', in Ralph Miliband and John Saville (eds), *The Socialist Register 1973* (London: Merlin, 1974), p. 214 and Graham Murdock and Peter Golding, 'Capitalism, Communication and Class Relations', in James Curran, Michael Gurevitch and Janet Woollacott (eds), *Mass Communication and Society* (London: Edward Arnold, 1977), pp. 23ff.

specialist interests; but these companies generally account for a relatively small proportion of total sales and remain highly vulnerable to market forces and takeover bids.

A significant degree of concentration also exists in the sphere of television. In the USA the three major networks still dominate the field in terms of audience share and revenue; a growing proportion of viewers are tuning in to cable channels, but most of the major cable systems are themselves owned by large media concerns. In Britain the independent television sector is dominated by the five major ITV companies (Thames, London Weekend, Central, Granada and Yorkshire); in 1972 these five majors served over 70 per cent of television homes, leaving the ten smaller ITV companies to serve the remaining homes. The five major companies are also the principal sources of television programmes for the ITV network. In 1980, 50 per cent of the material transmitted by a typical ITV company was supplied by the five majors, while less then 10 per cent was supplied by the ten smaller companies. Moreover, within the ITV companies themselves, share holdings are often concentrated in the hands of a few key individuals, or in the hands of other corporations with communications interests. In the case of Granada, the major shareholdings remain within the Bernstein family (62 per cent of voting shares in 1979); in the case of London Weekend and Yorkshire, the major holdings are represented by corporations with communications interests, including press corporations (47 per cent and 28 per cent respectively).[32] Hence the independent television sector, as with other sectors of the media industries, is characterized by a concentration of resources in the hands of a few large companies and, in some cases, by a concentration of shareholdings within these companies in the hands of a few key individuals, or in the hands of a few key corporations with communications interests.

2 In addition to the growing concentration of resources, the media industries have undergone increasing diversification in recent years. Diversification is the process by which companies expand their activities in different domains or product lines, either by acquiring companies which already operate in these domains or by investing capital in new developments. When diversification takes place in interrelated domains – for example, publishers acquiring typesetters, designers, printing plants, bookshops and so on – it becomes a means of enabling companies to control costs and to benefit from different stages in the development of a particular product. When diversification involves expansion into unrelated domains concerned with the production and distribution of different goods – as, for example, when the Rank Organization expanded into the fields of hotels, restaurants, television and hi-fi equipment – it becomes a means of creating

new profit centres within a company and cushioning it against the negative consequences of recession, unstable growth or long-term decline in certain domains. The diversification of activities among some of the larger British media companies is illustrated in table 4.7. Thus EMI, for instance, derived 7 per cent of its revenue in 1972 from broadcasting (it had a controlling interest in Thames Television), 15 per cent from film and cinema (it owned one of two major cinema chains), and 55 per cent from other media sources (it owned one of the largest record companies trading in the UK). In 1980 EMI was itself taken over by Thorn, which was already the largest manufacturer of TV hardware in Britain (Ferguson). The newly merged Thorn–EMI thus established an increasingly diversified base in which foreign operations account for about one-third of its annual turnover of £2.6 billion (1981–2).

The concentration and diversification of the media industries have led to the formation of *communication conglomerates* which have major interests in a variety of industries concerned with information and communication. Among the largest of these conglomerates is Time Warner, formed by the merger of Time, Inc. and Warner Communications in 1989. It is the largest magazine publisher in the United States, the second largest cable company in the world, one of the largest book publishers and the largest video company in the world. It has subsidiaries in Australia, Asia, Europe and Latin America, and its assets exceed the combined gross national product of Bolivia, Jordan, Nicaragua, Albania, Liberia and Mali. The American corporations RCA and CBS also emerged as two of the largest and most diversified communication conglomerates, although they have themselves recently been taken over by other corporations. In addition to owning one of the major broadcasting networks (NBC), RCA acquired substantial interests in publishing, the record industry, domestic and industrial electronics and a variety of other consumer goods and services; RCA was then bought by General Electric, the tenth largest US corporation, for $6.3 billion. CBS also controls one of the three major American networks and has interests in publishing, film production and the record industry; after incurring massive debts and fighting off a series of hostile takeover bids, CBS was eventually acquired by a large real estate corporation. Another huge communication conglomerate, the Bertelsmann group, has major interests in book and magazine publishing, in book clubs and distribution networks, in the printing industry, in the music and record industry, in television and in film. Originally based in West Germany, the Bertelsmann group is now one of the largest media concerns in the United States, where it owns the publishing firms Doubleday, Bantam Books, Dell and the Literary Guild, among other things. As communication conglomerates have become larger and more

Table 4.7

Distribution of turnover among some media companies in UK, 1972 (%)

Companies	Broadcasting	Film/cinema	Newspapers	Publishing	Other media/ leisure	Other
EMI	7	15			55	23
Granada	36	6		6	40	12
Associated Television Corporation	48	23			28	1
Rank		27			43	30
Pearson Longman			56	39		5
Thomson			40	24	27	9

Source: Adapted from Peter Golding, *The Mass Media* (Harlow, Essex: Longman, 1974), p. 50

diversified, they have become increasingly integrated into the higher levels of the banking and industrial sectors, both as clients and subsidiaries and through interlocking boards of directors.

The activities of communication conglomerates have recently been highlighted by the media attention bestowed on some of the more eccentric entrepreneurs. Rupert Murdoch, head of the sprawling multi-media conglomerate called News Corporation, has sought and received particular prominence in this regard. Table 4.8 lists some of the major assets of the News Corporation. Ownership of the *Sun* newspaper gives Murdoch control of 35 per cent of the popular daily newspaper market in Britain, in addition to controlling a substantial share of the quality daily and Sunday markets. The Sky Channel gives him a leading role in the emerging arena of satellite broadcasting. In the United States, Australia and the Pacific basin, the News Corporation has extensive and expanding interests in a wide range of media industries, from newspapers, magazines and book publishers to television stations, film studios and commercial printing concerns. Murdoch controls two-thirds of all newspaper circulation in Australia and nearly half in New Zealand. In the USA he controls Twentieth-Century Fox movie studios, the Fox Broadcasting network, and numerous newspapers, magazines, book publishers and TV stations. He is part owner of CBS–Fox Video and is the world's largest distributor of video cassettes. The News Corporation also has interests in non-media industries, including an airline and an oil and gas exploration company. In 1988 Murdoch launched a successful $3 billion takeover bid for the Annenberg family's Triangle Publications, publisher of *TV Guide*, the largest-circulation magazine in the USA. The breadth and diversity of the News Corporation illustrates well the kind of diversification characteristic of the media industries today. But Murdoch's multi-media conglomerate, however sprawling and prominent it may be, is relatively small in terms of overall assets and turnover compared to the major US-based corporations involved in communication and information tech-nologies.

3 The breadth of Murdoch's News Corporation illustrates another feature of the modern media industries: the increasing globalization of their activities. Of course, the trans-national character of the activities of the media industries is not a new phenomenon. As we have seen, the early development of the book trade involved the transport of printed materials across national boundaries; and the emergence of news agencies in the nineteenth century resulted in a global system of trans-national territorial domains for the collection and dissemination of news. But in recent decades, the globalization of the activities of the media industries has taken on new

forms and has become far more extensive and pervasive in character. We can distinguish several distinct aspects of this trend. In the first place, the media industries are part of communication conglomerates which are increasingly trans-national in terms of the range of their operations and activities. The process of transnationalization has been propelled to some extent by large-scale mergers and takeovers among the communication conglomerates. I have already mentioned some of these takeovers, and other examples can be easily added. In 1981 the British newspapers *The Times* and the *Sunday Times* were sold by the Canadian-based International Thomson Organization to Murdoch's News International, the British-based subsidiary of his multi-national News Corporation. In 1987 the Japanese electronics giant Sony bought the US-based CBS record label; the international record industry is now largely controlled by five labels – Sony-CBS, RCA, Warner, Thorn-EMI and Polygram – each of which is owned by a multi-national corporation. In 1986 the British-based Penguin books, itself part of the Pearson Longman group, gained entry into the American paperback market by acquiring the New American Library. In 1987 Random House – a subsidiary of the US-based Newhouse Corporation which has extensive interests in newspaper, book and magazine publishing – acquired a range of well-known British publishers including Chatto, Virago, Bodley Head and Jonathan Cape. In the same year the International Thomson Organization, bidding against stiff competition from the American-based Simon and Schuster, acquired the British group Associated Book Publishers, which itself em-braces Methuen, Routledge and Kegan Paul, Sweet and Maxwell, Chapman and Hall, and Croom Helm, among others. Through mergers and takeovers of this kind, the media industries have become increasingly trans-national in character, as particular companies become integrated into large communication conglomerates that span the globe.

A second aspect of the globalization of the media industries concerns the increasing role of exports and of the production of media goods for an international market. The export trade has always been part of the publishing industry, especially when printing books in languages which, as a result of prior colonial or military expansion and other factors, extend well beyond the boundaries of particular nation-states. In 1949 book exports accounted for 29 per cent of sales by British publishers; by 1969 they accounted for 47 per cent. The sale of educational texts to the Third World is a major component of this trade, accounting for 20 per cent of British book exports in 1972. The Commonwealth countries, the United States and, increasingly, Japan, are also major export markets for British publishers. Similarly, in the case of television, the sale of programmes in foreign markets is becoming an important source of revenue. In 1982 the ITV companies

Table 4.8
Major media assets of Rupert Murdoch's News Corporation, 1988

	Britain	United States	Australia	Pacific Basin
Newspapers	The Times The Sunday Times Today Sun News of the World	San Antonio Express-News Boston Herald	The Australian Over 120 regional titles	South China Morning Post (Hong Kong) Sunday Morning Post The Fiji Times The Sunday Times Post Courier (Papua New Guinea)
Magazines and books	Elle Sky Times supplements Geographia	Automobile Elle New York 19 other titles	TV Week Australasian Post Family Circle Better Homes & Gardens	Pacific Islands Monthly

	John Bartholemew	Harper & Row Publishers		Bay Books
	Robert Nicholson	Salem House		Angus & Robertson Publishers
		Zondervan		Herald & Weekly Times Books
TV and films	Sky Channel	Twentieth-Century Fox		
		Fox Broadcasting		
		TV stations in:		
		Dallas		
		Houston		
		Los Angeles		
		Chicago		
		Boston		
		New York		
		Washington DC		
Commercial printing	Eric Bemrose	World Printing		Over 20 companies

Source: Adapted from the *Guardian*, 19 August 1988, p. 11

earned £20 million through the sale of programmes abroad, representing 2.8 per cent of their total revenue; by 1984 this had risen to £47 million, or 5 per cent of the total. The BBC has also been increasingly successful in marketing its programmes overseas and it now sells programmes to over 100 countries; in 1984–5 the sale of programmes overseas accounted for 70 per cent of the £35 million revenue of BBC Enterprises, the commercial wing of the BBC.[33] However, international film and television programme sales are still largely dominated by American companies. In 1981 American films accounted for 94 per cent of foreign films broadcast on British television, 80 per cent of those broadcast on French television, and 54 per cent of those broadcast on West German television. In Western Europe as a whole, approximately 30 per cent of television broadcasting time was filled with imported programmes in 1983, and the bulk of imported programmes (44 per cent) originated in the USA; in Britain, American imports represented 75 per cent of all imported programmes. The share represented by US-originated programmes in other parts of the world is even greater. In Latin America, for instance, imports accounted for 46 per cent of television broadcasting time in 1983, and 77 per cent of all imported material originated in the US. By contrast, in the USA itself, imports accounted for only 2 per cent of broadcasting time in 1983.[34] It is this kind of dramatic asymmetry in terms of the international diffusion of films and programmes, coupled with other considerations such as the dependence of developing countries on Western-based news agencies, which underlies recent debates concerning the so-called 'cultural imperialism' of the West and the need, espoused by some critical commentators, to restructure and regulate the international system for the flow of information and communication.[35]

A third aspect of globalization stems from the deployment of technologies which facilitate the trans-national diffusion of information and communication. Again, this aspect of globalization is not altogether new. Printed materials were always capable of being transported across national boundaries, and broadcasting has often been conducted (and sometimes contested) in the international domain – especially in Europe, where signals can easily spill over the boundaries of nation-states. But the technological generation of globalization has increased dramatically in recent years, primarily as a result of advances in satellite technology. In the next section I shall discuss the application of satellite technology in systems of direct broadcasting, which is the use with which many people today are most familiar. Satellite technology has, however, an extensive range of uses throughout the domain of communication and information transmission. The initial development of satellite technology was a spin-off of the early American and Soviet space missions and of research in the military domain.[36]

The first Telstar satellite was launched in 1962, and by 1965 the Americans were able to place the first commercial telecommunications satellite, Early Bird, in a stationary orbit. A satellite in a stationary orbit – or a 'synchronous satellite' as it is called – will be continuously visible over about one-third of the earth. So a system of three synchronous satellites, properly positioned and linked, can provide global coverage, with the exception of the Arctic and Antarctic regions. In 1962 the US Congress set up the Communication Satellite Corporation (Comsat) to organize the commercial exploitation of satellite technology. Comsat was a private corporation, half of the shares in which were offered to private subscribers while the other half were held by the major American communication conglomerates. Following the forma-tion of Comsat, the United States proposed to establish an international organization, subsequently called Intelsat, which would enable commercial communications to be conducted by satellite among its members. The original members included the Western European countries, Canada, Australia and Japan. Commercial operation began across the Atlantic in 1965 and became global in 1969. Intelsat now has more than 100 members worldwide and serves as the carrier for national domestic services in several countries. The Soviet Union, which launched its first non-stationary communications satellite in 1965 and its first stationary one in 1974, founded a similar international organization in 1971, called Intersputnik, embracing the countries of Eastern Europe, Cuba and Outer Mongolia. In addition to these international satellite systems, there is now a range of regional and domestic systems which operate at the continental and national levels, as well as a variety of systems used exclusively for military, maritime and aeronautical purposes. The systems are capable of transmitting vast quantities of information on a global scale and virtually instantaneously. They are used heavily by multi-national corporations to transmit data and to communicate between their dispersed branches and subsidiaries. Texas Instruments, for example, has 50 major plants in 19 countries and uses a satellite-based system to link 8,000 terminals for worldwide planning, marketing, accounting and electronic mail. Citicorp, a trans-national financial services organization, employs a satellite-based system to link 2,300 branches and affiliate offices in 94 counties.[37] The use of satellite systems for commercial purposes is part of a more general process of trans-national data flow in which information or communication is increasingly becoming a commodity that can be exchanged and controlled in a global market.

4 Partly as a response to the changing technological bases of the media industries, many Western governments have sought to deregulate the activities of media organizations and to remove legislation that was

perceived as restrictive. The trend towards deregulation has been particularly pronounced in the sphere of broadcasting, which generally developed within a framework of strong government controls. In Britain and most other European countries, radio and television broadcasting was strictly regulated by the state, which licensed broadcasting institutions, allocated wavelengths and closely monitored output. In many cases, state or quasi-state broadcasting institutions were granted a monopoly to broadcast to the nation. The strict regulation of broadcasting was generally justified on the grounds that, within any particular territorial domain, there was a limited number of channels available for the transmission of radio and television signals. This justification was sometimes coupled with the view that broadcasting was essentially a public service and that, as such, it should be regulated in what might be judged to be the public interest. For some of the early British and European broadcasters and policy-makers, these explicit justifications for state regulation were reinforced by an abhorrence of commercialism and a generalized fear about the potentially harmful and disruptive consequences of uncontrolled broadcasting.

Although state monopolies on broadcasting were broken in some European countries at an early date, the term 'deregulation' is customarily used to refer to a series of political initiatives which characterized many Western societies in the 1970s and 1980s. The deregulation of the media was part of a more general attempt to increase competitiveness in a variety of industrial sectors and to remove legislation which was thought to restrict unduly the pursuit of commercial interests. In the United States, where state regulation of the media has traditionally been much weaker than in Europe, attempts were made in the late 1970s to rewrite the Communications Act of 1934 in a way that would have deregulated radio and relaxed the rules for television broadcasting, as well as shaking up the telecommunication monopolies and conglomerates. Although the proposed bills were ultimately withdrawn, the Federal Communications Commission effectively implemented policies of deregulation in the early 1980s, easing controls on radio and television broadcasting by curtailing requirements for public service broadcasting and allowing more air-time for commercial messages.[38] In many European countries, similar attempts at deregulation of the media were made in the 1970s and 1980s. Radio and television broadcasting in Italy had been traditionally monopolized by the state service, RAI. In 1975 this monopoly was challenged and broken, and since then a multiplicity of local and quasi-national channels has emerged, financed primarily by advertising revenue and subjected to minimal state regulation. In France, Germany, Belgium and The Netherlands, radio and television broadcasting outside of the established state service was gradually legalized in the 1970s and 1980s, allowing independent services, financed by advertising or subscription, to emerge.[39] In Britain the duopoly established by the introduction of commercial television in the 1950s remains largely intact, although radio broadcasting has been deregulated to some extent and it is likely that the BBC–ITV duopoly will undergo some transformation in the 1990s.

The process of deregulation has been spurred on by the development of new technologies in the sphere of telecommunications. With the deployment of cable and satellite systems of transmission, the traditional arguments about the limited number of channels – arguments which shaped the development of broadcasting from the 1920s to the 1970s – began to carry less weight. These new technologies created the possibility of a proliferation of channels of transmission, so that the grounds for restricting the right to transmit to a single state organization, or to a small number of strictly regulated organizations, began to appear less plausible. Moreover, commercial organizations were keen to exploit the new technologies and they actively pressed for a more liberalized framework in which they could do so. While deregulation has been welcomed by many as a necessary antidote to an overly regulated media sector, it has been criticized by others as an avenue for the acceleration of concentration in the media industries: by opening up broadcasting and the new technologies to commercial exploitation, deregulation may enable the communication conglomerates to increase their dominant role in the new global economy of information and communication. I shall return to the policy implications of these considerations in the next chapter.

The Social Impact of New Communication Technologies

I have referred on several occasions to the importance of new communication technologies in the current stage of development of the media industries. Of course, technological change has always been crucial in the history of cultural transmission: it alters the material substratum, as well as the means of production and reception, upon which the process of cultural transmission depends. The development of new technologies in the sphere of telecommunications and information processing has, in recent years, profoundly affected the activities of the media industries in a variety of domains, from newspaper printing and desk-top publishing to the reproduction of music on tape and compact disc, from computerized systems of information recall to the broadcasting of television programmes by satellite. In this final section I shall not attempt to review all of the many developments which are currently taking place as a result of technological change. I shall focus on a few of the developments which are taking place in the domain of television, considering especially the ways in which they affect the transmission and reception of television messages. The developments I shall discuss are these: (1) the introduction of *video cassette recorders* (VCRs) for domestic use; (2) the deployment of *cable systems* for the transmission of television programmes, sometimes in conjunction with satellite relay stations; and (3) the development of *direct broadcasting by satellite*. Finally, I shall consider (4) whether the emerging configuration of satellite and cable systems represents a continuation of the traditional means of broadcasting or the beginnings of a fundamentally different system of cultural transmission.

1   In a relatively short period of time, the video cassette recorder has become a familiar addition to the television set in many Western homes. The VCR is a compact unit which can be connected to an existing TV set; it enables the user to record programmes which are broadcast through the established networks, and to replay recorded programmes or pre-recorded films. VCRs are based on the technology of magnetic tape recording, originally developed for recording sound in the late 1940s. Magnetic recording is a form of information storage in which the channel consists of magnetized particles that coat a plastic tape. Information is fed into the channel in the form of a modulated electrical current which produces variations in a magnetic field, and these variations produce a pattern in the magnetized particles of the tape. The information can be decoded by passing the tape over another electromagnet, in which a modulated electric current, capable of amplification and projection, can be generated. In the late 1950s these principles were adapted to enable visual images to be recorded. Visual image recording requires a much higher degree of information storage (about 200 times more than sound recording) and the recorders therefore employ a more sophisticated mechanism for recording and decoding information.

The first video tape recorders were developed for studio use, but by the early 1970s compact units for domestic use were available. In the late 1970s and early 1980s the number of VCRs in domestic use increased at a dramatic rate, rising from around 1 million in the EEC countries together and in the USA in 1976, to more than 30 million in the EEC countries and to just under 40 million in the USA by 1986. Nearly a third (about 170 million) of all television households in the world had VCRs by the middle of the 1980s. The proportion of homes with television sets which have VCRs varies considerably from one country to another, as indicated in table 4.9. Britain has one of the highest rates of penetration, with an estimated 52 per cent of television homes possessing VCRs in 1986, compared with an estimated 45 per cent in the USA, 49 per cent in Australia, 37 per cent in West Germany

Table 4.9

Estimates of national sales of video cassette recorders, 1986

	Annual sales (thousands)	Annual growth (%)	VCR population (thousands)	Rate of penetration (%)
Australia	585	24.4	2,937	48.5
Canada	1,050	35.8	3,932	41.8
France	1,350	44.0	4,420	22.6
Germany (FDR)	1,750	26.0	8,343	36.9
Italy	380	57.3	1,043	7.2
Japan	4,700	26.2	21,960	62.2
United Kingdom	1,650	19.4	9,954	52.4
United States	13,850	50.7	39,115	45.4

Source: Adapted from 'Mid-Year Video Statistics Review', Screen Digest (June 1987), pp. 129–33

and 23 per cent in France. A substantial proportion of VCRs may be rented rather than purchased, however, and there is some evidence to suggest that the rate of penetration may vary considerably according to the class position and employment status of individuals within the household.[40] The rapid increase in the number of VCRs in domestic use has provided a major new source of revenue for the large electronics companies – mainly Japanese, but increasingly West German and South-East Asian – involved in producing recorders and cassettes for the world market.

The domestic use of VCRs has also modified in significant ways the channels of diffusion for audio-visual products and the extent of control which recipients can exercise over these channels. The channels of diffusion have been modified in two respects: first, VCRs enable recipients to disconnect viewing schedules from broadcasting schedules, so that broadcast material can be recorded and watched at a different time. 'Time-shifting', as this practice is known, is the most common use of VCRs; it accounts for more than 75 per cent of home video viewing in Britain, Belgium and Sweden. The practice of time-shifting marks a significant increase in the extent of control which recipients can exercise over the process of broadcasting. The programming schedules of broadcasting organizations can be adapted by recipients and, to some extent, re-programmed in order to integrate viewing activities into other aspects of their daily life. In this way, recipients gain some control over the space–time distanciation characteristic of television broadcasting, even though this use of VCRs remains dependent on, and derivative from, the systems of broadcasting.

There is a second respect in which the domestic use of VCRs has modified the channels of diffusion: it enables audio-visual products to be distributed through the sale or rental of video cassettes for private domestic use, rather than through a broadcasting system or network of cinemas. The extent to which VCRs can be used in this way depends on the availability of pre-recorded cassettes, and this varies from one country and locale to another. In Britain, where there is a buoyant market for pre-recorded cassettes and a high level of VCR penetration, the rental and sale of video cassettes is a major retail trade: in 1986 the total value of rentals and sales was nearly £500 million, which was around half of the total revenue of the BBC and more than twice the box-office takings of all cinemas. By creating a new distribution network for pre-recorded material, the domestic use of VCRs has provided a new source of revenue for the film industry while bypassing the established systems of broadcasting and cinema. At the same time, this use of VCRs has raised new problems concerning the capacity of the state to regulate the content of audio-visual material and the capacity of commercial organizations to control copyright. These problems, which have been on the political agenda in many countries for the last decade, are part of a broader range of policy issues raised by the development of new communication technologies.

2 A second major technological change which is currently affecting television is the deployment of cable systems for the transmission of programmes. The basic technology for cable transmission has been available for some time. From an early stage, radio and television employed coaxial cables – that is, cables consisting of two conductors, one inside the other – as a means of relaying signals. During the 1950s and 1960s, coaxial cables were used on a limited scale to improve TV reception in rural and mountainous regions. But the full exploitation of cable systems began in the 1970s, when they were linked to the supply of television programmes via satellite. Cable television typically involves the use of antennae (or receiver dishes if programmes are supplied via satellite) which pick up signals and relay them to the cable 'headend', from which they are transmitted to individual TV sets by means of cables. Recipients typically pay a subscription fee for the channel or channels received. Many separate programmes and other signals can be transmitted simultaneously over the cable – coaxial cables can transmit between 40 and 100 programmes simultaneously. Recent developments in fibre optic technology offer the possibility of greatly increased transmission capacity, as well as greater interactive control. Fibre optic cables transmit messages, in the form of light pulses based on digital signalling, through tiny glass tubes. Large numbers of signals can be transmitted simultaneously, and messages can be transmitted in both directions with minimal interference.

The deployment of cable systems proceeded rapidly in the USA during the 1970s and 1980s. In 1970 less than 10 per cent of American households were connected to cable systems. By 1986 over 40 million households were connected to cable, representing a penetration of nearly 47 per cent; and a penetration of 60 per cent is expected by the early 1990s. In most European countries, by contrast, the deployment of cable systems has proceeded more slowly. Belgium, Luxembourg and The Netherlands had achieved high levels of penetration by the mid-1980s, but France, West Germany and Britain lagged well behind. In most parts of southern Europe the levels of penetration remain negligible. Cabling has advanced quickly in France and West Germany, where cabling schemes have received active government support. In Britain progress has been markedly slower, partly as a result of a hands-off governmental policy coupled with a reluctance on the part of financial institutions to invest in what is perceived as a high-risk venture. By October 1988 the number of homes connected in Britain had risen to over 380,000, but this was still a tiny fraction of the 20 million TV households.

The deployment of cable systems in Britain is controlled by a statutory Cable Authority, established in 1984, which issues licences to install cables and grants monopoly franchises to provide cable services. The franchise holders must carry all BBC and local independent television transmissions, but otherwise can choose from available broadcasting services, provided that the programmes concur with what the Cable Authority regards as appropriate standards of taste and decency. Among the most popular services is Sky Channel, a satellite-based service controlled by Rupert Murdoch's News International. Supported by advertising and offering a 24–hour service, Sky Channel claimed to reach more than 10 million homes throughout Europe by 1987. It has its own channel on all 78 UK cable networks and surpasses both BBC2 and Channel 4 in terms of its weekly share of viewing.

The use of cable systems greatly increases the transmission capacity of television and creates new channels of diffusion for television programmes. Although in many cases cable systems transmit signals emitted from the traditional broadcasting services, they also transmit signals emitted from a variety of new broadcasting services: in the USA there were, by 1985, around 40 satellite-delivered programming services, in addition to the established national networks. The development of cable systems thus represents a major challenge to the traditional system of broadcasting. By greatly increasing the transmission capacity and relaying signals from a variety of sources, they offer the possibility of greater diversity and they undermine to some extent the traditional regulatory arguments based on the limited range of channels of supply. The more sophisticated cable systems can be used to provide an increasing number of other telecommunication services, including access to financial information and databases of various kinds, and they create new opportunities for two-way transmission. Until now, the interactive capacity of cable systems has been used mainly as a means of monitoring usage, but it could in principle be used in other ways – for example, as a means of programme selection and evaluation, as a means of responding to surveys and questionnaires, and even as a means of voting. However, it remains to be seen how far the possibilities offered by cable technology will be realized in practice, particularly in Europe and in those parts of the world where levels of penetration remain relatively low.

3 The third major technological change which is having a major impact on television is the development of direct broadcasting by satellite, or DBS. In the previous section I briefly discussed the emergence of satellite technology and its use in the trans-national diffusion of information and communication. From the outset, communication satellites were also used as relay stations and distribution points for television broadcasting. Today they form

an integral part of national network systems in the USA, the USSR and elsewhere, and they are used as distribution points to supply cable systems on a national and international basis. DBS differs from these established satellite systems in certain key respects. In the case of DBS, signals are transmitted at a higher power, so that programmes can be delivered directly to the point of consumption – that is, the household – by virtue of a small domestic antenna or receiving dish. Hence DBS bypasses both the national network broad-casting systems and the cable supply systems, allowing recipients to tune in directly to signals transmitted via satellites. Signals can be encoded or 'scrambled' in such a way that reception can be restricted to individuals possessing special decoders capable of unscrambling the message. Hence the consumption of programmes can, in principle, be monitored and controlled by the transmitting authority.

It is likely that DBS systems will become increasingly important in the closing decade of the twentieth century. By 1986 an estimated 1.5 million homes in the USA received programmes via backyard dishes, giving rise to growing concern among cable companies who feared a substantial loss of subscription revenue. In Europe the French and German governments have been particularly active in developing DBS systems, signing an agreement in 1979 for a bilateral DBS project called TV-SAT. In 1988 the Luxembourg-based Astra satellite was successfully launched, offering 16 channels of sufficient strength to be received domestically. Six of the Astra channels were taken over by Rupert Murdoch's Sky, which began offering a range of DBS services in 1989. Murdoch's major DBS competitor in the UK market was a consortium, British Satellite Broadcasting (BSB), which included several companies that were already heavily involved in the communication and information industries (Granada, Pearson, Reed, Anglia Television, the Bond Corporation and the French industrial holding company Chargeurs). BSB began transmitting on five channels in April 1990, and intense competition developed between Sky and BSB in an attempt to persuade consumers to purchase and install the receiving equipment appropriate to the respective satellites. After a brief period during which both companies incurred sub-stantial losses, in November 1990 the companies merged to form British Sky Broadcasting, in which Murdoch holds a 50 per cent stake. While the financial problems confronting BSkyB remain considerable, the merger has placed the company in a strong position to increase uptake among con-sumers and to compete against the major terrestrial-based systems of transmission.

As with cable systems, DBS greatly increases the transmission capacity of television, enabling consumers to receive a large number of channels transmitted via a plurality of satellites. It also creates new channels of diffusion which bypass the traditional, terrestrial-based networks of broadcasting. The old monopolies and duopolies which characterized the early development of broadcasting in many European countries are therefore threatened by the deployment of these new media – although the extent of the threat will depend, in practice, on the level of uptake secured by the new services. DBS, as well as integrated cable–satellite systems, present another challenge to traditional patterns of broadcasting: they challenge the capacity of governments to regulate the transmission of audio-visual material, since signals can be transmitted across national boundaries and received, either directly or indirectly, by the consumer. Transmission via satellite does not respect national boundaries, and hence is considerably more difficult to monitor and control by the regulatory authorities of particular nation-states. The regulatory problems presented by satellite broadcasting – not only in the sense of monitoring the content of transmission, but also in the sense of regulating the ownership of and access to the new media of transmission – are among the most important political issues raised by the development of new communication technologies.

4 I want to consider, lastly, whether the development of new technologies, and especially the deployment of cable, cable–satellite and DBS systems, represents the continuation of traditional means of broadcasting or the emergence of a fundamentally different system of cultural transmission. There are clear continuities with the traditional broadcasting systems: cable and satellite technologies have, for some while, been an integral part of traditional systems; the domestic TV set remains the principal apparatus of reception; and much of the audio-visual material which is transmitted by cable and satellite systems is similar to, or identical with, the content of traditional broadcasting. Nevertheless, there are significant differences, and these differences are sufficiently profound to suggest that, with the increasing deployment of cable and satellite systems, we are witnessing the emergence of a new modality, or cluster of modalities, of cultural transmission. In drawing this chapter to a close, let me summarize some of the features of this modality and draw out some of their implications.

In the first place, the deployment of cable and satellite systems greatly augments the capacity for the transmission of audio-visual material. Whereas the traditional systems of television broadcasting were based on a limited number of channels of supply (in some cases only two or three channels), cable and satellite systems offer a large number of channels. The traditional scarcity of channels is rapidly being replaced by a bewildering multiplicity. Moreover, the rapid expansion in the number of channels available for the diffusion of audio-visual material is generally taking place outside of the traditional institutions of broadcasting – though many of the institutional actors who have been important so far in the development of cable and satellite systems are actors with major stakes in other sectors of the communication and information industries. The replacement of scarcity by multiplicity in terms of channels of diffusion has fundamental implications for the ways in which audio–visual material is regulated by state authorities and for the ways in which it is received by consumers. Traditional regulatory principles that were based on limited channels of supply cannot be applied directly to systems of transmission where scarcity of channels is no longer the key factor. The proliferation of channels also offers consumers the possibility of greater choice in the selection and reception of audio–visual material, although the extent to which this possibility becomes a reality will depend on a variety of factors which go beyond the technical capacities of the media as such.

A second feature of the development of new communication technologies is that they greatly increase the trans-national character of audio–visual transmission. By relaying signals via satellites, they extend the availability of audio–visual material in space while retaining the virtually instantaneous character of telecommunication. Again, this feature of satellite and cable-satellite systems differs significantly from traditional systems of television broadcasting, which were developed largely within the territorial boundaries of particular nation-states. For the institutional actors involved in European satellite broadcasting, the different European populations are treated as part of a potential pan-European audience, and air-time is sold to advertisers on the grounds that their products will be promoted in a pan-European market. These developments have far-reaching implications for the processes of globalization to which I referred earlier, implications that are only beginning to be recognized and assessed. They also have fundamental implications, as I indicated above, for the capacity of particular governments to regulate and control the transmission of audio–visual material originating from external sources, that is, sources external to the regions circumscribed by the traditional boundaries of the nation-state.

Third, the development of new communication technologies offers the possibility of an increasingly integrated set of communication and information services. This possibility is associated primarily with the development of sophisticated cable systems, employing fibre optic technology, but it is linked more generally to the codification of information and communication in a digital form. The shift from analog to digital systems of information codification, combined with the deployment of high-capacity cables which integrate different information services – the so-called Integrated Services Digital Network or ISDN – are creating a new technical scenario in which different kinds of information and communication converge on a common carrier.[41] This scenario is still some way off in most modern industrial societies, but the growing integration of information and communication services is a process that is already with us. This represents a significant departure from traditional broadcasting systems, in so far as the latter generally supplied a single service to an indefinite number of recipients. The development of new communication technologies offers not only a greatly expanded provision of the same kind of service but also a greatly expanded range of services supplied through a common carrier system.

Finally, the development of new communication technologies also offers the possibility of a more personalized and interactive form of communication, in the sense that they give recipients greater choice in the selection of channels and services and greater capacity to transmit messages of their own through the system. Once again, these new possibilities are associated primarily with the development of cable technology, and especially fibre optic cables which greatly increase the interactive capacity of cable systems. But the exploitation of the interactive capacity of fibre optic cables remains largely a matter for the future: today, most communication through cable and satellite systems remains overwhelmingly one-way. Nevertheless, the deployment of new systems of communication will certainly give recipients a greater range of channels and services from which to choose, and will in certain respects give individuals more control over the sources of their information and entertainment.

In view of these considerations, I think it is plausible to maintain that the emerging configuration of cable and satellite systems represents the development of a new modality of cultural transmission, a modality which differs significantly from the traditional systems of television broadcasting. For the foreseeable future it is likely that this new modality will co-exist with traditional broadcasting systems, providing a steadily increasing range of channels and services to individuals who continue to receive a significant proportion of their viewing material through the traditional networks. In the longer term, the emerging configuration of cable and satellite systems may have a more disruptive impact on the organization of the media industries. The long-term impact will depend partly on the ways in which existing media institutions and state authorities respond to the new systems, partly on the rate of uptake of the services offered and partly on the capacity of the media industries to generate audio-visual material of sufficient quantity and quality to fill the rapidly increasing number of available channels and to command the attention of viewers. For the transformation brought about by the deployment of cable and satellite systems is a transformation in the modality of transmission; it does not directly transform, but rather depends upon, the ongoing production of audio-visual materials. Whether this transformation in the modality of transmission will serve to stimulate new and innovative kinds of productive activity, or will tend on the contrary to consolidate the production of low-budget formula programming, is a question that remains open.

In this chapter I have traced the development of the technical media and institutions of cultural transmission, concentrating on the developments associated with the rise of mass communication from the late fifteenth century to the present day. The rise of mass communication, I have argued, is a fundamental constitutive feature of modern societies. It is a process which has been closely interwoven with the development of industrial capitalism and with the rise of the modern nation-state. It is also a process which has profoundly transformed the ways in which symbolic forms are circulated in modern societies. With the rise of mass communication, the process of cultural transmission becomes increasingly mediated by a cluster of institutions concerned with the commodification and extended circulation of symbolic forms. In recent decades these institutions have become increasingly integrated into large-scale communication conglomerates, and the circulation of symbolic forms has become increasingly global in character. The deployment of new communication technologies has followed and facilitated these trends, while at the same time marking the beginning of a significant new departure in the history of modalities of cultural transmission.

In the next chapter I shall move beyond this largely historical account and seek to outline a more theoretical approach to the nature of mass communication. Although 'mass communication' is a broad term and can legitimately be used – as I have used it here – to refer to a wide range of technical media and institutions concerned with the production and diffusion of symbolic goods, in the next chapter I shall focus primarily on the medium of television as it has developed within the existing frameworks of broadcasting. I shall not consider in further detail the possible impact of new communication technologies, except in so far as these technologies have become an issue in current policy debates. My concern will be primarily with the forms of television experience and with the organization of broadcasting institutions as they have existed hitherto.

Towards a Social Theory of
Mass Communication

The advent of mass communication, and especially the rise of mass circulation newspapers in the nineteenth century and the emergence of broadcasting in the twentieth, has had a profound impact on the modes of experience and patterns of interaction characteristic of modern societies. For most people today, the knowledge we have of events which take place beyond our immediate social milieu is a knowledge largely derived from our reception of mass-mediated symbolic forms. The knowledge we have of political leaders and their policies, for instance, is a knowledge derived largely from newspapers, radio and television, and the ways in which we participate in the institutionalized system of political power are deeply affected by the knowledge so derived. Similarly, our experience of events which take place in contexts that are spatially and temporally remote, from strikes and demonstrations to massacres and wars, is an experience largely mediated by the institutions of mass communication; indeed, our experience of these events as 'political', as constitutive of the domain of experience which is regarded as politics, is partly the outcome of a series of institutionalized practices which endow them with the status of news. The role of the media is so fundamental in this regard that it would be partial at best to portray the nature and conduct of politics at a national and international level without reference to the processes of mass communication.

In this chapter I want to begin to explore some of the ways in which the advent of mass communication has transformed the modes of experience and patterns of interaction characteristic of modern societies. I shall not try to deal equally with the many different media of mass communication, but shall give particular attention to the nature and impact of television broadcasting, as it has emerged and developed hitherto. Drawing on my earlier analysis of technical media and their development, I shall begin by delineating some general characteristics of mass communication. I shall then focus on what I call *the interactional impact of technical media*, that is, the ways in which the development of mass communication affects the social organization of everyday life. Here I shall be concerned to stress that the deployment of technical media should be seen, not merely as the establishment of new channels of diffusion which exist alongside pre-existing social relations, but rather as a potential reorganization of social relations themselves, in the sense that new media make possible new forms of action and interaction in the social world. In the third section I shall explore some of the ways in which the deployment of technical media of mass communication has reconstituted the boundaries between public and private life in modern societies. The fourth section will examine some of the relations between institutions of mass communication, on the one hand, and institutions of the market economy and the state, on the other. This discussion will be more normative in tone and will address issues of a more practical, policy-orientated kind. I shall reappraise some traditional liberal ideas about the nature and role of media institutions in modern societies, juxtaposing these ideas to the developmental trends characteristic of the media industries; and, against this backcloth, I shall put forward an alternative view of the ways in which media institutions could be developed in contemporary societies, as a range of organizations located between market and state. Finally, in the closing section of the chapter, I shall return to the theme of ideology and consider how the analysis of ideology should be rethought in the era of mass communication.

This chapter represents a preliminary contribution to a social theory of mass communication. My aim is to prepare the way for a systematic theoretical reflection on the developments which constitute the mediazation of modern culture. The account which I offer here is at most a prolegomenon to a systematic reflection of this kind, a reflection which I shall pursue in a subsequent work. Here my aims are more limited: I shall seek to highlight some characteristics of mass communication, and some of the ways in which the deployment of technical media has transformed the nature of experience and interaction in modern societies, with a view to reflecting on certain problems of a theoretical and practical kind. The theoretical and practical problems on which I focus here, while central to current debates, comprise only a selection of the issues that would have to be addressed by a systematic attempt to come to terms with the theoretical and political implications of the mediazation of modern culture.

Some Characteristics of Mass Communication

Let me begin by analysing some of the general characteristics of what is commonly called 'mass communication'. It has often been pointed out that, while 'mass communication' is a convenient label for referring to a broad range of media institutions and products, the term is misleading in certain respects. It is worth dwelling for a moment on some of the respects in which this term can lead astray. The expression 'mass' derives from the fact that the messages transmitted by the media industries are generally available to relatively large audiences. This is certainly the case in some sectors of the media industries and at some stages in their development, such as the mass circulation newspaper industry and the major television networks. However, during other periods in the development of the media industries (e.g. the early newspaper industry) and in some sectors of the media industries today (e.g. some book and magazine publishers), the audiences were and remain relatively small and specialized. Hence the term 'mass' should not be construed in narrowly quantitative terms; the important point about mass communication is not that a given number or proportion of individuals receive the products, but rather that the products are available in principle to a plurality of recipients. Moreover, the term 'mass' is misleading in so far as it suggests that the audiences are like inert, undifferentiated heaps. This suggestion obscures the fact that the messages transmitted by the media industries are received by specific individuals situated in particular social-historical contexts. These individuals attend to media messages with varying degrees of concentration, actively interpret and make sense of these messages and relate them to other aspects of their lives. Rather than viewing these individuals as part of an inert and undifferentiated mass, we should leave open the possibility that the reception of media messages is an active, inherently critical and socially differentiated process – a theme which I shall explore in more detail in the following chapter.

If the term 'mass' may be misleading in this context, the term 'communication' may also be, since the kinds of communication generally involved in mass communication are quite different from those involved in ordinary conversation. I shall examine some of these differences in the course of the following discussion. Here I shall call attention to one important difference: namely, that mass communication generally involves a one-way flow of messages from the transmitter to the receiver. Unlike the dialogical situation of a conversation, in which a listener is also a potential respondent, mass communication institutes a fundamental *break* between the producer and receiver, in such a way that recipients have relatively little capacity to contribute to the course and content of the communicative process. Hence it may be more appropriate to speak of the 'transmission' or 'diffusion' of messages rather than of 'communication' as such. Yet even in the circumstances of mass communication, recipients do have some capacity to contribute, in so far as recipients are also consumers who may sometimes choose between various media products and whose views are sometimes solicited or taken into account by the organizations concerned with producing and diffusing these products. Moreover, it is possible that new technological developments – such as those associated with fibre optic cables – will increase the interactive capacity of the medium of television and give viewers greater control over the transmission process, although the extent to which this will become a practical reality remains to be seen.

In the light of these preliminary qualifications, I want to offer a broad conceptualization of mass communication and to highlight some of its key characteristics. We may broadly conceive of mass communication as *the institutionalized production and generalized diffusion of symbolic goods via the transmission and storage of information/communication*. By conceiving of mass communication in terms of the production and diffusion of symbolic goods, I wish to stress the importance of viewing mass communication in relation to the institutions concerned with the commodification of symbolic forms. What we now describe as mass communication is a range of phenomena and processes that emerged historically through the development of institutions seeking to exploit new opportunities for the fixation and reproduction of symbolic forms. I briefly sketched the development of some of these institutions in the previous chapter. I now want to analyse mass communication in a more theoretical way by focusing on the following four characteristics: the institutionalized production and diffusion of symbolic goods; the instituted break between production and reception; the extension of availability in time and space; and the public circulation of symbolic forms. In discussing these characteristics I shall draw on my earlier comments concerning aspects of cultural transmission, adapting them to the purpose of analysing mass communication.

The first characteristic of mass communication is *the institutionalized production and diffusion of symbolic goods*. Mass communication presupposes the development of institutions – that is, relatively stable clusters of social relations and accumulated resources – concerned with the large-scale production and generalized diffusion of symbolic goods. These activities are 'large-scale' in the sense that they involve the production and diffusion of multiple copies or the provision of materials to numerous recipients. This is rendered possible by the fixation of symbolic forms in technical media and by the reproducibility of the forms. *Fixation* may involve processes of encoding whereby symbolic forms are translated into information which can be stored in a particular medium or material substratum; the symbolic forms may be transmitted as information and then decoded for the purposes of reception or consumption. The symbolic forms diffused by mass communication are inherently *reproducible* in the sense that multiple copies may be produced or made available to numerous recipients. The reproduction of forms is generally controlled as strictly as possible by the institutions of mass communication, since it is one of the principal means by which symbolic forms are subjected to economic valorization. Forms are reproduced in order to be exchanged on a market or through a regulated type of economic transaction. Hence they are *commodified* and treated as objects to be sold, as services to be paid for or as media which can facilitate the sale of other objects or services. In the first instance, therefore, mass communication should be understood as part of a range of institutions concerned, in varying ways, with the fixation, reproduction and commodification of symbolic forms.

A second characteristic of mass communication is that *it institutes a fundamental break between the production and reception of symbolic goods.* These goods are produced for recipients who are generally not physically present at the place of production and transmission or diffusion; they are, literally, *mediated* by the technical media in which they are fixed and transmitted. This characteristic is not, of course, unique to mass communication: the fixation and transmission of symbolic forms on papyrus or stone also involved a break between production and reception. But with the rise of mass communication, the range of producers and receivers affected by this process has greatly expanded. Moreover, as I noted earlier, the mediation of symbolic forms via mass communication generally involves a one-way flow of messages from the producer to the recipient, such that the capacity of the recipient to influence or intervene in the processes of production and transmission or diffusion is strictly limited. One consequence of this condition is that the processes of production and transmission or diffusion are characterized by a distinctive form of *indeterminacy*. Symbolic forms are produced for audiences and transmitted or diffused in order to reach these audiences, but these processes generally take place in the absence of a direct and continuous monitoring of the audiences' responses. In contrast to face-to-face interaction, where the interlocutors can question one another and observe one another's responses, in mass communication the personnel involved in the production and transmission or diffusion are generally deprived of immediate feedback from the recipients. Since the economic valorization of mass-mediated symbolic forms may depend crucially on the nature and extent of reception, the personnel involved typically employ a variety of strategies to cope with this indeterminacy.[1] They draw upon past experience and use it as a guide to likely future outcomes; they use well-tried formulas which have a predictable audience appeal; or they try to obtain information about recipients through market research or through the routine monitoring of audience size and response. These and other techniques are institutionalized mechanisms which enable personnel to reduce the indeterminacy stemming from the break between production and reception, and to do so in a way which concurs with the overall aims of the institutions concerned.

A third characteristic of mass communication is that *it extends the availability of symbolic forms in time and in space*. Again, this characteristic is not unique to mass communication: all forms of cultural transmission involve some degree of space-time distanciation. But the media of mass communication generally involve a relatively high degree of distanciation in both space and time; and, with the development of telecommunications, space-time distanciation is severed from the physical transportation of symbolic forms. The transmission of symbolic forms via telecommunications – for example, via a network of terrestrial and satellite relays – enables the institutions of mass communication to achieve a high degree of spatial distanciation in a minimal amount of time. Moreover, since the symbolic forms are generally fixed in a relatively durable medium, such as paper, photographic film or electromagnetic tape, they also have extended availability in time and can be preserved for subsequent use. The space-time distanciation involved in mass communication is also affected by the conditions under which symbolic forms are received and consumed. By virtue of the instituted break between production and reception, the nature and extent of distanciation may depend on the social practices and technical conditions of reception. For example, the extension of availability of a book in time and space may depend as much on the ways in which the book is received – whether it is recommended or ignored, incorporated into curriculae or actively suppressed, and so on – as it depends on the channels of diffusion and the nature of the technical medium itself. Similarly, the extension of availability of a television programme or film may depend on whether potential recipients have the technical means to receive the programme, whether the scheduling concurs with the social organization of their everyday lives, and so on.

A fourth characteristic of mass communication is that *it involves the public circulation of symbolic forms*. The products of mass communication are produced in principle for a plurality of recipients. In this respect, mass communication differs from forms of communication – such as telephone conversations, teleconferencing, or private video recordings of various kinds – which employ the same technical media of fixation and transmission but which are orientated towards a single or highly restricted range of recipients. As I remarked in the previous chapter, this basic difference between established forms of mass communication and other forms of electronically mediated interaction may be called into question by the increasing deployment of new communication technologies, but this is a development which has yet to be fully realized. As the institutions of mass communication have developed hitherto, their products circulate within a 'public domain', in the sense that they are available in principle to anyone who has the technical means, abilities and resources to acquire them. While the nature and scope of this public domain may be unlimited in principle, it is always limited in practice by the social-historical conditions of production, transmission and reception. The institutions of mass communication often aim to reach as large an audience as possible, since the size of the audience may directly affect the economic valorization of the products concerned. Today the audiences for some films and television programmes may amount to hundreds of millions of viewers worldwide; a single Christmas Day television broadcast can command more than 30 million viewers in Britain alone. The nature and scope of the audiences for the products of mass communication vary enormously from one medium to another, and from one product to another within the same medium. The ways in which these products are appropriated by the recipients – whether, for example, they are appropriated by a collective gathering in a cinema or by a private viewing in the home – also vary considerably, depending on the medium, the product, the channels of diffusion and the social and technical conditions of reception. One consequence of the intrinsically public character of media products is that the development of mass communication has been accompanied by attempts to exercise control, on the part of state authorities and other regulatory bodies, over the institutions of mass communication. The very capacity of these institutions to make symbolic forms available to a potentially vast audience is a source of concern for authorities which seek to maintain order and regulate social life within the territories under their jurisdiction. I shall return to these issues later in this chapter, in the context of discussing the relations between institutions of mass communication, the market economy and the state.

In considering some of the general characteristics of mass communication, I have mentioned various respects in which particular media and media products differ from one another. In order to analyse these differences further, we would have to examine certain media and media products in more detail and in relation to the social and technical conditions of their deployment and diffusion. We can use the notion of modalities of cultural transmission, introduced in the previous chapter, to describe media which involve determinate and relatively stable conditions of deployment. The development of the newspaper industry, of the retail book trade, of the recorded music industry and of television network broadcasting can all be regarded as the emergence of modalities of cultural transmission in this sense. These modalities involve certain typical clusters of technical media, institutions of production, forms of reproduction, channels of diffusion, conditions of reception, and so on. Some of the features of the various modalities of mass communication, and of the products of these modalities, can be analyzed in terms of the aspects listed in the right-hand column of figure 5.1. These aspects indicate some of the variable features of modalities and their products, that is, some of the features which vary from one modality to another. These aspects are related in turn to the characteristics of mass communication, as distinguished and defined above. So, for example, variations in the nature of productive institutions and technical media are related to the fact that mass communication involves the institutionalized production and diffusion of symbolic goods, while variations in the nature

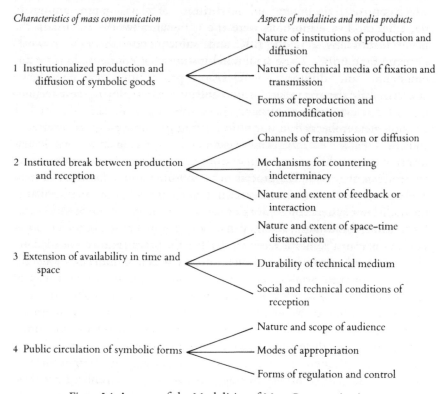

Figure 5.1 Aspects of the Modalities of Mass Communication

and scope of audiences are related to the fact that mass communication involves the public circulation of symbolic forms. In proposing that these aspects indicate some of the variable features of modalities of mass communication, I do not want to suggest that a variation in terms of any one feature is sufficient to constitute a new modality: matters are, of course, much more complicated than this. By virtue of the growing interconnections within the media industries themselves and the range and diversity of their activities and products, the lines of demarcation between the modalities of mass communication are becoming increasingly blurred. Nevertheless, there is a series of partially overlapping and partially divergent features which serve to define relatively distinct clusters of characteristics. The technical media of fixation and transmission are central components of these clusters, but one must also consider the broader social conditions and contexts of production, diffusion and reception.

We can use the example of television transmission, documented in the previous chapter, to illustrate these points. The development of television broadcasting in the 1940s and 1950s took place within a range of institutions which controlled the production and diffusion of television programmes. In the USA the key institutions were the national networks; in Britain the major institutions were the BBC and, subsequently, the ITV network, overseen by the IBA. These traditional institutional configurations for the production and diffusion of television programmes are now being challenged by the emergence of new institutions employing new technologies for television transmission. The combination of cable and satellite technologies, embedded in institutions offering a new range of services to audiences that are potentially more extended in space, making possible new forms of commodification and undermining traditional forms of regulation and control, may be in the process of establishing a new modality of mass communication. In certain respects this emergent configuration is similar to the traditional systems of network broadcasting – many of the products may be the same, for instance, and they may be consumed by means of an audio-visual display in a domestic receiving set. But the products are embedded in a new cluster of institutions and technologies which significantly alter the conditions of their production, diffusion and reception. Hence it may be appropriate to speak of the emergence of a new modality of mass communication, even though we cannot draw a sharp line of demarcation between this modality and the traditional system of network broadcasting.

In emphasizing the technical and institutional aspects of the modalities of mass communication, I do not wish to downplay the importance of analysing the *content* of the messages or products transmitted by these modalities, or of examining the *modes of appropriation* of these messages or products. Both the content of the messages and the ways in which they are appropriated by recipients are of great interest; and, as I shall try to show in the following chapter, an adequate framework for the analysis of mass communication must make room for the study of the content and reception of media messages as well as their production and diffusion. Here I have been concerned to stress, however, that the analysis of mass communication must begin by considering the nature and development of the range of institutions involved in the large-scale production and generalized diffusion of symbolic goods. Only in this way can we make sense of media products *qua* commodified and reproducible symbolic forms which are made available, in extended reaches of time and space, for public circulation and reception.

Mass Communication and Social Interaction

The analysis of the general characteristics of mass communication provides a backcloth against which I want to consider some of the ways in which the development of mass communication has transformed the nature of social interaction and the modes of experience in modern societies. Here I shall be concerned, not so much with the specific 'effects' of particular media messages, but rather with the ways in which the deployment of technical media serve to reorganize and reconstitute social interaction. I shall argue that the deployment of different media of mass communication should not be seen as a mere supplement to pre-existing social relations, as the introduction of neutral channels which diffuse symbolic goods within society but leave social relations unchanged. On the contrary, the deployment of technical media has a fundamental impact on the ways in which people act and interact with one another. This is not to say that the technical medium *determines* social organization in some simple, mono-causal way; the deployment of technical media is always situated within a broader social and institutional context which limits the available options. But new technical media *make possible* new forms of social interaction, modify or undermine old forms of interaction, create new foci and new venues for action and interaction, and thereby serve to restructure existing social relations and the institutions and organizations of which they are part.

It is to the credit of the so-called media theorists, such as Harold Innis and Marshall McLuhan, that they highlighted the fact that the nature of social interaction may be affected by the very *form* of media transmission.[2] These theorists argued, rightly in my view, that different technical media help to create different environments for action and interaction; they argued that the *form* of the medium itself, quite apart from the specific *content* of the messages it conveys, has an impact on the nature of social life. The ways in which Innis and McLuhan develop this general theme are, I think, of considerably less interest than the theme itself. Innis draws questionable conclusions from what he calls the 'bias' of communication in time and space: he suggests, for instance, that societies in which the dominant medium is biased towards temporal durability, such as stone carvings, will tend to be small and stable, whereas societies with media which are biased towards spatial mobility will tend to be large and imperial, like the Roman Empire. I do not wish to follow this rather sweeping and speculative line of reflection. However, I do wish to pursue the general theme highlighted by the media theorists and to examine some of the ways in which the development of technical media have transformed the nature of social interaction, have created new contexts for action and interaction and new arenas for self-presentation and the perception of others.

In pursuing this theme I shall adopt a selective approach, focusing primarily on the modality of television broadcasting as it has developed in the post-war period. Television broadcasting does not operate in isolation from other modalities of mass communication, but it does play a central role in the contemporary constellation of technical media. By focusing on some aspects of television and comparing these with the characteristics of other media, we can examine some of the ways in which social interaction has been transformed by the advent and widespread deployment of the televisual medium. We can thereby highlight certain respects in which cultural experience in modern societies is different from the forms of cultural experience which were characteristic of societies in which symbolic forms were transmitted exclusively or primarily by oral or written means. Today we live in societies in which the diffusion of symbolic forms via electronic media has become a common, and in certain respects primary, mode of cultural transmission. Modern culture is, to an ever greater extent, an *electronically mediated culture* in which oral and written modes of transmission have been supplemented, and to some extent displaced, by modes of transmission based on electronic media. Here I shall not attempt to explore in detail the comparison between oral, written and electronically mediated forms of transmission, although such a comparison raises issues which merit systematic analysis.[3]

Taking the medium of television as the primary focus, my aim in this section will be to elucidate what I shall describe as the *interactional impact of technical media*. I shall distinguish four dimensions of this interactional impact: (1) media facilitate interaction across time and space; (2) they affect the ways in which individuals act *for* others, in so far as the others for whom they are acting may comprise an audience which is extended, dispersed and remote in time and space; (3) they affect the ways in which individuals act *in response to* others, in so far as they are able to act in response to others who are located in distant contexts; and (4) media also affect the ways in which individuals act and interact in the process of reception, that is, they affect the social organization of those spheres of everyday life in which the reception of mediated messages is a routine activity. In this section I shall examine each of these dimensions. In the subsequent section I shall consider a related aspect of mass communication, namely, the ways in which the deployment of technical media serve to reconstitute the boundaries between public and private life, thereby altering the modes of access to information and communication.

1 Interaction across time and space

Technical media may enable individuals to interact with one another across spatial and temporal distances, although the nature of mediated interaction may differ significantly from the kinds of interaction which are typical of face-to-face situations. In an earlier chapter I used the notion of space–time distanciation to discuss the ways in which symbolic forms are detached from their contexts of production and transmitted via technical media to contexts which are spatially and temporally remote. Here I want to focus on a particular aspect of this process: namely, the impact of space–time distanciation on the nature and patterns of social interaction. By virtue of space–time distanciation, *the deployment of technical media separates social interaction from physical locale*, so that individuals can interact with one another even though they do not share a common spatial–temporal setting.[4] A letter enables individuals to communicate with one another at a distance, and it introduces a temporal delay in the process of communication which is determined by the time required physically to transmit the letter from its origin to its destination. The telephone also enables individuals to communicate at a distance, but it virtually eliminates the temporal delay characteristic of letter transmission. Telephone interaction combines extended availability in space with temporal simultaneity; and it enables individuals to communicate in an oral mode which is similar to face-to-face conversation, although it also displays some distinctive social and discursive properties.[5] In differing ways both letter writing and telephone conversation enable individuals to establish, sustain and develop forms of social interaction which are independent of a shared physical locale.

The development of technical media of mass communication has further consequences for the spatial and temporal constitution of social interaction. The media of mass communication extend the availability of symbolic forms in time and space, and they do so in a way which permits specific kinds of mediated interaction between producers and recipients. Since mass communication institutes a fundamental break between the production and reception of symbolic forms, it makes possible a specific kind of interaction across time and space which we may describe as *mediated quasi-interaction*.[6] It is 'interaction' because it involves individuals communicating to others who respond to them in certain ways and who may form bonds of friendship, affection or loyalty with them. But it is '*quasi*-interaction' in so far as the flow of communication is predominantly one-way and the modes of response through which recipients can communicate with the principal communicator are strictly limited. The development of television has greatly increased the importance and pervasiveness of mediated quasi-interaction in modern societies, and it has transformed its character. In the case of printed media such as books and newspapers, the communicating individuals often remain indefinite and may be little more than a name to most readers. With the advent of electronic media and especially television, however, communicating individuals become *personalities* with a voice, a face, a character and a history, personalities with whom recipients can sympathize or empathize, whom they can like or dislike, detest or revere. These personalities acquire a physical presence which is mediated and managed rather than direct, and they become the objects of complex processes of economic and symbolic valorization which are controlled to some extent by the media industries. Hence TV personalities have an 'aura' which is sustained in part by the distance that separates personalities from viewers. In exceptional circumstances this distance may be bridged – as, for example, when a viewer meets a television personality or a fan meets a star. But the exceptional and sometimes awkward character of such encounters attests to the fact that the relationship established through mediated quasi-interaction is a relationship that does not normally involve the sharing of a common physical locale.

The specific spatial and temporal characteristics of electronically mediated quasi-interaction depend on a variety of factors including the nature of the technical medium, the institutional apparatus of diffusion, the contexts and conditions of reception, and the nature and content of the symbolic forms transmitted. Consider an example: an interview with the President of the United States, televised and transmitted via satellite, and watched by individuals in a domestic context in Britain. This quasi-interaction involves the establishment of a relationship between individuals who are situated in contexts which are widely divergent both in terms of their spatial location and in terms of their social and institutional characteristics. It is unlikely that the recipients, however positively predisposed they may feel towards the President and however well they may feel they know him, will ever share a common physical locale with him. Watching the interview is part of a relationship which extends through time without ever overlapping in space, and indeed if it ever were to overlap in space – if, in the unlikely event, viewers were to encounter the President in the street or entertain him in their home – this occasion would no doubt be accompanied by considerable awkwardness, anxiety or confusion. While watching the interview is a quasi-interaction that takes place across divergent spatial contexts, it also makes the spatial context of the President, and the President himself, *available to* the recipients, albeit in a mediated form. If the interview takes place in a domestic setting, such as the President's living room, accompanied perhaps by his wife and children, then the quasi-interaction may acquire a certain *intimacy* which may enable the President to communicate public matters in a personal way or personal matters in a public way; but it may also expose him to unprecedented political risks, a possibility that I shall examine in more detail later. The quasi-interaction of watching the interview may involve virtual simultaneity by virtue of satellite transmission, although this may be, and often is, attenuated by pre-recording, editing and scheduled diffusion. The virtual simultaneity of the live interview offers unique opportunities but also carries high risks. It enables the President to appear informal, spontaneous, versatile and in command, and it enables him to communicate with the audience as if they were conversational partners, as if they were participants in an ongoing dialogue. But live interviews also carry risks: the President may just as easily appear incompetent, inconsistent, ill-informed or simply *ordinary*. More-over, since live interviews are recorded and can be shown on subsequent occasions, any displayed incompetence may be reviewed or recalled in future quasi-interactions, thereby affecting in a potentially permanent way the nature of the relationship sustained between the President and his audience.

I have chosen the example of watching an interview with the US President in order to illustrate some of the ways in which mediated quasi-interaction may be spatially and temporally constituted. I could of course focus on other examples – quasi-interaction with television chat-show personalities or news broadcasters, with soap-opera characters or film stars, etc. – and these examples, analysed in relation to such factors as the institutional apparatus of diffusion and the conditions of reception, would display specific spatial and temporal characteristics. But there is no need to proliferate examples. The general point I wish to make is that the deployment of technical media of mass communication, and in particular electronic media such as television, is accompanied by the development of new forms of mediated quasi-interaction between communicators and recipients, and these forms of quasi-interaction are typically divorced from the sharing of a common physical locale. The distinctive characteristics of mediated quasi-interaction have important consequences for the ways in which communicators and recipients behave and relate to others and to themselves.

2 Acting for distant others

Technical media enable individuals to communicate with others in new and effective ways, and individuals adapt their communicative behaviour to concur with the opportunities offered by the deployment of technical media. The acquisition of a telephone generally changes an individual's pattern of interaction with others as well as the nature of the interaction itself. Telephone conversation is simultaneous dialogical interaction which is severed from shared physical locale and devoid of visual cues, so that an individual, in speaking to another over the telephone, must monitor and adapt his or her utterances in the light of responses which are entirely aural. The telephone greatly expands the range of relationships that an individual can form, and it enables individuals to sustain these relationships through time and space and yet in the absence of physical encounters. But the spatial and temporal constitution of interaction mediated by the telephone also restricts the nature of the relationships formed through such interaction. An individual known only through telephone conversations is literally faceless and, in most cases, is unlikely to become the object of a strong emotional bond; we relate to such individuals primarily as absent interlocutors rather than as close personal friends. Of course, a great deal of telephone conversation takes place between individuals who also interact with one another in other ways, and in such cases the nature of the relationships formed is less dependent on the particular characteristics of telephone interaction.

By separating social interaction from physical locale, the deployment of technical media also affects the ways in which, and the extent to which, individuals are able to manage their self-presentation. Any action or performance takes place within a particular interactive framework which involves a whole series of assumptions, conventions and points of reference. An individual acting within this framework will, to some extent, adapt his or her behaviour to it, projecting a self-image which is more or less compatible with the framework. Actions and aspects of self which are felt to be inappropriate may be suppressed and reserved for other settings or encounters – that is, for settings which are, in Goffman's terms, 'back regions' relative to the 'front regions' of the primary interactive framework.[7] The use of a technical medium serves partially to define the interactive framework, and therefore also defines in part those settings which are front and back regions. In the course of a telephone conversation with a business associate, for example, an individual may seek to suppress noises which arise in the physical locale from which he or she is speaking – the sound of a television, the comments or laughter of a friend or colleague, etc. – as such noises may be regarded as back-region behaviour relative to the primary interactive framework.

In considering the ways in which interactive frameworks may be transformed by the deployment of technical media of mass communication, let me restrict myself again to the medium of television. The instituted break between production and reception implies that behaving for and communicating to television audiences are activities that take place largely in the absence of direct and continuous feedback, of either an oral or a visual kind. Earlier in this chapter I noted that this interactive indeterminacy is generally mitigated by means of various strategies which enable production personnel to achieve relatively predictable effects in the absence of direct and continuous feedback. These strategies thus constrain and guide the actions and utterances of individuals communicating, or seeking to communicate, via television. Precisely how, and to what extent, these strategies constrain and guide individuals depends on a variety of factors, including the nature of the programme, the position and status of the individual, and the technical possibilities and practical opportunities. I shall not examine these factors here. I shall emphasize instead a point which is of general significance. Given the role that television (and indeed other media of mass communication) have come to assume as sources of information concerning news and current affairs, the very existence of this medium may have an impact on the actions of individuals who seek to communicate to a distant and extended audience, or who happen to find themselves in a situation which is deemed worthy of being televised. *The very existence of the medium of television gives rise to a category or categories of action which is carried out with the aim of being televisable*, that is, capable of being regarded as worthy of transmission via television to a spatially distant and potentially vast audience. Today part of the purpose of actions such as mass demonstrations and hijackings, summit meetings and state visits, is to generate televisable events which will enable individuals or groups to communicate with remote and extended audiences. The possibility of being televised is one of the conditions for carrying out the action itself, or for the staging and performance of a sequence of actions which may be viewed and heard by an indeterminate number of absent individuals.

The medium of television presents communicators and potential communicators with new opportunities and new problems in terms of the management of self-presentation. The production process defines a primary interactive framework which is spatially remote from the recipients of the television programme and in which the lines of demarcation between front regions and back regions are determined independently of direct recipient response. Hence viewers may see a television character acting in ways and in situations which, in the course of their everyday lives, would be strictly back-region behaviour. Part of the shock value of television and other media – and a feature about which much controversy has raged – is that it routinely makes available behaviour which, in most contexts of face-to-face inter-action, would generally be regarded as belonging to back regions. The importance of redefining front-region and back-region behaviour, and of managing the presentation of self within this interactive framework, is well understood by political leaders and other public figures, who generally take great care in determining the boundaries of their televisable selves. The medium of television offers unprecedented opportunities for political leaders to appear before extended audiences and to manage their self-presentation, but it also carries enormous risks, both because leaders may appear incompetent or ill-informed and because they may expose, or have exposed by others, too much of their back-region behaviour. Much that may be regarded as *scandalous* in the modern political arena is probably not uncommon in other spheres of life and is probably not new; what are new are, among other things, the means available for recording and transmitting back-region behaviour and hence the capacity to expose, on an unprece-dented scale and with vivid realism, activities that previously would have remained hidden from public view. The shock experienced by many people on listening to the Watergate Tapes or reading the transcripts was not so much the discovery that the President may have been involved in a criminal conspiracy or a cover-up, as many people had long suspected this; rather, it was the discovery that, behind the carefully managed presentation of Nixon and his administration, there was a back region of behaviour, and associated forms of back-region conversation, which seemed altogether inappropriate for the incumbent of the White House.

3 Acting in response to distant others

Just as technical media may enable individuals to act for distant others, so too they may create new opportunities for individuals to act in response to others who are spatially and temporally remote. In the case of telephone conversation, the responsive action is often part of the conversation itself. Indeed, some form of responsive action is partly constitutive of telephone conversation, which is essentially dialogical: an extended silence from a telephone interlocutor will generally lead to a breakdown of the conversation. But telephone conversation also gives rise to forms of responsive action which are not integral to the conversation as such. This happens, for instance, when a telephone conversation gives rise to an action or further conversation which is carried out or conducted after the initial conversation has been concluded. In such cases individuals are engaging in forms of action or interaction which are generated in response to others who are spatially and temporally distant, and whose generative role has been made possible by the technical media of transmission.

With the development of mass communication and especially television, the nature and scope of responsive action is both greatly increased and rendered less determinate. It is greatly increased in the sense that a plurality of individuals may act in response to distant others: messages are now received by audiences which may comprise thousands or millions of individuals, spread across a diverse array of spatial and temporal contexts; and these individuals may act, in one way or another, in response to the messages they receive. Such responsive action is less determinate than that characteristic of telephone conversation in the sense that, in the case of mass communication, responsive action is not constitutive of the interaction itself. That is, the mediated quasi-interaction does not require an ongoing and active response from recipients, and the production and diffusion of mass-mediated messages generally takes place in the absence of immediate feedback. Hence the forms of responsive action to which a mass-mediated message may give rise are not easily monitored by the communicator: he or she is speaking to recipients who are largely unknown, and whose ways of responding to what is said or shown may be difficult to predict. Moreover, since responsive action is not constitutive of mediated quasi-interaction, the nature of the responsive action is not directly constrained by the quasi-interaction itself (unlike the case of telephone conversation, where the recipient of a call has to make some kind of response, even if a minimal one). The recipients of mass-mediated messages are generally able to respond in a variety of ways to the messages they receive, and the constraints which operate on their action derive less from the nature of the mediated quasi-interaction than from the conditions under which the process of reception takes place.

In many cases, the action that occurs in response to mass-mediated messages may be extremely varied and diverse, reflecting the diversity of the contexts within which these messages are received. But it is also clear that, in some cases, the actions of distant others, relayed via media such as television, can give rise to what we may term *concerted forms of responsive action*. It seems likely, for instance, that the extensive and vivid television coverage of the Vietnam War was at least partially responsible for the strength and concerted character of the anti-war movement. The vivid images of napalm attacks, wounded soldiers and civilians, screaming children and frightened refugees, as well as regular reports of US military setbacks, fuelled the controversy in the United States concerning the legitimacy of the intervention and provided individuals with readily available grounds for protest. In the light of the Vietnam experience, it seems probable that military establishments in the United States and elsewhere will seek to exercise greater control over the media coverage of armed conflicts and skirmishes. (British media coverage of the Falklands conflict in 1982 was quite strictly controlled by the Ministry of Defence.) Other examples of concerted responsive action could easily be added. It is difficult to believe that the revolutionary upheavals in Eastern Europe in 1989 would have occurred as they did – with breathtaking speed and with similar results in different countries – in the absence of continuous media coverage. Not only did television provide individuals in Eastern Europe (and especially East Germany) with a flow of images of the West, portraying life conditions which contrasted sharply with their own, but it also provided Eastern Europeans with an account of the actions and demonstrations that were taking place in neighbouring countries, and in neighbouring cities or locales in their own countries. In Czechoslovakia the brutal suppression of the demonstration of 17 November 1989 was filmed by foreign television networks and subsequently screened, amid much controversy, within Czechoslovakia itself. Even in Romania, where the national media were strictly controlled by the state, individuals were able to learn about the dramatic changes taking place elsewhere in Eastern Europe, and elsewhere in their own country, by tuning in to TV broadcasts from the Soviet Union, Hungary and Yugoslavia. It seems likely that the concerted action displayed in the streets of Leipzig, Berlin, Prague, Timisoara, Bucharest and elsewhere in Eastern Europe was, to some extent, action in response to the activities of distant others whose successes and failures had been relayed via the media of mass communication.

By creating the possibility for new kinds of responsive action, of action that responds, sometimes concertedly, to individuals and events that are spatially and temporally remote, the development of mass communication has introduced a new and fundamentally important element into social and political life. The transmission of messages via the mass media, and especially television, may spark off or intensify forms of concerted action which may be difficult to resist or contain with the established mechanisms of state power. The importance of this phenomenon is attested to by the fact that, during the revolutionary upheavals in Eastern Europe, control of the means of television broadcasting became a crucial stake in the battle. But the events in Eastern Europe also illustrate that, in the era of modern mass communication, the battlefield itself can no longer be strictly delimited in spatial and temporal terms, since the means of communication make possible forms of action and reaction which are extended or compressed in time and which transcend the boundaries of particular nation-states.

4 The social organization of receptive activity

The deployment of technical media affects action and interaction in yet another respect: it establishes new contexts and forms of interaction in which individuals are routinely engaged in the reception and appropriation of mediated messages. The activities of receiving mediated messages are socially, spatially and temporally organized, and the organization of receptive activities typically intersects in complex ways with other routine aspects of everyday life. The installation of a telephone in a house will turn a particular area of domestic space into a primary interactive framework. The area may be chosen in a way which will enable it to be easily insulated (e.g. by closing a door) from back regions, and hence from potential participants or eavesdroppers whom an individual may wish to exclude from the conversation. The telephone enables individuals to initiate interaction over distance with great ease, and to do so in a way which intrudes on the temporal organization of others' activities. The temporal intrusion of telephone-initiated interaction is generally accepted as an unavoidable feature of modern life, although complex sets of assumptions and conventions govern the temporal organization of telephone practices, and although it is increasingly common for telephone recorders to be used as a means of regulating intrusion. In many contexts it would be inappropriate to telephone a business associate at home in the evening or at the weekend, unless the circumstances were exceptional or the associate could be regarded as a personal friend. In addition to being spatially and temporally organized, telephone interaction is also embedded in a broader social context involving relations of power and inequality. Not everyone in a household, for instance, has the same right or responsibility to answer a telephone or to use a telephone at certain times and for certain periods. Like other aspects of domestic social life, the use of the telephone is subject to some extent to the relations of power which prevail between the members of the household.

When we turn our attention to the technical media of mass communication, we can see that the social, spatial and temporal organization of reception is different in certain respects. Some of these differences are high-lighted by figures 5.2 and 5.3. Figure 5.2 illustrates the social organization of technically mediated interaction which is effectively or potentially two-way (or multi-way), such as a telephone conversation. Here the primary interactive framework encompasses the front regions of both conversational partners, and each front region is associated with a series of back regions which

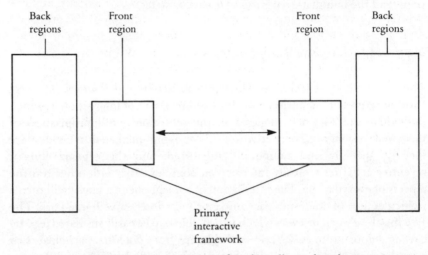

Figure 5.2 The Social Organization of Technically Mediated Interaction

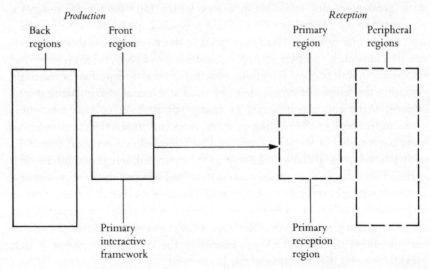

Figure 5.3 The Social Organization of Technically Mediated Quasi-interaction
(Mass Communication)

are generally excluded from the primary interactive framework. Figure 5.3, by contrast, illustrates the social organization of the technically mediated quasi-interaction characteristic of certain forms of mass communication, such as television. In this case, the primary interactive framework is constituted by the front region of the production sphere; this region has its own back regions which are typically excluded from the framework. Since the transmission of messages is predominantly one-way, the regions in the reception sphere do not directly enter into the constitution of the primary interactive framework, and hence they are not, strictly speaking, front regions and back regions relative to this framework. Within the sphere of reception we can distinguish between the primary reception region, within which the activity of reception takes place, and those peripheral regions which are typically excluded from it. In many cases the primary reception region serves not only as a setting for the quasi-interaction mediated by the television or other technical form, but it also constitutes a primary interactive framework in its own right, serving as a setting in which individuals interact *with one another*, or engage in some other activity, while participating in the process of reception.

The primary reception region is typically situated in a particular physical locale. In the case of television, the locale is often a particular room or rooms in a house, and the importance of the quasi-interaction mediated by television is attested to by the fact that the television set often occupies a central space (e.g. the living room) and often determines or strongly influences the layout of the room. The temporal patterns of receptive activity are determined by a variety of factors including the programming schedules, the tastes and preferences of recipients, and the temporal organization of the routine aspects of their daily lives. The scheduling of particular programmes may be a key point of reference around which individuals organize their activities in the course of a day or an evening; and in the case of serials, this organizational process may extend over several days, weeks or even months. The deployment of new technologies such as VCRs is particularly important in this respect, since it enables recipients to exercise greater control over the scheduling of programmes, and hence over the temporal organization of their activities as a whole. The process of reception is also embedded within a broader context of social relations which affects the nature of this process and the control over its location, timing and content. Relations of power between parents and children, and between men and women, are often crucial in determining the selection of programmes and in deciding which programmes can be watched by whom.[8]

In addition to analysing the spatial, temporal and social characteristics of the activity and context of reception, it is important to emphasize that receptive activities are complex social practices which involve varying degrees of skill and attention, which are accompanied by differing degrees of pleasure and interest, and which intersect in complicated ways with other activities and interactions taking place in the primary reception region. All too often it has been assumed by theorists and commentators on the media that the reception of media messages is a fairly straightforward and unproblematic process, an assumption which allows them to concentrate on analysing the content of media messages, supplementing this perhaps with some statistical data on audience viewing levels and responses. It seems clear, however, that this approach seriously underestimates the complexity of the processes whereby media messages are actually received and appropriated by individuals situated in particular contexts, and the ways in which these receptive activities intersect with other aspects of everyday life. I shall return to these issues in the following chapter.

Reconstituting the Boundaries between Public and Private Life

By making messages available to audiences which are extended and dispersed in time and space, the deployment of technical media of mass communication also serves to reconstitute the boundaries between public and private life. The private lives of individuals can be turned into public events by being publicized through the mass media; and public events can be experienced in private settings, as happens when affairs of state are watched or read about in the privacy of the home. The nature of what is public and what is private, and the demarcation between these domains, are transformed in certain ways by the development of mass communication, and this in turn has implications for the ways in which political power, at the level of state institutions, is acquired, exercised and sustained in modern societies.

In order to examine these issues further, we have to draw some broad distinctions between the public and private domains. The terms 'public' and 'private' have acquired a wide variety of senses in modern social and political discourse, and any attempt to identify broad distinctions is bound to be a selective and simplifying task. Nevertheless, this task is worthwhile and important for analysing the nature and impact of mass communication. Although the public–private dichotomy can be traced back to the philosophical debates of Classical Greece and to the early development of Roman law, here I shall focus on some of the senses which this dichotomy has come to assume in early modern and modern Western societies characterized by capitalist economic relations and a constitutional state incorporating democratic institutions.[9] In this context, we can distinguish between two basic senses of the public–private dichotomy. According to the first sense, the public–private dichotomy refers to the distinction between, on the one hand, the domain of institutionalized political power which was increasingly vested in the hands of a sovereign state, and, on the other, the domains of private economic activity and personal relations which fell outside the direct control of the state. Of course, this broad distinction was never rigid or clear-cut; the early development of capitalist economic activity was a process that took place within a legal framework that was established and continuously modified by state authorities, and the activities of the state were, in turn, influenced and constrained in varying degrees by the development of the capitalist economy. Moreover, since the late nineteenth century, a range of economic and welfare organizations have been created within, or brought into, the public domain, as a result of policies of state intervention aimed partly at offsetting the erratic character of capitalist economic growth, thus rendering the distinction between private and public domains more complex.

Figure 5.4 summarizes some aspects of the distinction between private and public domains as it has developed in the course of the nineteenth and twentieth centuries. The private domain includes privately owned economic organizations operating in a market economy and orientated primarily towards profit, as well as a range of personal and familial relations which may be informal or formally sanctioned by legal means (e.g. marriage). The public domain includes state-owned economic organizations, such as nationalized industries and state-owned public utilities, as well as a wide range of state and quasi-state organizations, from parliamentary institutions, the civil service and the police to a variety of welfare services and organizations which have expanded rapidly in most Western societies in the post-Second World War period. Between the private and public domains, a wide range of intermediate organizations has grown up and flourished, organizations which are neither state-owned nor lodged wholly within the private domain – for example, charities which are non-profit-making; mutual benefit associations (such as clubs and trade associations); political parties and pressure groups (such as anti-nuclear and ecological groups) which seek to articulate particular viewpoints; and economic organizations which are owned and operated on a co-operative basis.[10] These intermediate organizations are non-state private institutions in terms of their legal status, but they are legally and operationally distinct from organizations established primarily to earn profits for private owners.

The public–private dichotomy, as it has emerged in Western social and

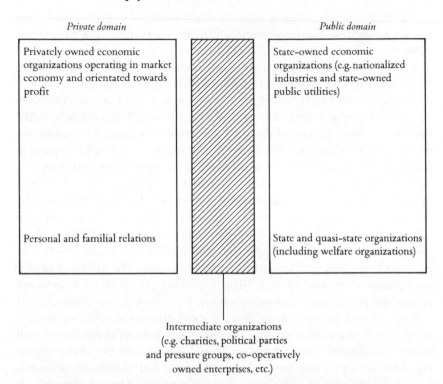

Figure 5.4 Private and Public Domains in Contemporary Western Societies

political discourse, has a second basic sense which must be separated off from the distinction elaborated above. According to this second sense, 'public' means 'open' or 'available to the public'. What is public, in this sense, is what is visible or observable, what is performed in front of spectators, what is open for all (or many) to see or hear or hear about; what is private, by contrast, is what is hidden from view, what is said or done in privacy or secrecy or among a restricted circle of people. In this sense, the public-private dichotomy has to do with *publicness versus privacy*, with *visibility versus invisibility*. This second sense of the dichotomy does not coincide with the first, but rather overlaps with it in complex and historically varying ways. In the traditional monarchical states of medieval and early modern Europe, the affairs of state were conducted in the relatively closed circles of the court, in ways that were largely invisible to most of the subject population. When officials of the state appeared before their subjects, they did so in ways that were carefully staged and managed: their principal aim was to affirm their power publicly (visibly), not to render public (visible) the grounds and deliberations which entered into their decision-making processes. The privacy of their decision-making processes was justified by recourse to the *arcana imperii* – that is, to the doctrine of state secrecy, which held that the power of the prince is more effective and true to its aim if it is hidden from the gaze of the people and, like divine will, invisible.[11] The invisibility of power was assured institutionally by the fact that decision-making processes took place in a closed space, the secret cabinet, and by the fact that decisions themselves were only occasionally and selectively made public. With the development of the modern constitutional state, however, the invisibility of power and the privacy of decision-making processes were limited in certain ways. The secret cabinet was replaced or supplemented by a range of political institutions that were more open and accountable to the people, and the doctrine of *arcana imperii* was transformed into the modern principle of official secrecy and restricted in its application to those issues regarded as vital to the security and stability of the state. Power was rendered more visible and decision-making processes became more public, although this broad trend was neither uniform nor complete: new forms of invisibility and privacy have emerged, and the exercise of state power in modern societies remains in many ways shrouded in secrecy and hidden from the public gaze.

Against the backcloth of these distinctions, we can consider the ways in which the development of mass communication has reconstituted the boundaries between public and private life. The basis for this reconstitution is that, *with the development of mass communication, the publicness (visibility) of events or individuals in the public and private domains is no longer linked directly with the sharing of a common locale*, and hence events or individuals can acquire a publicness which is independent of their capacity to be observed or heard directly by a plurality of individuals. The development of mass communication has thus facilitated and promoted the emergence of two types of events which have distinctive characteristics and consequences: we can describe these as *mediated public events* and *mediated private events*. Mediated public events are events which originally take place in an institutional setting within the public domain, but which acquire a new status by virtue of the fact that they are recorded in a technical medium of transmission and thereby made available to a range of recipients who were not present to witness the original occurrence of the event. Similarly, mediated private events are events which originally take place in the private domain, but which acquire a new status by being recorded and diffused through the media of mass communication. Figure 5.5 is a classification of these two types of events. As this figure makes clear, mediated events are sub-categories of publicized events, in the sense that transmission via the mass media is one way in which events taking place in the private and public

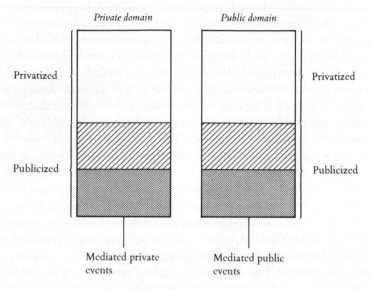

Figure 5.5 The Classification of Mediated Events

domains can be *made public*. It is important to stress that the mediazation of private and public events is a process which not only endows old events with a new status (publicness), but which also changes the nature of events themselves. The debate over the televising of parliamentary sessions in Britain – to take a recent and topical example – is largely a debate over this issue: to what extent should events which take place in the public domain, and which potentially affect the interests of everyone, be rendered visually and orally available to the public at large, and what consequences would this mediated publicness have for the nature of the events themselves? (Would MPs feel obliged to turn up more often, for instance, and would they feel more reluctant to shout at one another across the benches?)

While both public and private events can be given a new publicness by mediazation, these mediated events are generally experienced by others within their own private domains. The development of mass communication, and especially of television, is characterized by what we may describe as *the privatized reception of mediated events*. Events which take place in public and private domains can be experienced in private domestic settings which are remote in space and perhaps distant in time from the contexts in which the events originally took place. By virtue of the technical media of mass communication *the private domain of modern societies – in particular, the private domestic setting - has become a principal site of mediated publicness.* In modern societies most individuals typically experience events which take place in the public domain, and events which take place in those regions of the private domain which are beyond their immediate milieu, by watching, reading or hearing about these events in the context of their private domestic settings: their experience is both mediated and privatized. The privatized reception of mediated events is also typically *fragmentary*, in the sense that receptive activities typically take place in locales which are segregated and dispersed in time and space; but this does not mean that receptive activities are non-social. On the contrary, the privatized reception of mediated events involves two distinctive kinds of interaction: the quasi-interaction characteristic of the reception process, and what we may call *the discursive elaboration of media messages*. Figure 5.6 represents some of the elements involved in the reception process. Through mediated quasi-interaction, individuals situated in private domestic contexts are able to experience public and private events. But the nature of this experience is peculiar, since the flow of messages is predominantly one-way and the capacity for recipients to respond to the principal communicator is limited. Hence individuals are able to experience events which take place in the public and private domains without directly

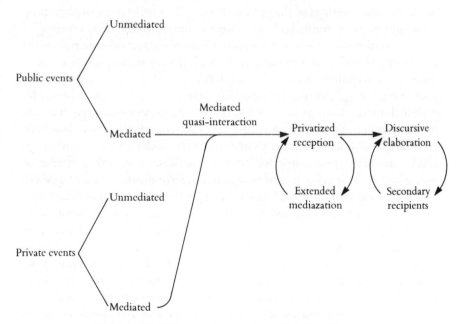

Figure 5.6 The Privatized Reception of Mediated Events

participating in these domains; their participation is, at most, a 'quasi-participation' in which there are definite limits on the range of responses available to recipients. The messages received via television and other media are commonly subjected to discursive elaboration: they are discussed by individuals in the course of their everyday lives, both within the primary reception region and in a variety of other interactive contexts in the private and public domains. In this way mediated messages may acquire an additional audience of secondary recipients who did not themselves participate in the mediated quasi-interaction, but who assimilate some version of the message through interaction with the primary recipients. The messages may also be taken up by media organizations and incorporated in new media messages, a process that may be described as *extended mediazation*. Through discursive elaboration and extended mediazation, messages received via the media are adapted and dispersed to an ever-widening circle of secondary recipients, who may thereby acquire information about events which they neither experienced directly nor witnessed via the media.

Thus the development of mass communication has not only facilitated the process of making public the events or individuals which take place or who act in the public or private domains, but it has also enabled the publicness of events or individuals to be experienced or otherwise received in the domestic settings of the private domain. The experience of publicness no longer requires individuals to share a common locale. The severing of publicness from the context of co-presence involves a transformation in the nature of publicness and in the ways in which individuals participate in it. Since access to publicness is no longer dependent on physical co-presence, a wider range of individuals, and especially individuals in so far as they inhabit private domestic settings, are able to experience a greater spectrum of events in the public and private domains. The advent of television has been particularly important in this regard, since the codes and conventions of access are often less restrictive than is the case with other media of transmission, such as books and newspapers. *Hence any individual situated in a private domestic setting equipped with a TV set has potential access to the sphere of publicness created and mediated by television*. It is the very accessibility of mediated publicness which has given rise to new opportunities as well as new problems. New opportunities, in the sense that the greater accessibility of mediated publicness may enable a wider range of individuals to participate, in a certain way, in spheres of information and communication. Thanks to the development of new modes of mass communication, especially television, more individuals than ever before are able to experience events which take place in spatially and temporally remote regions, and to participate in an ever-widening and increasingly global sphere of mediated publicness. But these opportunities may also present new problems, for greater accessibility and participation may make it more difficult for those who exercise power, whether in the public or the private domain, to control and restrict access to information, a control upon which their power may, to some extent, depend. This is part of what is at stake in the continuing debate about children and television, for the debate is, in part, about what can and should be transmitted on a medium which enables reception to take place in the relatively uncontrolled and uncontrollable contexts of private domestic life. With the advent of television, children have acquired a new and accessible means of learning about the events and activities which take place in public and private domains, including those forms of behaviour which adults generally reserve for the back regions of the private domestic context. And this in turn may present new problems for adults, who may feel that mediated messages intended primarily for themselves have become, by virtue of the accessibility of the medium, a source of information, entertainment or harm for children, and hence have come into conflict with their perceived responsibility to regulate and control the educative process of children. The levelling of access to material transmitted via television creates new problems for those individuals who, rightly or wrongly, are concerned with the regulation of access to information and communication, whether this bears on the education of children or, more generally, on the knowledge and experience of the population at large.

I have argued that the development of mass communication has transformed the nature and experience of publicness in the modern world. By severing publicness from the sharing of a common locale, it has rendered more events more public (more visible) and has rendered their publicness more accessible to more people. But there are some commentators who would interpret the development of mass communication as a largely negative force in the historical unfolding of public life. These commentators see the privatized and fragmentary character of the reception process as a sign that public life in modern societies is all but dead – not that the development of mass communication by itself has killed public life, but that the deployment of technical media, with their one-way flow of messages pouring into the privacy of the home, has sealed the coffin of a once-thriving public sphere.[12] This interpretation would, I think, be an overly negative view of the significance of mass communication in the modern world. It is true that the reception of mediated messages is generally a fragmentary and privatized process, but from this it does not follow that reception is non-social: on the contrary, the reception of mediated messages generally involves, as I have indicated, a range of distinctive social activities, including the discursive elaboration of mediated messages. It is true that mass communication generally involves a one-way flow of messages, in such a way that those who receive mediated messages have relatively little capacity to respond. But from this it does not follow that recipients have no control over the communicative process, nor that the process of reception does not involve some form of participation – albeit a distinctive and limited form. On the contrary, as I have suggested, the process of reception is a much more active, creative and critical process than many commentators are inclined to assume.

The most serious shortcoming of the argument that the development of mass communication has destroyed a once-thriving public sphere is that it fails to take account of the ways in which the deployment of technical media has transformed the very nature of publicness. The argument is based on a notion of publicness which is essentially *spatial* and *dialogical* in character: that is, publicness implies an ensemble of individuals meeting in an open place, a public space, within which they can directly discuss issues of common concern. This is a notion of publicness derived from the assemblies of the Classical Greek city-states, a notion which could still be applied to some extent to the salons and coffee-houses of early modern Europe. But with the development of mass communication, and especially television, the nature of publicness has changed. An individual need no longer be present at an event in order to witness it; the publicness (visibility) of an event no longer depends on the sharing of a common locale. Hence the notion of publicness has become de-spatialized and increasingly divorced from the idea of a dialogical conversation in a shared locale. Publicness has become increasingly linked to the distinctive kind of visibility produced by, and achievable through, the technical media of mass communication. Television and other media have generated a new type of public realm which has no spatial limits, which is not necessarily tied to dialogical conversation and which is accessible to an indefinite number of individuals who may be situated within privatized domestic settings. Rather than sounding the death knell of public life, the development of mass communication has created a new kind of publicness and has transformed fundamentally the conditions under which most people are able to experience what is public and participate today in what could be called a public realm.

It is important to emphasize that, with regard to the exercise of institutionalized political power, the kind of publicness or visibility created by the development of mass communication is a double-edged sword. In the new political arena produced and sustained by the media of mass communication, political leaders are able to appear before their subjects in a way and on a scale that had never existed previously. The relationship between political leaders and subjects becomes increasingly mediated by mass communication, that is, becomes a form of technically mediated quasi-interaction, through which bonds of loyalty and affection (as well as feelings of repugnance) can be formed. Skilful politicians exploit this circumstance to their advantage. They seek to create and sustain a basis of support for their power and their policies by controlling their self-presentation, by *managing the visibility which they have within the mediated arena of modern politics*. Today the management of visibility is widely recognized as a fundamental aspect of institutionalized politics. From fireside chats to party conventions, from local walkabouts to superpower summits, political leaders and their organizations preoccupy themselves with the management of visibility and with the nurturing of a relationship produced and sustained by mediated quasi-interaction. By virtue of the very nature of mass communication, this management activity is not localized in time or in space. Political leaders appear before an audience which extends well beyond those individuals who may be assembled within a common locale. The audience may extend to the boundaries of a nation-state and beyond, for the mediated arena of modern politics is potentially global in character.

While the development of mass communication has created unprecedented opportunities for the management of visibility, it has also created unprecedented risks for political leaders and for the exercise of political power. Prior to the advent of mass communication, political leaders could restrict the activity of managing visibility to the relatively closed circle of the assembly or the court, while generally maintaining a distance and aloofness from the population as a whole. The legitimacy of their power was sustained, to some extent, by the very distance they maintained from the subjects over whom they ruled, a distance which nourished the cultivated aura of regality. Today it is no longer possible to restrict the management of visibility in this way. The mediated arena of modern politics is open and accessible in a way that traditional assemblies and courts were not. Moreover, given the nature of mass communication, the messages transmitted by the media may be received in ways that cannot be directly monitored and controlled by communicators. Hence the visibility created by mass communication may also be the source of a new kind of fragility: *however much political leaders may seek to manage their visibility, the very phenomenon of visibility may slip out of their control and undermine whatever support they may have or may seek*. Political leaders can be destroyed by an emotional outburst, an impromptu remark or an ill-judged action: the fall from power can be breathtakingly quick. More importantly, the exercise of political power today takes place in an arena which is increasingly *open to view*, however hard political leaders may try to control and restrict the visibility. Hence the deployment of American troops in South-East Asia or Central America, or the suppression of demonstrations in China, South Africa or the West Bank, are activities which take place in a new kind of public realm: they are visible, observable, capable of being witnessed simultaneously by millions of individuals dispersed across the globe. The exercise of political power is subjected to a kind of *global scrutiny* which simply did not exist prior to the advent of mass communication, and especially of television. Given the possibility of such scrutiny, political actions carry unprecedented risks and may expose a regime to international condemnation and to political and economic isolation. The visibility created by mass communication is a double-edged sword: today political leaders must seek continuously to manage it, but they cannot completely control it. Mediated visibility is an unavoidable condition of institutionalized politics in the modern era, but it has uncontrollable consequences for the exercise of political power.

Mass Communication between Market and State

In the previous sections I have analysed some of the characteristics of mass communication and examined some of the social and political implications of the deployment of technical media. I now want to focus more sharply on the institutional organization of mass communication and consider some of the arguments that have been put forward, from the nineteenth century to the present day, to explicate and justify the role of media institutions in social and political life. I shall try to show that these arguments are flawed in various ways and that, to some extent, they are inapplicable to the circumstances in which we find ourselves in the late twentieth century, even though they are sometimes invoked in political debates as if nothing had changed. Although I shall proceed by considering certain historical arguments about the media, my primary concern is to assess the relevance of these arguments to present-day problems and possibilities: my main interest here is not to examine these arguments in relation to the particular social-historical contexts in which they were originally propounded, but rather to consider whether these arguments have any enduring relevance to the circumstances in which we find ourselves today. I shall begin by considering the traditional liberal theory of the free press, according to which the press is conceived as a critical and independent watchdog on state power – what is sometimes called the 'Fourth Estate of the Realm'. I shall then examine the principle of public service broadcasting, a principle which has been central to the development of broadcasting institutions in Britain and elsewhere. Finally, adopting a more normative approach, I shall offer some constructive suggestions about how an institutional framework for mass communication could be developed which would preserve some of the tasks traditionally assigned to the media while taking account of the actual circumstances in which media institutions operate today. My thesis is that media institutions should occupy a space between the unbridled operation of market forces, on the one hand, and direct control by the state, on the other. Only by developing a form of *regulated pluralism* in the organization and operation of media institutions can we sustain today some of the traditional and justifiable ideas of thinkers who were preoccupied with the social and political role of mass communication.

Liberal theory and its limits

Contemporary debates about the political role of mass communication in modern societies have been strongly influenced by a range of views which emerged in the course of a long and often bitter struggle for the establishment of a 'free press' in Britain and elsewhere. There is no need to review this history here, since it has been well documented elsewhere.[13] I shall focus instead on one of the key ideas that animated the early struggle for the freedom of the press and seek to assess its continued relevance to the circumstances of mass communication today. The development of the newspaper and publishing industries in the seventeenth, eighteenth and nineteenth centuries was accompanied by continuous attempts, on the part of state authorities, to control, restrict and suppress the publication of newspapers, pamphlets and books which were commonly regarded by government officials as dangerous and depraving, as 'vehicles of falsehood and of bad principles', in the words of the Tory journalist William Cobbett.[14] The early struggle for the freedom of the press was essentially a struggle against state controls, which assumed a variety of forms, from taxation and subsidies to overt censorship. To some extent this struggle coincided with, and found an effective voice in, the development of liberal democratic thought, which was concerned, among other things, with defining and defending the liberty of individuals against the excessive and repressive exercise of state power. Writing in the early nineteenth century, at a time when the newspaper industry in Britain was campaigning against the stamp duties (the so-called 'taxes on knowledge'), the early liberal thinkers like Jeremy Bentham, James Mill and John Stuart Mill gave an eloquent and influential defence of the freedom of the press. They saw the free expression of opinion through the organs of an independent press as a principal means by which a diversity of viewpoints could be expressed, an enlightened public opinion could be formed, and the abuses of state power by corrupt or tyrannical governments could be checked.[15] While the views of the early English liberals differed in various respects, they were generally united on the view that a free and independent press was a vital safeguard against the despotic use of state power. A free and independent press would play the role of a critical watchdog: not only would it articulate a diversity of opinions and thereby enrich the sphere of knowledge and debate, but it would also expose and criticize the activities of those who rule and the principles upon which their decisions are based.

The early struggle for the freedom of the press was not without success, and in the course of the eighteenth and nineteenth centuries the principle of the free expression of thoughts and opinions was incorporated into the constitutions of many Western states. In Britain, the Act of Parliament which imposed censorship on the press expired in 1695 and was never renewed, so that individuals were formally at liberty to publish what they wished so long as it was not blasphemous, seditious, obscene or defamatory, in which case they would be answerable in a court of law. But the suppression of texts deemed to be blasphemous or seditious remained a fraught political issue and was exacerbated by the fact that the stamp duties had a disproportionate effect on the cheap radical newspapers and pamphlets. It was only in the first half of the nineteenth century that the special duties and taxes on the press were removed: the tax on pamphlets was repealed in 1833; the newspaper stamp duty was reduced to a penny in 1836 and then altogether eliminated in 1855; and the paper duty was repealed in 1861. These legal reforms paved the way for the expansion of the newspaper and publishing industries, which were already undergoing rapid technological change. The subsequent development of these industries in Britain and other Western societies thus took place within a political and legal framework that formally recognized the principle of freedom of expression: individuals had a *right* to express their opinions in a free and independent press, subject only to the constraints, which have varied historically and from one national context to another, that what is said is not deemed to be blasphemous, seditious, obscene, defamatory or, in general, libellous; and the constraints which circumscribe this right are not to be applied pro-actively in the form of state censorship or control, but only retro-actively by requiring an individual accused of libel to be answerable in a court of law.

The political and legal recognition of freedom of expression is an important feature of many Western states. It is a testimony to the efforts of many individuals who fought, often fiercely, against the entrenched opposition of conservative and reactionary officials of the state, and it is a tribute to the political insight of early liberal democratic thought. Moreover, the issues raised by the historical struggle are by no means of mere historical interest: whether one considers the current controversies on freedom of expression in the societies of Eastern Europe and the Soviet Union, or the recent attempts to suppress publications or programmes of various kinds in Western societies like Britain, one can see that the principle of free expression retains its radical and critical potential today. In a world where the political suppression of information and ideas is commonplace, John Stuart Mill's eloquent defence of the liberty to express thoughts and opinions, however unpopular they may be or however uncomfortable for established authorities, still has a topical ring. Nevertheless, the nature and organization of the media industries have changed enormously since the early nineteenth century, and in the light of these developments, we can see that the traditional liberal theory of the free press is, at best, of limited value for thinking about the role of media institutions in modern societies. The most important developments in this regard are (1) the growing concentration and commercialization of the media industries; and (2) the development of new media technologies. There is a further problem with the traditional liberal theory which concerns (3) the nature of legitimate constraints on the freedom of expression. Let me consider each of these points in turn.

1 The traditional liberal theory of the free press took it for granted that free enterprise was the foundation of freedom of expression. The free expression of thoughts and opinions could be practically achieved only in so far as the institutions of the press were independent of the state and were situated in the private domain where they could carry out their activities with a minimum of constraint: in traditional liberal theory, a *laissez-faire* approach to economic activity was the natural counterpart to individual liberty, including the liberty of thought and expression.[16] And, indeed, it was on this basis that the newspaper and publishing industries developed in Britain and other Western societies in the course of the nineteenth and twentieth centuries. But the consequence of the growth of these industries is that, by the early twentieth century, the freedom of expression was increasingly confronted by a new threat: a threat stemming not from the repressive exercise of state power, but rather from the unhindered growth of the newspaper and publishing industries *qua* commercial concerns. In the previous chapter I traced the development of mass circulation newspapers in the late nineteenth century, and the growing concentration of resources in the newspaper industry, and in the media industries generally, in the course of the twentieth century. The press and, more generally, media institutions have increasingly become large-scale economic organizations orientated towards

the production and diffusion of mass circulation symbolic goods, and they have become increasingly integrated into diversified trans-national communication conglomerates. These developments seriously call into question the relevance of the traditional liberal theory to the social and economic conditions of mass communication in the late twentieth century. While the press and some other media institutions may have sustained a large degree of independence from state power, many of these institutions have been caught up in a process resulting in an unprecedented degree of concentration – both of resources and of power – in the private domain. In these circumstances, the traditional liberal theory of the free press, viewed as a vehicle for the free expression of diverse thoughts and opinions, is of limited value. The theory rightly emphasizes that the independence of media institutions *vis-à-vis* the state is a vital feature of modern democracy and an essential precondition for the capacity of individuals to comment critically and publicly on the exercise of state power; but the theory underestimates the dangers that stem from the dependence of media institutions on a highly competitive and increasingly global process of capital accumulation, a process which has resulted in a steady decline in the number of newspapers and a growing concentration of resources in the hands of multi-media conglomerates and idiosyncratic entrepreneurs. A more satisfactory account of the institutional conditions of the freedom of expression in the late twentieth century would have to take account of the fact that such freedom is threatened, not just by the unrestricted exercise of state power, but also by the unhindered growth of media organizations in the private domain.

2 A second limitation of the traditional liberal theory of the free press is that it was developed primarily with regard to the newspaper and publishing industries, and its relevance to those sectors of the media industries which have assumed such significance in the twentieth century – in particular, television broadcasting – is not immediately clear. As I emphasized earlier, there are important differences between the technical media used in different sectors of the media industries, and between the institutional apparatuses within which these media are deployed. The traditional liberal theory tends to assume a conception of media institutions as a multiplicity of independent organizations which, by virtue of their multiplicity as well as their independence, assure the expression of differing views. But this conception is called into question, not only by the developments referred to in the previous paragraph, but also by the fact that, in certain sectors of the media industries, the nature of the technical media place limits on the extent to which a multiplicity of independent organizations can be established and sustained. These limits derive both from the capacity of the technical

medium to accommodate the transmissions of different organizations, and from the entry costs associated with industries dependent on relatively high capital investment. It was primarily for these reasons that the development of broadcasting institutions, and particularly those associated with television, occurred within a cluster of institutional frameworks which differed significantly from that envisaged by the traditional liberal theory of the free press. The architects of the early systems of television broadcasting generally assumed that there would be a limited number of supply channels, and the institutional frameworks which they helped to forge were based either on the principle of restricted competition within a network system operating in the private domain, or on the principle of public service broadcasting by organizations located within the public domain. I shall examine below the principle of public service broadcasting and some of its shortcomings. Here I wish simply to note that neither of the institutional frameworks within which television broadcasting has developed over the last fifty years concurs very well with the traditional liberal theory of the free press. Neither the principle of restricted competition within a network system nor the principle of public service broadcasting corresponds to the conception of media institutions as a multiplicity of independent organizations which freely compete with one another in the private domain. It may well be that the most recent developments in cable and satellite technologies, coupled with government policies on deregulation, will significantly alter existing institutional frameworks. But it seems doubtful, as I shall indicate later, that these developments, left to themselves, would lead to a situation which approximated that envisaged by the traditional liberal theory.

3 There is a further problem that arises when we attempt to assess the relevance of the traditional liberal theory of the free press to the conditions of mass communication in the modern world: this is the problem of the nature of legitimate constraints on the freedom of expression. Even in those societies today where the principle of free expression is institutionalized in the legal and political system, it is commonly argued that the state can legitimately restrict the publication or transmission of certain kinds of information or communication. Here we are dealing not simply with retro-active cases of libel against individuals or organizations, but rather with pro-active intervention by state authorities to restrict or suppress the diffusion of symbolic forms. There are two main areas in which such intervention is both common and controversial: in the area of obscenity and in the area of state security. The issues raised in both of these areas are extremely complex and there is certainly room for legitimate disagreement. Here I do not want to pursue the arguments for and against state intervention in these areas, but

want simply to consider whether the traditional liberal theory is of any help in trying to resolve these disputes. In fact, John Stuart Mill does not address in any detail the question of the nature of legitimate constraints on the freedom of expression, and the passages in his classic essay 'On Liberty' which bear on this issue are vague and ambiguous at best. On the one hand, Mill's 'principle of harm', according to which the actions of individuals can be legitimately sanctioned by the state only if they cause harm to others or are prejudicial to the interests of others, might be interpreted as a justification for minimal state interference in the diffusion of symbolic forms which an individual may choose to consume or ignore, and which, if they choose to consume, they may consume privately, in the seclusion of their own home. On the other hand, the same principle could be interpreted as a justification for extensive state intervention in the sphere of mass communication, since it could be argued that obscene publications or the disclosure of politically sensitive information 'causes harm to others' or is 'prejudicial to the interests of others' – much depends on how these key expressions are understood. Mill remarks, in passing, that offences against decency are not in themselves sanctionable, but 'if done publicly, are a violation of good manners, and coming thus within the category of offences against others, may rightly be prohibited'.[17] But this qualification, if applied consistently to the large-scale production and diffusion of symbolic forms in the era of mass communication, could result in a highly restrictive media policy which would differ little from that demanded by present-day conservative campaigners like Mary Whitehouse. Hence, while the traditional liberal theory of the free press remains an important reference point for contemporary debates, it cannot, I think, be said to provide an altogether clear and satisfactory approach to some of the key questions of media policy today.

The principle of public service broadcasting

The advent of radio and television broadcasting in the twentieth century altered, in certain respects, the terms of the debate concerning the role of mass communication in modern societies. The nature of the technical media was such that broadcasting institutions could not develop in a way that was directly comparable to newspaper and publishing organizations. The limited channels of supply required the state, or quasi-state institutions, to be directly involved in allocating licences or franchises and in regulating transmission; and the relatively high costs associated with the production and diffusion of programmes tended to favour the concentration of resources in the hands of large-scale broadcasting organizations. As I indicated in the previous chapter, the development of broadcasting took place within different institutional frameworks and varied from one national context to another. These developments have often taken place in an *ad hoc* way, as a result of specific commercial initiatives or policy recommendations, and have not necessarily been accompanied by the formulation of a general theoretical account of the aims and methods of broadcasting. However, there is one such account which has been particularly influential in the development of broadcasting – especially in Britain, but also in many other countries where broadcasting institutions were to some extent modelled on those initially established in Britain. We may describe this account as the principle of public service broadcasting. Originally formulated by John Reith, the first Director General of the BBC, the principle of public service broadcasting has underpinned the development of the BBC since its inception and has had an enormous impact on the course of broadcasting. Although this principle is currently the subject of intensive political debate in Britain and its future is uncertain, there can be no doubt that it has played a major role in the institutional development of mass communication hitherto.

What is the principle of public service broadcasting? In his 1924 book, *Broadcast over Britain*, Reith characterized public service broadcasting in terms of four elements: the rejection of commercialism, the extension of availability of programmes to everyone in the community, the establishment of unified control over broadcasting, and the maintenance of high standards, 'the provision of the best and the rejection of the hurtful'.[18] These elements were embodied in the organizational structure and practice of the BBC, which was conceived of by Reith as having 'founded a tradition of public service and of devotion to the highest interest of community and nation'.[19] As an institution, the BBC was and remains located in the public domain, relying for its revenue on the income raised by a licence fee; and, until the arrival of commercial television in the 1950s and apart from the illegal incursions of offshore radio stations, it exercised a monopoly on broadcasting services in Britain. While located in the public domain, the BBC was formally insulated from the government of the day and has always regarded its political independence as an essential feature. Reith himself was not a member of any political party, but he was a strong-willed individual with a clear vision and the determination necessary to implement it. He conceived of his task primarily in cultural and educational terms: public service broadcasting should seek to inform and enlighten the people of the nation as a whole, and to entertain them with programmes of high standards and good taste.

The BBC has certainly changed since its early Reithian years. Not only has it grown enormously in size and output, but it has lost some of its missionary zeal, tempered in part by the competitive anxiety induced by the advent of commercial television. Nevertheless, the principle of public service broadcasting remains fundamental to the BBC and, in the context of current debates about the future of broadcasting, it is championed by individuals of widely differing political persuasions. I think there can be no doubt that the BBC, under the guidance of this principle, has produced some material of outstanding quality and enduring value. Many BBC programmes are a testimony to the fact that broadcasting institutions can operate very effectively within the public domain, that is, within an institutional framework that is not privately owned and not orientated towards profit realization. However, if we scrutinize the ways in which the BBC has operated *in practice*, it is also clear that there are serious shortcomings to the principle of public service broadcasting, at least in the form originally elaborated by Reith. Once again, let me restrict myself to three considerations: (1) the concentration of power in the hands of a bureaucratic elite; (2) the susceptibility of broadcasting institutions to the exercise of state power and governmental pressure; and (3) the difficulty of sustaining the traditional principle of public service broadcasting in the face of new media technologies.

1 One of the risks associated with the principle of public service broadcasting is that, when embedded in a specific institutional framework, it may facilitate the concentration of power in the hands of a bureaucratic elite. The development of the BBC provides ample evidence of this risk. Under Reith's leadership, the BBC was organized in a strictly hierarchical way, with a small group of individuals constituting an executive control board responsible to the Director General, who himself exercised a great deal of control over the direction and output of the institution. In the organizational structure of the BBC, the Director General is formally accountable to a Board of Governors who are appointed by the government of the day. Although the Governors rarely intervene in the day-to-day operations of the BBC, they are responsible for appointing or replacing the Director General and their views can be crucial in times of crisis. The direction of accountability is strictly upwards, and considerable power is vested in the hands of the Director General. For an institution entrusted with a total or partial monopoly in the field of broadcasting, this kind of hierarchical organization is certainly questionable. It vests overall control of the institution in the hands of an elite which, by virtue of the appointment system, tends to comprise individuals drawn from a relatively narrow and privileged social background. If we examine the social backgrounds of the Governors and Directors General of the BBC since the 1920s, we find that nearly half were Oxbridge graduates; around one in four was drawn from finance or business, whereas only one in

fifteen had a trade union background; and most have been white and male.[20] Of course, as in all complex organizations, power is not vested solely in the hands of this bureaucratic elite. The day-to-day running of the BBC involves a continuous and complex process of decision-making at many different levels of the institution. But the overall ethos and direction of the institution are influenced by the values of the elite, whose views can, in particular circumstances, be decisive.

The fact that the BBC has developed as a strongly hierarchical organiza-tion, and the fact that the upper echelons of this institution have been filled by individuals drawn from a relatively restricted social background, do not by themselves demonstrate that the principle of public service broadcasting is flawed. It may be that the institutional framework within which the principle was embedded in Britain owed as much to the distinctive personality of Reith, whose autocratic and elitist inclinations were well-known, as it owed to the principle of public service broadcasting as such. Nevertheless, there is a serious risk of facilitating the concentration of power when broadcasting is organized according to a principle which calls for the establishment of a unified control over broadcasting by an institution entrusted with the maintenance of high standards and good taste. Judgements of quality and taste do not operate in a social vacuum; they are conditioned by socially differentiated processes of cultivation.[21] The more such judgements are vested in the hands of a small circle of appointed individuals, the greater the risk that the output will reflect the cultivated sensibilities of particular social groups or strata. When the *Listener* began to carry out audience research in 1936, if found a fair degree of disaffection among working-class listeners, who had had their fill of Toscanini concerts and frequently tuned in to foreign commercial stations for some respite from high culture.[22] The fact that even today, under the duopolistic system of television broadcasting, the BBC channels are significantly more popular than ITV among upper-middle-class viewers, and ITV is more popular than BBC among unskilled manual workers, tends to confirm the view that the risks associated with the principle of public service broadcasting are not purely hypothetical. The principle of public service broadcasting carries the risk of a kind of *cultural paternalism* in which the cultivated sensibilities of particular social groups are institutionalized as the norm to be maintained in the production and appreciation of mediated symbolic forms. I shall argue below that the best way to avoid this and associated risks is to seek explicitly to de-concentrate power in the sphere of broadcasting by establishing a multiplicity of decision-making bodies – what I shall describe as regulated pluralism. But before I elaborate this proposal, I want to address some related problems in the principle of public service broadcasting.

2 Since the advent of radio and television, broadcasting institutions have been particularly susceptible to the exercise of power by members of the government and officials of the state. By the early twentieth century, the struggle to establish a formally free press had been achieved to a significant extent in many Western societies, and the constraints that operated in the field of the press increasingly assumed the form of economic imperatives stemming from the commercial character of the newspaper industry rather than overt political sanctions. However, with the development of broad-casting under the principle of public service broadcasting, a new set of relations was established between state and government institutions, on the one hand, and institutions of mass communication, on the other. Reith retained something of the traditional liberal idea of a free press, but substantially reworked this idea in the context of a medium which had a strictly limited number of channels of transmission and over which a unified control operating in the public interest was, he thought, essential. The control agency could sustain the traditional liberal idea in this new context only by remaining scrupulously neutral with regard to political parties and organized interest groups, and by insulating itself from the government of the day by the mechanism of the licence fee, which provided the BBC with a source of revenue independent of government-allocated funds. The neutrality espoused by the BBC is an *operative ideal* which is essential to its character as a public service broadcasting institution – that is, as an institution which, in spite of its monolithic character and its location within the public domain, can claim to be independent of state or governmental pressure and to be acting in the public interest.

The difficulty is that this operative ideal has, all too often, been compromised in practice. From its origins to the present day, the BBC has often found itself in difficult situations where conflicting interests were at stake, and where decisions had to be made about what to broadcast and how to broadcast it. Given the institutional framework of the BBC, there was always a risk that this decision-making process would, in cases where serious conflict or national security were at stake, systematically favour the concerns of state or government officials. As is well known, this is exactly what happened in the first major crisis of this kind which confronted the BBC: the General Strike of 1926. Reith resisted the attempts by some members of the government to 'commandeer' the BBC, arguing that such an action would be both counter-productive and unnecessary: 'If the Government be strong and their cause right they need not adopt such measures. Assuming the BBC is for the people and that the Government is for the people, it follows that the BBC must be for the Government in this crisis too.'[23] Reith's argument is significant for what it reveals about the hidden risks of public service broadcasting: at times of crisis, the difficulty of defining 'the public interest' can be resolved, he suggested, by temporarily aligning the broadcasting institution with the government, who must in principle have the welfare of the people as a whole in mind. For those concerned with the freedom of broadcasting institutions from the state, the dangers inherent in this temporary expedient are clear. The point is not simply that, on the occasion of the General Strike or on various occasions since then, the BBC has favoured the government or bowed to pressure from the government or other agencies of the state; rather, the point is that the principle of public service broadcasting, by advocating a unified control over broadcasting, by locating broadcasting institutions within the public domain and charging them with the task of pursuing the public interest, *carries with it the risk* that the neutrality sought for by these institutions will be compromised in practice by the systematic favouring of the concerns and perspectives of officials of the government and the state. This is a risk which is amply exemplified not only by the history of the BBC, but also by the history of those broadcasting institutions elsewhere in the world which have been modelled on the British system of public service broadcasting.

3 Of the four elements in terms of which Reith originally characterized the principle of public service broadcasting, there was one which, in fact, was never achieved: the establishment of unified control over broadcasting. While a near monopoly existed during the 1930s and 1940s, control over radio broadcasting was never entirely concentrated in the BBC's hands, since foreign-based and pirate radio stations were capable of transmitting programmes to British listeners. The first few years of television broad-casting were wholly dominated by the BBC, but this monopoly was soon broken by the establishment of the independent television network and, subsequently, by the addition of Channel 4. Hence, in the case of Britain, the institutional realization of the principle of public service broadcasting has always fallen short, to some extent, of the original Reithian conception: broadcasting institutions have never been wholly subjected to unified control, and in recent decades several quasi-state regulatory bodies have existed to regulate the different sectors of the industry. But today there are new developments which are likely to militate against any attempt to establish a unified control over broadcasting. The deployment of new communication technologies, and especially those associated with cable and DBS, is creating new media of transmission with a much greater capacity than has existed hitherto, and with a potential range of transmission which easily exceeds national boundaries. In these circumstances it would be difficult to argue that the principle of public service broadcasting,

understood as a *comprehensive* approach to broadcasting policy, could be sustained in anything like its original Reithian form. Stripped of its comprehensive ambitions, the question that remains is whether the principle of public service broadcasting has any role to play within the new configuration of technical media and institutions which are being ushered in by the deployment of new technologies.

The deployment of new communication technologies has highlighted another feature of cultural transmission in the modern world which tends to run counter to the principle of public service broadcasting as originally formulated by Reith: namely, its globalized and globalizing character. In its original formulation, the principle of public service broadcasting was set within the context of the nation-state. The main broadcasting institution, in Reith's vision, would be a national institution, capable of reaching simultaneously every home in the land. 'Broadcasting should be operated on a national scale, for national service and by a single national authority,' asserted the *BBC Yearbook* for 1933.[24] The problem with this vision of public service broadcasting on a national scale is two-fold: on the one hand, the attempt to forge a national broadcasting service may lead to the exclusion or marginalization of local and regional interests and concerns, a point which has been extensively debated in recent decades; on the other hand, this attempt may be undercut by the increasing globalization of cultural transmission in the modern world. At a time when films and television programmes are increasingly sold in an international market, and when the technical media of transmission are increasingly capable of diffusing audio-visual material across national boundaries, it will become increasingly difficult to attempt to insulate broadcasting institutions from international and trans-national pressures and processes. In the following section I shall suggest that, rather than embarking on some rearguard action in the hope of sustaining an idea whose time has in many ways passed, we need to rethink the organization and role of broadcasting institutions in a way which creatively takes advantage of the opportunities opened up by the development of the media industries and the deployment of new communication technologies.

Towards a regulated pluralism

In attempting to think about the future of media institutions, we can begin by drawing some general lessons from the past. The traditional liberal theory of the free press emphasized, rightly in my view, the importance of maintaining a distance between media institutions, on the one hand, and the major institutions of state and government, on the other: only by maintaining this distance can media institutions comment critically on the exercise of institutionalized political power. However, the traditional liberal thinkers did not sufficiently take account of the dangers which would stem from the unhindered growth of media institutions as commercial concerns. In the newspaper and publishing industries, and increasingly across the media industries as a whole, this growth has resulted in the concentration of resources in the hands of large-scale organizations in the private domain. It was partially in order to avert this outcome in the sphere of broadcasting that the principle of public service broadcasting was introduced. The main strength of this principle was its claim that broadcasting institutions should be governed by criteria other than strictly commercial considerations, and this claim retains its relevance today. But the principle of public service broadcasting, in the form elaborated and institutionalized by Reith, tended to concentrate resources within a single institution and to concentrate power in the hands of a bureaucratic elite, whose proximity to state and government officials would make it difficult in practice to avoid compromising the sought-for neutrality of broadcasting institutions. As a response in part to the Scylla of unhindered commercialism, the principle of public service broadcasting raised once again the Charybdis of state interference in, and control over, the institutions of mass communication.

The future development of media institutions should be governed, in my view, by what I shall describe as *the principle of regulated pluralism*. By this I mean that *an institutional framework should be established which would both accommodate and secure the existence of a plurality of independent media institutions in the different spheres of mass communication*. In the sphere of the press and of publishing more generally, the importance of a plurality of independent institutions was emphasized by traditional liberal thinkers, who regarded such plurality as a way of ensuring the expression of diverse and differing views. While this insight retains its relevance today, it is equally important to ensure, through legislation enacted and enforced by states, that the plurality of institutions is not radically reduced by the large-scale corporate concentration of resources in the private domain. This is not just a matter of legislating against monopolistic activities which disadvantage the consumer by restricting competition: what is at stake is not simply the consumer's freedom to choose, but also the availability of a multiplicity of public fora in which differing views can be expressed. The individual is not only a consumer who deserves some choice in selecting objects of consumption; he or she is also a participant in a political community or communities in which the formation of opinion and the exercise of judgement today depends, to some extent, on the availability of information and the expression of differing ideas through the media of mass communication. The corporate concentration of resources in the media industries is not just a threat to the individual *qua* consumer: it is also a threat to the individual *qua* citizen. In the sphere of broadcasting, one of the principal justifications for the restriction of pluralism has always been the technical limitations imposed by the relatively narrow range of wavebands available for channels of supply. With the development of new communication technologies, however, this justification is rapidly losing whatever force it may have had. Cable and satellite technologies have already greatly increased the available channels in some countries and will, during the coming decades, continue to do so in others. But it may be reasonably doubted whether, left to market forces alone, the expansion in the supply capacity brought about by the deployment of these new technical media will result in a significant increase in pluralism rather than a further increase in the concentration of resources in the hands of the large communication conglomerates.[25]

Hence the principle of regulated pluralism calls, in the first instance, for a *de-concentration of resources in the media industries*. The trend towards the concentration of resources in the media industries should be arrested and reversed through legislation which limits the activities of communication conglomerates; and, in the sphere of broadcasting, the original Reithian idea that broadcasting should be subsumed to a unified control is an idea that should be firmly put aside. While the principle of regulated pluralism calls for legislative intervention in the media industries, at the same time it requires, so far as the routine operation of media institutions is concerned, *the clear separation of media institutions from the exercise of state power*. The importance of this independence was underlined both by the liberal theorists of the free press and by the founders of public service broadcasting – although I have argued that the institutional realization of public service broadcasting has compromised this independence in certain respects. These twin aspects of the principle of regulated pluralism – the de-concentration of resources in the media industries, the separation of media institutions from the exercise of state power – define a broad institutional space for the development of media organizations. The space is very broad indeed, and intentionally so: there is room for a variety of different forms of ownership and control, within the public domain, the private domain and what I described earlier as the domain of intermediate organizations. But this space is not without limits. It is a space *between* the unhindered operation of market forces, on the one hand, and the direct control of media institutions by the state, on the other. It is by locating media institutions in the space between market and state that the principle of regulated pluralism can most effectively be enacted.

The specific ways in which media institutions can be developed within this space, and the forms of regulation which may be necessary and appropriate, will vary from one sphere of mass communication to another, and I shall not undertake to examine these issues in detail here.[26] I shall simply note that, in the sphere of television, it may be appropriate to draw a sharper distinction today between the institutional apparatuses of transmission, on the one hand, and the institutions involved in the production of television programmes, on the other. The processes of production and transmission do not have to be merged in the same institution, although historically they have often been combined. As available channels of transmission increase, more opportunities are created in principle for the diffusion of programmes which may be produced by independent production companies, although whether these opportunities are realized in practice will depend, among other things, on how the emerging channels are regulated and controlled. The organization of Channel 4 in Britain is based on this kind of institutional division of labour between production and transmission, and it seems likely that the BBC will draw an increasing proportion of its programmes from the independent sector. But the effective development of this institutional division in the context of changing technologies will require a range of regulatory mechanisms to ensure, first, that the channels of transmission are developed in a way that is both pluralistic and responsive to the needs and interests of recipients; and second, that production organizations have access to different sources of funding, both public and private, so that organizations engaged in producing high-cost programmes, or in catering for minority interests and tastes, will not be automatically eliminated by the flow of funds into programmes which promise the highest return for the lowest investment.

Since the deployment of new communication technologies is rendering mass communication increasingly global in character, the principle of regulated pluralism must itself be placed within a trans-national context. Viewed from the perspective of this principle, the increasing globalization of mass communication presents both new opportunities and new dangers. New opportunities, in the sense that new markets are created for the distribution of programmes produced by independent organizations, and in the sense that the process of transmission itself can no longer be conceptualized purely in terms of the boundaries and interests of the nation-state. But new dangers too, in the sense that, without careful regulation, the development of the new media may simply repeat the course taken by the newspaper and publishing industries during the last fifty years – that is, the course of the growing concentration of resources in the hands of communication conglomerates. Given the trans-national character of the new media of transmission, the regulation necessary to avert this outcome will have to be both national and international. Particular states, as well as states in association with one another, will have to take steps to ensure that the new channels of transmission which are being opened up by the deployment of new technologies will not be controlled in such a way that pluralism and responsiveness will be sacrificed on the altar of free enterprise. This regulatory responsibility must be openly and directly faced; to fail to do so would be to lose, or significantly and perhaps irreversibly to diminish, an unprecedented opportunity for the enrichment of social and political life in modern societies.

Rethinking Ideology in the Era of Mass Communication

In drawing this chapter to a close, I want to return to some of the questions which were central to earlier chapters and re-address them in the light of the considerations offered here. In particular, I want to ask how, in the light of these considerations, the analysis of ideology should be understood and pursued today. In chapter 2 I criticized a variety of different approaches to the analysis of ideology, arguing that these approaches either neglected or misconstrued the role of mass communication in modern societies, and hence misinterpreted the significance of mass communication for the analysis of ideology. So how, we may now ask, should the analysis of ideology be understood in the era of mass communication? To answer this question fully will require us to move to a kind of analysis which, in the course of this chapter, we have not confronted: we shall have to move from a pre-occupation with the nature of technical media and the organization of media institutions to a kind of analysis which, while informed by these considerations, is orientated towards the *content* of media messages and the ways in which this content is employed and appropriated in particular circumstances. A methodological framework for this kind of analysis will be developed in the following chapter. Here I shall restrict myself to some considerations of a general kind concerning the analysis of ideology today. I shall proceed by putting forward four theses which will provide a set of theoretical guidelines for a re-orientation of the analysis of ideology in the era of mass communication.

Thesis 1: The analysis of ideology in modern societies must give a central role to the nature and impact of mass communication, although mass communication is not the only site of ideology. As I tried to show in an earlier chapter, the analysis of ideology has often been couched within a general theoretical account concerning the cultural transformations associated with the rise of modern industrial societies – what I called the grand narrative of cultural transformation. This account placed primary emphasis on the decline of traditional religious beliefs and practices, and on the progressive rationalization of social life; the analysis of ideology was thus conceived of primarily in terms of the analysis of the secular belief systems which accompanied the development of industrial capitalism. But we live in a world today in which cultural experience is profoundly shaped by the diffusion of symbolic forms through the various media of mass communication. It is this mediazation of modern culture, rather than the alleged secularization and rationalization of social life, which should provide the principal frame of reference with regard to which the analysis of ideology is reconsidered today. Drawing on the critical conception of ideology which I outlined in chapter 1, we can analyse ideology in terms of the ways in which the meaning conveyed by symbolic forms serves to establish and sustain relations of domination; and we can acknowledge that, in societies characterized by the development of mass communication, the analysis of ideology should be centrally concerned with the symbolic forms transmitted by the technical media of mass communication. Rather than focusing on the secular belief systems formulated and espoused by organized political groups, the analysis of ideology should be orientated primarily towards the multiple and complex ways in which symbolic phenomena circulate in the social world and intersect with relations of power. The technical media of mass communication are of central concern not only as channels for the circulation and diffusion of symbolic forms, but also as mechanisms which create new kinds of action and interaction, new kinds of social relations which are extended in time and space. Hence the analysis of ideology must address both the symbolic forms which are produced and diffused by media institutions, and the contexts of action and interaction within which these mediated symbolic forms are produced and received.

While mass communication is of central concern to the analysis of ideology, it is important to stress that it is by no means the only site for the operation of ideology in modern societies. I have characterized ideological phenomena as meaningful symbolic forms in so far as they serve, in particular social–historical circumstances, to establish and sustain relations of domination; and such phenomena can be discerned in a variety of contexts, from everyday conversations between friends to Presidential or ministerial addresses (mediated or not), from banter and jokes to serious declarations of policy and principle. Acknowledging the centrality of mass communication as a site for the production and diffusion of ideology does not imply that one must neglect the operation of ideology in contexts other than those involving the transmission of symbolic forms via mass communication. Moreover, as I indicated earlier, symbolic forms transmitted via mass communication are often taken up in contexts of everyday life and incorporated in the symbolic content of social interaction. This discursive elaboration of mediated messages may transform the meaning of the messages themselves and modify their impact and role in the lives of both primary and secondary recipients. The study of ideology must be sufficiently broad to take account of the diversity of contexts within which symbolic forms circulate, whether these forms are mediated by mass communication, elaborated in subsequent discussion, or simply exchanged in the course of everyday social interaction.

Thesis 2: The development of mass communication greatly expands the scope for the operation of ideology in modern societies, for it enables symbolic forms to be transmitted to extended and potentially vast audiences which are dispersed in time and space. If we conceive of ideology in terms of the ways in which the meaning conveyed by symbolic forms serves to establish and sustain relations of domination, then we can see that the development of mass communication, and especially electronic media, has enormous consequences for the propagation and diffusion of ideological phenomena. With the development of printed media of mass communication, the circulation of symbolic forms was increasingly severed from the sharing of a common physical locale, and hence the mobilization of meaning in symbolic forms was increasingly capable of transcending the immediate social context in which symbolic forms were produced. It was only with the development of printed media of mass communication that ideological phenomena could emerge as *mass* phenomena, for prior to that the circulation of symbolic forms was restricted to particular locales or to specific strata or networks of individuals. The advent of electronic media, and especially television, has further accentuated the mass character and mass potential of ideological phenomena. Electronic media enable symbolic forms to be circulated on an unprecedented scale, to reach vast audiences, far-flung in space, more or less contemporaneously. Never before has the circulation capacity of symbolic forms been so great as in the era of electronically mediated mass communication.

In addition to augmenting circulation capacity, the development of electronically mediated mass communication has modified the modes of access to the production and reception of symbolic forms. Broadcasting institutions in modern societies are organized in determinate ways, some of which I sketched in an earlier chapter, and these organizational characteristics serve to restrict access to the production and diffusion of electronically mediated symbolic forms. The nature of these restrictions is varied and constantly changing, especially with the deployment of new technologies in the field of broadcasting. But for the foreseeable future it is likely that the modes of access to the production and diffusion of symbolic forms in the field of broadcasting will remain highly restrictive and primarily determined by the organizational features of large-scale media institutions and communication conglomerates. In contrast to the restricted access on the side of production and diffusion, the symbolic forms transmitted by electronic media such as television are characterized by relatively unrestricted accessibility on the side of reception. Certain material, technical, financial and legal conditions may have to be satisfied in order for receptive activity to take place – individuals may have to acquire a television set, for example, and to pay a licence or subscription fee; but once these conditions are satisfied, access to the reception of mediated messages is relatively unrestricted. Of course, restrictions of various kinds do operate in domestic and other contexts of reception, and I have alluded to these in an earlier section of this chapter. But it is important to stress that, compared to other forms of mass communication such as books, newspapers and magazines, the messages transmitted by electronic media like television are in principle accessible to, and are typically received by, a larger and broader audience. To some extent this is due to the fact that the television set is commonly a domestic appliance which occupies a central position in the home, and which is a focal point around which much social interaction takes place. It is also due to the fact that the skills required to decode the messages received via television are often less sophisticated, and involve less specialized training, than those required to decode messages transmitted by other media such as printed matter. This two-fold character of electronically mediated mass communication – restricted access to the production and diffusion of symbolic forms, relatively unrestricted access to the reception of symbolic forms – shapes the ways in which, and the extent to which, electronically mediated symbolic forms are a site for the operation of ideology in modern societies.

Thesis 3: We cannot analyse the ideological character of mass communication by analysing only the organizational features of media institutions or the characteristics of media messages; rather, media messages must also be analysed in relation to the specific contexts and processes in which they are appropriated by the individuals who receive them. As I indicated in chapter 2, a number of contemporary theorists have been concerned with the ways in which mass communication has become a major medium of ideology in modern societies. Thus the mass media are commonly given a central role as a mechanism of reproduction in what I described as the general theory of state-organized and ideologically secured social reproduction. Moreover, authors such as Horkheimer, Adorno and Habermas have tried, in differing ways, to analyse the ideological character of media products. Apart from the specific criticisms that can be made of these various approaches, there is one shortcoming that they share in common: the tendency to interpret the ideological character of mass communication in terms of the features or functions of media institutions and the characteristics of media messages. This is a shortcoming because it cannot be assumed that the messages diffused by media institutions will have, by virtue of the organization of these institutions or the characteristics of the messages themselves, a given effect when the messages are received and appropriated by individuals in the course of their everyday lives. It cannot be assumed that the individuals who receive media messages will, by the very fact of receiving them, be impelled to act in an imitative and conforming way and thereby be bound to the social order which their actions, and the messages which allegedly impel them, serve to reproduce. The fact that the continuous and reverent portrayal of Ceauşescu and his entourage on Romanian state television did little to win them a secure place in the hearts and minds of the Romanian people is vivid testimony to the weakness of this assumption. Based on what I termed the fallacy of internalism, this whole approach to the ideological character of mass communication takes too much for granted and must be replaced by an approach which considers more carefully the specific contexts and processes in which the messages produced and diffused by media institutions are appropriated by the individuals who receive them.

We can begin to make this re-orientation by situating the analysis of the ideological character of mass communication within the framework of what I have called technically mediated quasi-interaction. The structure and content of media messages must be analysed in relation to their production within the primary interactive framework and their reception within the primary reception region, as well as in relation to the quasi-interaction sustained between communicators and recipients and the subsequent social interactions in which the content of media messages is incorporated and elaborated. Moreover, these interlocking frameworks of interaction are always embedded in broader sets of social relations and institutions which are structured in certain ways. It is only by analysing the structure and content of media messages in relation to these frameworks of interaction and encompassing sets of social relations that we can examine the ideological character of media products. For these products, like all symbolic forms, are not ideological in themselves; rather, they are ideological only in so far as, in particular social-historical circumstances, they serve to establish and sustain relations of domination. The circumstances which are of particular importance in this regard are those of the primary reception region and the frameworks of interaction and quasi-interaction which are linked to it, as well as the broader sets of social relations and institutions in which these frameworks are embedded. Since mass communication, and especially electronic media, has the capacity to diffuse symbolic forms in a vast range of dispersed reception regions which are remote in space (and perhaps also in time) from the place of production, the ideological character of media messages is both greatly enhanced in principle and yet dependent in practice on a diverse range of circumstances which lie beyond the context in which the message is produced. Hence whatever strategy of symbolic construction may be employed by the principal communicator, the ways in which media messages are received and understood, and the consequences which they may have for the maintenance or disruption of relations of power, will depend on a range of circumstances which lie beyond the production context and, to some extent, beyond the control of the producers. If the scope for the operation of ideology in modern societies has been greatly enhanced by the development of mass communication, the complexity and ambiguity of ideological phenomena have also increased, by virtue of the fact that symbolic forms now circulate in a multiplicity of contexts which are remote in space (and time), which are structured in differing ways and in which symbolic forms may be interpreted, assimilated, discussed or contested in ways that cannot be fully anticipated or controlled by the principal communicators.

Thesis 4: The various media of mass communication, and the nature of the quasi-interactions which they make possible and sustain, define broad parameters within which the messages transmitted by these media acquire an ideological character, but they do not constitute these messages as ideological. These broad parameters are boundary conditions within which ideological phenomena emerge, but they do not determine these phenomena as such. I noted earlier, for example, that electronic media such as television make possible a quasi-interaction in which communicators become recognizable personalities who can speak directly to recipients, and with whom recipients can sympathize. The audio-visual character of this medium, and its capacity to transmit messages virtually instantaneously, provide the communicator with opportunities for symbolic construction which are not provided by other media. A communicator can, for instance, accentuate symbols of familiarity – a domestic setting, casual dress, informal speech, personal anecdotes, etc. – and thereby seek to achieve a mediated intimacy which may be difficult to establish in the same way, and on the same scale, with other media. There can be no doubt that the advent of television has thus facilitated what we may describe as a *generalized personalization of political issues* – that is, political figures are able to appear on a national and international stage as *personalities* with whom recipients can enter into a certain kind of relationship, whom they can like or dislike, admire or detest. Today political figures have little choice but to act within the opportunity space provided by the deployment of the technical media of mass communication. They typically employ strategies of symbolic construction which seek to present themselves as likeable and accessible personalities, as competent and unswerving leaders, and so on. In the era of electronically mediated mass communication, the study of ideology must take account of the new strategies of symbolic construction, and of the symbolic organization of self-presentation, which are constitutive features of the managed visibility of political leaders.

However, if the nature of media and mediated quasi-interactions define broad parameters within which messages acquire an ideological character, it is essential to relate these messages to the particular contexts within which they are received. It is only within these contexts that mediated messages may, or may not, be constituted as ideological; it is only here that a message constructed in order to sustain power will succeed, or not succeed, in sustaining it. Hence the new opportunities offered by mass communication, and especially television, are also new risks. The political personalities who appear on the new stage of mediated quasi-interaction are fragile symbolic constructs who are faced not only with questions and tasks of unprecedented complexity, but also with audiences who can observe, with unprecedented immediacy, their ways of responding to them. In seeking to cultivate their personalities and to establish a mediated intimacy with a multitude of individuals who are remote in space and time, political figures also run the risk of presenting themselves to some of these individuals as unworthy of the very positions of power which they hold or seek. What is constructed as an intimate, affable and likeable personality may be perceived, in the diverse and remote contexts of reception, as a rather ordinary and uninteresting character, or even as one whose personal attributes and back-region behaviour are slightly disgusting. The generalized personalization of political issues which is facilitated by mass communication carries the risk that the constructed personalities may be received and perceived as charlatans, and hence the process of personalization may give rise to new forms of scepticism, cynicism and distrust.

In this chapter I have outlined a general theoretical account of mass communication and its role in modern societies. I began by conceptualizing mass communication as the institutionalized production and diffusion of symbolic goods via the transmission and storage of information or communication. I then examined some of the ways in which the development of mass communication may affect the manner in which individuals act and interact – what I called the interactional impact of technical media. I also examined the ways in which mass communication creates a new kind of mediated publicness or visibility in modern societies, thereby reconstituting the boundaries between public and private life. In a more normative tone, I considered some of the arguments that have been developed historically concerning the institutional organization of the media and their role in social and political life. Finally, in drawing the chapter to a close, I returned to the theme of ideology and asked how the analysis of ideology should be rethought today, in a world where mass communication plays an increasingly important role.

In the sixth and final chapter, I shall pick up some of the issues raised by the attempt to rethink the analysis of ideology in the era of mass communication and pursue them on a methodological level. Beginning from the theoretical accounts which I have presented in this and previous chapters, I shall ask how, concretely, we can analyse symbolic forms and ideological phenomena in specific circumstances. I shall try to move beyond a purely theoretical account of culture, ideology and mass communication and to show that, by drawing on this account, we can elaborate a methodological framework which is systematic, justifiable and practical. For I want to argue that the approach developed here makes a difference in practice – both in the practice of social analysis, understood as a systematic interpretative activity, and potentially in the practice of the subjects who make up, in part, the social–historical world.

The Methodology of Interpretation

In previous chapters I have developed a general theoretical account of culture, ideology and mass communication, but I have not addressed in detail questions of a properly methodological kind. I have indicated in broad outline how we might approach the analysis of culture and ideology, but I have not pursued these indications in any depth. In this chapter I want to take up these methodological issues in a systematic way. I want to follow through the methodological implications of my earlier discussions; I want to show that these discussions, while largely theoretical, make a difference in practice, and that practical analysis has a bearing on theoretical discussion and debate. The division between theoretical discussion and practical analysis runs deep in the social sciences, often leaving the practitioners of each on the opposite sides of a yawning chasm. Taken to extremes, this division is deleterious and can only work to the mutual detriment of theory and research. In this chapter I shall try to break down this division and to explore some of the links between theoretical debates about culture, ideology and mass communication, on the one hand, and the practical analysis of symbolic forms, on the other.

In pursuing issues of a methodological kind, I shall seek to develop a particular argument, or series of arguments, concerning the analysis of symbolic forms. I shall argue that the analysis of symbolic forms can be most appropriately conceptualized in terms of a methodological framework that I shall describe as 'depth hermeneutics'. This framework highlights the fact that the object of analysis is a meaningful symbolic construction which calls for interpretation. Hence we must give a central role to the process of interpretation, for only in this way can we do justice to the distinctive character of the object domain. But symbolic forms are also embedded in social and historical contexts of various kinds; and, as meaningful symbolic constructions, they are internally structured in various ways. In order to take account of the social contextualization of symbolic forms and of their internal structural features, we must employ other methods of analysis. I shall try to show that depth hermeneutics provides a framework within which these various methods of analysis can be systematically interrelated, their strengths appreciated and their limits defined. Depth hermeneutics provides a framework which enables us to follow through, at the methodological level, with the kind of re-orientation that I have outlined on a more theoretical plane in previous chapters.

As a general methodological framework for the analysis of symbolic forms, depth hermeneutics can readily be adapted to the analysis of ideology and the analysis of mass communication. This development of the depth-hermeneutical approach requires us to take account of the distinctive characteristics of ideology and mass communication, as identified and discussed in previous chapters. However, in developing the approach in this way, I do not wish to suggest that there is a single, simple method which is uniquely tailored to the analysis of culture, ideology and mass communication. These phenomena are extremely complex, they display many different aspects and may be approached in differing ways. Indeed, the literature abounds with countless examples of research carried out from diverse points of view, focusing on a wide range of characteristics and problems. My aim in this chapter is neither to provide a general review of this literature, nor to suggest that depth hermeneutics provides a simple and hitherto unconsidered alternative. Instead, I shall draw on a highly selective range of examples, chosen in order to develop a general methodological argument; and I shall try to show that depth hermeneutics provides, not so much an alternative to existing methods of analysis, but rather a general methodological framework within which some of these methods can be situated and linked together. It enables us to draw out the value of certain methods of analysis, while at the same time highlighting their limitations. It enables us to show how different approaches to the analysis of culture, ideology and mass communication can be interrelated in a systematic way, combined within a coherent movement of thought which illuminates different aspects of these multi-faceted phenomena.

I shall begin by discussing the relevance of hermeneutics to social-historical inquiry and outlining the methodological framework of depth hermeneutics. This framework will then be applied to the analysis of ideology: as we shall see, the analysis of ideology can be conducted within the depth-hermeneutical framework; but by emphasizing the interrelations of meaning and power, this analysis takes on a distinctive, critical character. The fourth section of the chapter will be concerned with the study of mass communication. Consistent with my earlier account of mass communication, I shall outline what may be described as a 'tripartite approach' to the analysis of mass communication, seeking to show how the depth-hermeneutical framework is relevant to each phase of this approach. I shall dwell in particular on the third phase of the tripartite approach, a phase which is concerned with the reception and appropriation of media messages. For I shall argue that it is only by careful consideration of what is involved in the everyday appropriation of media messages that we can avoid the pitfalls which characterize much previous work on the ideological character of mass communication. Finally, the concluding section of the chapter will explore some of the relations between the methodology of interpretation, the conduct of critique and the process of self-reflection.

Some Hermeneutical Conditions of Social-Historical Inquiry

In this chapter I shall develop a methodological framework which draws on the tradition of hermeneutics. This ancient tradition, stemming from literary debates in Classical Greece, has undergone many transformations since its emergence two millenia ago; and it is the developments associated with the work of nineteenth- and twentieth-century hermeneutical philosophers – especially Dilthey, Heidegger, Gadamer and Ricoeur – which are of particular relevance to our concerns. These thinkers remind us, in the first place, that *the study of symbolic forms is fundamentally and inescapably a matter of understanding and interpretation*. Symbolic forms are meaningful constructions which call for interpretation; they are actions, utterances, texts which, *qua* meaningful constructions, can be understood. This fundamental emphasis on the processes of understanding and interpretation retains its value today. For in the social sciences, as in other disciplines concerned with the analysis of symbolic forms, the legacy of nineteenth-century positivism is strong. There is a constant temptation to treat social phenomena in general, and symbolic forms in particular, as if they were natural objects, amenable to various kinds of formal, statistical and objective analysis. My argument here is *not* that this temptation is completely misguided, that it must be resisted at all costs, that the legacy of positivism must be eradicated once and for all: this may be the view of some radical proponents of what is sometimes called 'the interpretative approach' in social analysis, but it is not my view. Rather, my argument, which I shall elaborate below, is that, while various kinds of formal, statistical and objective analysis are perfectly appropriate and indeed vital in social analysis generally and in the analysis of symbolic forms in particular, nevertheless these kinds of analysis comprise at best a *partial* approach to the study of social phenomena and symbolic forms. They are partial because, as the tradition of hermeneutics reminds us, many social phenomena are symbolic forms and all symbolic forms are meaningful constructs which, however thoroughly they may be analysed by formal or objective methods, inescapably raise distinctive problems of understanding and interpretation. Hence processes of understanding and interpretation should be regarded, not as a methodological dimension which radically excludes formal or objective analyses, but rather as a dimension which is both complementary and indispensable to them.

But surely, it might be said, all disciplines in whatever field of inquiry, whether social or natural sciences, whether sociology or astronomy, raise problems of understanding and interpretation. The observations of the astronomer require interpretation no less than do the results of a sociological survey. This is no doubt true, but the issue cannot be left there. For the tradition of hermeneutics also reminds us that, in the case of social inquiry, the constellation of issues is significantly different from the constellation that exists in the natural sciences, since in social inquiry *the object of our investigations is itself a pre-interpreted domain*. The social–historical world is not just an object domain which is there to be observed; it is also a *subject domain* which is made up, in part, of subjects who, in the routine course of their everyday lives, are constantly involved in understanding themselves and others, and in interpreting the actions, utterances and events which take place around them. It is the work of Heidegger, above all, which has brought out the importance of regarding the process of understanding, not as some specialized procedure employed by the analyst in the social–historical sphere, but rather as a fundamental characteristic of human beings as such: understanding is something that we, *qua* human beings, already do all the time anyway, and the more specialized procedures of interpretation employed by social analysts take for granted, and build upon, the pre-established bases of everyday understanding.[1] So when social analysts seek to interpret a symbolic form, for example, they are seeking to interpret an object which may itself be an interpretation, and which may already have been interpreted by the subjects who make up the object domain of which the symbolic form is part. The analysts are offering an interpretation of an interpretation, they are re-interpreting a pre-interpreted domain; and it may be important to consider, as I shall do later, just how this re-interpretation is related to, and how it may be informed by, the pre-interpretations which exist (or existed) among the subjects who make up the social–historical world.

If hermeneutics reminds us that the object domain of social inquiry is also a subject domain, so too it reminds us that *the subjects who make up the subject-object domain are, like social analysts themselves, subjects capable of understanding, of reflecting, and of acting on the basis of this understanding and reflection.* Here again, we find a fundamental difference between social inquiry, on the one hand,

and the conduct of the natural sciences, on the other. When the social analyst puts forward theories, findings or interpretations of some kind, these results stand in what we may describe as a *relation of potential appropriation* by the subjects who make up the social world. That is, these results stand in a relation of potential feedback with the very subject–object domain about which the results are formulated, in a way that has no direct parallel in the natural sciences. Of course, natural scientific knowledge can be used to transform the natural world, as when this knowledge is employed in technological developments. But in this case, it is once again the scientist or the technologist who employs the knowledge; it is not the constituents of the object domain who employ this knowledge to transform themselves. In social inquiry, by contrast, it is the latter situation which may in principle, and often does in practice, obtain. The results of social inquiry may be in principle, and often are in practice, appropriated by the subjects who make up the subject–object domain about which these results are formulated, and this domain may itself be transformed in the very process of appropriation. There are many familiar examples of this intrinsic relation of potential feedback: the results of an opinion poll about voting intentions may itself affect voting intentions; an analysis of systematic inequalities may stimulate protests aimed at reducing or eliminating inequalities; and so on. I shall return to some of the implications of this intrinsic relation at a later stage. Here it may suffice to say that this relation should be construed, not as an unfortunate *problem* for social inquiry, but rather as a *condition of possibility* of the kind of knowledge that can be attained in the social–historical sphere. It is because social inquiry is concerned with an object domain which is made up in part of subjects capable of understanding, reflection and action that the results of this inquiry can in principle be appropriated by the subjects who make up this domain, even if in practice, for all sorts of reasons, the results may not be appropriated.

There is a further and related respect in which hermeneutics retains its relevance today: it reminds us that *the subjects who in part make up the social world are always embedded in historical traditions.* Human beings are *part of* history, and not merely observers or spectators of it; historical traditions, and the complex clusters of meaning and value which are handed down from generation to generation, are partly constitutive of what human beings are. This point has been forcefully developed by Gadamer, whose conception of understanding as a fusion of historical horizons, as a creative production of meaning which implicitly draws on the resources of traditions, helped to emphasize the fact that human beings are always part of broader social–historical contexts and that the process of understanding is always more than an isolated encounter between minds.[2] Gadamer among others has helped to highlight what we could call *the historicity of human experience*. What I mean by this is that human experience is always historical, in the sense that new experience is always assimilated to the residues of what is past, and in the sense that in seeking to understand what is new we always and necessarily build upon what is already present. Indeed, our very understanding of new experience as *new* is an indication of the fact that we relate it to what has come before, with regard to which we perceive it as new. But there is another aspect to the historicity of human experience, an aspect which is brought out less well by Gadamer's work. The residues of the past are not only a basis upon which we assimilate new experiences in the present and the future: these residues may also serve, in specific circumstances, to conceal, obscure or disguise the present. It is this aspect to which Marx was calling attention in *The Eighteenth Brumaire of Louis Bonaparte*, when he observed that, at times of rapid social change and conflict, human beings are inclined to 'conjure up the spirits of the past' in order to disguise the present and to reassure themselves of their continuity with the past.[3] Moreover, as I noted earlier, many of the traditions with which we are familiar today are in fact *invented* traditions of relatively recent date, even though they may have established themselves so firmly in the collective imagination that they seem to be much more ancient than they actually are.[4] Hence, while hermeneutics is right to emphasize the fact that human beings are always embedded in historical traditions, it is also important to recognize that the symbolic residues which comprise traditions may have specific characteristics and uses which merit further analysis. As we shall see, it is this recognition that helps to create the space for a hermeneutically informed approach to the analysis of ideology.

The Methodological Framework of Depth Hermeneutics

It may be that hermeneutics can remind us of some of the conditions of social-historical inquiry, but it is less clear that it can offer methodological guidelines of a more concrete character for the study of symbolic forms in general, and for the analysis of ideology in particular. Was not the intellectual revolution associated with Heidegger and Gadamer an attempt to turn hermeneutics away from a preoccupation with 'method' and turn it towards a philosophical reflection on the character of being and on the constitutive role of understanding? And if so, how can we draw upon this philosophical reflection while at the same time orientating ourselves towards questions of a methodological kind? Moreover, it might be remarked, has not the tradition of hermeneutics been concerned primarily with problems of meaning and understanding, with the ways in which the social-historical world is created by speaking and acting individuals whose meaningful utterances and actions can be understood by others who partake of this world? And if so, how can this tradition provide us with the methodological resources to take account, not only of the meaningful constitution of the social-historical world, but also of its constitution as a *field of force*, a realm of power and conflict in which 'meaning' may be a mask for repression? In short, can we draw from the tradition of hermeneutics something more than a set of general conditions of social-historical inquiry? Can we draw from it a methodological framework which can be employed for the study of symbolic forms in general, and for the analysis of ideology in particular?

We can find the beginnings of a response to these questions in the work of Paul Ricoeur, Jürgen Habermas and others. Ricoeur's work is of particular interest in this regard because he has sought to build upon the insights of Heidegger and Gadamer without abandoning methodological concerns. He has sought explicitly and systematically to show that hermeneutics can offer both a philosophical reflection on being and understanding, and a methodological reflection on the nature and tasks of interpretation in social inquiry. The key to this path of reflection is what Ricoeur and others have called 'depth hermeneutics'.[5] The idea underlying depth hermeneutics is that, in social inquiry as in other domains, the process of interpretation can be, and indeed demands to be, mediated by a range of explanatory or 'objectifying' methods. When dealing with a domain which is constituted as much by force as by meaning, or when analysing an artefact which displays a distinctive pattern through which something is said, it is both possible and desirable to mediate the process of interpretation by employing explanatory or objectifying techniques. Hence 'explanation' and 'interpretation' should not be regarded, as they sometimes are, as mutually exclusive or radically antithetical terms; rather, they may be treated as complementary moments in a comprehensive interpretative theory, as mutually supportive steps along 'a unique *hermeneutical arc*'.[6] While I concur with the overall aims of Ricoeur's work, the methodological framework that I shall develop will differ significantly from his account of depth hermeneutics. For Ricoeur places too much emphasis on what he calls 'the semantic autonomy of the text', and he thus abstracts too readily from the social-historical conditions in which texts, or analogues of texts, are produced and received. I have developed this criticism elsewhere and I shall not pursue it further here.[7] Leaving aside the details of Ricoeur's account, I shall draw on the underlying idea of depth hermeneutics in order to outline a methodological framework for the study of symbolic forms. I shall subsequently adapt this approach for the purposes of analysing ideology and mass communication.

In outlining a general methodological framework for the study of symbolic forms, I shall seek to elaborate, at a methodological level, the structural conception of culture which I formulated in chapter 3. According to this conception, cultural analysis can be construed as the study of symbolic forms in relation to the historically specific and socially structured contexts and processes within which, and by means of which, these symbolic forms are produced, transmitted and received – in short, it is the study of the meaningful constitution and social contextualization of symbolic forms. I shall try to show that depth hermeneutics can provide a methodological framework for the conduct of cultural analysis in this sense. I shall go on to argue, in the next section, that this framework can also be used for the analysis of ideology. The analysis of ideology, as I have defined it, is also concerned with symbolic forms in relation to social–historical contexts; hence the analysis of ideology can be regarded methodologically as a particular form of depth hermeneutics. But by focusing our attention on the interrelations between meaning and power, on the ways in which symbolic forms can be used to establish and sustain relations of domination, the analysis of ideology assumes a distinctive, critical character. It raises new questions concerning the uses of symbolic forms and the relations between interpretation, self-reflection and critique.

Let me begin the discussion of depth hermeneutics with a preliminary but fundamental observation: in so far as the object of our investigations is a pre-interpreted domain, the depth-hermeneutical approach must acknowledge and take account of the ways in which symbolic forms are interpreted by the subjects who comprise the subject–object domain. In other words, *the hermeneutics of everyday life is the primordial and unavoidable starting point of the depth-hermeneutical approach*. Hence the depth-hermeneutical approach must be based, so far as possible, upon an elucidation of the ways in which symbolic forms are interpreted and understood by the individuals who produce and receive them in the course of their everyday lives: this ethnographic moment is an indispensable preliminary to the depth-hermeneutical approach. By means of interviews, participant observation and other kinds of ethnographic research, we can reconstruct the ways in which symbolic forms are interpreted and understood in the varied contexts of social life. Of course, this reconstruction is itself an interpretative process; it is an interpretation of everyday understanding – or, as I shall describe it, an *interpretation of doxa*, an interpretation of the opinions, beliefs and understandings which are held and shared by the individuals who comprise the social world. The importance of undertaking the interpretation of doxa has been emphasized by a variety of authors in recent years. Analysts drawing on the philosophy of the later Wittgenstein, on the phenomenological writings of Husserl and Schutz, and on the ethnomethodological approach of Garfinkel, Cicourel and others, have all emphasized in differing ways the methodological significance of the interpretation of doxa. Nevertheless, this dimension is commonly neglected in social analysis, including the analysis of symbolic forms. All too often symbolic forms are analysed in isolation from the contexts in which they are produced and received by individuals who routinely make sense of these forms and integrate them into other aspects of their lives. To neglect these contexts of everyday life, and the ways in which the individuals situated within them interpret and understand the symbolic forms which they produce and receive, is to disregard a fundamental hermeneutical condition of social–historical inquiry, namely that the object domain of our investigation is also a subject domain in which symbolic forms are pre-interpreted by the subjects who comprise this domain.

But to stress the importance of the interpretation of doxa is not to suggest that the study of symbolic forms should amount to nothing more than this. The interpretation of doxa is an indispensable starting point of analysis, but it is not the end of the matter. Indeed, the problem with much of the work inspired by Wittgensteinian philosophy, phenomenology and ethnomethodology is that, while rightly emphasizing the importance of the interpretation of doxa, it rarely moves beyond this level of analysis; what should be treated as an indispensable aspect of the inquiry becomes the whole of the inquiry, and other aspects are either neglected or dismissed. This exclusive preoccupation with the interpretation of doxa is just as misleading as the failure to take this dimension into account. In order to avoid this shortcoming, we must make what I shall describe as a *methodological break with the hermeneutics of everyday life*. Without ignoring the interpretation of doxa, we must move beyond this level of analysis in order to take account of other aspects of symbolic forms, aspects which stem from the constitution of the object domain. Symbolic forms are meaningful constructs which are interpreted and understood by the individuals who produce and receive them, but they are *also* meaningful constructs which are structured in definite ways and which are embedded in specific social and historical conditions. To take account of the ways in which symbolic forms are structured, and of the social–historical conditions in which they are embedded, we must move beyond the interpretation of doxa and engage in kinds of analysis which fall within the methodological framework of depth hermeneutics.

As I shall develop it, depth hermeneutics is a broad methodological framework which comprises three principal phases or procedures. These phases should be regarded, not so much as discrete stages of a sequential method, but rather as analytically distinct dimensions of a complex interpretative process. Figure 6.1 summarizes the various phases of the depth-hermeneutical approach, situating this approach in relation to the hermeneutics of everyday life. The three phases of the depth-hermeneutical approach may be described as *social-historical analysis, formal or discursive analysis*, and *interpretation/re-interpretation*. In explicating these phases I shall introduce further distinctions, but these additional distinctions should be understood primarily as a means of illustration. The ways in which these phases of analysis are most suitably followed through in practice will depend on the specific objects of analysis and the kinds of information available to the researcher. While I wish to advocate and defend the methodological framework of depth hermeneutics, I do not wish to suggest that questions concerning the most appropriate methods of research can be answered *a priori*. Within each phase of the depth-hermeneutical approach, a variety of methods of research may be available, and some methods may be more appropriate than others given the specific object of analysis and the specific circumstances of the research.

The first phase of the depth-hermeneutical approach is what may be described as *social-historical analysis*. Symbolic forms do not subsist in a vacuum: they are produced, transmitted and received in specific social and historical conditions. Even works of art which seem timeless and universal are characterized by definite conditions of production, circulation and reception, from relations of patronage in sixteenth-century Florence to the showrooms of a modern gallery or art museum, from the courts of eighteenth-century Vienna to the concert halls, television screens or

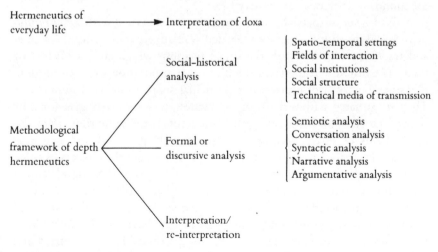

Figure 6.1 Forms of Hermeneutical Inquiry

compact discs of today. *The aim of social–historical analysis is to reconstruct the social and historical conditions of the production, circulation and reception of symbolic forms.* The ways in which these conditions may be most appropriately examined will vary from one study to another, depending on the particular objects and circumstances of inquiry. But we can distinguish between several different kinds of conditions which may, in particular cases, be relevant. Here we can draw upon the discussion in chapter 3 of some of the typical characteristics of social contexts. I distinguished between four basic aspects of social contexts and I suggested that each of these aspects defined a distinct level of analysis. Let me briefly recall these aspects. In the first place, we may seek to identify and describe the specific *spatio-temporal settings* in which symbolic forms are produced and received. Symbolic forms are produced (uttered, enacted, inscribed) and received (seen, listened to, read) by individuals situated in specific locales, acting and reacting at particular times and in particular places, and the reconstruction of these locales is an important part of social–historical analysis. Symbolic forms are also typically situated within certain *fields of interaction.* We can analyse a field as a space of positions and a set of trajectories, which together determine some of the relations between individuals and some of the opportunities available to them. In pursuing courses of action within fields of interaction, individuals draw upon the various kinds and quantities of resources or 'capital' available to them, as well as upon a variety of rules, conventions and flexible 'schemata'. These schemata are not so much explicit and well-formulated precepts as implicit and unformulated guidelines. They exist in the form of practical knowledge, gradually inculcated and continuously reproduced in the mundane activities of everyday life.

A third level of social–historical analysis is concerned with *social institutions.* Social institutions may be regarded as relatively stable clusters of rules and resources, together with the social relations which are established by them. The BBC and Rupert Murdoch's News Corporation are institutions in this sense. Social institutions give a particular shape to fields of interaction. They are situated within fields of interaction, to which they give form by fixing a range of positions and trajectories; but, at the same time, they also create fields of interaction by establishing new positions and new trajectories. To analyse social institutions is to reconstruct the clusters of rules, resources and relations which constitute them, to trace their development through time and to examine the practices and attitudes of the individuals who act for them and within them. We can distinguish the analysis of social institutions in this sense from the analysis of what I have called *social structure.* I use the latter term to refer to the relatively stable asymmetries and differentials which characterize social institutions and fields of interaction.

To analyse social structure is to focus on asymmetries, differentials and divisions. It is to seek to determine which asymmetries are systematic and relatively stable – that is, which are manifestations not simply of individual differences, but of collective and durable differences in terms of the distribution of, and access to, resources, power, opportunities and life chances. Analysing social structure also involves the attempt to ascertain the criteria, categories and principles which underlie these differences and account for their systematic and durable character. The analysis of social structure thus demands a more theoretical level of reflection, for it requires the analyst to propose criteria, formulate categories and draw distinctions which may help to organize and illuminate the evidence of systematic asymmetries and differentials in social life. The analysis of the formation and reproduction of social classes, or the analysis of the division between men and women and associated forms of asymmetry and inequality, are instances of what is involved in the analysis of social structure in this sense.

Finally, for the purposes of this discussion, we can distinguish a further set of conditions which are of particular relevance to the study of symbolic forms: the technical media of inscription and transmission. In so far as symbolic forms are exchanged between individuals, they necessarily involve some medium of transmission, whether it be simply modulated airwaves, as in the case of utterances in a face-to-face situation, or complex mechanisms of electronic codification and transmission, as in the case of radio and television broadcasting. As I explained in chapter 4, a technical medium is a material substratum in which, and by means of which, symbolic forms are produced and transmitted. Technical media endow symbolic forms with certain characteristics – with a certain degree of fixation, a certain kind of reproducibility, and a certain scope for participation among the subjects who employ the medium. Of course, technical media do not exist in isolation. They are always embedded in particular social–historical contexts; they always presuppose certain skills, rules and resources for encoding and decoding messages, attributes which are themselves unevenly distributed among individuals; and they are often deployed within specific institutional apparatuses which may be concerned with regulating the production and circulation of symbolic forms. Hence the social–historical analysis of technical media of inscription and transmission cannot be a narrowly technical inquiry, but must seek to elucidate the broader social contexts in which these media are embedded and deployed.

The various kinds of social–historical inquiry are differing ways of trying to grasp what I have described as the social contextualization of symbolic forms. The production, circulation and reception of symbolic forms are processes that take place within historically specific and socially structured contexts or fields. The production of meaningful objects and expressions – from everyday utterances to works of art – is production made possible by the rules and resources available to the producer, and it is production orientated towards the anticipated circulation and reception of the objects and expressions within the social field. This orientation may be part of an explicit strategy pursued by the producers, as when television personnel seek to produce a programme for a particular market and modify the contents accordingly. But the orientation may also be an implicit aspect of the productive process, in so far as the aims and orientations of the producer may already be adapted to the conditions of circulation and reception of the objects produced, in such a way that the orientation does not have to be formulated as part of an explicit strategy. If the production of meaningful objects and expressions involves the utilization of rules and resources available to the producer, so too the circulation of these objects and expressions requires technical media and may involve a determinate set of institutions, with their own clusters of rules, resources and social relations. Similarly, the reception of symbolic forms is a process situated in definite social-historical contexts, in which individuals employ various kinds of resources, rules and conventions in order to understand and appropriate symbolic forms. The task of the first phase of the depth-hermeneutical approach is to reconstruct the social-historical conditions and contexts of the production, circulation and reception of symbolic forms, to examine the rules and conventions, the social relations and institutions, and the distribution of power, resources and opportunities by virtue of which these contexts form differentiated and socially structured fields.

The meaningful objects and expressions which circulate in social fields are also *complex symbolic constructions which display an articulated structure*. It is this characteristic which calls for a second phase of analysis, a phase that we may describe as *formal or discursive analysis*. Symbolic forms are the products of situated actions which draw upon the rules, resources, etc. available to the producer; but they are *also* something else, for they are complex symbolic constructions through which something is expressed or said. Symbolic forms are contextualized products *and* something more, for they are products which, by virtue of their structural features, are able to, and claim to, say something about something. It is this additional and irreducible aspect of symbolic forms which calls for a different kind of analysis, a different way of looking at symbolic forms. It establishes the basis for a type of analysis which is concerned primarily with the internal organization of symbolic forms, with their structural features, patterns and relations. This type of analysis, which I have described as formal or discursive analysis, is a perfectly legitimate, indeed indispensable, undertaking; it is rendered possible by the very constitution of the object domain. But this type of analysis becomes misleading when it is removed from the methodological framework of depth hermeneutics and pursued in isolation from social–historical analysis and from what I shall describe below as interpretation (or re-interpretation). Taken on its own, formal or discursive analysis can become an abstract exercise, disconnected from the conditions of production and reception of symbolic forms and oblivious to what is being expressed by the symbolic forms whose structure it seeks to unveil.

As with social–historical analysis, there are various ways in which formal or discursive analysis can be carried out, depending on the particular objects and circumstances of inquiry. Here again, we can distinguish several methods or types of analysis. Among the most widely known and widely practised types of formal analysis is what could be called, broadly speaking, *semiotic analysis*. 'Semiotics' is, of course, a very general term, and there are many different authors, from Saussure and Peirce to Barthes, Eco and Voloshinov, whose work could be described as a contribution to 'semiotics' in some sense. I do not wish to review this wide-ranging body of literature here. For the purposes of this discussion I shall regard semiotic analysis as the study of the relations between the elements which compose a symbolic form or sign, and of the relations between these elements and those of a broader system of which this symbolic form or sign may be part. Semiotic analysis, understood in this sense, generally involves a methodological abstraction from the social–historical conditions of the production and reception of symbolic forms. It focuses on the symbolic forms themselves and seeks to analyse their internal structural features, their constitutive elements and interrelations, and to connect these to the systems and codes of which they are part. In chapter 3 we considered the example, drawn from Barthes's *Mythologies*, of the cover illustration on *Paris-Match*, in which a young black soldier in French uniform is saluting, with eyes slightly uplifted and askance: this juxtaposition of images constitutes a distinctive structure through which the meaning of the message is conveyed.[8] It would be easy to multiply examples of this kind of semiotic analysis. Advertisements offer a particularly rich field of analysis, for much advertising is based on a logic of symbolic association or displacement, in which goods are promoted by being associated with desirable objects, authoritative persons, etc., and in which the association is established through the juxtaposition of words and images in the symbolic form or forms which make up the ad.[9] Semiotic analysis can do much to illuminate the ways in which ads and other symbolic forms are constructed; it can help to identify the constitutive elements and their interrelations, by virtue of which the meaning of a message is constructed and conveyed. But, as I have stressed, this kind of analysis is at best a partial approach to the study of symbolic forms. It is concerned primarily with the internal constitution of symbolic forms, with their distinctive elements and their interrelations. It often takes for granted, but fails to consider in a systematic way, the social–historical contexts in which symbolic forms are produced and received, as well as what I described earlier as the 'referential aspect' of symbolic forms – that is, the ways in which the elements combine to say something about something. These limitations of semiotic analysis do not undermine its usefulness, but they do imply that this type of analysis should be regarded, not as a self-sufficient approach to the study of symbolic forms, but as a partial step in a more comprehensive interpretative procedure.

So far we have been considering the analysis of symbolic forms which consist of images or words and images, but the structural features of linguistic expressions can also be analysed formally. In such cases we may speak of 'discursive analysis', that is, the analysis of the structural features and relations of discourse. I am using the term 'discourse' in a general way to refer to *actually occurring instances of communication*. Hence the object of discursive analysis is not some well-honed example designed to test our linguistic intuitions, but rather actual instances of everyday communication: a conversation between friends, a classroom interaction, a newspaper editorial, a television programme. These instances form linguistic units which generally exceed the limits of a single sentence. They often involve a concatenation of sentences or expressions, which are combined together in a specific way to form an ordered, supra-sentential linguistic unit. The expressions which make up an instance of discourse – especially oral discourse – are often ungrammatical, if compared with the rules of grammar which appear in grammarians' rule-books. The use of expressions in everyday communication is ordered, but this order derives from and reproduces a practical grammar, a *practical syntax*, which is both acquired and employed in the ongoing exchange of linguistic expressions in everyday life. Thus, while instances of discourse are always situated in particular social–historical circumstances, they also display structural features and relations which can be analysed formally, with the aid of various methods of what I have called discursive analysis.

What are these methods? Once again, I do not wish to pre-empt methodological deliberations concerning the most appropriate methods to adopt in specific cases. Nevertheless, by reflecting on a range of research which has already been carried out, we can distinguish – by way of exemplification and without seeking to be exhaustive – several different methods of discursive analysis. One such method is what is commonly described as *conversation analysis*. This term refers to a broad stream of research which was initiated by Harvey Sacks, Emanuel Schegloff and others, and which, since the mid-1960s, has been concerned with studying the systematic properties of various forms of linguistic interaction.[10] The key methodological principle of conversation analysis is to study instances of linguistic interaction in the actual settings in which they occur; and, by attending carefully to the ways in which they are organized, to highlight some of the systematic or 'structural' features of linguistic interaction. Moreover, it is assumed that the systematic features of linguistic interaction are not merely characteristics which the analyst discerns in the complex data of discourse, but rather are the mechanisms by means of which the participants produce their interaction in an organized way. That is, the orderliness of linguistic interaction is itself the outcome of an ongoing process in which participants *produce order* through the routine and recursive application of conversational rules and devices. In this respect, conversation analysis displays its affiliation to Garfinkel's ethnomethodology, which is concerned with the ordered properties and ongoing achievements of every-day social practices.[11] A significant part of the literature of conversation analysis has focused on the sequential organization of conversation, examining the intricate mechanisms by means of which conversational partners succeed in taking turns, and allowing others to take turns, without overriding one another's talk by talking at the same time. While illuminating in many respects, the main limitation of conversation analysis as it is commonly practised is that it is rarely conjoined with a satisfactory account of the social–historical conditions of linguistic interaction, a point that I shall develop further in the following section.

Instances of discourse can also be studied by virtue of what we may describe as *syntactic analysis*. This type of analysis is concerned with practical syntax or practical grammar – not with the grammarian's grammar, but with the grammar or syntax which is operative in everyday discourse. A distinctive and fruitful version of syntactic analysis can be found in the work of Robert Hodge, Gunther Kress and their associates.[12] Drawing on the linguistic writings of Halliday, Hodge and Kress examine some of the ways in which grammatical forms operate in ordinary discourse, combining, conflating and deleting elements through processes of transformation. In an earlier chapter I mentioned two common types of transformation, namely nominalization and passivization. Other important grammatical characteristics of discourse include the markers of modality, by means of which speakers indicate the degree of certainty or reality associated with a statement (e.g. 'might', 'maybe', 'possibly'); the system of pronouns employed, which may imply differences in terms of power and familiarity (especially in languages which have two forms of pronoun for the second person singular, e.g. *vous* and *tu*); and markers associated with gender differences, where the grammatical gender of linguistic expressions may serve as a vehicle to convey assumptions about the sexes (e.g. the use of 'man' or masculine pronouns in a generic sense).[13] The analysis of these and other aspects of practical grammar or syntax may help to highlight some of the ways in which meaning is constructed within everyday discursive forms.

Another way in which instances of discourse can be studied is by analysing their *narrative structure*. The analysis of narrative structure, stemming from Propp's pioneering work on the Russian folktale, is now a well-established approach in the fields of literary and textual analysis, in the study of myth and, to a lesser extent, in the study of political discourse. It is an approach which has been adopted and developed in differing ways by a number of contemporary authors, including Barthes, Lévi-Strauss, Bremond, Greimas, Todorov and Genette.[14] A narrative may be regarded, broadly speaking, as a discourse which recounts a sequence of events - or, as we commonly say, which 'tells a story'. The story generally consists of a constellation of characters and a succession of events, combined in a way which displays a certain orientation or 'plot'. The sequentiality of the plot may differ from the temporal succession of events, as when the story is told by means of counter-temporal devices such as flashbacks. The characters within the story may be real or imaginary, but their properties *qua* characters are defined in terms of their relations to one another and their roles in the development of the plot. In studying narrative structure, we can seek to identify the specific narrative devices which operate within a particular narrative, and to elucidate their role in the telling of the story - in the way, for example, that Genette analyses the techniques which operate in Proust's *A la recherche du temps perdu*. But we can also examine - and this is the main emphasis of the kinds of analysis initiated by Propp - the patterns, characters and roles which are common to a set of narratives and which constitute a common underlying structure. This approach is followed through most rigorously and ambitiously by Greimas, who seeks to establish a basic set of roles or 'actants' which would suffice to account for the surface organization of the narrative. Whatever the merits of Greimas's approach (which may be somewhat extreme),[15] it can be illuminating to focus on a particular set of narratives, whether traditional Russian folktales or modern romance novels, and to seek to identify the basic patterns, characters and roles which are common to them.

A final type of discursive analysis which I shall consider here is what may be called *argumentative analysis*. Forms of discourse, as supra-sentential linguistic constructions, may comprise chains of reasoning which can be reconstructed in various ways. These chains of reasoning do not generally amount to valid arguments, in the traditional sense of formal or syllogistic logic; they are better construed as patterns of inference which lead from one theme or topic to another, in a way that is more or less cogent, more or less implicit. The aim of argumentative analysis is to reconstruct and render explicit the patterns of inference which characterize the discourse. Various methods have been developed to facilitate this type of analysis.[16] These methods enable the analyst to break up the discursive corpus into sets of claims or assertions organized around certain topics or themes, and then to map out the relations between these claims and topics in terms of certain logical, or quasi-logical, operators (implication, contradiction, presupposition, exclusion, etc.). Argumentative analysis is particularly useful for the study of overtly political discourse – that is, the speeches or discourse of officials or government ministers who exercise power within the modern nation-state – since such discourse is often presented in the form of an argument: a series of claims or assertions, topics or themes, strung together in a more or less coherent way and seeking, often with the aid of rhetorical flourishes, to persuade an audience. Whether a particular argument is a *good* argument, and whether the individuals who comprise its audience are in fact persuaded by it, are important questions raised by argumentative analysis, but they are questions which lead us beyond this particular phase of the depth-hermeneutical approach.

The third and final phase of the depth-hermeneutical approach is what I shall call *interpretation/re-interpretation*. The phase of interpretation is facilitated by, but distinct from, the methods of formal or discursive analysis. The latter methods proceed by *analysis*: they break down, divide up, deconstruct, seek to unveil the patterns and devices which constitute, and operate within, a symbolic or discursive form. Interpretation builds upon this analysis, as well as upon the results of social-historical analysis. But interpretation involves a new movement of thought: it proceeds by *synthesis*, by the creative construction of possible meaning. This movement of thought is a necessary adjunct to formal or discursive analysis. Although there are some practitioners of formal or discursive analysis who claim to offer nothing other than *analysis*, who claim to resolve symbolic or discursive forms into a set of elements and their interrelations (and nothing more), this claim can represent at best a partial approach to the study of symbolic or discursive forms. *However rigorous and systematic the methods of formal or discursive analysis may be, they cannot abolish the need for a creative construction of meaning, that is, for an interpretative explication of what is represented or what is said.* Symbolic or discursive forms have what I have described as a 'referential aspect': they are constructions which typically represent something, refer to something, say something about something. It is this referential aspect that we seek to grasp in the process of interpretation.

Located within the depth-hermeneutical framework, the process of interpretation can be mediated by the methods of social-historical analysis as well as those of formal or discursive analysis. These methods may enable the analyst to see a symbolic form in a new way, in relation to the contexts of its production and reception and in the light of the patterns and devices which constitute it. But the process of interpretation goes beyond the methods of social-historical analysis and formal or discursive analysis. It transcends the contextualization of symbolic forms treated as socially situated products, and the closure of symbolic forms treated as constructions displaying an articulated structure. Symbolic forms represent something, they say something about something, and it is this transcending character which must be grasped by the process of interpretation.

The process of interpretation, mediated by the methods of the depth-hermeneutical approach, is simultaneously a process of *re-interpretation*. For, as I emphasized earlier in this chapter, the symbolic forms which are the object of interpretation are part of a pre-interpreted domain: they are already interpreted by the subjects who make up the social-historical world. In developing an interpretation which is mediated by the methods of the depth-hermeneutical approach, we are re-interpreting a pre-interpreted domain; we are projecting a possible meaning which may diverge from the meaning construed by subjects who make up the social-historical world. Of course, we can see this as a divergence only in so far as we have grasped, via the hermeneutics of everyday life, the ways in which symbolic forms are routinely and mundanely understood. But the interpretation of doxa, while an indispensable preliminary, is not the end point of the interpretative process. Symbolic forms can be analysed further, in relation both to their social-historical conditions and to their internal structural features, and they can thereby be re-interpreted. As a re-interpretation of a pre-interpreted object domain, the process of interpretation is necessarily risky, conflict-laden, open to dispute. *The possibility of a conflict of interpretation is intrinsic to the very process of interpretation*. And this is a conflict that may arise, not simply between the diverging interpretations of analysts employing different techniques, but also between an interpretation mediated by the depth-hermeneutical approach, on the one hand, and the ways in which symbolic forms are interpreted by the subjects who make up the social-historical world, on the other. It is this possibility of a conflict of interpretations, a divergence between lay interpretation and depth interpretation, between pre-interpretation and re-interpretation, that creates the methodological space for what I shall describe as *the critical potential of interpretation*, a theme to which I shall return later in this chapter.

In outlining the methodological framework of depth hermeneutics, I have tried to show how different types of analysis can be integrated in a systematic, coherent way. Depth hermeneutics provides an intellectual template, as it were, which enables us to see how symbolic forms can be analysed systematically and appropriately – that is, in a way which does justice to their character as socially and historically situated constructs which display an articulated structure through which something is represented or said. The methodological framework of depth hermeneutics enables us to appreciate the merits of particular methods of analysis – whether of social-historical analysis or of formal or discursive analysis – while at the same time enabling us to determine their limits. Particular methods of social-historical analysis may shed light on the conditions of production and reception of symbolic forms; but these methods tend to neglect the structure and content of symbolic forms and, if generalized into a self-sufficient approach, they can lead to the *fallacy of reductionism*, by which I mean the fallacy of assuming that symbolic forms can be analysed exhaustively in terms of the social-historical conditions of their production and reception. Particular methods of formal or discursive analysis may shed light on the patterns and devices which structure symbolic forms; but these methods tend to neglect the conditions under which symbolic forms are produced and received and, if pursued on their own, they can lead to what I have described as the *fallacy of internalism*, by which I mean the fallacy of assuming that one can read off the character-istics and consequences of symbolic forms by attending to the symbolic forms alone, without reference to the social-historical conditions and everyday processes within which and by means of which these symbolic forms are produced and received. The methodological framework of depth hermeneutics enables us to make use of particular methods of analysis while alerting us to their limits and their attendant fallacies. It is an intellectual template for a movement of thought which probes the distinctive features of symbolic forms without falling into the twin snares of internalism or reductionism.

The Interpretation of Ideology

I now want to show how the methodological framework of depth hermeneutics can be employed for the purposes of interpreting ideology. I shall regard the interpretation of ideology as a specific form of depth hermeneutics. It implements the different phases of the depth-hermeneutical approach in order to analyse the social contextualization and meaningful constitution of symbolic forms; but the concern with the ideological aspects of symbolic forms gives it a distinctive, critical turn. The interpretation of ideology draws upon each of the phases of the depth-hermeneutical approach, but it employs these phases in a particular manner, with a view to highlighting the ways in which meaning serves to establish and sustain relations of domination. The interpretation of ideology is an interpretation of symbolic forms which seeks to illuminate the interrelations of meaning and power, which seeks to show how, in specific circumstances, the meaning mobilized by symbolic forms serves to nourish and sustain the possession and exercise of power. Hence the interpretation of ideology, while implementing the different phases of the depth-hermeneutical approach, gives a critical inflection to these phases: it employs them with the aim of disclosing meaning in the service of power.

We can follow through this critical inflection by considering in turn each phase of the depth-hermeneutical approach. At the level of social–historical analysis, the concern with ideology directs our attention towards the *relations of domination* which characterize the context within which symbolic forms are produced and received. As I explained in an earlier chapter, relations of domination are a particular type of power relation; they are relations of power which are systematically asymmetrical and relatively durable. Among the asymmetries which are most important and most enduring in modern societies are those based on divisions of class, gender, ethnicity and nation-state: these are some of the elements which structure social institutions and fields of interaction. But these are not, of course, the only divisions and elements which structure the social field, nor the only bases of systematic and durable asymmetries of power. When employed in the interpretation of ideology, social–historical analysis must give particular attention to the relations of domination which characterize social institutions and fields of interaction. For what we are interested in is the ways in which these relations are nourished and sustained by the symbolic forms which circulate in the social field. We cannot grasp the ideological character of symbolic forms without highlighting the relations of domination which these forms may, in specific circumstances, serve to establish and sustain.

If the concern with ideology directs social–historical analysis towards the study of relations of domination, then it focuses formal or discursive analysis on the *structural features of symbolic forms which facilitate the mobilization of meaning*. There are many structural features of symbolic forms which may facilitate the mobilization of meaning, and the conduct of formal or discursive analysis must be sufficiently flexible to take account of these differing features. But we can begin to develop the connection between the analysis of the structural features of symbolic forms, on the one hand, and the interpretation of ideology, on the other, by returning to the schema outlined in table 1.2 (see p. 60). This table summarizes the relations between certain general *modi operandi* of ideology and some typical strategies of symbolic construction. When I initially introduced this schema, I did so by distinguishing five general modes of operation of ideology – legitimation, dissimulation, unification, fragmentation and reification – and then identifying some of the strategies of symbolic construction which are typically associated with them. But in the actual conduct of formal or discursive analysis, the pattern of inference will generally be in the opposite direction. That is, we may begin by analysing the structural features of symbolic forms, and may seek to establish these features as instances of particular strategies or processes of symbolic construction. We may then try to argue that, in the specific circumstances of the production and reception of these symbolic forms, the strategies or processes of symbolic construction can be linked to certain modes of operation of ideology. So, for example, we may seek to show that the extensive use of nominalized verbs and the passive tense are indicative of strategies or processes of nominalization and passivization; and we may further undertake to argue that, in specific circumstances, these strategies or processes serve to sustain relations of domination by reifying social–historical phenomena, that is, by representing a transitory, historical state of affairs as if it were permanent, natural, outside of time.

In undertaking such an argument, we are already moving beyond the phase of formal or discursive analysis strictly speaking and engaging in what I have called interpretation (or re-interpretation). Here too, the concern with ideology gives a distinctive turn to this phase. To interpret ideology is *to explicate the connection between the meaning mobilized by symbolic forms and the relations of domination which that meaning serves to establish and sustain.* The interpretation of ideology is a process of creative synthesis. It is creative in the sense that it involves the active construction of meaning, the creative explication of what is represented or what is said. Meaning is determined and re-determined through the ongoing process of interpretation. The interpretation of ideology also has the role of synthesis in the sense that it seeks to draw together the results of social–historical and formal or discursive analysis, showing how the meaning of symbolic forms serves to establish and sustain relations of domination. Formal or discursive analysis can provide only an initial access to the modes of operation of ideology. In order to employ the study of syntactic devices or of narrative structures for the analysis of ideology, one must seek to show how such devices or structures facilitate the construction of meaning which serves, in specific social–historical circumstances, to support relations of domination; in other words, one must develop an argument about the interrelations between meaning and power. The interpretation of ideology is thus charged with a double task: the creative explication of meaning, the synthetic demonstration of how this meaning serves to establish and sustain relations of domination. It is a task which demands both sensitivity to the structural features of symbolic forms and awareness of the structured relations between individuals and groups. By linking symbolic forms to relations of domination, the process of interpretation seeks to show how these symbolic forms may operate as ideology in specific social-historical circumstances.

To undertake the interpretation of ideology is to engage in a risky, conflict-laden activity. It is risky because the meaning of a symbolic form is not given, fixed, determinate; to offer an interpretation is to project a possible meaning, one of several possible meanings which may diverge from, or conflict with, one another. This potential conflict assumes a distinctive form in the case of interpreting ideology. For the interpretation of ideology involves not only the projection of possible meaning, but also the claim that such meaning serves, in certain circumstances, to establish and sustain relations of domination. The interpretation of ideology thus enters the realm of claim and counter-claim, of argument and counter-argument; it is not only a projection of possible meaning but a potential intervention in social life, that is, a projection that may intervene in the very social relations that the object of interpretation serves to sustain. To interpret a symbolic form as ideology is to open the possibility of a critique, not only of other interpretations (including those of the subjects who make up the social world), but also of the relations of domination in which subjects are enmeshed.

So far I have developed my account of the interpretation of ideology in a general methodological way. I have tried to show that the depth-hermeneutical approach provides a suitable framework for the interpretation of ideology, but that the latter gives a distinctive, critical turn to the various phases of depth hermeneutics. I now want to render this discussion more concrete by considering an example in some detail. I shall focus on the telling of a dirty joke, as recorded and analysed by Harvey Sacks.[17] This example is particularly useful because it is an instance of routine, mundane interaction: the telling is a very ordinary event, and yet it displays an elaborate organization by means of which the joke is told and received. The following extract is a fragment of the conversation within which the joke is told. The teller (Ken) is a male teenager around seventeen years old. He tells the joke to two male peers (Roger and Al) and to one male adult (Dan), who is a therapist in a group therapy session which the others attend. The conversation goes like this:

KEN: You wanna hear – My sister told me a story last night.
ROGER: I don't wanna hear it. But if you must.
          (0.7 second)
AL: What's purple and an island. Grape, Britain. That's what his sister told him.
KEN: *No*. To stun me she says eh,
          (0.8 second)
KEN: There was these three girls and they just got married?
ROGER: hhhh-hhh
AL: heh heh heh
KEN: And uh,
ROGER: Hey waita second. Drag that by again heh
KEN: There was these three girls. And they were all sisters. And they'd just got married to three *bro*thers.
ROGER: You better have a long talk with your sister.
AL: Waita second heh!
ROGER: *Oh*. Three *bro*thers.
KEN: And uh, so,
AL: The brothers of these sisters.
KEN: No they're *dif*ferent you know *dif*ferent families.
ROGER: That's closer than be*fore* (I think).
KEN: So–
AL: hhhh*hah*
          (0.7 second)
KEN: *Qui*et. So, *first* of all, that night they're on their honeymoon the mother in law says well why don't you all spend the night here and then you can go on your honeymoon in the morning. The *f*irst night, the mother walks up to the first door and she hears this '*uu*ooo-ooo-ooo', second door is '*HHHOHHhhh*', third door there's *NO*thin. She stands there for about twenty five minutes waitin for somethin to happen. *No*thin.
          (1.0 second)
KEN: Next morning she talks to the first daughter and she says 'How come you – how come you went *YAAAaaa* last night' and the daughter says 'Well it *ti*ckled, Mommy'. Second girl, 'How come you *scre*amed'. '*Oh, Mo*mmy it *hu*rts'. Third girl, walks up to her. 'Why didn't you *say* anything last night'. 'Well *you* told me it was always impolite to talk with my mouth full'.
          (1.3 seconds)
KEN: hhhhyok hyok. Hyok.
          (2.5 seconds)
AL: *HA-A-A-A!*
KEN: heh-heh-huh-huh
ROGER: Delayed reaction.

AL: I had to think about it awhile you know?
ROGER: Sure.
              (1.0 second)
ROGER: hih heh You mean the *deep* hidden *m*eaning there doesn't *hit*
           you right away heh
AL: hhih
DAN: It's pretty interesting.
AL: What he *m*eant to say is that – that um.
ROGER: Kinda got psychological overtones.
KEN: Little sister's gettin older.
AL: eh-hih-hih
KEN: yihh hih-hih That's what I *m*ean to say.
DAN: *Sounds* like it.
KEN: For twelve years old tellin me – *I* didn't even know –
ROGER: How do you know she's just not repeating what she heard and
           doesn't know what it means.
AL: Did she have to explain it to you Ken?
KEN: Yeah she had to explain it in detail to me.
AL: Okay Ken, glad you got a sister that knows somethin.
KEN: She told me she was eatin a hot dog.
              (3.0 seconds)
ROGER: What does *th*at mean.
AL: Yeah come on. Explain it to us. Explain –
KEN: *I DON'T KNOW* I just said that.
AL: Explain everything you know, Ken. Explain everything.[18]

How can we analyse this joke and the conversational interaction of which it is part? I shall begin by following the analysis offered by Sacks. I shall then employ the methodological framework elaborated above to highlight what seem to me to be the main deficiencies of Sacks's account. This will prepare the way for a somewhat different interpretation of the joke which will bring out its potential ideological character.

Sacks's analysis of the joke and its telling falls into three distinct phases. The first phase of his analysis concerns the sequential organization of the telling within the context of the conversation as a whole. In order to tell a joke (or, more generally, a story), the intending teller must secure a suspension of the turn-taking machinery which operates in ordinary conversation (that is, the machinery according to which one person speaks, another responds, etc., in such a way that one person speaks at a time). This suspension is secured by a *preface sequence* in which the intending teller makes an offer to tell the joke, provides an initial characterization of it, gives some reference to a person or place from whom it may have been acquired, and so on. The preface sequence may inform the potential recipients about the kind of response which the teller is seeking ('To *stun* me she says'), and hence may aid the recipients in listening and in producing the kind of response intended by the teller. The potential recipients may immediately accept the offer to tell; or they may, as is the case with this telling, provisionally reject the offer, make a counter-offer, etc., thereby extending the preface sequence until the intending teller can succeed in suspending the turn-taking machinery ('*Quiet*'). At this point the preface sequence gives way to the *telling sequence*. Having secured the suspension of the turn-taking machinery, the teller can now proceed to tell the joke (or story) until completion. If recipients wish to talk, they may have to do so by interrupting the teller, a process that may require special justification (e.g. the recipient failed to hear something or encountered some other 'understandability problem'). The completion of the telling sequence is marked by the punchline, and is followed by the *response sequence*. The response sequence may consist entirely of laughter, but the timing and the character of the laughter may be crucial. On the completion of a joke, laughing has priority over talking, so any delay in the occurrence of laughter is itself significant. In order to appreciate this significance, we must see that jokes are 'understanding tests': they present recipients with a test, namely to 'get' the joke and to get it quickly. Given that failure to get a joke can be treated as a sign of one's lack of sophistication, and given that recipient laughs can be differentiated in terms of their relative starts, it follows that the timing of laughs can provide a basis for comparatively assessing the wit of recipients – what Sacks calls 'the recipient comparative wit assessment device'. This device encourages recipients to laugh as soon as possible; and, once laughter has begun, it encourages others to join the laughter, so that their wit will not be negatively assessed relative to the others. But if no one laughs immediately (as in the case of this joke), then the device may be turned against the teller, in such a way that the concerted absence of laughter becomes a negative assessment of the joke or of its teller. In the response sequence of the joke under discussion, the silence is broken first by the teller, who laughs mirthlessly, thereby taking some distance from the joke in order pre-emptively to deflect a negative assessment of himself. This is followed by loud mirthless laughs from Al, laughter which, by mocking the joke, occasions the transition to talk which assesses the comparative wit of the teller, of the recipients and of the alleged source (Ken's twelve-year-old sister).

The second phase of Sacks's analysis concerns the temporal and sequential organization of the joke itself. The joke takes the form of a story which proceeds in a simple temporal order, an order which may be seen as preserving the temporal pattern of the alleged events described in the story. The joke also has a distinctive sequential structure which overlaps with the temporal order. The sequential structure is crucial to the joke, since this structure sets up a puzzle whose solution is the punchline of the joke. The joke consists of two interrelated sequences: the 'first night' sequence and the 'next morning' sequence. The first night sequence yields a puzzle in a way which is perfectly economical, for you need at least three instances, but no more, to produce silence as problematic. The next morning sequence is connected to the preceding sequence by means of a temporal reference ('next morning') and by means of a parallel sequential structure (first door, second door, third door; first daughter, second daughter, third daughter). The first two steps of the next morning sequence employ a pronoun, 'it', which has no prior-named referent; but the information provided by the teller in the preface sequence (they just got married, this was their 'first night', etc.) enable the recipients to interpret 'it' as an allusion to sexual intercourse. The third step of the next morning sequence is set up as a solution to the puzzle presented by the third step of the first night sequence. This solution is the punchline, 'Well *you* told me that it was always impolite to talk with my mouth full'. The punchline is itself a puzzle which the recipients have to solve (to 'get') by superimposing two interpretative codes: on the one hand, the code employed in the first two steps of the next morning sequence, which enabled 'it' to be interpreted as an allusion to sexual intercourse; and, on the other hand, a code derived from the mother-daughter relation in which the daughter ought to obey the mother's pre-scriptions with regard to, among other things, the polite manner of eating food. The superimposition of these two codes, which are implied without being explicitly provided by the teller, enables the recipients to interpret the punchline as an allusion to oral sex. Figure 6.2 summarizes these various aspects of the sequential organization of the joke.

In the third and final phase of his analysis, Sacks draws on some general considerations about the nature and role of dirty jokes in order to develop a novel re-interpretation of the punchline. A dirty joke can be regarded, Sacks suggests, as a 'rational institution' concerned with packaging and trans-mitting information. The obscene character of the dirty joke operates as a censor to restrict the circulation of the joke; hence the dirtiness of the joke should be seen, not as what the joke is *about*, but rather as a mechanism which restricts the circulation of the information conveyed by the joke. What is the information in this case? Here Sacks puts forward a somewhat surprising argument:

> I want to argue that the joke we're examining is a joke with information relevant for, and passage intendedly restricted to, 12-year-old girls. In our data it's told by a 17-year-old boy to other 17-year-old boys, and it's

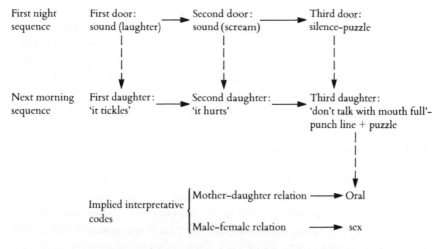

Figure 6.2 The Sequential Organization of a Dirty Joke

specifically told by the boy as having been told him by his 12-year-old sister. Now, the boys know they understand it and figure it's not very funny, and they also doubt that the girl would have understood it. I'll argue that the *boys* don't understand it, that the girl would, and that it involves some information distinctly interesting to 12-year-old girls.[19]

The joke is interpreted by the boys as a joke about oral sex, but it would be interpreted differently, Sacks suggests, by 12-year-old girls. For the latter, the obscene character of the joke is merely a vehicle for the transmission of a message which has nothing to do with oral sex. The message, in part, is this: daughters can overturn the authority of their mothers by following the very rules which their mothers taught them. If accused of violating a rule, daughters can come up with another rule to excuse their action. Of course, this could be said of children in general, of boys as well as girls; but the joke directs the message specifically towards girls, since it focuses on the relation between daughters and their mothers in such a way that girls can identify with the daughters while boys cannot. Hence girls can interpret the punchline as a *squelch* of the mothers by the daughters, as an overturning of the authority of the mother by means of a rule prescribed by the mother. This interpretation of the joke is completely missed by the boys. The joke sets up the child as victor, inverting the hierarchy of parent–child relations in a way that only daughters can understand.

In developing some critical remarks on Sacks's account, I want to focus on the interpretation which he offers in the final phase of the analysis. The first two phases, in which Sacks analyses the sequential organization of the conversational interaction and of the joke itself, seem to me to be both insightful and illuminating. They amply display the usefulness of Sack's distinctive methods of analysis, methods which bring out the mechanisms and structural features by means of which the participants of a conversation produce their interaction in an ordered way. However, I shall argue that the interpretation offered by Sacks in the final phase of his analysis is less than plausible. I shall suggest that the joke can be interpreted differently, in a way that highlights its potential ideological character.

What grounds does Sacks offer in support of his interpretation? The first ground provided by Sacks is that the teller (Ken) introduces the joke as a joke that was told to him the night before by his twelve-year-old sister. But, of course, this by no means establishes the fact that it was actually told to him by his sister: as Sacks himself observes, the attribution of a source may itself be part of the joke and may serve various functions, one of which is to deflect the criticism that would be directed at the teller if the joke were to flop. The second ground is that, as it turns out, the joke does flop. The response sequence is marked by an initial silence, then by mirthless laughter by Ken, then by exaggerated laughter from one of the recipients, then by a laughter-ridden discussion about the joke itself, the teller and the alleged source. But this hardly shows, as Sacks maintains, that the boys do not 'understand' the joke, nor even that they do not find it funny, humorous or titillating; for the ways in which the recipients respond to the joke are conditioned by the specific circumstances of the telling. We do not, in fact, know much about these circumstances. Sacks informs us that the three male teenagers are participants in a group therapy session and that an adult male therapist (Dan) is present; he also notes that the teenagers have been telling dirty jokes for about 20 minutes before this one comes up. From the fragment transcribed by Sacks it appears that the teenagers are locked in a battle of wits, testing one another's competence by probing their sophistication with regard to sexual matters, all under the general supervision of Dan. As soon as Ken declares his intention to enter the ring, his two peers declare their intention to test him. Hence from the outset a battle line is drawn between Ken and his audience, in such a way that the latter are seeking to test Ken's competence, and to display their own competence by putting down Ken. The fact that the joke flops does not demonstrate that the boys fail to understand or enjoy it, for it may well be that they *allow* it to flop in order to undermine the competence of Ken. Their silence is an effective weapon in the battle of wits.

Sacks offers two further grounds for his interpretation, both of which concern the content of the joke. The third ground is the fact that the joke is about three daughters who got married at the same time. This unlikely event would appeal to twelve-year-old girls, Sacks surmises, because it would express a fantasy which they already have, namely the fantasy that, by marrying as a 'pack', they could reconcile monogamous marriage with their desire to travel into the future as a group. The fourth ground is that the joke, if understood as a squelch of the mother by the daughter, is the sort of thing that one (Sacks) might well imagine that twelve-year-old girls would enjoy. These two grounds offered by Sacks are very speculative indeed. He provides no evidence to back up his claim that, in general, girls have a fantasy of getting married in a pack; no evidence to support the view that twelve-year-old girls understand the joke, and enjoy the joke, in the way that Sacks imagines they would; no evidence which would give us any reason to believe that the joke actually does circulate among twelve-year-old girls as Sacks alleges. The fact that the joke is told by a male teenager to two male peers is, Sacks concludes, 'a chance feature of these data' and, while it goes nowhere with them, 'it continues to circulate among those for whom it is relevant and who understand it for the information it contains specifically for them'.[20] But this conclusion is simply not supported by the evidence adduced by Sacks.

Can the joke, as told and received in the circumstances noted by Sacks, be interpreted differently? Rather than speculating on how the joke might be understood by twelve-year-old girls, I shall take as given that it is told and received by three seventeen-year-old boys in the company of a male adult. It seems reasonable to assume, as indicated above, that the boys are engaged in a light-hearted sparring match in which the telling and appraising of dirty jokes is a means of assessing one another's competence. Ken's joke presents his audience with an understanding test: the punchline forms a puzzle which they can solve, and which they do in fact appear to solve, by superimposing two interpretative codes, thereby understanding the joke as a joke about oral sex. In understanding the joke in this way, the teller and his recipients make, we may propose, two further assumptions. The first assumption is that the third daughter, in explaining her silence on the first night by reference to table manners, has *misapplied a rule of etiquette*: when the recipients solve the puzzle by superimposing the two interpretative codes, they do so at the expense of the daughter, whose confusion between the rules of the dinner table and the practices of the bedroom is the basis of the puzzle. We may describe this as the assumption of female ignorance. The second assumption is that the daughters are sources of gratification for men. This assumption is combined with the first in the punchline, when the capacity of the third daughter to gratify a man is enhanced by her confusion over the application of a rule. Although men do not feature in the joke, you cannot understand it as a joke about oral sex unless you presuppose that the third daughter is alluding to a penis. Hence the second assumption: their understanding of the joke involves a phallocentric conception of sexual relations in which women are regarded as objects to satisfy male desire.[21]

By bringing out these assumptions we can re-interpret the joke in a way which does not reject the understanding of it by Ken and his peers, but which builds upon their understanding and attempts to show how, in being understood in this way in these circumstances, it may sustain or disrupt relations of power. There are two sets of power relations which are particularly relevant here. There are relations of power between Ken and the members of his audience (including one adult, Dan, who evidently has a relatively stable and institutionally endowed authority); and there are relations of power between the members of this group, taken as a whole, and the members of other groups who are not present – in particular, the group comprising women, who feature prominently in the joke but who are absent from the circumstances of its telling. The relation between men and women is, in the society of which these teenagers are part, structured asymmetrically, and these asymmetrical relations are thus part of the broader context of the telling of the joke. If we view the telling of the joke, and its understanding as a joke about oral sex, in the context of these two sets of relations, we can see that the joke serves, in the immediate milieu of its telling, to display and contest the competence of Ken and his peers among whom there are fluid and shifting relations of power, while at the same time serving, in the broader context of asymmetrically structured gender relations, to affirm the collective superiority and sexual self-importance of the boys with regard to the group who feature in the joke but who are absent from its telling. Ken's competence is on trial, but the joke is on women. In the aftermath of the joke, Ken's peers effectively challenge his competence (while Dan offers avuncular support), and Ken defends himself by putting down his twelve-year-old sister, whose capacity to understand the joke is doubted by the boys. The joke has become a token in a battle of wits between male teenagers who, precisely because they understand it as a joke about oral sex, take for granted (and appear not to question) certain assumptions about women and about their relations to women, even though women are absent from the telling.

I have offered a re-interpretation of the joke which highlights what we may describe as its potential ideological character – that is, its character as a symbolic form which serves, in these circumstances, to sustain an asymmetrical relation of power between the sexes. Had the joke been told under different circumstances – among twelve-year-old girls, for instance – it may have been understood differently and may have played a different role. But, even with regard to the actual circumstances of its telling, I describe the ideological character of the joke as 'potential', simply because, with the evidence at our disposal, this interpretation is at best a conjecture. I think that it is a plausible conjecture, but, in the absence of more information about the circumstances of the telling and the understanding of the recipients, it is difficult to say more than that. It may be, for instance, that the recipients had doubts about the assumptions implicit in the joke and felt that it was simply too crude, and it may be that the flopping of the joke could be partly explained in terms of this recipient doubt. It may also be that the presence of an older authority figure at the telling of the joke had important consequences for its reception. These are speculations that, with the evidence at our disposal, we are not in a position to resolve. Here I have restricted myself to an analysis of the available data on the joke and its telling, using this as a means of showing how the methodological framework of depth hermeneutics can be employed for the analysis of symbolic forms as they are produced, received and understood in everyday life, and how these mundane symbolic forms can be interpreted – plausibly if tentatively – as ideological.

Analysing Mass Communication: The Tripartite Approach

So far I have been discussing the analysis of symbolic forms in a general way, without reference to the specific issues raised by the production and transmission of symbolic forms within the context of mass communication. We have seen in earlier chapters that mass communication affects the character of symbolic forms and their circulation in certain respects, and I now want to draw out the implications of these considerations at a methodological level. We may begin by recalling one of the principal characteristics of mass communication: that it institutes a fundamental break between the production and reception of symbolic forms. The institutions of mass communication produce symbolic forms for recipients who are generally not physically present at the place of production and transmission or diffusion. Moreover, the mediation of symbolic forms by technical media of various kinds generally involves a one-way flow of messages from the producer to the recipient, in such a way that the capacity of the recipient to intervene in the communicative process is often very limited. The break between production and reception is a structured break in which the producers of symbolic forms, while dependent to some extent on recipients for the economic valorization of symbolic forms, are institutionally empowered and obliged to produce symbolic forms in the absence of direct responses from recipients.

Bearing this characteristic in mind, we may approach the analysis of mass-mediated symbolic forms by distinguishing three aspects or object domains – what I shall describe as the 'tripartite approach'. The first aspect is the *production and transmission or diffusion* of symbolic forms, that is, the process of producing the symbolic forms and of transmitting or distributing them via channels of selective diffusion. These processes are situated within specific social–historical circumstances and generally involve particular institutional arrangements. The second aspect is the *construction* of the media message. The messages transmitted by mass communication are products which are structured in various ways: they are complex symbolic constructions which display an articulated structure. The third aspect of mass communication is the *reception and appropriation* of media messages. These messages are received by individuals, and groups of individuals, who are situated within specific social–historical circumstances, and who employ the resources available to them in order to make sense of the messages received and to incorporate them into their everyday lives. These three distinguishable aspects of mass communication enable us to define three object domains of analysis. We can focus our attention on each of these domains in turn, analysing their characteristic forms and processes. But the fact that each of these object domains is constituted by abstracting from the other aspects of mass communication implies that an analysis focused on a single object domain will be limited in certain respects. A comprehensive approach to the study of mass communication requires the capacity to relate the results of these differing analyses to one another, showing how the various aspects feed into and shed light on one another.

By distinguishing these three aspects of mass communication, we can also see that the depth-hermeneutical approach is applicable in differing ways to the analysis of the respective object domains. The processes of the production and transmission or diffusion of media messages can be most appropriately analysed by means of a combination of social–historical analysis and ethnographic research (what I have called the interpretation of doxa). By means of social–historical analysis we can seek to determine, for instance, the characteristics of the institutions within which media messages are produced and through which they are transmitted or diffused to potential recipients. We can examine the patterns of ownership and control within media institutions; the relations between media and non-media institutions, including the state organizations responsible for monitoring media output; the techniques and technologies employed in production and transmission; the recruitment of media personnel; and the routine procedures followed by individuals in carrying out their everyday tasks, from writing to editing, filming to scheduling, fund-raising to marketing.[22]

We can also adopt a more interpretative approach and seek to elucidate the understanding of the individuals involved in producing and transmitting media messages, that is, the ways in which they understand what they are doing, what they are producing and what they are trying to achieve. This interpretation of everyday understanding, of 'doxa', may help to illuminate the rules and assumptions implicit in the production process, including assumptions about the audience and its needs, interests and abilities. These rules and assumptions are part of the social conditions and codes upon which media personnel draw in producing and transmitting media messages. Together with other aspects of the social–historical context, these conditions and codes both facilitate and circumscribe the processes of production and transmission, thereby enabling the media message to be produced and diffused as a meaningful symbolic construction.

The second aspect of mass communication is the construction of the media message. When we focus on this aspect we give priority to what I have called formal or discursive analysis: that is, we analyse the media message as a complex symbolic construction which displays an articulated structure. For example, in analysing a television programme we can examine the juxta-position of words and images; the angles, colours and sequences of the imagery used; the syntax, style and tone of the language employed; the struc-ture of the narrative or argument; the extent to which the narrative or argu-mentative structure allows for sub-plots, digression or dissent; the use of specific devices such as flashbacks and voice-overs; the ways in which narrative tension is combined with features such as humour, sexuality and violence; the interconnections between programmes which form part of a finite or open-ended sequence; and so on.[23] The analysis of the internal structural features of media messages is a perfectly legitimate undertaking. But it is also a *limited* undertaking, and all too often it goes astray when it is pursued in isolation from those aspects of mass communication which it necessarily presupposes but heuristically ignores, namely the production/transmission and reception/appropriation of media messages.

The reception and appropriation of media messages defines a third object domain of analysis. As with the analysis of production and transmission, the analysis of the processes of reception and appropriation can be carried out by a combination of social–historical analysis and ethnographic research. By means of social–historical analysis, we can examine the specific circumstances and the socially differentiated conditions within which media messages are received by particular individuals. The specific circumstances: in what contexts, with what company, with what degree of attention, consistency and commentary, do individuals read books, watch television, listen to music, etc? The socially differentiated conditions: in what ways does the reception of media messages vary according to considerations such as class, gender, age, ethnic background and the geographical location of the recipient?[24] Such social-historical analyses can be conjoined with a more interpretative form of inquiry in which we seek to elucidate how particular individuals, situated in specific circumstances, make sense of media messages and incorporate them into their daily lives. This interpretation of the everyday understanding of media messages may help to highlight the rules and assumptions which recipients bring to bear upon media messages, and by means of which they understand these meanings in the way that they do. It may also help to highlight the consequences which media messages have for the individuals who receive them, including their consequences for the relations of power in which these individuals are enmeshed.

I have tried to show how the tripartite approach to mass communication can be developed in methodological terms, in such a way that each aspect of mass communication can be analysed by means of a particular phase of depth hermeneutics, combined in some cases with the interpretation of doxa. We can now develop this account one step further by showing how we can situate the interpretation of the ideological character of media messages within this overall approach. Rather than assuming that the ideological character of media messages can be read off the messages themselves (an assumption that I have called the fallacy of internalism), we can draw upon the analysis of all three aspects of mass communication - production/ transmission, construction, reception/appropriation - in order to interpret the ideological character of media messages. Figure 6.3 summarizes this methodological development of the tripartite approach. The analysis of production and transmission is essential to the interpretation of the ideological character of media messages because it sheds light on the institutions and social relations within which these messages are produced and diffused, as well as on the aims and assumptions of the producers. The study of the construction of media messages is essential because it examines the structural features by virtue of which they are complex symbolic phenomena, capable of mobilizing meaning. Finally, the study of the reception and appropriation of media messages is essential because it considers both the social-historical conditions within which messages are received by individuals, and the ways in which these individuals make sense of the messages and incorporate them into their lives. In drawing upon the analysis of these three aspects of mass communication, the process of interpretation may seek to explicate the connections between particular media messages, which are produced in certain circumstances and constructed in certain ways, and the social relations within which these messages are received and understood by individuals in the course of their everyday lives. In this way the process of

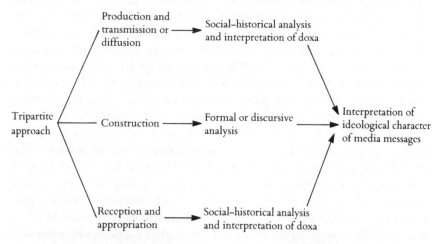

Figure 6.3 The Methodological Development of the Tripartite Approach

interpretation can begin to explicate the ideological character of media messages, that is, the ways in which the meaning mobilized by particular messages may serve, in certain circumstances, to establish and sustain relations of domination. For what these relations of domination are, and whether this meaning serves to sustain or subvert them, to establish or undermine them, are questions that can be answered only by linking the production/transmission and construction of media messages to the ways in which they are received and appropriated by individuals situated within specific social–historical contexts.

Consider an example. In an outstanding study of romance fiction, Janice Radway brings together the analysis of conditions of production, the analysis of the structure of media messages and the analysis of their modes of reception, showing how these analyses can inform a creative interpretation of romance novels and the role they play in the lives of their readers.[25] Let us follow the main lines of her account. Radway is particularly concerned to avoid what I have called the fallacy of internalism, which in this case would take the form of an analysis of the content of romance novels, considered in isolation from the social–historical conditions under which they are produced, diffused, purchased and read. Hence she gives some attention to the institutional and technological context within which the genre of romance novels has emerged. The production of cheap paperback novels orientated towards a mass market has been a prominent feature of the American publishing industry since the early twentieth century. From the outset this type of publishing relied heavily on the development of particular categories or genres of literature as a way of increasing the reliability of predicted sales and reducing the risks associated with over-production. Mass-market publishing was initially dominated by the mystery or detective story, but the popularity of this genre declined in the 1950s. Partially as a response to the decline, several of the large publishers began experimenting with 'gothic' romance novels, the sales of which grew dramatically during the 1960s and early 1970s. As sales began to tail off in the mid-1970s, a new sub-genre appeared, the 'sweet savage' romance, named after the second entrant in the field, Rosemary Roger's *Sweet Savage Love*. The new line was developed rapidly by the major mass-market publishers, including Avon, Harlequin, Fawcett, Dell, and Simon & Schuster. The Canadian-based firm, Harlequin Enterprises, which had initially risen to prominence by reprinting the romances of Mills & Boon in the 1950s and 1960s, played a particularly important role in the new surge in romance fiction. It developed extremely successful strategies for marketing cheap paperbacks, including audience research, supermarket sales and subscription services. By 1980 Harlequin could claim that its million-dollar advertising campaigns reached one out of every ten American women and that 40 per cent of those reached could usually be converted into Harlequin readers.

Against the backcloth of these developments, Radway focuses on the experiences of a group of women who were regular, and fairly typical, romance readers. This group of 42 women lived in a sprawling suburb of a medium-sized, Mid-Western city ('Smithton'); most of the women were married mothers with children between the ages of five and eighteen. The women were all customers of a bookshop in which Dorothy ('Dot') Evans worked. Dot had gained some notoriety within the romance trade by writing a review newsletter for bookshops and editors. Her advice on the best buys of the month became so influential that New York editors began to send her proofs of new books in order to secure reviews in the newsletters. The 42 Smithton women were among the many who relied on Dot to help them sift through the monthly outpouring of new titles. Through Dot as intermediary, Radway asked these women to complete a detailed questionnaire on their reading practices and their attitudes towards romance fiction. She also conducted in-depth interviews with Dot and with a selection of the women. In this way she generated a body of data on the social circumstances, reading practices, attitudes and understandings of a group of women for whom the reading of romance is an integral feature of everyday life.

This data enables Radway to distinguish between novels which are judged *by the readers themselves* to be successful (what she calls the 'ideal romance') and novels which they judge to be unsuccessful (the 'failed romance'). She then analyses the narrative structures of these two categories of romance in an attempt to see whether there are structural features which would help to explain the appeal of romance. Employing a modified version of Propp's method of narrative analysis, she is able to show that the ideal romance contains thirteen narrative functions which are related in a systematic fashion. Despite the individual preoccupation with phenomena such as reincarnation, adultery and amnesia, all of the successful stories are built upon a common narrative structure which is summarized in figure 6.4. Like most narratives, the ideal romance is composed of three basic stages: an initial situation which sets up a tension (functions 1–6), a final situation which transforms the initial situation and resolves the tension (functions 8–13), and an intermediate intervention (function 7) which provokes and eventually explains the transformation. Each of the functions in the initial situation is paired with a function in the final situation, and the link between the two is revealed gradually, as the story reaches a conclusion. Thus the ideal romance generally begins with the removal of the heroine from a familiar, comfortable realm usually associated with her childhood and family. She encounters an aristocratic man and reacts antagonistically to his behaviour, which she interprets as evidence of a purely sexual interest in her. The heroine responds with anger or coldness to the hero, who retaliates by punishing her. Then a break occurs: the hero and heroine are separated in some way. This prepares the way for a reversal of the emotional stand-off produced by the initial situation. The hero suddenly displays an act of tenderness which is not fully explained at this point of the story, and this triggers a process of re-interpretation in which the heroine comes to see the hero's earlier behaviour in a new light. The hero openly declares his love for the heroine, who responds emotionally and sexually, thus culminating in a happy reconciliation of the pair.

The analysis of the narrative structure of the ideal romance enables us to see that the successful novels repeatedly tell a certain story about women, about men, and about their interrelations. The novels tell their readers that a woman needs the love and care of a man, that she can find this love and care by trusting that, beneath the harsh and impassive exterior of a man, there is warmth and tenderness, and that, when this warmth and tenderness is displayed and understood, a genuinely reciprocal and mutually satisfying relationship will ensue. By contrast with the ideal romance, the failed romance generally fails to reconcile fully the estranged partners, either because the hero is never fully transformed into a caring and tender companion, or because other characters become entangled in the core relationship and obstruct or deflect its development. The ideal romance is a

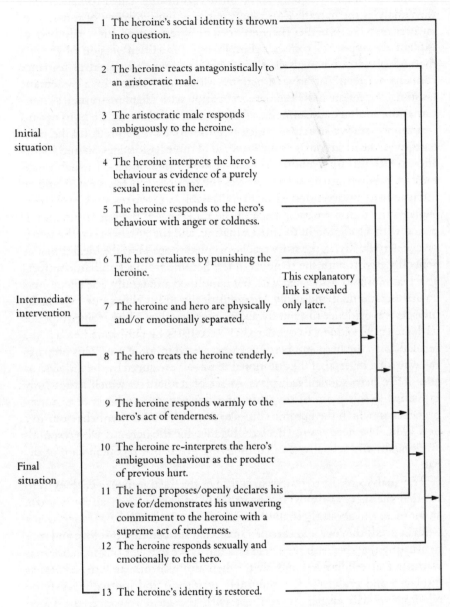

Initial situation

1 The heroine's social identity is thrown into question.

2 The heroine reacts antagonistically to an aristocratic male.

3 The aristocratic male responds ambiguously to the heroine.

4 The heroine interprets the hero's behaviour as evidence of a purely sexual interest in her.

5 The heroine responds to the hero's behaviour with anger or coldness.

6 The hero retaliates by punishing the heroine.

Intermediate intervention

7 The heroine and hero are physically and/or emotionally separated.

This explanatory link is revealed only later.

‑ ‑ ‑ ‑ ‑ →

8 The hero treats the heroine tenderly.

Final situation

9 The heroine responds warmly to the hero's act of tenderness.

10 The heroine re-interprets the hero's ambiguous behaviour as the product of previous hurt.

11 The hero proposes/openly declares his love for/demonstrates his unwavering commitment to the heroine with a supreme act of tenderness.

12 The heroine responds sexually and emotionally to the hero.

13 The heroine's identity is restored.

Figure 6.4 The Narrative Structure of the Ideal Romance

Source: Adapted from Janice A. Radway, *Reading the Romance: Women, Patriarchy, and Popular Literature* (Chapel Hill, NC: University of North Carolina Press, 1984; London: Verso, 1987), p. 150.

story of tension based on misunderstanding, and of reconciliation based on trust. It provides its female readers with a set of instructions about *how to read a man*, how to re-interpret male behaviour in a way that will remove ambiguity, resolve tension and enable both partners to display tenderness and affection in a mutually satisfying way. The romance also enables its readers to experience vicariously a form of pleasure and to imagine themselves temporarily to be the focal point of a man's care and attention, experiences that are generally denied to them in the actual circumstances of their day-to-day life where they are largely preoccupied with caring for others. For the Smithton woman, reading romances thus has a reassuring, therapeutic value. It reassures her that, if she has doubts or covert fears about men or heterosexual relationships, these doubts or fears are in all likelihood based on a misunderstanding which can be put right. It has therapeutic value in that it provides her, in a vicarious and yet pleasurable way, with a sense of being cared for and attended to by a man to whom she is attracted and whom she has succeeded in attracting to herself. The capacity of the romance to be both reassuring and therapeutic co-exists with, and helps to reproduce, a structured set of social relations in which these women are situated and in which they carry out certain tasks and roles, particularly tasks associated with attending to the needs of others. Hence by reading romances these women are able to experience – vicariously and temporarily – a form of care and attention which they are generally denied in the practical conduct of their day-to-day lives.

If the reading of romance fiction thus serves to sustain and reproduce the socially structured relations of everyday life, it is also important to see, Radway argues, that this activity enables the Smithton women to take some distance from these relations. In order to appreciate this point, we must distinguish between the *meaning of mediated messages as received and interpreted*, on the one hand, and the *significance of the activity of reception*, on the other. The latter refers to the fact that, apart from the meaning that the messages may have, the very activity of receiving these messages may be meaningful for the recipients. In the case of the Smithton women, reading romances is understood by them primarily as a way of relaxing and of creating a time and a space which are their own, separate from the domestic sphere in which they are preoccupied with catering for the needs of others. They enjoy the activity of reading because it enables them temporarily to take some distance from the context of familial relations, within which they do most of their relating to others, and to define a domain within which they can be by themselves and attend vicariously to their own needs. In this regard, the *private* character of the act of reading is important, for the women enjoy reading romances because it enables them to establish a private domain in which they are temporarily released from the demands imposed by domestic life.

Viewed in this light, the interpretation of the ideological character of romance fiction requires qualification. If we focus on the activity of reading as distinct from the texts which are read, we can see that reading romances is, to some extent, a way of resisting or protesting against a situation which the Smithton women experience as unfulfilling. It is a way of coping with a situation that is structured in a manner which requires them to service the needs of others while their own needs are left unmet. In this respect, the activity of reading romance fiction has, for these women in these circumstances, a certain *critical character*: it represents a form of resistance, albeit partial and not articulated as such, to a set of social relations which are asymmetrically structured and experienced as unfulfilling. But the critical character of the activity of reading is, in this case, probably overshadowed by the *compensatory character* of the texts which are read. While the activity of reading creates temporarily a time and space which are removed from the contexts of everyday life, the meaning conveyed by the texts which are read serves to reassure the readers and to fulfil vicariously their unmet needs, thereby enabling them to continue their day-to-day lives without altering in any fundamental way the social relations which characterize them. Just how the balance between these two aspects of romance reading – the critical and the compensatory – will work out over time is a question that Radway, quite reasonably, leaves open. To answer it properly would require a much more extended analysis of the lives of these recipients and of the ways in which their lives are changed, if at all, by a reading practice that has become vital to them.

I have considered this example in some detail because it seems to me to combine, in an exemplary way, a concern with the production, construction and reception of media messages, and to show how the analysis of these different aspects can inform the interpretation of the ideological character of mass-mediated symbolic forms. Of course, there are features of Radway's study that can be criticized; for example, she is much better on the analysis of processes of reception than on the analysis of the production and transmission of romance fiction, and her heavy reliance on Chodorow's account of the formation of the female psyche is certainly questionable.[26] But she has rightly emphasized the importance of studying the ways in which mass-mediated products are received and understood by individuals in the course of their everyday lives, and she has shown how we can develop a critical interpretation of media products in a way which avoids an exclusive focus on the conditions of production and transmission of media messages or on the structure and content of the messages themselves. Moreover, in focusing our attention on the ways in which media messages are received and understood, she has emphasized – again rightly, in my view – that we must consider not only the ways in which media messages are ordinarily understood and appraised, but also the nature and significance of the activity of reception, that is, the role that this activity plays in the lives of recipients. By examining these two dimensions of the activity of reception, we can begin to explore the ways in which the meaning mobilized by mass-mediated symbolic forms becomes part of the everyday lives of recipients. We can begin to grasp the extent to which this meaning serves, in the structured contexts of everyday life, to reaffirm or challenge traditional assumptions and established divisions, to sustain or disrupt existing social relations; and hence we can begin to grasp the extent to which the symbolic forms produced and diffused by the technical media of mass communication are ideological.

The Everyday Appropriation of Mass-Mediated Products

If we follow through with the methodological framework that I outlined in the previous section, we can see that the analysis of mass communication in general, and the interpretation of the ideological character of media messages in particular, must give attention to what may be called *the everyday appropriation of mass-mediated products*. Not that this aspect of mass communication should be studied at the expense of the production/transmission and construction of media messages: on the contrary, all three aspects are integral to a comprehensive approach to mass communication. But the everyday appropriation of mass-mediated products has been neglected in much of the literature to date. A great deal of research has been done on the nature and size of audiences, the short-term and long-term effects of media messages, the ways in which audiences use the media and the gratifications which they derive from them. But these kinds of research, however interesting they may be, pay insufficient attention to the particular social-historical contexts within which individuals and groups of individuals receive media messages, make sense of them, appraise them and integrate them into other aspects of their lives. In the previous section I indicated how these and other characteristics of the everyday appropriation of media messages could be studied through a combination of social-historical analysis and ethnographic research. I now want to pursue this theme further by identifying some general features of the everyday appropriation of mass-mediated products and indicating how these features can be analysed in specific cases. I shall concentrate on six features: (1) the typical modes of appropriation of mass-mediated products; (2) the social-historical characteristics of contexts of reception; (3) the nature and significance of activities of reception; (4) the meaning of messages as interpreted by recipients; (5) the discursive elaboration of mediated messages; and (6) the forms of interaction and mediated quasi-interaction established through appropriation.

1 Let me begin by considering the typical modes of appropriation of mass-mediated products. In approaching this issue it is helpful to focus on the technical media of transmission, as distinct from the structure and content of the message transmitted. This focus is helpful because it enables us to see that some of the characteristics of everyday appropriation are linked to the nature of the technical media of transmission, to the availability of the skills, capacities and resources required to decode the messages transmitted by particular media and to the rules, conventions and practical exigencies associated with such decoding. If we consider again the everyday appropriation of romance fiction, we see that some of the key characteristics of this process stem from the fact that the books are read privately, by one individual in isolation from others, although this individual may get some assistance in the choosing, decoding and appraising of particular books. But the private character of romance reading is neither a feature of reading as such, nor a characteristic shared by the reception of messages transmitted by other kinds of media. It is not a feature of reading as such because there are other circumstances in which reading is, or has been, a collective, social activity. Although the practice of reading privately – on one's own, silently, without moving the lips – is today a typical mode of appropriating written materials, it seems likely that this reading practice is a particular historical development and that it co-existed throughout the early modern period with other, more social and more public, reading practices. It seems likely that books and other written materials were often read out loud to a group of individuals who had assembled to hear the written word, and who could thereby appropriate the messages inscribed in print without possessing the capacity to read.[27] Moreover, if we consider other technical media of transmission, we may find that the ways in which mediated products are received and appropriated vary significantly from those involved in reading texts. For example, the practice of watching television in Western industrial societies generally takes place in private domestic contexts, although the activity is often social in the sense that programmes are watched in the presence of others and viewers may interact with one another in the course of watching.

By examining the ways in which mediated products are received and appropriated by individuals and groups situated in particular social-historical contexts, we can elucidate *the typical modes of appropriation of mass-mediated products*. To elucidate typical modes of appropriation is to identify some of the characteristic ways in which mass-mediated products are received and taken up by individuals – the characteristic ways in which romance fiction is read, television programmes are watched, etc. This kind of analysis requires one to abstract from idiosyncrasies and to seek to specify features which are common to a plurality of reception practices, in the way, for instance, that we can seek to specify some of the features common to the reading of romance fiction by a plurality of readers, or the watching of television soap operas by a plurality of viewers. Modes of appropriation are generally circumscribed by the nature of the technical media of transmission, and changes in these media (e.g. the introduction of VCRs) can alter significantly the modes of appropriation. But the technical media of transmission do not determine the typical modes of appropriation, as these modes are also dependent on the conditions, conventions and competencies which characterize the contexts of reception and the recipients. It is only by analysing the technical media of transmission in relation to the actual circumstances in which mass-mediated products are received and taken up that we can attempt to elucidate the typical modes of appropriation of these products.

2 A second feature of the everyday appropriation of mass-mediated products concerns the social–historical characteristics of contexts of reception. The reception and appropriation of mass-mediated products must be seen as *situated practices*, that is, as practices which take place in particular social–historical contexts, in particular times and places, in isolation or in the company of others, and so on. In analysing reception and appropriation as situated practices, we are pursuing what I have described as the social–historical analysis of contexts of reception. We may seek to analyse, among other things, the spatial and temporal features of reception contexts (e.g., in the case of television viewing, who watches particular programmes when, for how long, in what places, etc.); the relations of power and the distribution of resources among recipients (who controls the choice of programme, who has the capacity to acquire the technical means of reception, etc.); the rules and conventions which govern reception practices and related patterns of interaction (who is allowed to watch when, how does viewing fit in to the routines of day-to-day living, etc.); the social institutions within which receptive activity takes place (often, but by no means always, particular families); the systematic asymmetries and differentials which characterize the contexts of reception and the relations among recipients (asymmetries between men and women, adults and children, differentials between one context and another, etc.); the technical media employed for reception (whether television, VCR, DBS, etc.) and the ways in which these media affect the activity of reception.

3 We can distinguish the social-historical analysis of contexts of reception from the analysis of a third feature of everyday appropriation: the nature and significance of activities of reception. It is important to recognize that what we regard as receptive activities – reading books, watching television, listening to music – are complex and highly skilled accomplishments which involve the application of a great deal of acquired knowledge, and which overlap in complicated ways with other activities in the routine organiza-tion of everyday life. For example, television may be watched while preparing or eating dinner, while reading a paper or playing with children, or it may simply be 'on' as a background accompaniment to other activity; hence it may be watched with varying degrees of interest, attentiveness and concentration.[28] If we view receptive activities from this perspective, we can see how misleading it would be to try to infer the consequences of media messages from the messages alone (what I have called the fallacy of internalism), since such inferences would take no account of the specific ways in which these messages are attended to (or ignored) by the individuals who receive them. Moreover, as Radway emphasized in her study of romance fiction, the very activity of reception may be meaningful for recipients. *Ways of receiving mass-mediated messages are ways of acting*; and within the contexts of day-to-day living, these ways of acting may be meaningful for the individuals concerned, may be understood by them as ways of relaxing, of sharing experiences with others, of escaping tem-porarily from the demands of everyday life. In examining the nature and significance of receptive activities, we treat these activities as skilled accomplishments by individuals for whom these activities are, or may be, meaningful, and we seek to analyse the practical characteristics of these activities and the significance which they have for the individuals concerned.

4 A fourth feature of the everyday appropriation of mass-mediated products concerns the meaning of the messages as received and interpreted by recipients. I have stressed throughout this work that mass-mediated products are not only products to be consumed: they are also messages to be understood, and the analysis of the everyday appropriation of these messages must be concerned, in part, with the ways in which they are understood by the individuals who, in the course of their daily lives, receive them. This is an aspect of what I described earlier as the interpretation of doxa – that is, the interpretation of the everyday understandings and beliefs of the individuals who make up the social world. In receiving mass-mediated messages, individuals draw upon and employ conventions of various kinds which enable them to decode and make sense of the messages, and in this process

they may also evaluate the messages, endorse them or reject them, take up a stand *vis-à-vis* them, and so on. In seeking to analyse the meaning of messages as received and interpreted, we are seeking, among other things, to reconstruct the sense which recipients make of the messages they receive, to render explicit the conventions implicitly employed to decode the messages and to examine the stances they take, explicitly or implicitly, *vis-à-vis* the messages. And we may pursue further this feature of everyday appropriation: we may relate the everyday understanding of media messages to the social–historical characteristics of the contexts of reception, and seek thereby to ascertain whether everyday understanding varies systematically in relation to social–historical characteristics – for example, in relation to the class background, ethnic background, sex or age of the recipients.[29] In these ways we may take up and pursue the hermeneutical insight that 'the meaning of the message' is not a fixed property of the message itself, but is a characteristic that is constantly renewed and transformed in the very process of appropriation.

5 A fifth feature of everyday appropriation is what I have described as the discursive elaboration of mediated messages. The messages transmitted by technical media are not only received by particular individuals in particular contexts, but are also commonly discussed by recipients in the course of reception or subsequent to it, and are thereby elaborated discursively and shared with a wider circle of individuals who may or may not have experienced directly the process of reception (who may or may not have read the book, watched the programme, etc.). Moreover, media messages may be taken up by media personnel and incorporated into the content of new media messages, so that they are presented or re-presented to recipients through extended mediazation. In these ways media messages may be relayed well beyond the primary contexts of reception and transformed through a process of telling and re-telling, interpretation and criticism. *The appropriation of mediated messages does not necessarily coincide with the initial reception of messages*: on the contrary, it often involves an ongoing process of discursive elaboration. This ongoing process may take place in a variety of contexts – in the home, on the telephone, in the workplace – and it may involve a variety and plurality of participants.[30] It may provide a narrative framework within which individuals recount aspects of their own lives, interweaving personal experiences with the re-telling of mediated messages or with the re-telling of messages thereby re-told. The analysis of the discursive elaboration of mediated messages is crucial to an account of everyday appropriation, since the process may influence the ways in which individuals understand and appraise mediated messages, and since it is, to

some extent, through this process that messages are interwoven with other aspects of individuals' lives.

6 Finally, we should consider the forms of interaction and mediated quasi-interaction established through appropriation. This feature of everyday appropriation is complicated and it may be helpful to distinguish between four broad types of interaction and quasi-interaction. First, there is the interaction that may take place among recipients, or between recipients and non-recipients, within the primary reception region – for example, the conversation that may take place between individuals who are watching a television programme. Second, there is the interaction that may take place in the course of the subsequent discursive elaboration of mediated messages. As I noted above, this second type of interaction may involve individuals who were not present at the initial context of reception, or who did not experience directly the reception of mediated messages. These two types of interaction among primary and secondary recipients must be distinguished from the kind of mediated quasi-interaction established between recipients, on the one hand, and the individuals involved in the production of, or represented in the construction of, mediated messages, on the other. Recipients may become involved with the individuals who produce mediated messages (e.g. the author of a sequence of novels) or with the individuals represented in them (e.g. the characters of a television soap opera), and these forms of involvement may affect the ways in which recipients understand and appraise messages, the ways in which they talk about them and the loyalty with which they continue to receive them. In addition to mediated quasi-interaction, the everyday appropriation of mediated messages establishes what we may describe as a *virtual community of recipients* who may not interact with one another directly or indirectly, but who share in common the fact that they receive the same messages and who thereby comprise a collectivity that may be extended across time and space. While the individuals who make up this collectivity may not interact among themselves, the knowledge that they are not alone in receiving mediated messages, that they are part of a virtual community of recipients that may extend across time and space, may be an integral part of the pleasure and importance that the reception of messages has for them.

In examining these various features of everyday appropriation, I have sought to identify some of the lines along which the analysis of processes of reception and appropriation can, in actual circumstances, be pursued. But I have also highlighted some aspects of reception and appropriation which are of more general theoretical and methodological interest. I have emphasized that, while the reception of mediated messages always takes place in particular contexts, the appropriation of mediated messages is a continuing process that may involve other contexts, other individuals, other messages interwoven with those initially received. 'Appropriation', to use the terminology of hermeneutics, is the process of 'making one's own' something that is new, alien or strange; what I have argued here is that the process of 'making one's own' should be understood in relation to the particular individuals who, in the course of their everyday lives, receive mediated messages, talk about them with others and, through an ongoing process of discursive elaboration, integrate them into their lives. This is an active and potentially critical process in which individuals are constantly involved in an effort to understand, an effort to make sense of the messages they receive, appraise them, relate to them and share them with others. The idea that the recipients of mediated message are passive onlookers, inert sponges that simply absorb the material poured into them, is a misleading myth which bears no resemblance to the actual character of appropriation as an ongoing process of interpretation and incorporation. The myth of the passive recipient goes hand-in-hand with the fallacy of internalism: it is the methodological equivalent, on the side of reception/appropriation, of the fallacious attempt to infer the consequences of mediated messages from the structure and content of the messages alone. If the recipients of mediated messages are involved in a continuing effort to understand, they are also involved in an ongoing process of understanding and re-understanding themselves through the messages they receive. This process of self-understanding and self-formation is not a sudden, once-and-for-all event; it is a gradual process which takes place slowly, imperceptibly, from day to day and year to year. It is a process which takes place in the course of making sense of messages and relating to them, and in the to-ing and fro-ing of re-telling them to others and hearing them re-told to oneself. In this continuing process individuals gain an understanding not only of the things these messages are about, but also of themselves as individuals who understand, have views, needs and desires, are embedded in social relations of certain kinds, etc. Understanding mediated messages is, at the same time, a process of self-understanding and self-formation in which individuals are engaged, in varying ways and to differing extents, in understanding themselves and perhaps changing themselves in the course of the ongoing appropriation of messages received. Hence the everyday appropriation of mediated messages carries within itself the potential for criticism and self-criticism, even if, in actual circumstances, the critical potential of the process of appropriation may be limited or unfulfilled.

Interpretation, Self-Reflection and Critique

I shall conclude this chapter by considering the theme of criticism and self-criticism, and by using this theme to develop the links between the methodology of interpretation and the everyday appropriation of mass-mediated products. I have developed a methodological framework in which the process of interpretation/re-interpretation can be regarded as a complex procedure mediated by different phases of analysis, phases that I have described as social–historical analysis and formal or discursive analysis. When this framework is employed for the analysis of ideology, it enables us to show, or seek to show, how symbolic forms serve, in specific circumstances, to establish and sustain relations of domination. The task of the interpretation of ideology is, on the account that I have developed here, to explore the interconnections between the meaning mobilized by symbolic forms and the relations of domination which this meaning may, in particular contexts, support. Understood as a version of the depth-hermeneutical procedure, the interpretation of ideology draws upon the phases of social–historical analysis and formal or discursive analysis – but it also goes beyond these phases: it puts forward an interpretation, a creative and synthetic proposition, concerning the interrelations between meaning and power. Like all interpretations, the interpretation of ideology is risky, conflict-laden, open to dispute. It makes a claim about something which may differ from other views, including the views of the subjects who make up the social world and whose everyday understanding may be the object of interpretation. This is one respect in which the interpretation of ideology implies a critical potential: I shall describe it as the *interpretative transformation of doxa*. It can be distinguished from a second respect in which the interpretation of ideology may imply a critical potential: it may open the possibility for a critical reflection on the relations of domination in which subjects are enmeshed. It is in this second respect that the interpretation of ideology bears an internal connection to what we may call the *critique of domination*. Let me take up in turn each of these critical aspects of the interpretation of ideology.[31]

To offer an interpretation, I suggested a moment ago, is to make a claim which is risky and open to dispute. When we offer an interpretation we lay ourselves on the line; we make a claim which could, we suppose, be defended or sustained in some way. We do not necessarily suppose that our interpretation is the only possible or only sensible interpretation, but we do suppose that it is a justifiable one, that is, that it *could* be justified if we were called upon to do so. There are, of course, many different ways of seeking to justify our claims. How we do so, what kinds of evidence and arguments we employ, will depend on a variety of factors, such as the general field of inquiry and the specific circumstances of the claim. It would be neither feasible nor helpful to try to map out these numerous possibilities here. But we can abstract from these variations and ask whether there are any general conditions which must be fulfilled in order for a claim to be justified. It is with this question in mind that I shall put forward the following thesis: in supposing that an interpretation is justifiable, we presuppose that it could *not* be justified by being *imposed*. We presuppose, in other words, that there is a distinction between justifying an interpretation and imposing it on others, or having it imposed on ourselves. To justify is to provide reasons, grounds, evidence, elucidation; to impose is to assert or re-assert, to force others to accept, to silence questioning or dissent. To justify is to treat the other as an individual capable of being convinced; to impose is to treat the other as an individual who must be subjected. This distinction suggests that an interpretation would be justified only if it could be justified without being imposed, that is, only if it could be justified under conditions which included the suspension of asymmetrical relations of power. I shall call this *the principle of non-imposition*. It is a principle which defines one of the formal conditions under which an interpretation could be justified. It defines a necessary condition but not a sufficient one. The condition is not sufficient because it tells us nothing about the specific criteria that may be invoked, the particular kinds of evidence and argument that may be used, in attempting to sustain or defeat a particular claim. The specific criteria and the particular kinds of evidence and argument may vary from one field of inquiry to another, and from one instance of analysis to another; what is relevant or sufficient evidence in one context may not be relevant or sufficient evidence in another. But the fact that the criteria, evidence and arguments we employ in attempting to justify an interpretation may vary according to the context of inquiry does not imply that all attempts at justification are no more than arbitrary whim.

We can illustrate this point with an example we have considered already: Sacks's analysis of a dirty joke. We have seen how Sacks analyses the sequential organization of the joke and its telling and, on the basis of this analysis, develops a novel interpretation of the joke as a message intended specifically for girls, a message conveying information which only young girls would understand. How good is this interpretation? How are we to assess whether it is plausible or not? The only way we can proceed is to look carefully at the grounds that Sacks provides (or could have provided) for his interpretation, to examine the evidence and arguments that he adduces (or could have adduced) and to seek to determine whether they are sufficient and convincing – and to do this irrespective of who it is who is offering the interpretation and irrespective of the institutionalized power and prestige of the interpreter (which, in this case, was and remains considerable). This is what I tried to do in my assessment of Sacks's interpretation, and I came to the conclusion that Sacks's account was wanting. I put forward an alternative interpretation of the joke which took account of the actual circumstances of its telling and which highlighted its potential ideological character. This alternative interpretation deserves no more, nor any less, respect than that of Sacks; it stands or falls on the basis of the evidence and arguments that can be adduced to support it. The character of the evidence and arguments that can be adduced depends on the specific features and circumstances of the joke and its telling and on the nature and extent of the available information. But the judgement of whether the evidence and arguments are sufficient and convincing, and hence of whether the interpretation is plausible or implausible (or more plausible than another), is a judgement made by individuals engaged in a deliberation on reasons and grounds – that is, a deliberation, under conditions of non-imposition, on whether an interpretation is justified.

So far I have been concerned to show that the justification of an interpretation presupposes a principle of non-imposition and that, within the broad contours established by this principle, we can develop arguments in specific contexts in order to defend or criticize a particular interpretation, to demonstrate that it is plausible or implausible, justifiable or unjustifiable, in the light of the evidence and grounds that may be adduced in this context of inquiry. I now want to call attention to another general principle which comes into play when we are concerned with the interpretation of ideology. Recalling some of the hermeneutical conditions of social–historical inquiry, we may note that when we engage in the interpretation of ideology, we are engaging in the interpretation of symbolic forms which are produced and received by subjects capable of understanding. Our interpretations are about an object domain which consists of, among other things, subjects like ourselves; and the specific forms we are seeking to interpret are already understood, in some sense, by the subjects who make up the social world and who produce, receive and understand symbolic forms as a routine part of their everyday lives. In the light of these considerations, I shall put forward the following principle: if our interpretations are justifiable, then they are justifiable in principle not only for us *qua* analysts, but also for the subjects who produce and receive the symbolic forms which are the object of interpretation. I shall call this *the principle of self-reflection*. It is a matter of self-reflection because it indicates that, in dealing with an object domain which is also a subject domain, the process of interpretation is connected in principle to the subjects who make up this domain, and that this connection in principle may serve in practice to stimulate reflection among and by these subjects.

This brings us to the point at which we can clarify the sense in which the interpretation of ideology involves the interpretative transformation of doxa. The symbolic forms which are the object of interpretation are, as I have remarked, already understood by the individuals who produce and receive them in the course of their day-to-day lives. The interpretation of the everyday understanding of symbolic forms – what I have called the interpretation of doxa – is an essential preliminary to a more elaborate interpretation of symbolic forms. Mediated by the phases of the depth-hermeneutical approach, this more elaborate interpretative process may enable the analyst to interpret (or re-interpret) symbolic forms in a way which differs from the everyday understanding of lay actors. If the analyst is concerned to bring out the ideological character of symbolic forms, to highlight the ways in which they may serve, in particular circumstances, to establish and sustain relations of domination, then the potential divergence between depth interpretation and everyday understanding may assume a charged and conflictual character. *The depth interpretation becomes a potential intervention in the very circumstances about which it is formulated.* A depth interpretation is itself a symbolic construction, capable in principle of being understood by the subjects enmeshed in the circumstances which form in part the object of interpretation. As an interpretation which may differ from their own everyday understanding, the depth interpretation may enable them *to see themselves differently*; it may enable them to re-interpret a symbolic form in relation to the circumstances of its production and reception, to question or revise their prior understanding and prior assessment of the symbolic form and, in general, to alter the horizons of their understanding of themselves and others. It is in this sense that the process of interpretation, and in particular the interpretation of ideology, implies the possibility of the interpretative transformation of doxa. The transformation is interpretative in the sense that it is stimulated by the process of interpretation and re-interpretation, the framework of which I have outlined above. The transformation is also a *self*-transformation, in the sense that the critical questioning and revision of everyday understanding is not an activity undertaken by the analyst alone (though it may be undertaken by the analyst as well): rather, it is an activity which may be undertaken by the very individuals whose everyday understanding is called into question by the process of interpretation.

I have argued that the process of interpretation implies the *possibility* of the interpretative transformation of doxa, but from this it does not follow that the process of interpretation necessitates such a transformation, nor does it follow that such a transformation is a condition of plausibility of a preferred interpretation. The process of interpretation does not necessitate the interpretative transformation of doxa because, for a variety of practical reasons, a depth interpretation, however plausible, may not stimulate a process of critical self-reflection on everyday understanding. The practical obstacles are numerous, formidable and, in some respects, obvious: a depth interpretation may not be transmitted to lay actors, may not be read or heard by them, may be resisted or regarded as implausible by them, and so on. But whatever practical obstacles there may be, the fact that the process of interpretation implies the possibility of the self-transformation of doxa is not insignificant, for it attests to the fundamental link between the activity of interpretation carried out within the framework of depth hermeneutics, on the one hand, and the self-understanding of the subjects who make up the object domain of analysis, on the other. Whether the interpretation offered by the analyst is plausible or not does not depend on whether it stimulates a process of critical self-reflection. The plausibility or otherwise of the interpretation is a matter of judgement based on a consideration, under conditions of non-imposition, of the evidence and arguments adduced in support of the interpretation. But this consideration, this process of deliberation and judgement, is a process which is open in principle to the subjects who make up the social world. The point is not that the participation of the subjects who make up the social world is a *sine qua non* for the plausibility of the interpretation; rather, the point is that, if the interpretation is plausible in the light of the evidence and arguments adduced in its support, then it may in principle be plausible not only for the analysts involved in the to and fro of interpretation and counter-interpretation, but also for the subjects who make up the social world. For these subjects are also actors capable of, and routinely engaged in, processes of deliberation, in weighing up evidence and arguments, in seeking to persuade (and in being persuaded by others). Hence, while the plausibility of an interpretation does not depend on its acceptance by the subjects about whom it is formulated, an interpretation which is plausible may stimulate a process of critical self-reflection among subjects who, as actors capable of deliberation, may regard the interpretation as plausible and worthy of recognition.

So far I have been considering the sense in which the interpretation of ideology may give rise to the interpretative transformation of doxa. I now want to turn to the second respect in which the interpretation of ideology may imply a critical potential: it may open the possibility for a critical reflection, not only on the everyday understanding of lay actors, but also on the relations of power and domination in which these actors are enmeshed. I have argued that the interpretation of symbolic forms as ideological involves the analysis both of the construction of meaning and of the specific social relations and contexts within which the symbolic forms are produced and received. By highlighting these social relations and contexts, and by showing how symbolic forms may serve in these contexts to sustain certain kinds of social relations, the interpretation of ideology may stimulate a critical reflection on the relations of power and domination characteristic of social life. This is one of the reasons why the interpretation of ideology may elicit strong reactions: it touches the nerves of power, it highlights the positions of those who benefit and those who suffer from social relations that are structured asymmetrically, it brings into the open what often remains implicit, taken for granted or hidden from view in the day-to-day conduct of social life. Once again, this stimulation of critical reflection is not necessarily restricted to the sphere of social analysts: it is capable, in principle, of spilling over into the broader social domain, and hence of generating or contributing to debates and conflicts which are an integral and continuous feature of social life. It is in this sense that *the interpretation of ideology bears an internal connection to the critique of domination*: it is methodologically predisposed to stimulate critical reflection of relations of power and domination, and this reflection includes in principle the reflection of the subjects who are enmeshed in these relations.

But while the connection between the interpretation of ideology and the critique of domination is internal, it is not immediate, in the sense that the critical reflection on relations of power and domination is governed by its own logic, its own argumentative structure and criteria of assessment, distinct from the criteria that may be employed in assessing the plausibility of an interpretation. In pursuing a critical reflection on relations of power and domination, one is engaged in an inquiry which is different in character from the assessment of the plausibility or otherwise of an interpretation, even if it was the interpretation which stimulated the reflection. The critical reflection on relations of power and domination raises new questions, new issues, calls for new kinds of evidence and argument. It is concerned, not with the question 'Is this interpretation justifiable?' but rather with the question 'Are these social relations just?' There is no simple procedure, no convenient rule of thumb, by means of which the latter question can be answered. It is a question which calls for judgement and for the careful consideration of arguments for and against particular institutions and societal arrangements. To pursue this question here would take us well beyond the scope of our present concerns. But I shall conclude by venturing the suggestion that the critical reflection on relations of power and domination should be governed by what may be called *the principle of non-exclusion*: a deliberation on whether particular institutions and societal arrangements are just and worthy of support should be a deliberation in which all those individuals who are affected by the institutions and arrangements have the right in principle to participate. Hence the deliberation should include in principle those individuals who, in the actual circumstances of everyday life, may be excluded from positions of power. For if the institutions and arrangements are just and worthy of support, then their justness and worthiness are features which should be acknowledged in principle by all those who are affected by them, and not only by those who, in actual circumstances, benefit most from them. And if the principle of non-exclusion has the effect of turning the tables in favour of those who, in actual circumstances, are generally excluded from positions of power, then it seems to me that this is neither a surprising nor an undesirable outcome. It is not surprising because, when the individuals and groups who have hitherto occupied subordinate social positions are given a voice, then it is likely that their needs and desires, their preferences and priorities, will have to be taken into account in the process of deliberation. And the outcome is not undesirable because, in a society where all individuals are treated as subjects capable of understanding and reflection, the institutions and social arrangements within which individuals live out their lives should concur so far as possible with what these individuals will to be the case, rather than with what some individuals will to be the case and most others accept as inevitable or unalterable. So if the critical reflection on relations of power and domination displays an effective bias in favour of those who, in actual circumstances, are generally excluded from positions of power, it does so in the sense that, and in so far as, it is governed by a principle which calls for the participation of all those affected in a process of deliberation, including those who benefit least, and suffer most, from the organization of social life as it exists and has existed hitherto. That there is plenty of scope for critical reflection of this kind is a proposition that cannot be doubted by anyone familiar with the multiple forms of inequality and conflict which remain pervasive, explosive and seemingly intractable features of the modern world.

My aim in this chapter has been to pursue, at the level of methodology, some of the arguments and proposals put forward in earlier chapters. I have tried to formulate a hermeneutically informed approach to the study of symbolic forms, and I have tried to show how this approach can be developed for the interpretation of ideology and the analysis of mass communication. By following this approach we can avoid the problems which vitiate much of the literature on ideology and mass communication. In particular, we can avoid the tendency, pervasive in the literature, to read off the ideological character of media messages from the messages themselves, without reference to the specific social–historical contexts within which these messages are produced, circulated and received. The methodological approach developed here enables us to see how the concept of ideology can play a role – albeit a restricted and carefully defined role – within a social theory informed by hermeneutics and orientated towards critique, that is, towards the critical self-reflection of the subjects who make up the social–historical world.

Conclusion: Critical Theory and Modern Societies

Critical social theory has always been concerned with the task of analysing the emergence of modern industrial societies and understanding their distinctive developmental trajectories. If we conceive of critical social theory in a narrow sense – as a body of thought associated with the Frankfurt School or directly influenced by it – then we can see that this task has generally been pursued within a framework derived primarily from Marx, and secondarily from Max Weber. Within this framework, it was the emergence and development of industrial capitalism that stood out as the fundamental constitutive feature of the modern era. It was the rapid expansion of industrial capitalism, with its restless search for new markets, its incessant commodification and its exploitative class relations, which was the driving force of modern societies. And it was this force, above all, that had to be tamed. For the early critical theorists, the taming of industrial capitalism was conceived of primarily in terms of the socialization of the means of production and the continuation of industrialism on a new, non-capitalist basis. Of course, the early critical theorists were aware of some of the difficulties and dangers inherent in this project. They were aware that the radical transformation of society would require a level of generalized political commitment that might be lacking, or that might be hijacked for other, more reactionary aims. They were aware that the socialization of the means of production carried with it the risk that power might be increasingly concentrated in the hands of a bureaucratic elite. And they surmised that the development of industrial capitalism was, in any case, part of a much broader process of social and cultural rationalization whose origins lay far in the past and whose consequences would be felt well into the future.

Today we can find other, more serious grounds for doubting the social and political vision inherent in the early project of critical theory. In the late twentieth century we have the benefit of hindsight: some of the ideals and aspirations which animated their work have been tarnished by the sobering, and sometimes sordid, realities of history. More generally, we may doubt whether the theoretical framework within which they pursued their analysis of modern societies was adequate for the task. We may suspect that the emphasis on industrial capitalism as the key constitutive feature of modern societies was an over-emphasis which tended to blur the significance of other developmental processes and other bases of domination and inequality. We may doubt whether the risks associated with the socialization of the means of production, and the associated bureaucratization of social and political organizations, had been fully recognized and appraised. We may wonder whether they had given adequate attention to the institutional forms through which individuals could best express their wishes and needs, and through which they could protect themselves from the excessive use of state power. We may express scepticism about the idea, taken from Max Weber and generalized into a sweeping vision of history, that modern societies are caught up in a process of rationalization which increasingly permeates every aspect of social life, rendering individuals increasingly dependent on a reified and administered totality that threatens to overwhelm them.

These doubts and reservations may be of sufficient weight to incline us to abandon much of the early project of critical theory. But they do not oblige us to give up the task with which the early critical theorists were concerned – namely, the task of analysing the distinctive development trajectories of modern societies, of reflecting on the shortcomings of these societies and the opportunities afforded by their development. This task retains its relevance today, even if the framework within which it is pursued must be funda-mentally recast. In this book I have sought to make a contribution to the continuing task of developing a critical theory of modern societies. I have argued that the mediazation of culture is a fundamental constitutive feature of modern societies, that is, one of the features by virtue of which the societies in which we live today are 'modern'. The mediazation of modern culture is a process that has gone hand–in–hand with two other constitutive trends: on the one hand, the development of industrial capitalism and the related attempts to develop non–capitalist (or state–socialist) forms of industrial organization; on the other hand, the rise of the modern state and the associated emergence of mass political movements orientated towards the exercise of influence over, and the increased participation in, political institutions. Together these developmental processes have moulded, and continue to mould, the major institutions of modern societies. Together they have shaped modern societies as relatively discrete entities and, at the same time, incorporated these societies into a globalized social system. If today we live in a world which is increasingly interwoven economically, which displays some common features in terms of political organizations and movements, and which is increasingly traversed by the products and institutions of the media industries, then it is because our societies have been shaped by a set of processes which are constitutive of the modern world.

It is against the backcloth of the mediazation of modern culture that I have tried to re-assess what is involved in the analysis and critique of ideology. The critique of ideology has always been a central preoccupation of critical theory: indeed, in the writings of some of the earlier critical theorists, the critique of ideology was the main preoccupation. But the concept of ideology has been used so diffusely in recent years, and criticized so heavily in certain quarters, that it has lost some of its analytical usefulness and theoretical appeal. I have tried to formulate a conception of ideology which has some precision and which retains, none the less, the critical edge traditionally associated with critical theory. I have tried to show how this conception of ideology can be integrated into a theoretical framework which focuses on the nature of symbolic forms, the characteristics of social contexts, the organization and reproduction of power and domination. I have indicated how the phenomenon of ideology acquires a new scope and complexity when it becomes part of the extended circulation of symbolic forms brought about by the mediazation of modern culture. Finally, I have outlined a methodological framework within which the critical analysis of ideology can be pursued concretely, as part of an interpretative approach to the study of contextualized symbolic forms.

In seeking to reformulate rather than jettison the idea of a critical analysis of ideology, I betray an indebtedness to the project of critical theory – even though I have sought, in other respects, to distance myself from it. Whatever the shortcomings of the work of the critical theorists, they were right, in my view, to emphasize the enduring significance of domination in the modern world; they were right to stress that individuals are self-reflective agents who can deepen their understanding of themselves and others and who can, on the basis of this understanding, act to change the conditions of their lives; and they were right to regard the critical analysis of ideology as one phase in the dynamic relation between domination and action, between the establishment and reproduction of forms of domination, on the one hand, and the process of critical self-reflection which may enable individuals to challenge these forms, on the other. These are emphases and perspectives which have been lost in some recent debates in social and political theory. Some recent theorists have become so preoccupied with diversity and difference, with the sheer variety and variability of forms of life, that they fail to take full account of the fact that, in the actual circumstances of modern societies, diversity and difference are commonly embedded in social relations which are structured in systematically asymmetrical ways. We must not be so blinded by the spectacle of diversity that we are unable to see the structured inequalities of social life. In the account that I have developed here, the critical analysis of ideology retains its value as part of a broader concern with the nature of domination in the modern world, with the modes of its reproduction and the possibilities for its transformation. This is not to say that the cluster of problems associated with the analysis of ideology and domination are the only worthwhile concerns of critical theory today – there is no need to adopt such a restrictive approach. But to suggest that we can now leave these problems behind, treat them as a residue of nineteenth-century thought which has no place in the modern (or 'post-modern') world, would be decidedly premature.

Notes

CHAPTER 1 THE CONCEPT OF IDEOLOGY

1 Detailed accounts of the history of the concept of ideology may be found in Hans Barth, *Truth and Ideology*, trans. Frederick Lilge (Berkeley: University of California Press, 1976); Jorge Larrain, *The Concept of Ideology* (London: Hutchinson, 1979); and George Lichtheim, 'The Concept of Ideology', in his *The Concept of Ideology and Other Essays* (New York: Random House, 1967), pp. 3–46.

2 For accounts of Destutt de Tracy's life and work, see Emmet Kennedy, *A 'Philosophe' in the Age of Revolution: Destutt de Tracy and the Origins of 'Ideology'* (Philadelphia: The American Philosophical Society, 1978); and François Picavet, *Les idéologues. Essais sur l'histoire des idées et des théories scientifiques, philosophiques, religieuses, etc. en France depuis 1789* (Paris: Félix Alcan, 1891).

3 Destutt de Tracy, 'Mémoire sur la faculté de penser', quoted in Kennedy, *A 'Philosophe' in the Age of Revolution*, p. 47.

4 Ibid.

5 Destutt de Tracy, *Élémens d'Idéologie*, vol. 1 (Paris: Courcier, 1803; repr. Librairie Philosophique J. Vrin, 1970), p. xiii.

6 Cited in Kennedy, *A 'Philosophe' in the Age of Revolution*, p. 81.

7 Napoleon 1er, 'Réponse à l'adresse du Conseil d'État', quoted in Kennedy, *A 'Philosophe' in the Age of Revolution*, p. 215.

8 The literature on the concept of ideology in Marx and Marxism is extensive. For a selection see Jorge Larrain, *Marxism and Ideology* (London: Macmillan, 1983); Bhikhu Parekh, *Marx's Theory of Ideology* (London: Croom Helm, 1982); Joe McCarney, *The Real World of Ideology* (Brighton: Harvester, 1980); Martin Seliger, *The Marxist Conception of Ideology: A Critical Essay* (Cambridge: Cambridge University Press, 1977); and Centre for Contemporary Cultural Studies, *On Ideology* (London: Hutchinson, 1977).

9 Karl Marx and Frederick Engels, *The German Ideology*, part 1, ed. C. J. Arthur (London: Lawrence & Wishart, 1970), p. 37.

10 Ibid., p. 41.

11 Ibid., p. 47.

12 Ibid.
13 See, for example, Sarah Kofman, *Camera obscura: de l'idéologie* (Paris: Galilée, 1973); and Wolfgang Fritz Haug et al., *Die Camera obscura der Ideologie: Philosophie, Ökonomie, Wissenschaft* (Berlin: Argument, 1984).
14 Marx and Engels, *The German Ideology*, pp. 51–2.
15 Ibid., p. 48.
16 Ibid., p. 64.
17 Karl Marx, 'Preface to *A Contribution to the Critique of Political Economy*', in Karl Marx and Frederick Engels, *Selected Works in One Volume* (London: Lawrence & Wishart, 1968), p. 182.
18 Ibid.
19 Karl Marx and Frederick Engels, *Manifesto of the Communist Party*, in *Selected Works in One Volume*, p. 38.
20 In outlining this alternative view of history, and the conception of ideology which is linked to it, I am indebted to the work of Claude Lefort; see especially 'Marx: From One Vision of History to Another', in his *The Political Forms of Modern Society: Bureaucracy, Democracy, Totalitarianism*, ed. John B. Thompson (Cambridge: Polity Press, 1986), pp. 139–80. See also Paul-Laurent Assoun, *Marx et la répétition historique* (Paris: Presses Universitaires de France, 1978).
21 Karl Marx, *The Eighteenth Brumaire of Louis Bonaparte*, in *Selected Works in One Volume*, p. 96.
22 Ibid., p. 97.
23 See Karl Marx, *The Class Struggles in France, 1848 to 1850* (Moscow: Progress Publishers, 1952), pp. 107–22. The first three chapters of this work were written by Marx in winter 1849–50 and originally published in the *Neue Rheinische Zeitung* in January, February and March 1850. The fourth chapter was written later by Marx and Engels and published in the last issue of the journal in autumn 1850. By contrast, *The Eighteenth Brumaire of Louis Bonaparte* was written by Marx, as a series of articles, in 1852 – that is, after the *coup d'état*.
24 Marx, *The Eighteenth Brumaire of Louis Bonaparte*, p. 168.
25 Ibid., p. 171.
26 Ibid., p. 98.
27 V. I. Lenin, *What Is To Be Done? Burning Questions of Our Movement* (New York: International Publishers, 1969), p. 41.
28 Georg Lukács, *History and Class Consciousness: Studies in Marxist Dialectics*, trans. Rodney Livingstone (London: Merlin Press, 1971), p. 76
29 See especially Jorge Larrain, *Marxism and Ideology*, ch. 2; Neil Harding, *Lenin's Political Thought: Theory and Practice in the Democratic and Socialist Revolutions* (London: Macmillan, 1983); Andrew Arato and Paul Breines, *The Young Lukács and the Origins of Western Marxism* (New York: Seabury Press, 1979); and Gareth Stedman Jones, 'The Marxism of the Early Lukács: An Evaluation', *New Left Review*, 70 (1971), pp. 27–64.
30 Lukács, *History and Class Consciousness*, p. 228.
31 For general discussions of Mannheim's work see A. P. Simonds, *Karl Mannheim's*

Sociology of Knowledge (Oxford: Oxford University Press, 1978); Susan J. Hekman, *Hermeneutics and the Sociology of Knowledge* (Cambridge: Polity Press, 1986); and Jorge Larrain, *The Concept of Ideology*, ch. 4.

32 Karl Mannheim, *Ideology and Utopia: An Introduction to the Sociology of Knowledge*, trans. Louis Wirth and Edward Shils (London: Routledge & Kegan Paul, 1936), p. 4.

33 Ibid., p. 69.

34 Ibid.

35 Ibid., p. 184.

36 Cf. ibid., pp. 69, 238–9.

37 See John B. Thompson, *Studies in the Theory of Ideology* (Cambridge: Polity Press, 1984).

38 See Max Weber, *Economy and Society: An Outline of Interpretive Sociology*, ed. Guenther Roth and Claus Wittich (Berkeley: University of California Press, 1978), ch. 3.

39 Suggestive examples of the invention of tradition may be found in Eric Hobsbawm and Terence Ranger (eds), *The Invention of Tradition* (Cambridge: Cambridge University Press, 1983).

40 Menachem Begin, in an interview on American television reported in the *Guardian* (22 June 1982). Begin's definition of 'invasion' may be compared with that offered by the OED: 'an entrance or incursion with armed force; a hostile inroad'.

41 A perceptive overview and analysis of trope, especially of metaphor, may be found in Paul Ricoeur, *The Rule of Metaphor: Multi-disciplinary Studies of the Creation of Meaning in Language*, trans. Robert Czerny with Kathleen McLaughlin and John Costello (London: Routledge & Kegan Paul, 1978). For a suggestive discussion of some of the links between trope and ideology, see Olivier Reboul, *Langage et idéologie* (Paris: Presses Universitaires de France, 1980), ch. 4.

42 Margaret Thatcher, in an interview conducted by the Press Association, reported in the *Guardian* (4 January 1988), p. 3.

43 Editorial comment in the *Sun* (30 June 1982), p. 6.

44 Lefort, *The Political Forms of Modern Society*, p. 201.

45 A detailed discussion of these and other devices may be found in Gunther Kress and Robert Hodge, *Language as Ideology* (London: Routledge & Kegan Paul, 1979); Roger Fowler, Bob Hodge, Gunther Kress and Tony Trew, *Language and Control* (London: Routledge & Kegan Paul, 1979); and Robert Hodge and Gunther Kress, *Social Semiotics* (Cambridge: Polity Press, 1988).

CHAPTER 2 IDEOLOGY IN MODERN SOCIETIES

1 Karl Marx and Frederick Engels, *Manifesto of the Communist Party*, in *Selected Works in One Volume* (London: Lawrence & Wishart, 1968), p. 38.

2 Max Weber, *The Protestant Ethic and the Spirit of Capitalism*, trans. Talcott Parsons (London: Unwin, 1930), pp. 181–2.

3 See Karl Mannheim, *Ideology and Utopia: An Introduction to the Sociology of Knowledge*, trans. Louis Wirth and Edward Shils (London: Routledge & Kegan Paul, 1936), pp. 5ff. For recent and differing statements of this argument, see Claude Lefort, 'Outline of the Genesis of Ideology in Modern Societies', in his *The Political Forms of Modern Society: Bureaucracy, Democracy, Totalitarianism*, ed. John B. Thompson (Cambridge: Polity Press, 1986); and Alvin W. Gouldner, *The Dialectic of Ideology and Technology: The Origins, Grammar and Future of Ideology* (London: Macmillan, 1976).

4 See Raymond Aron, *The Opium of the Intellectuals*, trans. Terence Kilmartin (London: Secker & Warburg, 1957) and *The Industrial Society: Three Essays on Ideology and Development* (London: Weidenfeld and Nicolson, 1967); Daniel Bell, *The End of Ideology: On the Exhaustion of Political Ideas in the Fifties* (Glencoe, Ill.: Free Press, 1960); Seymour Lipset, *Political Man: The Social Bases of Politics* (London: Heinemann, 1959); Edward Shils, 'Ideology and Civility: On the Politics of the Intellectual', *The Sewanee Review*, 66 (1958), pp. 450–80; Chaim I. Waxman (ed.), *The End of Ideology Debate* (New York: Funk & Wagnalls, 1968).

5 Although there has been a decline in regularized participation in Christian churches in many Western industrial societies since the nineteenth century, it remains the case that a large proportion of people declare religious beliefs of some kind. A recent Gallup Poll in Britain found that 75 per cent of people questioned said they believed in God, and nearly 60 per cent said they believed in heaven (see *Gallup Polls 1979* (London: Social Surveys Ltd, 1979), table 3)); comparable figures for the United States are generally higher (see Rodney Stark and William S. Bainbridge, *The Future of Religion: Secularization, Revival and Cult Formation* (Berkeley: University of California Press, 1985)). Moreover, Christian churches continue to exercise some influence in the social and political affairs of modern nation-states, although the nature of this influence varies considerably from one national context to another (see David Martin, *A General Theory of Secularization* (Oxford: Basil Blackwell, 1978) and Patrick Michel, *Politics and Religion in Eastern Europe*, trans. Alan Braley (Cambridge: Polity Press, 1991)).

6 See Gouldner, *The Dialectic of Ideology and Technology*, pp. 175–91.

7 See especially Louis Althusser, *For Marx*, trans. Ben Brewster (Harmondsworth, Middx: Penguin, 1969); and 'Ideology and Ideological State Apparatuses (Notes towards an Investigation)', in *Lenin and Philosophy and other Essays*, trans. Ben Brewster (London: New Left Books, 1971), pp. 121–73; Nicos Poulantzas, *Political Power and Social Classes*, trans. Timothy O'Hagan et al. (London: Verso, 1973) and 'The Problem of the Capitalist State', in Robin Blackburn (ed.), *Ideology in Social Science: Readings in Critical Social Theory* (London: Fontana/Collins, 1972), pp. 238–53.

8 See Antonio Gramsci, *Selections from the Prison Notebooks*, ed. and trans. Quentin Hoare and Geoffrey Nowell Smith (London: Lawrence & Wishart, 1971).

9 Among the many relevant works influenced by Althusser, Poulantzas and Gramsci are the following: Centre for Contemporary Cultural Studies, *On Ideology* (London: Hutchinson, 1977); Ernesto Laclau, *Politics and Ideology in Marxist Theory: Capitalism, Fascism, Populism* (London: New Left Books, 1977); Michel Pêcheux, *Language, Semantics and Ideology: Stating the Obvious*, trans. Harbans Nagpal (London: Macmillan, 1982); Colin Sumner, *Reading Ideologies: An Investigation into the Marxist Theory of Ideology and Law* (London: Academic Press, 1979); and Göran Therborn, *The Ideology of Power and the Power of Ideology* (London: New Left Books, 1980).

10 See, for example, Ted Benton, *The Rise and Fall of Structural Marxism: Althusser and his Influence* (London: Macmillan, 1984); Bob Jessop, *Nicos Poulantzas: Marxist Theory and Political Strategy* (London: Macmillan, 1985); and Chantal Mouffe (ed.), *Gramsci and Marxist Theory* (London: Routledge & Kegan Paul, 1979). I have discussed the work of some authors influenced by Althusser in *Studies in the Theory of Ideology* (Cambridge: Polity Press, 1984).

11 See Michael Mann, 'The Social Cohesion of Liberal Democracy', *American Sociological Review*, 35 (1970), pp. 423–39.

12 Brief surveys of the relevant literature may be found in Nicholas Abercrombie, Stephen Hill and Bryan S. Turner, *The Dominant Ideology Thesis* (London: Allen & Unwin, 1980), pp. 140–51, and David Held, 'Power and Legitimacy', in his *Political Theory and the Modern State: Essays on State, Power and Democracy* (Cambridge: Polity Press, 1989), pp. 99–157.

13 See Paul E. Willis, *Learning to Labour: How Working Class Kids Get Working Class Jobs* (Westmead, Farnborough, Hants: Saxon House, 1977).

14 The term 'dominant ideology thesis' is taken from the insightful study by Abercrombie et al. referred to in note 12 above.

15 See Althusser, 'Ideology and Ideological State Apparatuses', pp. 135–40. Nicos Poulantzas offers a somewhat more elaborate defence of this view in his essay 'The Problem of the Capitalist State', pp. 250–3.

16 The writings most often referred to in this regard are Engels's letter to J. Bloch (21 September 1890), in Marx and Engels, *Selected Works in One Volume*, pp. 682–3; and Marx's *The Eighteenth Brumaire of Louis Bonaparte*, in *Selected Works in One Volume*, pp. 96–179.

17 See especially Max Weber, 'Politics as a Vocation', in *From Max Weber: Essays in Sociology*, ed. and trans. H. H. Gerth and C. Wright Mills (London: Routledge & Kegan Paul), pp. 77–128. For recent works which have emphasized territoriality and military power in analysing the emergence and development of the modern state, see Theda Skocpol, *States and Social Revolutions: A Comparative Analysis of France, Russia and China* (Cambridge: Cambridge University Press, 1979); Anthony Giddens, *The Nation-State and Violence: Volume Two of A Contemporary Critique of Historical Materialism* (Cambridge: Polity Press, 1985); and Michael Mann, *The Sources of Social Power*, vol. 1, *A History of Power from the Beginning to AD 1760* (Cambridge: Cambridge University Press, 1986).

18 For a particularly clear statement of this view, see Ralph Miliband, *The State in*

Capitalist Society: An Analysis of the Western System of Power (London: Weidenfeld and Nicolson, 1969), ch. 8.

19 Detailed accounts of the history of the Frankfurt School and the views of the individuals associated with it may be found in Martin Jay, *The Dialectical Imagination: A History of the Frankfurt School and the Institute of Social Research 1923-50* (London: Heinemann, 1973); David Held, *Introduction to Critical Theory: Horkheimer to Habermas* (Cambridge: Polity Press, 1980); Helmut Dubiel, *Wissenschaftsorganisation und politische Erfahrung: Studien zur frühren kritische Theorie* (Frankfurt: Suhrkamp, 1978); and Rolf Wiggershaus, *Die Frankfurter Schule: Geschichte, Theoretische Entwicklung, Politische Bedeutung* (Munich: Carl Hanser, 1986).

20 See Max Horkheimer and Theodor W. Adorno, *Dialectic of Enlightenment*, trans. John Cumming (New York: Seabury Press, 1972); and Max Horkheimer, *Eclipse of Reason* (New York: The Seabury Press, 1974).

21 See, for example, Max Horkheimer and Theodor W. Adorno, 'The Culture Industry: Enlightenment as Mass Deception', in *Dialectic of Enlightenment*, pp. 120-67; Theodor W. Adorno, 'Culture Industry Reconsidered', trans. Anson G. Rabinbach, *New German Critique*, 6 (Fall 1975), pp. 12-19; Theodor W. Adorno, 'On the Fetish-Character in Music and the Regression of Listening', in *The Essential Frankfurt School Reader*, ed. Andrew Arato and Eike Gebhardt (New York: Urizen Books, 1978), pp. 270-99; Theodor W. Adorno, 'Television and the Patterns of Mass Culture', in *Mass Culture: The Popular Arts in America*, ed. Bernard Rosen and David Manning White (Glencoe, Ill.: Free Press, 1957); and Theodor W. Adorno, 'The Stars Down to Earth: The Los Angeles Times Astrology Column', *Telos*, 19 (Spring 1974), pp. 11-89.

22 Adorno, 'Culture Industry Reconsidered', p. 12.

23 Horkheimer and Adorno, *Dialectic of Enlightenment*, p. 158.

24 The Frankfurt Institute for Social Research, *Aspects of Sociology*, with a preface by Max Horkheimer and Theodor W. Adorno, trans. John Viertel (London: Heinemann, 1973), p. 202.

25 Adorno, 'On the Fetish-Character in Music and The Regression of Listening', p. 280.

26 See especially Theodor W. Adorno, 'Anti-Semitism and Fascist Propaganda', in Ernst Simmel (ed.), *Anti-Semitism: A Social Disease* (New York: International Universities Press, 1946); and 'Freudian Theory and the Pattern of Fascist Propaganda', in Geza Roheim (ed.), *Psychoanalysis and the Social Sciences* (New York: International Universities Press, 1951).

27 Adorno, 'The Stars Down to Earth', p. 18.

28 Horkheimer and Adorno, *Dialectic of Enlightenment*, p. 4.

29 See Robert Hodge and David Tripp, *Children and Television: A Semiotic Approach* (Cambridge: Polity Press, 1986).

30 See Jürgen Habermas, *The Structural Transformation of the Public Sphere: An Inquiry into a Category of Bourgeois Society*, trans. Thomas Bürger with Frederick Lawrence (Cambridge: Polity Press, 1989).

31 For general accounts of Habermas's work as a whole, see especially Thomas

McCarthy, *The Critical Theory of Jürgen Habermas* (Cambridge: Polity Press, 1978); and John B. Thompson and David Held (eds.), *Habermas: Critical Debates* (London: Macmillan, 1982).

32 This omission is partly explained by the fact that *The Structural Transformation of the Public Sphere* was published in English in 1989, 27 years after its original publication in German.

33 See Karl Marx, *On the Jewish Question*, in Karl Marx and Frederick Engels, *Collected Works* (London: Lawrence & Wishart, 1975), vol. 3, pp. 146–74.

34 Habermas, *The Structural Transformation of the Public Sphere*, p. 161.

35 Ibid., p. 207.

36 Ibid., p. 235.

37 Ibid., p. 195.

38 See especially Jürgen Habermas, *The Theory of Communicative Action*, vol. 1: *Reason and the Rationalization of Society*, trans. Thomas McCarthy (Cambridge: Polity Press: 1984), and *The Theory of Communicative Action*, vol. 2: *Lifeworld and System: A Critique of Functionalist Reason*, trans. Thomas McCarthy (Cambridge: Polity Press, 1987). For a critical overview of this project, see John B. Thompson, 'Rationality and Social Rationalization: An Assessment of Habermas's Theory of Communicative Action', in *Studies in the Theory of Ideology* (Cambridge: Polity Press, 1984), pp. 279–302. See also the various contributions in Richard J. Bernstein (ed.), *Habermas and Modernity* (Cambridge: Polity Press, 1985) and Axel Honneth and Hans Joas (eds), *Communicative Action: Essays on Jürgen Habermas' 'The Theory of Communicative Action'*, trans. Jeremy Gaines and Doris L. Jones (Cambridge: Polity Press, 1991).

39 Habermas, *The Theory of Communicative Action*, vol. 2, p. 355.

40 Ibid., p. 354.

41 Ibid., p. 355.

CHAPTER 3 THE CONCEPT OF CULTURE

1 For general discussions of the concept of culture, see A. L. Kroeber and Clyde Kluckhohn, *Culture: A Critical Review of Concepts and Definitions* (Cambridge, Mass.: Papers of the Peabody Museum of American Archaeology and Ethnology, Harvard University, 1952); Raymond Williams *Keywords: A Vocabulary of Culture and Society* (London: Fontana, 1976) and *Culture* (London: Fontana, 1981).

2 See Norbert Elias, *The Civilizing Process*, vol. 1: *The History of Manners*, trans. Edmund Jephcott (Oxford: Basil Blackwell, 1978), ch. 1.

3 Immanuel Kant, cited in Grimm's *Wörterbuch* and quoted in Kroeber and Kluckhohn, *Culture*, p. 11.

4 See J. C. Adelung, *Versuch einer Geschichte der Cultur des Menchlichen Geschlechts* (Leipzig: Gottlieb Hertel, 1782).

5 See J. G. von Herder, *Ideen zur Philosophie der Geschichte der Menschheit*, repr. as

vols. 13 and 14 of Herder's *Sämmtliche Werke*, ed. Bernhard Suphan (Berlin: Weidmannsche Buchhandlung, 1887). An English edition of *Ideen* appeared under the title *Outlines of a Philosophy of the History of Man*, trans. T. Churchill (London: J. Johnson, 1800).

6 J. G. von Herder, *Outlines of a Philosophy of the History of Man*, p. v (translation modified).

7 See Gustav Klemm, *Allgemeine Cultur-Geschichte der Menschheit* (Leipzig: B. G. Leubner, 1843–52), esp. vol. 1.

8 Edward B. Tylor, *Primitive Culture: Researches into the Development of Mythology, Philosophy, Religion, Language, Art, and Custom*, vol. 1 (London: John Murray, 1903), p. 1.

9 Ibid., p. 8.

10 Ibid., p. 1.

11 See Bronislaw Malinowski, *A Scientific Theory of Culture and Other Essays* (Chapel Hill, NC: University of North Carolina Press, 1944).

12 Bronislaw Malinowski, 'Culture', in *Encyclopaedia of the Social Sciences*, vol. 4 (London: Macmillan, 1931), pp. 621, 623.

13 Leslie A. White, *The Science of Culture: A Study of Man and Civilization* (New York: Farrar, Strauss and Cudahy, 1949), p. 363.

14 Clifford Geertz, *The Interpretation of Cultures* (New York: Basic Books, 1973), p. 5.

15 Ibid., pp. 89, 44; cf. also pp. 10, 216, 363.

16 See especially Paul Ricoeur, *Hermeneutics and the Human Sciences: Essays on Language, Action and Interpretation*, ed. and trans. John B. Thompson (Cambridge: Cambridge University Press, 1981) and *Interpretation Theory: Discourse and the Surplus of Meaning* (Fort Worth: Texas Christian University Press, 1976). I shall discuss the theory of interpretation in more detail in chapter 6.

17 See Clifford Geertz, 'Deep Play: Notes on the Balinese Cockfight', in *The Interpretation of Cultures*, pp. 412–53.

18 Some of the methodological problems in Geertz's work are discussed by Vincent Crapanzano, 'Hermes' Dilemma: The Masking of Subversion in Ethnographic Description', in James Clifford and George A. Marcus (eds), *Writing Culture: The Poetics and Politics of Ethnography* (Berkeley: University of California Press, 1986), pp. 51–76.

19 See Geertz, *The Interpretation of Cultures*, pp. 10, 448, 449. See also Clifford Geertz, *Local Knowledge: Further Essays in Interpretive Anthropology* (New York: Basic Books, 1983), pp. 30–1.

20 Geertz, *Local Knowledge*, p. 31.

21 For detailed discussion and criticism of Ricoeur's views, see John B. Thompson, *Critical Hermeneutics: A Study in the Thought of Paul Ricoeur and Jürgen Habermas* (Cambridge: Cambridge University Press, 1981) and 'Action, Ideology and the Text: A Reformulation of Ricoeur's Theory of Interpretation', in *Studies in the Theory of Ideology* (Cambridge: Polity Press, 1984), pp. 173–204.

22 See H. P. Grice, 'Meaning', *Philosophical Review*, 66 (1957), pp. 377–88, and the somewhat revised account in 'Utterer's Meaning and Intentions', *Philosophical*

Review, 78 (1969), pp. 147–77; and Eric D. Hirsch, Jr, *Validity in Interpretation* (New Haven, CT: Yale University Press, 1967).

23 See Peter Winch, *The Idea of Social Science and its Relation to Philosophy* (London: Routledge & Kegan Paul, 1958); see also R. S. Peters, *The Concept of Motivation* (London: Routledge & Kegan Paul, 1958); A. J. Melden, *Free Action* (London: Routledge & Kegan Paul, 1961); and A. R. Louch, *Explanation and Human Action* (Oxford: Basil Blackwell, 1966). For a pertinent criticism of Winch, see Alisdair MacIntyre, 'The Idea of a Social Science', in Bryan R. Wilson (ed.), *Rationality* (Oxford: Basil Blackwell, 1970), pp. 112–30. For a more extended critical discussion of Winch's account of meaningful action, see Thompson, *Critical Hermeneutics*, pp. 121–3 and 151–3.

24 See Ferdinand de Saussure, *Course in General Linguistics*, ed. Charles Bally and Albert Sechehaye, trans. Wade Baskin (London: Fontana/Collins, 1974).

25 See Roland Barthes, *Mythologies*, trans. Annette Lavers (St Albans: Paladin, 1973), p. 116.

26 See de Saussure, *Course in General Linguistics*, pp. 65–7. For a pertinent critical discussion of Saussure's notion of the sign, see Emile Benveniste, 'The Nature of the Linguistic Sign', in his *Problems in General Linguistics*, trans. Mary Elizabeth Meek (Cora Gables, Fla: University of Miami Press, 1971), pp. 43–8.

27 See P. F. Strawson, 'Truth', in his *Logico-Linguistic Papers* (London: Methuen, 1971), pp. 190–213.

28 Barthes, *Mythologies*, p. 116.

29 A critical review of different uses of the concept of structure may be found in the work of Anthony Giddens, who also offers a novel reformulation of the concept. See especially his *New Rules of Sociological Method: A Positive Critique of Interpretative Sociologies* (London: Hutchinson, 1976); *Central Problems in Social Theory: Action, Structure and Contradiction in Social Analysis* (London: Macmillan, 1979); and *The Constitution of Society: Outline of the Theory of Structuration* (Cambridge: Polity Press, 1984). For critical discussions of Giddens's proposed reformulation of the concept of structure, see the essays by Zygmunt Bauman and myself in David Held and John B. Thompson (eds), *Social Theory of Modern Societies: Anthony Giddens and his Critics* (Cambridge: Cambridge University Press, 1989).

30 In outlining this framework I am amplifying remarks which I made earlier in *Critical Hermeneutics*, pp. 139–49, and *Studies in the Theory of Ideology*, pp. 127–30.

31 Among the most relevant works by Bourdieu are the following: Pierre Bourdieu, *Outline of a Theory of Practice*, trans. Richard Nice (Cambridge: Cambridge University Press, 1977); *Distinction: A Social Critique of the Judgement of Taste*, trans. Richard Nice (Cambridge, Mass: Harvard University Press, 1984); *Homo Academicus*, trans. Peter Collier (Cambridge: Polity Press, 1988); *The Logic of Practice*, trans. Richard Nice (Cambridge: Polity Press, 1990); and *Language and Symbolic Power*, ed. John B. Thompson, trans. Gino Raymond and Matthew Adamson (Cambridge: Polity Press, 1991).

32 Some relevant analyses and critical discussions of Bourdieu's work may be found in Nicholas Garnham and Raymond Williams, 'Pierre Bourdieu and the

Sociology of Culture: An Introduction', *Media, Culture and Society*, 2 (1980), pp. 209–23; Rogers Brubaker, 'Rethinking Classical Social Theory: The Sociological Vision of Pierre Bourdieu', *Theory and Society*, 14 (1985), pp. 745–75; Axel Honneth, 'The Fragmented World of Symbolic Forms: Reflections on Pierre Bourdieu's Sociology of Culture', trans. T. Talbot, *Theory, Culture and Society*, 3/3 (1986), pp. 55–66; and John B. Thompson, 'Symbolic Violence: Language and Power in the Writings of Pierre Bourdieu', in *Studies in the Theory of Ideology*, pp. 42–72.

33 For extended discussions of strategies of conversion and reconversion, see Pierre Bourdieu and Luc Boltanski, 'Formal Qualifications and Occupational Hierarchies: The Relationship Between the Production System and the Reproduction System', trans. Richard Nice, in Edmund J. King (ed.), *Reorganizing Education: Management and Participation for Change* (London and Beverly Hills: Sage, 1977), pp. 61–9, and Bourdieu, *Distinction*, pp. 125–68.

34 This point has been emphasized with particular clarity by Anthony Giddens; see especially his *The Constitution of Society*, chs 1 and 4.

35 This strategy is analysed in an exemplary way by Bourdieu in *Distinction*, chs 1 and 3.

36 The attitudes of the courtly aristocracy have been analysed in detail by Norbert Elias; see especially his *State Formation and Civilization* (vol. 2 of *The Civilizing Process*), trans. Edmund Jephcott (Oxford: Basil Blackwell, 1982); and *The Court Society* (Oxford: Basil Blackwell, 1983).

37 For an analysis of the role of pretension and related strategies in the production of linguistic expressions, see Bourdieu, *Language and Symbolic Power*, chs 1 and 2.

38 In addition to the work of Elias cited above, see Jonas Frykman and Orvar Löfgren, *Culture Builders: An Historical Anthropology of Middle-Class Life*, trans. Alan Crozier (New Brunswick, NJ: Rutgers University Press, 1987); and Orvar Löfgren, 'Deconstructing Swedishness: Culture and Class in Modern Sweden', in *Anthropology at Home*, ed. Anthony Jackson (London: Tavistock, 1987), pp. 74–93.

39 See Bourdieu's account of the 'taste for necessity' characteristic of the working class in contemporary France, in *Distinction*, ch. 7.

40 See Paul E. Willis, *Learning to Labour: How Working Class Kids Get Working Class Jobs* (Westmead, Farnborough, Hants: Saxon House, 1977) and Stuart Hall and Tony Jefferson (eds), *Resistance through Rituals: Youth Subcultures in Post-War Britain* (London: Hutchinson, 1976).

41 See Raymond Williams, *The Long Revolution* (Harmondsworth, Middx: Penguin, 1961).

CHAPTER 4 CULTURAL TRANSMISSION AND MASS COMMUNICATION

1 For a general discussion of the relation between mass reproduction and works of art, see the classic essay by Walter Benjamin, 'The Work of Art in the Age of

Mechanical Reproduction', in his *Illuminations*, trans. Harry Zohn (London: Fontana, 1973), pp. 219–53.

2 See G. J. Fyfe, 'Art and Reproduction: Some Aspects of the Relations Between Painters and Engravers in London 1760–1850', *Media, Culture and Society*, 7 (1985), pp. 399–425.

3 See Harold A. Innis, *Empire and Communications* (Oxford: Oxford University Press, 1950) and *The Bias of Communication* (Toronto: University of Toronto Press, 1951). See also Anthony Giddens, *A Contemporary Critique of Historical Materialism*, vol. 1: *Power, Property and the State* (London: Macmillan, 1981), *The Constitution of Society: Outline of the Theory of Structuration* (Cambridge: Polity Press, 1984) and *The Nation-State and Violence: Volume Two of A Contemporary Critique of Historical Materialism* (Cambridge: Polity Press, 1985).

4 The term 'distanciation' derives from the work of Paul Ricoeur, who uses it to describe the ways in which written discourse (texts) is distinguished from spoken discourse. See especially Paul Ricoeur, *Hermeneutics and the Human Sciences: Essays on Language, Action and Interpretation*, ed. and trans. John B. Thompson (Cambridge: Cambridge University Press, 1981). The way in which I use the term 'distanciation' does not coincide with Ricoeur's use.

5 See I. J. Gelb, *A Study of Writing: The Foundations of Grammatology* (London: Routledge & Kegan Paul, 1952); David Diringer, *Writing* (London: Thames and Hudson, 1962); and Jack Goody, *The Domestication of the Savage Mind* (Cambridge: Cambridge University Press, 1977).

6 See Thomas Francis Carter, *The Invention of Printing in China and its Spread Westward* (New York: Ronald Press Company, 1925).

7 Ibid., chs 19 and 24.

8 See S. H. Steinberg, *Five Hundred Years of Printing* (Harmondsworth, Middx: Penguin, 1974), pp. 17ff.; Elizabeth L. Eisenstein, *The Printing Revolution in Early Modern Europe* (Cambridge: Cambridge University Press, 1983), pp. 12ff; and Lucien Febvre and Henri-Jean Martin, *The Coming of the Book: The Impact of Printing, 1450–1800*, trans. David Gerard (London: New Left Books, 1976), pp. 45ff.

9 See Joseph Frank, *The Beginnings of the English Newspaper 1620–1660* (Cambridge, Mass.: Harvard University Press, 1961), pp. 3ff.

10 See Michael Harris, 'The Structure, Ownership and Control of the Press, 1620–1780', in George Boyce, James Curran and Pauline Wingate (eds), *Newspaper History from the Seventeenth Century to the Present Day* (London: Constable, 1978), p. 87.

11 For more extended discussions of the early practices of censorship in Europe, see Steinberg, *Five Hundred Years of Printing*, pp. 260–72; Febvre and Martin, *The Coming of the Book*, pp. 244–7; and F. S. Siebert, *Freedom of the Press in England, 1476–1776* (Urbana, Ill.: University of Illinois Press, 1952).

12 The development of the newspaper industry in the United States during the nineteenth century is documented by Harold A. Innis, 'Technology and Public Opinion in the United States', in his *The Bias of Communication*, pp. 156–89. For

relevant material on France, see Irene Collins, *The Government and the Newspaper Press in France, 1814-1881* (Oxford: Oxford University Press, 1959).

13 See Ivon Asquith, 'The Structure, Ownership and Control of the Press, 1780-1855', in Boyce et al., *Newspaper History from the Seventeenth Century to the Present Day*, p. 102.

14 For a more detailed discussion of the rise of the popular press in the nineteenth century, see Alan J. Lee, *The Origins of the Popular Press in England 1855-1914* (London: Croom Helm, 1976).

15 The nature and development of the major news agencies are documented in Graham Storey, *Reuters' Century 1851-1951* (London: Max Parrish, 1951); Oliver Boyd-Barrett, *The International News Agencies* (London: Constable, 1980); and Anthony Smith, *The Geopolitics of Information: How Western Culture Dominates the World* (London: Faber, 1980).

16 See Boyd-Barrett, *The International News Agencies*, pp. 40-9. It should be noted that, while Africa is under-represented by the American agencies, a substantial proportion of AFP's overseas bureaux are located in Africa, due to the strong historical links between France and many African countries.

17 For a full discussion of the development of broadcasting in the United States, see Sidney W. Head, *Broadcasting in America: A Survey of Television and Radio* (Boston: Houghton Mifflin, 1976), part 2. The development of broadcasting in France is documented in Patrice Flichy, *Les Industries de l'imaginaire: pour une analyse économique des media* (Grenoble: Presses Universitaires de Grenoble, 1980).

18 See Asa Briggs, *The History of Broadcasting in the United Kingdom*, vol. 1: *The Birth of Broadcasting* (London: Oxford University Press, 1961) and Tom Burns, *The BBC: Public Institution and Private World* (London: Macmillan, 1977).

19 See Asa Briggs, *The History of Broadcasting in the United Kingdom*, vol. 4: *Sound and Vision* (London: Oxford University Press, 1979), pp. 239ff.

20 See Peter Golding, *The Mass Media* (Harlow, Essex: Longman, 1974), p. 35.

21 See Jeremy Tunstall, *The Media in Britain*, p. 61, and *Social Trends*, 15 (London: HMSO, 1985), p. 150.

22 See Peter Masson, 'The Effects of Television on Other Media', in James Halloran (ed.), *The Effects of Television* (London: Panther, 1970), pp. 138-80.

23 See the *Report of the Committee on Financing the BBC*, Chairman Alan Peacock (London: HMSO, 1986).

24 See Ivan Reid, *Social Class Differences in Britain*, 2nd edn (London: Grant McIntyre, 1981), pp. 266-8.

25 *Broadcasting in the '90s: Competition, Choice and Quality* (London: HMSO, 1988).

26 See Roger G. Noll, J. Peck Merton and John McGowan, *Economic Aspects of Television Regulation* (Washington, DC: Brookings, 1973), p. 61.

27 See Head, *Broadcasting in America*, p. 224. For details of corporate underwriting, see James Roman, 'Programming for Public Television', *Journal of Communication*, 30/3 (1980), pp. 150-6.

28 See Elihu Katz and George Wedell, *Broadcasting in the Third World: Promise and Performance* (Cambridge, Mass.: Harvard University Press, 1977).

29 Ibid., pp. 60–2.

30 For material on the United States, see Ben H. Bagdikian, *The Media Monopoly*, 3rd edn (Boston: Beacon Press, 1989). For material on France, see Flichy, *Les Industries de l'imaginaire*. For material on Germany, see Helmut H. Diederichs, *Konzentration in der Massenmedien: Systematischer Überblick zur Situation in der BRD* (Munich: Hanser, 1973).

31 See Bagdikian, *The Media Monopoly*, pp. 21ff.

32 See Graham Murdock, 'Large Corporations and the Control of the Communications Industries', in Michael Gurevitch, Tony Bennett, James Curran and Janet Woolacott (eds), *Culture, Society and the Media* (London: Methuen, 1982), pp. 136ff.

33 See *Independent Broadcasting Authority Annual Report and Accounts 1984–85* (London: HMSO, 1985); and *BBC Handbook, Incorporating the Annual Report and Accounts 1984–85* (London: BBC, 1985), pp. 90–3.

34 See Tapio Varis, *International Flow of Television Programmes*, UNESCO Reports and Papers on Mass Communication, no. 100 (Paris: UNESCO, 1986).

35 For further discussion of this theme, see Herbert I. Schiller, *Mass Communication and American Empire* (New York: Augustus M. Kelly, 1969); Jeremy Tunstall, *The Media are American: Anglo-American Media in the World* (London: Constable, 1977); and Oliver Boyd-Barrett, 'Media Imperialism: Towards an International Framework for the Analysis of Media Systems', in James Curran, Michael Gurevitch and Janet Woollacott (eds), *Mass Communication and Society*, (London: Edward Arnold, 1977), pp. 116–135.

36 The historical and technical aspects of satellite communications are discussed in Abram Chayes, James Fawcett, Masami Ito, Alexandre-Charles Kiss and others, *Satellite Broadcasting* (London: Oxford University Press, 1973); Jonathan F. Galloway, *The Politics and Technology of Satellite Communications* (Lexington, Mass.: D. C. Heath, 1972); and Marcellus S. Snow, 'Intelsat: An International Example', *Journal of Communications*, 30/2 (1980), pp. 147–56.

37 See Don Schiller, 'Business Users and the Telecommunications Network', *Journal of Communications*, 32/4 (1982), pp. 84–96, and R. Aldich, 'Emerging Issues in Transborder Data Flows', in *International Telecommunications Policy: A Sourcebook* (Washington, DC: Yurrow, 1983).

38 A more extensive discussion of broadcasting policy and deregulation in the USA can be found in Muriel G. Cantor and Joel M. Cantor, 'Regulation and Deregulation: Telecommunications Politics in the United States', in Marjorie Ferguson (ed.), *New Communication Technologies and the Public Interest: Comparative Perspectives on Policy and Research* (London and Beverly Hills: Sage, 1986), pp. 84–101.

39 For material on deregulation in Europe, see Denis McQuail and Karen Siune (eds), *New Media Politics: Comparative Perspectives in Western Europe* (London and Beverly Hills: Sage, 1986).

40 See Peter Golding and Graham Murdock, 'Unequal Information: Access and Exclusion in the New Communications Market Place', in Ferguson, *New Communication Technologies and the Public Interest*, pp. 71–83.

41 For an insightful discussion of the implications of ISDN and related developments, see G. A. Mulgan, *Communication and Control: Networks and the New Economies of Communication* (Cambridge: Polity Press, 1990).

CHAPTER 5 TOWARDS A SOCIAL THEORY OF MASS COMMUNICATION

1 See Denis McQuail, 'Uncertainty About the Audience and the Organization of Mass Communication', in Paul Halmos (ed.), *The Sociology of Mass-Media Communicators* (*Sociological Review Monograph* 13: University of Keele, 1969), pp. 75–84; and Tom Burns, 'Public Service and Private World', in *The Sociology of Mass-Media Communicators*, pp. 53–73.

2 Relevant works include Harold A. Innis, *Empire and Communications* (London: Oxford University Press, 1950) and *The Bias of Communication* (Toronto: University of Toronto Press, 1951); Marshall McLuhan, *The Gutenberg Galaxy: The Making of Typographic Man* (London: Routledge & Kegan Paul, 1962) and *Understanding Media: The Extensions of Man* (London: Routledge & Kegan Paul, 1964).

3 The impact of the spread of writing and literacy on traditional and predominantly oral cultures has been studied by anthropologists and others; see, for example, Jack Goody, *The Domestication of the Savage Mind* (Cambridge: Cambridge University Press, 1977); Jack Goody (ed.), *Literacy in Traditional Societies* (Cambridge: Cambridge University Press, 1968); and Walter J. Ong, *Orality and Literacy: The Technologizing of the Word* (New York: Methuen, 1982). On the nature and impact of printed materials in early modern Europe, see Roger Chartier, *The Cultural Uses of Print in Early Modern France*, trans. Lydia G. Cochrane (Princeton, NJ: Princeton University Press, 1987); and Roger Chartier (ed.), *The Culture of Print: Power and the Uses of Print in Early Modern Europe*, trans. Lydia G. Cochrane (Cambridge: Polity Press, 1989).

4 This point is elaborated in an insightful way by Joshua Meyrowitz in *No Sense of Place: The Impact of Electronic Media on Social Behavior* (New York: Oxford University Press, 1985).

5 For analyses of the ordered properties of telephone conversations, see Emanuel A. Schegloff, 'Sequencing in Conversational Openings', in John J. Gumperz and Dell Hymes (eds), *Directions in Sociolinguistics: The Ethnography of Communication*, pp. 349–80, and 'Identification and Recognition in Telephone Conversation Openings', in George Psathas (ed.), *Everyday Language: Studies in Ethnomethodology* (New York: Irvington Publishers, 1979), pp. 23–78; and Emanuel A. Schegloff and Harvey Sacks, 'Opening Up Closings', *Semiotica*, 8 (1973), pp. 289–327. See also A. A. L. Reid, 'Comparing Telephone with Face-to-Face Contact', in Ithiel de Sola Pool (ed.), *The Social Impact of the Telephone* (Cambridge, Mass.: MIT Press, 1977), pp. 386–414.

6 In an early article Horton and Wohl suggested, in a somewhat similar way, that

mass communication gives rise to a new type of social relationship which they call 'para-social interaction'; see Donald Horton and R. Richard Wohl, 'Mass Communication and Para-Social Interaction: Observations on Intimacy at a Distance', *Psychiatry*, 19 (1956), pp. 215–29.

7 See especially Erving Goffman, *The Presentation of Self in Everyday Life* (Harmondsworth, Middx: Penguin, 1969). Although Goffman's concepts of front region and back region are developed primarily with regard to face-to-face interaction, they can be usefully adapted for the purposes of analysing the interactional impact of technical media.

8 See James Lull, 'How Families Select Television Programmes: A Mass-Observational Study', *Journal of Broadcasting*, 26 (1982), pp. 801–11; and David Morley, *Family Television: Cultural Power and Domestic Leisure* (London: Comedia, 1986).

9 For more extended discussions of the nature and development of this dichotomy, see Jürgen Habermas, *The Structural Transformation of the Public Sphere: An Inquiry into a Category of Bourgeois Society*, trans. Thomas Bürger with Frederick Lawrence (Cambridge: Polity Press, 1989) and Norberto Bobbio, *Democracy and Dictatorship: The Nature and Limits of State Power*, trans. Peter Kennealy (Cambridge: Polity Press, 1989).

10 See Alan Ware, *Between Profit and State: Intermediate Organizations in Britain and the United States* (Cambridge: Polity Press, 1989).

11 See Bobbio, *Democracy and Dictatorship*, ch. 1.

12 See, for example, Richard Sennett, *The Fall of Public Man* (Cambridge: Cambridge University Press, 1974), pp. 282ff. Sennett's argument converges in some respects with that developed by Habermas in *The Structural Transformation of the Public Sphere*.

13 See S. H. Steinberg, *Five Hundred Years of Printing* (Harmondsworth, Middx: Penguin, 1955); Arthur Aspinall, *Politics and the Press, c. 1780–1850* (Brighton: Harvester, 1973); and George Boyce, James Curran and Pauline Wingate (eds), *Newspaper History from the Seventeenth Century to the Present Day* (London: Constable, 1978).

14 *Cobbett's Political Register* (14 May 1803), quoted in Aspinall, *Politics and the Press*, p. 10.

15 See especially James Mill, 'Liberty of the Press', in his *Essays on Government, Jurisprudence, Liberty of the Press and Law of Nations* (New York: Kelly, 1967); and John Stuart Mill, 'On Liberty', in his *Utilitarianism, On Liberty and Considerations on Representative Government*, ed. H. B. Acton (London: Dent, 1972).

16 See J. S. Mill, 'On Liberty', p. 150.

17 Ibid., p. 153.

18 See J. C. W. Reith, *Broadcast over Britain* (London: Hodder and Stoughton, 1924), pp. 57ff.; and Asa Briggs, *The Birth of Broadcasting* (London: Oxford University Press, 1961), pp. 234–9.

19 J. C. W. Reith, *Into the Wind* (London: Hodder and Stoughton, 1949), p. 103.

20 See Asa Briggs, *Governing the BBC* (London: British Broadcasting Corporation,

1979), ch. 2; and Stuart Hood, *On Television*, 2nd edn (London: Pluto Press, 1983), p. 41.

21 This point is amply demonstrated by Pierre Bourdieu in *Distinction: A Social Critique of the Judgement of Taste*, trans. Richard Nice (Cambridge, Mass.: Harvard University Press, 1984).

22 See Krishan Kumar, 'Public Service Broadcasting and the Public Interest', in Colin MacCabe and Olivia Stewart (eds), *The BBC and Public Service Broadcasting* (Manchester: Manchester University Press, 1986), pp. 50–1.

23 J. C. W. Reith, *Into the Wind*, p. 108.

24 *BBC Yearbook*, 1933, quoted in Kumar, 'Public Service Broadcasting and the Public Interest', p. 54.

25 The dangers of corporate concentration in the domains of the new communication technologies are, it seems to me, underplayed by Ithiel de Sola Pool in his otherwise thoughtful and illuminating study, *Technologies of Freedom* (Cambridge, Mass.: Harvard University Press, 1983).

26 For recent discussions of some relevant issues, see William H. Melody, 'Communication Policy in the Global Information Economy: Whither the Public Interest?', in Marjorie Ferguson (ed.), *Public Communication: The New Imperatives* (London and Newbury Park, Ca: Sage, 1990), pp. 16–39; and James Michael, 'Regulating Communications Media: From the Discretion of Sound Chaps to the Arguments of Lawyers', in ibid., pp. 40–60.

CHAPTER 6 THE METHODOLOGY OF INTERPRETATION

1 See Martin Heidegger, *Being and Time*, trans. John Macquarrie and Edward Robinson (Oxford: Basil Blackwell, 1978), especially ss. 31–3.

2 See Hans-Georg Gadamer, *Truth and Method* (London: Sheed & Ward, 1975), especially pp. 235–74.

3 Karl Marx, *The Eighteenth Brumaire of Louis Bonaparte*, in Karl Marx and Frederick Engels, *Selected Works in One Volume* (London: Lawrence & Wishart, 1968), pp. 96–179. See my discussion of this text in chapter 1.

4 See Eric Hobsbawn and Terence Ranger (eds), *The Invention of Tradition* (Cambridge: Cambridge University Press, 1983).

5 See especially Paul Ricoeur, *Hermeneutics and the Human Sciences: Essays on Language, Action and Interpretation*, ed. and trans. John B. Thompson (Cambridge: Cambridge University Press, 1981); *The Conflict of Interpretations: Essays in Hermeneutics*, ed. Don Ihde (Evanston, Ill.: Northwestern University Press, 1974); *Freud and Philosophy: An Essay on Interpretation*, trans. Denis Savage (New Haven, CT: Yale University Press, 1970); and *Interpretation Theory: Discourse and the Surplus of Meaning* (Fort Worth: The Texas Christian University Press, 1976). Similar views concerning the nature of depth hermeneutics may be found in the work of Jürgen Habermas and Karl-Otto Apel; see especially Jürgen Habermas, *Knowledge and Human Interests*, trans.

Jeremy J. Shapiro (Cambridge: Polity Press, 1987) and *On the Logic of the Social Sciences*, trans. Shierry Weber Nicholson and Jerry A. Stark (Cambridge: Polity Press, 1988); Karl-Otto Apel, *Towards a Transformation of Philosophy*, trans. Glyn Adey and David Frisby (London: Routledge & Kegan Paul, 1980) and *Understanding and Explanation: A Transcendental-Pragmatic Perspective*, trans. Georgia Warnke (Cambridge, Mass.: MIT Press, 1984).

6 Paul Ricoeur, 'What is a Text? Explanation and Understanding', in *Hermeneutics and the Human Sciences*, p. 161.

7 See John B. Thompson, *Critical Hermeneutics: A Study in the Thought of Paul Ricoeur and Jürgen Habermas* (Cambridge: Cambridge University Press, 1981), ch. 5; and 'Action, Ideology and the Text: A Reformulation of Ricoeur's Theory of Interpretation', in *Studies in the Theory of Ideology*, pp. 173–204.

8 See Roland Barthes, *Mythologies*, trans. Annette Lavers (St Albans: Paladin, 1973).

9 Judith Williamson draws on the work of Barthes to develop a semiotic analysis of advertisements in her *Decoding Advertisements: Ideology and Meaning in Advertising* (London: Marion Boyars, 1978). See also the contributions to part 3 of Howard Davis and Paul Walton (eds), *Language, Image, Media* (Oxford: Basil Blackwell, 1983).

10 Most of this research has been published in the form of articles; see, for example, Emanuel A. Schegloff and Harvey Sacks, 'Opening up Closings', *Semiotica*, 8 (1973), pp. 289–327; Harvey Sacks, Emanuel A. Schegloff and Gail Jefferson, 'A Simplest Systematics for the Organization of Turn-taking for Conversation', *Language*, 50 (1974), pp. 696–735; and Emanuel A. Schegloff, 'Sequencing in Conversational Openings', in John J. Gumperz and Dell Hymes (eds), *Directions in Sociolinguistics: The Ethnography of Communication* (New York: Holt, Rinehart and Winston, 1972), pp. 349–80. For helpful overviews of conversation analysis, see Stephen C. Levinson, *Pragmatics* (Cambridge: Cambridge University Press, 1983), pp. 294–370; and John C. Heritage, 'Recent Developments in Conversation Analysis', *Sociolinguistics*, 15/1 (1985), pp. 1–15.

11 See Harold Garfinkel, *Studies in Ethnomethodology* (Cambridge: Polity Press, 1984).

12 See especially Roger Fowler, Bob Hodge, Gunther Kress and Tony Trew, *Language and Control* (London: Routledge & Kegan Paul, 1979); Gunther Kress and Robert Hodge, *Language as Ideology* (London: Routledge & Kegan Paul, 1979); and Robert Hodge and Gunther Kress, *Social Semiotics* (Cambridge: Polity Press, 1988). For a critical appraisal of this material, see Thompson, *Studies in the Theory of Ideology*, pp. 118–26.

13 Further discussion of these grammatical characteristics may be found in Hodge and Kress, *Social Semiotics*; and Deborah Cameron, *Feminism and Linguistic Theory* (London: Macmillan, 1985).

14 See Roland Barthes, 'Introduction to the Structural Analysis of Narratives', in his *Image-Music-Text*, trans. Stephen Heath (Glasgow: Fontana/Collins, 1977), pp. 79–124; Claude Lévi-Strauss, 'The Structural Study of Myth', in his *Structural Anthropology*, trans. Claire Jakobson and Brooke Grundfest Schoepf (Har-

mondsworth, Middx: Penguin, 1963), pp. 206–31; Claude Bremond, *Logique du récit* (Paris: Seuil, 1973); A. J. Greimas, *Semantique structurale: recherche de méthode* (Paris: Larousse, 1966); A. J. Greimas, *Du Sens: essais semiotiques* (Paris: Seuil, 1970); Tzvetan Todorov, *The Poetics of Prose*, trans. Richard Howard (Oxford: Basil Blackwell, 1977); and Gerard Genette, *Narrative Discourse*, trans. Jane E. Lewin (Oxford: Basil Blackwell, 1980). Attempts to apply narrative analysis to political discourse may be found in Yves Delahaye, *La Frontière et le texte: pour une sémiotique des rélations internationales* (Paris: Payot, 1977); Yves Delahaye, *L'Europe sous les mots: le texte et la déchirure* (Paris: Payot, 1979); and Jean Pierre Faye, *Langages totalitaires: Critique de la raison/l'économie narrative* (Paris: Hermann, 1973).

15 For a sympathetic critique of Greimas's approach, see Paul Ricoeur, 'The Narrative Function', in *Hermeneutics and the Human Sciences*, pp. 274–96.

16 One method of argumentative analysis has been developed by Georges Vignaux and his associates; see Georges Vignaux, *L'Argumentation* (Genève: Droz, 1977); and Pierre Lascoumes, Ghislaine Moreau-Capdevielle and Georges Vignaux, 'Il y a parmi nous des monstres', *Communications*, 28 (1978), pp. 127–63. The method developed by Michel Pêcheux and his associates could also be understood as a rather formal contribution to the argumentative analysis of discourse; see John B. Thompson, 'Ideology and the Analysis of Discourse: A Critical Introduction to the Work of Michel Pêcheux' in *Studies in the Theory of Ideology*, pp. 232–54.

17 See especially Harvey Sacks, 'Some Technical Considerations of a Dirty Joke', in Jim Schenkein (ed), *Studies in the Organization of Conversational Interaction* (New York: Academic Press, 1978), pp. 249–69; and Harvey Sacks, 'An Analysis of the Course of a Joke's Telling in Conversation', in Richard Bauman and Joel Scherzer (eds.), *Explorations in the Ethnography of Speaking* (Cambridge: Cambridge University Press, 1974), pp. 337–53.

18 Adapted from Sacks, 'Some Technical Considerations of a Dirty Joke', pp. 250–2.

19 Sacks, 'Some Technical Considerations of a Dirty Joke', p. 263.

20 Ibid., pp. 268–9.

21 In fact, these assumptions seem to be fairly typical features of men's dirty jokes, a consideration which casts further doubt on Sacks's suggestion that this joke is really intended for circulation among twelve-year-old girls. See Gershon Legman, *Rationale of the Dirty Joke: An Analysis of Sexual Humour* (New York: Grove Press, 1968); and Michael Mulkay, *On Humour: Its Nature and Its Place in Modern Society* (Cambridge: Polity Press, 1988).

22 Various studies could be used to illustrate the social–historical analysis of media institutions and processes of production. For a selection of studies concerned with the production of television news, see Peter Golding and Philip Elliott, *Making the News* (London: Longman, 1979); Philip Schlesinger, *Putting 'Reality' Together: BBC News* (London: Constable, 1978); and Gaye Tuchman, *Making News: A Study in the Construction of Reality* (New York: Free Press, 1978).

23 There is an extensive literature dealing with the construction of media messages. For a selection see Karl Erik Rosengren (ed.), *Advances in Content Analysis* (London and Beverly Hills: Sage, 1981); Howard Davis and Paul Walton (eds),

Language, Image, Media; and Williard D. Rowland and Bruce Watkins (eds), *Interpreting Television: Current Research Perspectives* (London and Beverly Hills: Sage, 1985).

24 In recent years there has been a significant growth of sociologically informed literature on the nature of audiences and the conditions of reception of media messages. See, for instance, Anthony Piepe, Miles Emerson and Judy Lannon, *Television and the Working Class* (Westmead, Farnborough, Hants: Saxon House, 1975); David Morley, *The 'Nationwide' Audience: Structure and Decoding* (London: British Film Institute, 1980); David Morley, *Family Television: Cultural Power and Domestic Leisure* (London: Comedia, 1986); Robert Hodge and David Tripp, *Children and Television: A Semiotic Approach* (Cambridge: Polity Press, 1986); Ien Ang, *Watching Dallas: Soap Opera and the Melodramatic Imagination*, trans. Della Couling (London: Methuen, 1985); and Tamar Liebes and Elihu Katz, 'Patterns of Involvement in Television Fiction', *European Journal of Communication*, 1 (1986), pp. 151–71.

25 Janice A. Radway, *Reading the Romance: Women, Patriarchy, and Popular Literature* (Chapel Hill, NC: University of North Carolina Press, 1984). The book was republished with a new introduction in 1987 (London: Verso).

26 Radway follows Chodorow's feminist revision of Freud, arguing that the process of parenting constitutes the female child with an ongoing need for the style of care associated with her mother. Since this care cannot be provided by men, who have been conditioned to deny their capacities for gentle nurturance, women must seek to fulfil this constant need in other ways. Chodorow suggests that one way in which they seek to fulfil this need is through the mothering of others: see Nancy Chodorow, *The Reproduction of Mothering: Psychoanalysis and the Sociology of Gender* (Berkeley: University of California Press, 1978). Radway adds a new twist to the argument: she suggests that romance reading is an alternative way in which women seek to fulfil the need for nurturance which is constituted by the process of parenting but denied by the heterosexual relations of their everyday life. Reading romances is a ritual re-telling of the psychic processes through which their own identity was formed, and in this re-telling they experience vicariously the nurturance which is absent from their adult lives. I have not pursued this line of analysis because it seems to me to be one of the most speculative and questionable aspects of Radway's account.

27 On the history of reading practices, see Roger Chartier, *The Cultural Uses of Print in Early Modern France*, trans. Lydia G. Cochrane (Princeton, NJ: Princeton University Press, 1987); Roger Chartier (ed.), *The Culture of Print: Power and the Uses of Print in Early Modern Europe*, trans. Lydia G. Cochrane (Cambridge: Polity Press, 1989); and Paul Saenger, 'Silent Reading: Its Impact in Late Medieval Script and Society', *Viator. Medieval and Renaissance Studies*, 13 (1982), pp. 367–414.

28 For recent work on the mundane character of television viewing, see Morley, *Family Television*; Roger Silverstone, 'Television and Everyday Life: Towards an Anthropology of the Television Audience', in Marjorie Ferguson (ed.), *Public Communication: The New Imperatives* (London and Newbury Park, Ca: Sage, 1990),

pp. 173–89; and Peter Collett and Roger Lamb, *Watching People Watching Television* (Report to the Independent Broadcasting Authority, 1986).

29 Insightful contributions to this type of inquiry may be found in Hodge and Tripp, *Children and Television*; and Liebes and Katz, 'Patterns of Involvement in Television Fiction'.

30 For some thoughtful reflections on the ways in which women discuss soap operas at work, see Dorothy Hobson, 'Soap Operas at Work', in Ellen Seiter, Hans Borchers, Gabriele Kreutzner and Eva Maria Warth (eds), *Remote Control: Television Audiences and Cultural Power* (London: Routledge, 1989), pp. 150–67, and 'Women Audiences and the Workplace', in Mary Ellen Brown (ed.), *Television and Women's Culture: The Politics of the Popular* (London and Newbury Park, Ca: Sage, 1990).

31 In examining the relation between the interpretation of ideology and the nature of critique, I draw some inspiration from the recent work of Habermas, who has developed an original and valuable approach to the epistemological and normative problems confronting a critical theory of modern societies. See especially Jürgen Habermas, *Communication and the Evolution of Society*, trans. Thomas McCarthy (Cambridge: Polity Press, 1979) and *The Theory of Communicative Action*, vols. 1 and 2, trans. Thomas McCarthy (Cambridge: Polity Press, 1984, 1987). However, while I have drawn inspiration from Habermas's work, I have not followed his proposals in any detail, as I believe that there are serious, and in some respects irremediable, difficulties in his account. For a discussion of these difficulties, see John B. Thompson, *Studies in the Theory of Ideology*, pp. 253–302.

Index